PUNISHER
WAR JOURNAL
GOIN' OUT WEST

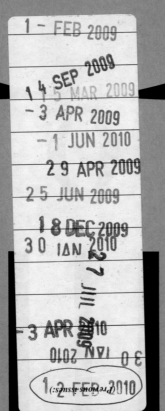

PUNISHER WAR JOURNAL

GOIN' OUT WEST

WRITER: **Matt Fraction**
ART *(Issues #5-10)*: **Ariel Olivetti**

ART, *Issue #11:*
PENCILER: **Leandro Fernandez**
INKER: **Francisco Paronzini**
COLORIST: **Val Staples**

LETTERER: **Virtual Calligraphy's Joe Caramagna**
COVER ART: **Ariel Olivetti**
ASSISTANT EDITORS: **Michael O'Connor & Aubrey Sitterson**
EDITOR: **Axel Alonso**

COLLECTION EDITOR: **Jennifer Grünwald**
ASSISTANT EDITORS: **Cory Levine & John Denning**
ASSOCIATE EDITOR: **Mark D. Beazley**
SENIOR EDITOR, SPECIAL PROJECTS: **Jeff Youngquist**
SENIOR VICE PRESIDENT OF SALES: **David Gabriel**
PRODUCTION: **Jerron Quality Color & Jerry Kalinowski**
VICE PRESIDENT OF CREATIVE: **Tom Marvelli**

EDITOR IN CHIEF: **Joe Quesada**
PUBLISHER: **Dan Buckley**

R JOURNAL VOL. 2: GOIN' OUT WEST. Contains material originally published in magazine form as PUNISHER WAR JOURNAL #5-11. First printing 2007. Hardcover ISBN# 978-0-7851-
er ISBN# 978-0-7851-2636-2. Published by MARVEL PUBLISHING, INC., a subsidiary of MARVEL ENTERTAINMENT, INC. OFFICE OF PUBLICATION: 417 5th Avenue, New York, NY 10016.
07 Marvel Characters, Inc. All rights reserved. Hardcover: $24.99 per copy in the U.S. and $40.00 in Canada (GST #R127032852). Softcover: $17.99 per copy in the U.S. and $29.00 in
R127032852). Canadian Agreement #40668537. All characters featured in this issue and the distinctive names and likenesses thereof, and all related indicia are trademarks of Marvel
No similarity between any of the names, characters, persons, and/or institutions in this magazine with those of any living or dead person or institution is intended, and any such similarity
t is purely coincidental. **Printed in the U.S.A.** ALAN FINE, CEO Marvel Toys & Publishing Divisions and CMO Marvel Entertainment, Inc.; DAVID GABRIEL, Senior VP of Publishing Sales &
VID BOGART, VP of Business Affairs & Editorial Operations; MICHAEL PASCIULLO, VP Merchandising & Communications; JIM BOYLE, VP of Publishing Operations; DAN CARR, Executive
ishing Technology; JUSTIN F. GABRIE, Managing Editor; SUSAN CRESPI, Production Manager; STAN LEE, Chairman Emeritus. For information regarding advertising in Marvel Comics or on
ase contact Joe Maimone, Advertising Director, at jmaimone@marvel.com or 212-576-8534.

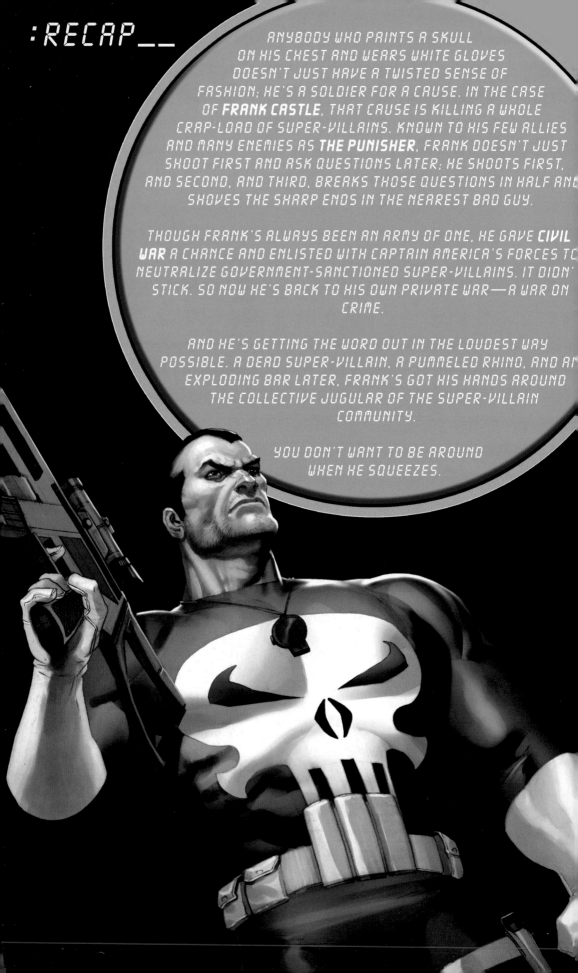

ANYBODY WHO PAINTS A SKULL ON HIS CHEST AND WEARS WHITE GLOVES DOESN'T JUST HAVE A TWISTED SENSE OF FASHION; HE'S A SOLDIER FOR A CAUSE. IN THE CASE OF **FRANK CASTLE**, THAT CAUSE IS KILLING A WHOLE CRAP-LOAD OF SUPER-VILLAINS. KNOWN TO HIS FEW ALLIES AND MANY ENEMIES AS **THE PUNISHER**, FRANK DOESN'T JUST SHOOT FIRST AND ASK QUESTIONS LATER; HE SHOOTS FIRST, AND SECOND, AND THIRD, BREAKS THOSE QUESTIONS IN HALF AND SHOVES THE SHARP ENDS IN THE NEAREST BAD GUY.

THOUGH FRANK'S ALWAYS BEEN AN ARMY OF ONE, HE GAVE **CIVIL WAR** A CHANCE AND ENLISTED WITH CAPTAIN AMERICA'S FORCES TO NEUTRALIZE GOVERNMENT-SANCTIONED SUPER-VILLAINS. IT DIDN'T STICK. SO NOW HE'S BACK TO HIS OWN PRIVATE WAR—A WAR ON CRIME.

AND HE'S GETTING THE WORD OUT IN THE LOUDEST WAY POSSIBLE. A DEAD SUPER-VILLAIN, A PUMMELED RHINO, AND AN EXPLODING BAR LATER, FRANK'S GOT HIS HANDS AROUND THE COLLECTIVE JUGULAR OF THE SUPER-VILLAIN COMMUNITY.

YOU DON'T WANT TO BE AROUND WHEN HE SQUEEZES.

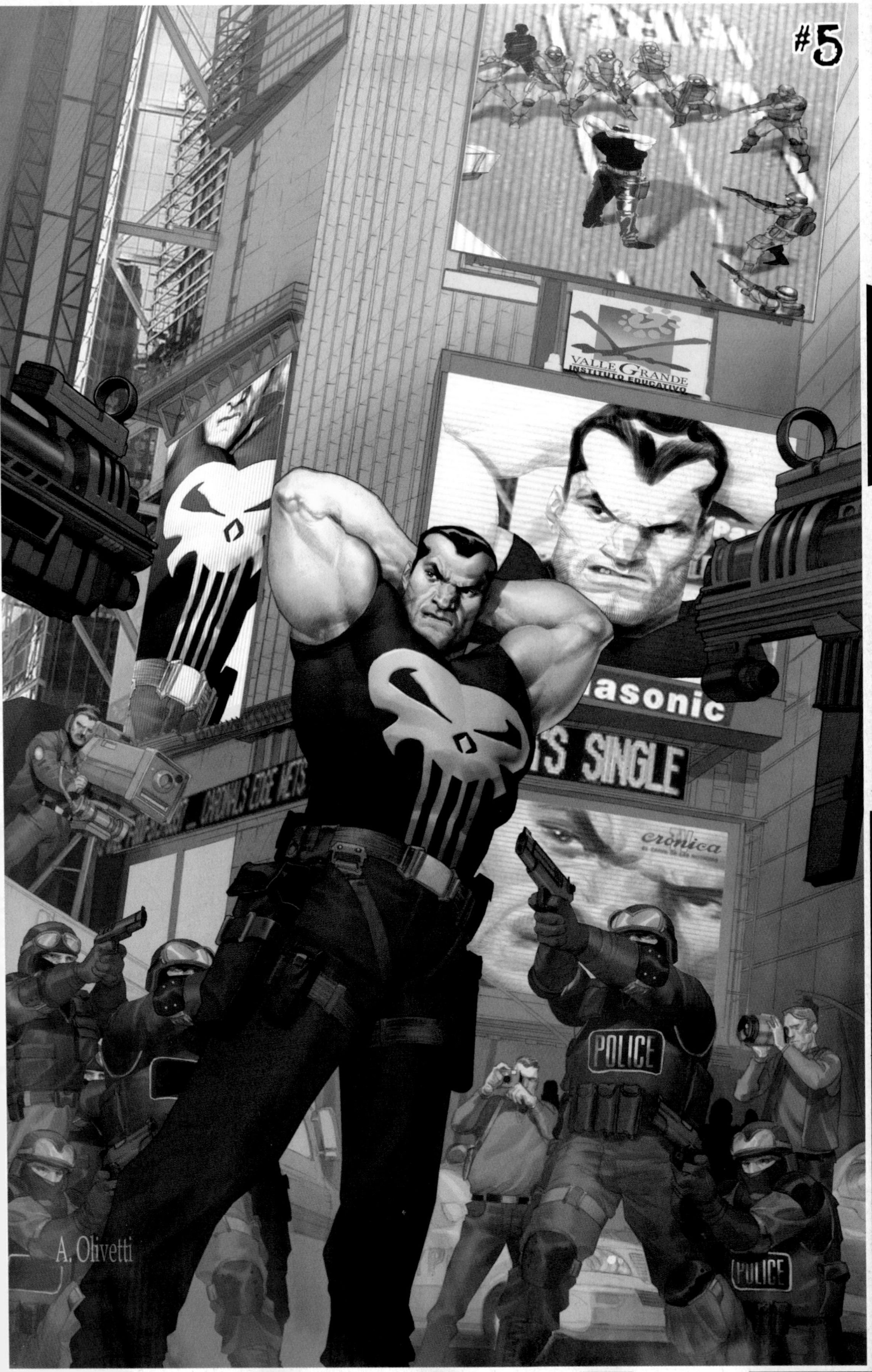
#5
VALLE GRANDE
INSTITUTO EDUCATIVO
SINGLE
crónica
POLICE
POLICE
A. Olivetti

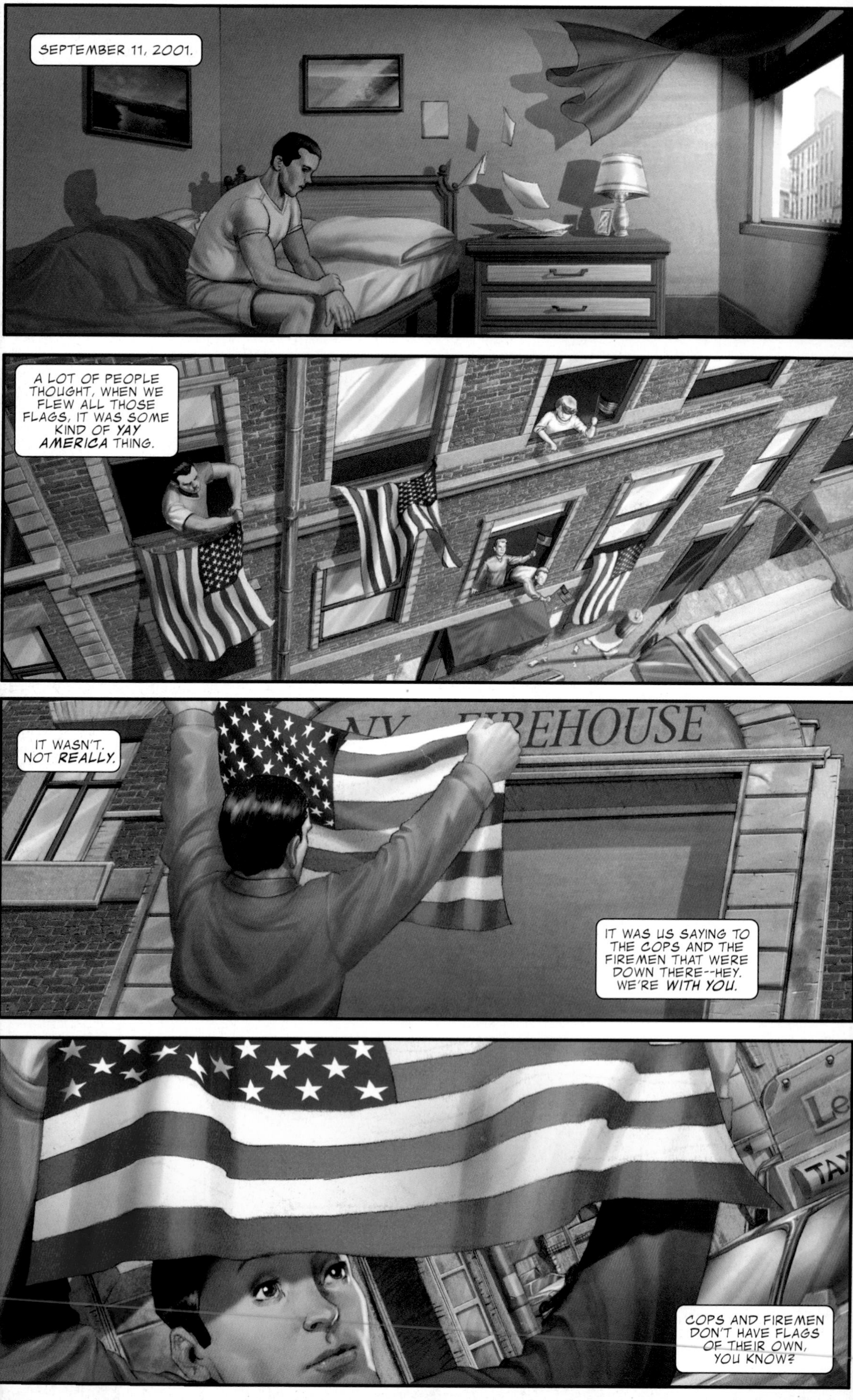
SEPTEMBER 11, 2001.
A LOT OF PEOPLE THOUGHT, WHEN WE FLEW ALL THOSE FLAGS, IT WAS SOME KIND OF YAY AMERICA THING.
IT WASN'T. NOT REALLY.
NY FIREHOUSE
IT WAS US SAYING TO THE COPS AND THE FIREMEN THAT WERE DOWN THERE--HEY. WE'RE WITH YOU.
COPS AND FIREMEN DON'T HAVE FLAGS OF THEIR OWN, YOU KNOW?

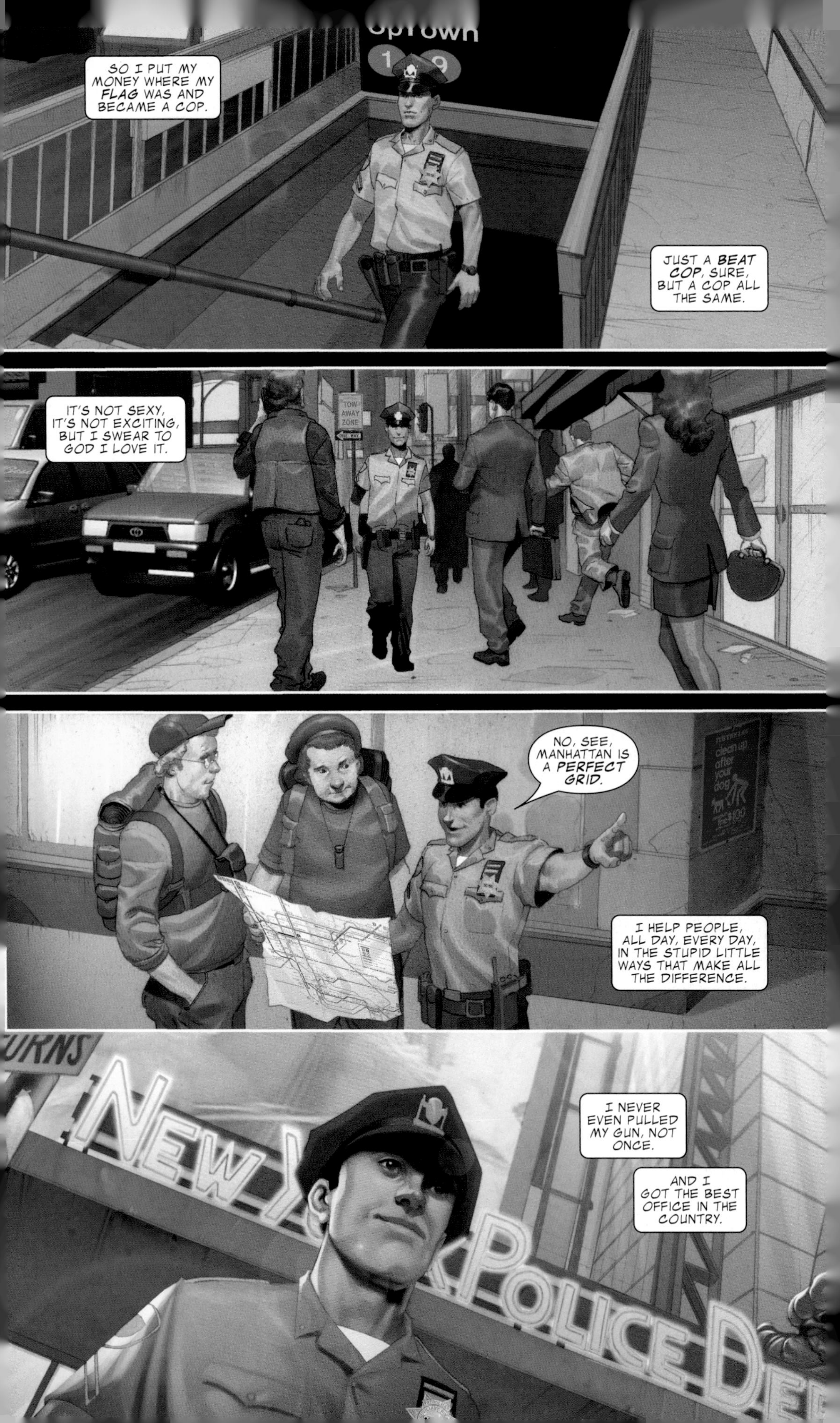
Uptown
SO I PUT MY MONEY WHERE MY FLAG WAS AND BECAME A COP.
JUST A BEAT COP, SURE, BUT A COP ALL THE SAME.
TOW AWAY ZONE
ONE WAY
IT'S NOT SEXY, IT'S NOT EXCITING, BUT I SWEAR TO GOD I LOVE IT.
NO, SEE, MANHATTAN IS A PERFECT GRID.
clean up after your dog
I HELP PEOPLE, ALL DAY, EVERY DAY, IN THE STUPID LITTLE WAYS THAT MAKE ALL THE DIFFERENCE.
I NEVER EVEN PULLED MY GUN, NOT ONCE.
AND I GOT THE BEST OFFICE IN THE COUNTRY.

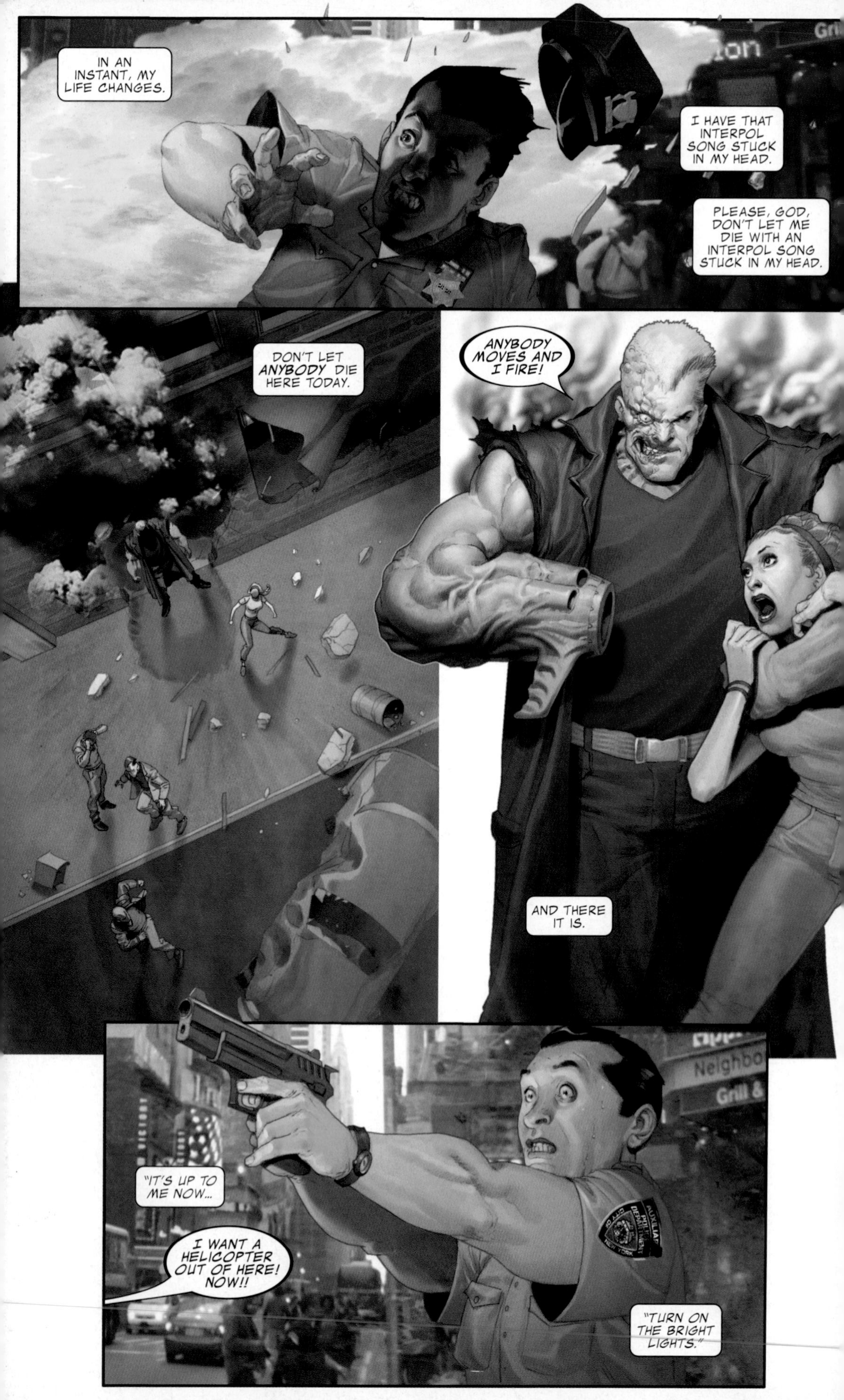
IN AN INSTANT, MY LIFE CHANGES.
I HAVE THAT INTERPOL SONG STUCK IN MY HEAD.
PLEASE, GOD, DON'T LET ME DIE WITH AN INTERPOL SONG STUCK IN MY HEAD.
DON'T LET ANYBODY DIE HERE TODAY.
ANYBODY MOVES AND I FIRE!
AND THERE IT IS.
"IT'S UP TO ME NOW...
I WANT A HELICOPTER OUT OF HERE! NOW!!
"TURN ON THE BRIGHT LIGHTS."

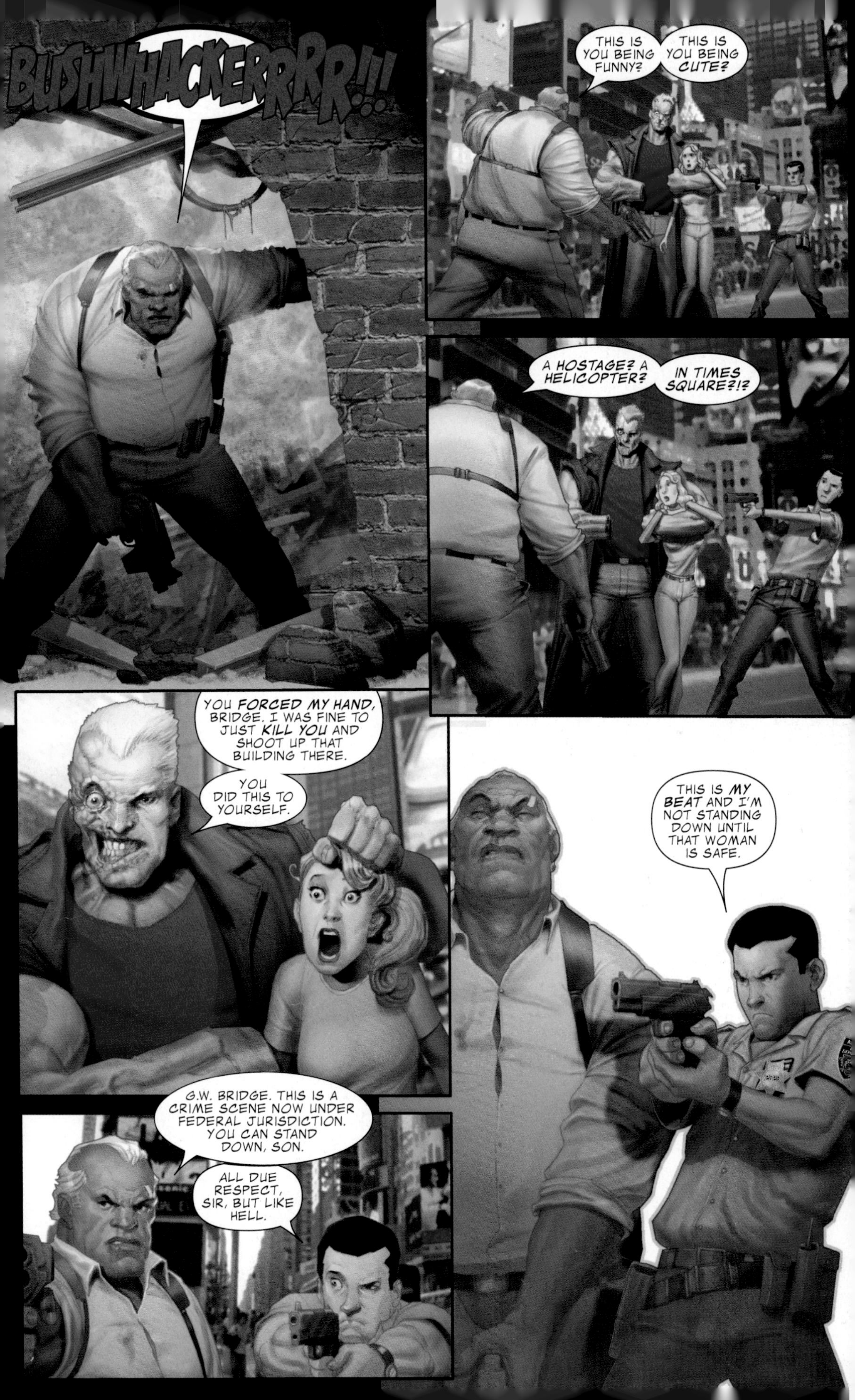
BUSHWHACKERRRR!!!
THIS IS YOU BEING FUNNY?
THIS IS YOU BEING CUTE?
A HOSTAGE? A HELICOPTER?
IN TIMES SQUARE?!?
YOU FORCED MY HAND, BRIDGE. I WAS FINE TO JUST KILL YOU AND SHOOT UP THAT BUILDING THERE.
YOU DID THIS TO YOURSELF.
G.W. BRIDGE. THIS IS A CRIME SCENE NOW UNDER FEDERAL JURISDICTION. YOU CAN STAND DOWN, SON.
ALL DUE RESPECT, SIR, BUT LIKE HELL.
THIS IS MY BEAT AND I'M NOT STANDING DOWN UNTIL THAT WOMAN IS SAFE.

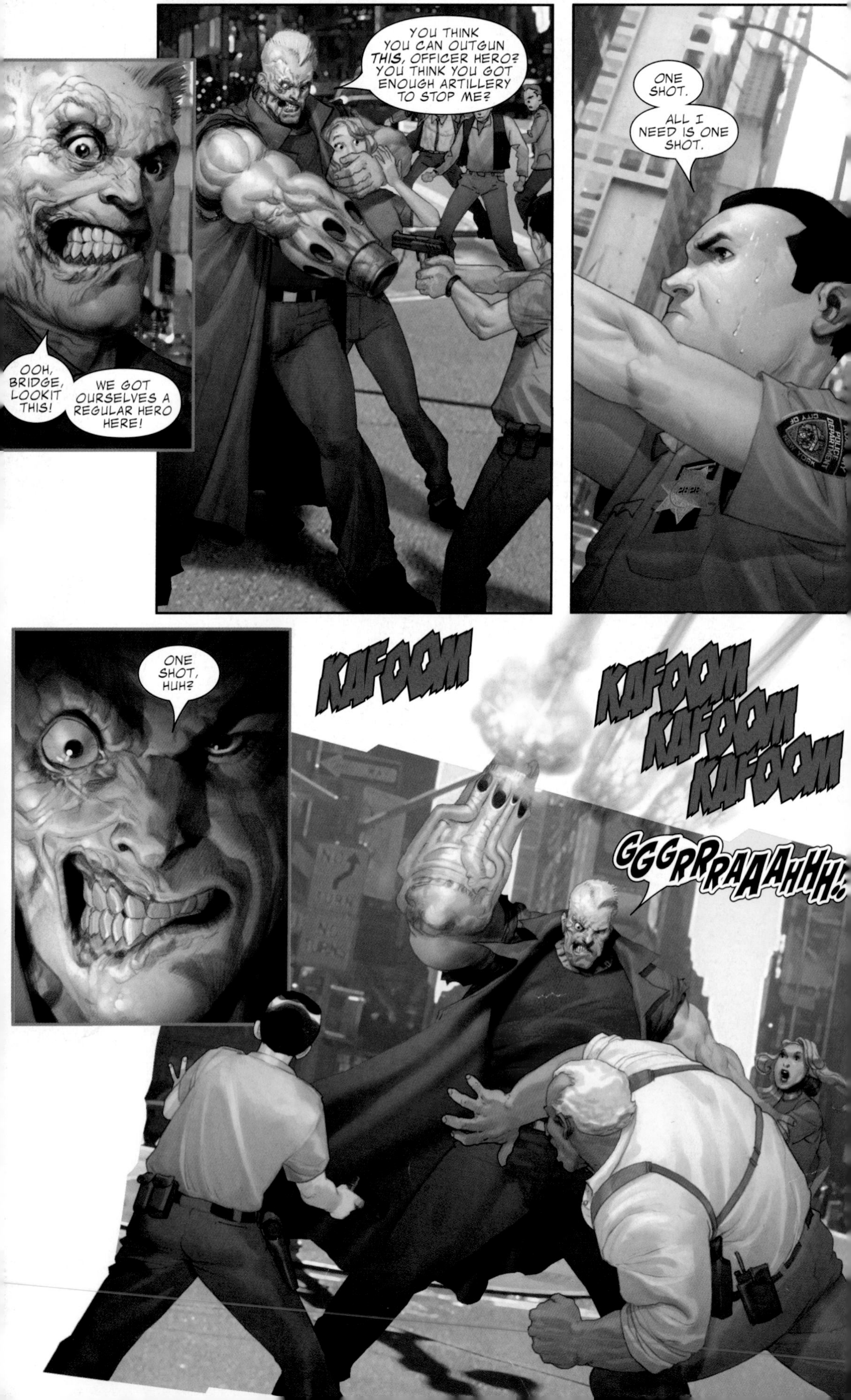
OOH, BRIDGE, LOOKIT THIS!
WE GOT OURSELVES A REGULAR HERO HERE!
YOU THINK YOU CAN OUTGUN THIS, OFFICER HERO? YOU THINK YOU GOT ENOUGH ARTILLERY TO STOP ME?
ONE SHOT.
ALL I NEED IS ONE SHOT.
ONE SHOT, HUH?
KAFOOM
KAFOOM KAFOOM KAFOOM
GGGRRRAAAHHH!

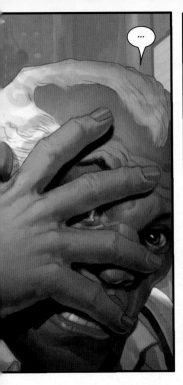

HEH.
YOU FLINCHED AT ALL *FOUR* SHOTS, SUPERCOP.

IT'S *BRIDGE*. I CAN'T IMAGINE EVERY PHONE IN *MIDTOWN* ISN'T DIALING 911 RIGHT NOW, BUT YOU GUYS ARE GONNA WANT TO GET A COUPLE DOZEN *CAPEKILLER* SQUADS DOWN TO TIMES SQUARE.

OOH-HOO-HOO, LOOK WHO DIDN'T *FLINCH*.

BUT, C'MON, IF YOU DIDN'T SHOOT ME AFTER *THAT*, WHAT'S IT GONNA ACTUALLY *TAKE?*

HARM ONE HAIR ON HER HEAD.

MAYBE YOU WOULD, LAW-MAN. MAYBE YOU WOULD.

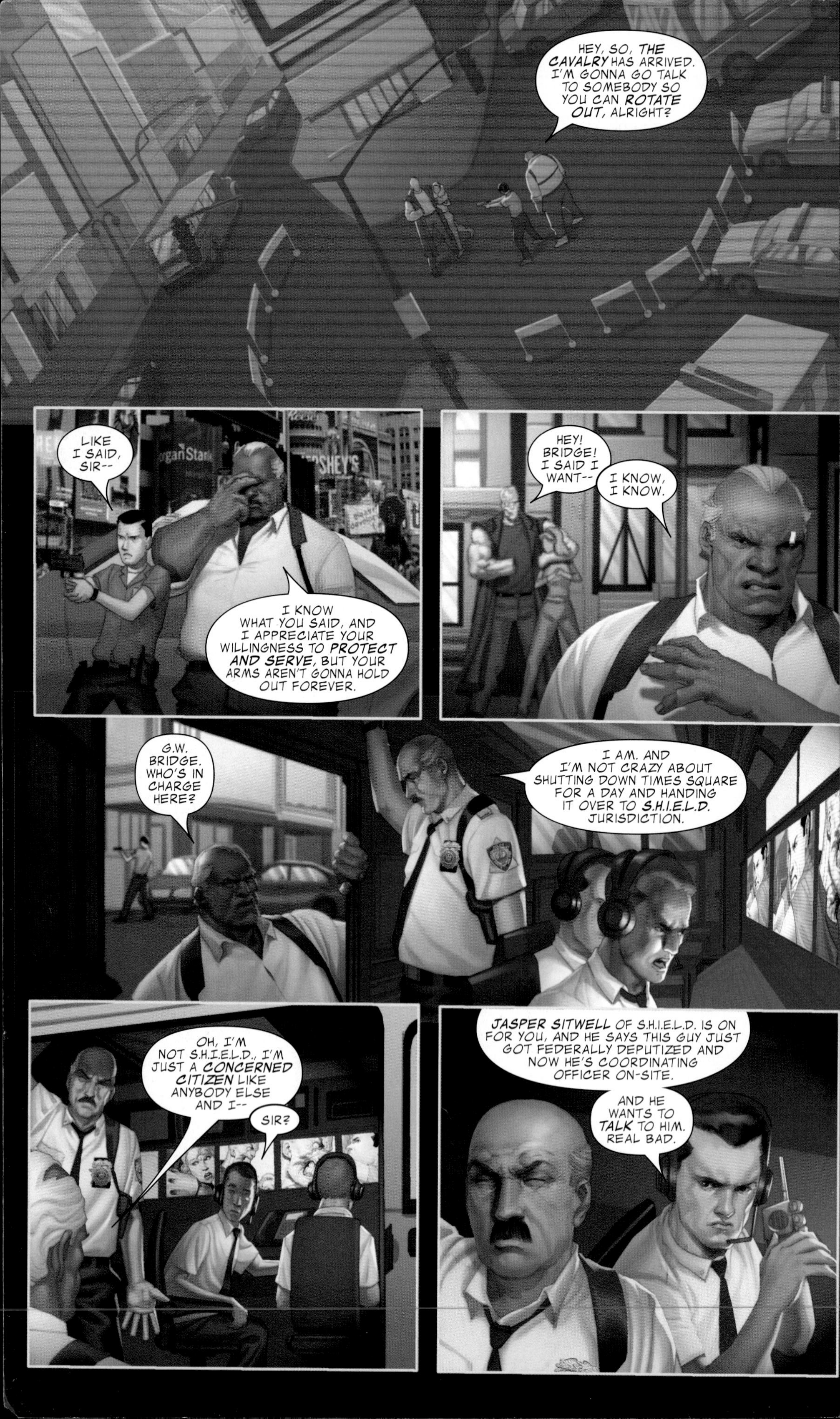
HEY, SO, THE CAVALRY HAS ARRIVED. I'M GONNA GO TALK TO SOMEBODY SO YOU CAN ROTATE OUT, ALRIGHT?
LIKE I SAID, SIR--
I KNOW WHAT YOU SAID, AND I APPRECIATE YOUR WILLINGNESS TO PROTECT AND SERVE, BUT YOUR ARMS AREN'T GONNA HOLD OUT FOREVER.
HEY! BRIDGE! I SAID I WANT--
I KNOW, I KNOW.
G.W. BRIDGE. WHO'S IN CHARGE HERE?
I AM. AND I'M NOT CRAZY ABOUT SHUTTING DOWN TIMES SQUARE FOR A DAY AND HANDING IT OVER TO S.H.I.E.L.D. JURISDICTION.
OH, I'M NOT S.H.I.E.L.D., I'M JUST A CONCERNED CITIZEN LIKE ANYBODY ELSE AND I--
SIR?
JASPER SITWELL OF S.H.I.E.L.D. IS ON FOR YOU, AND HE SAYS THIS GUY JUST GOT FEDERALLY DEPUTIZED AND NOW HE'S COORDINATING OFFICER ON-SITE.
AND HE WANTS TO TALK TO HIM. REAL BAD.

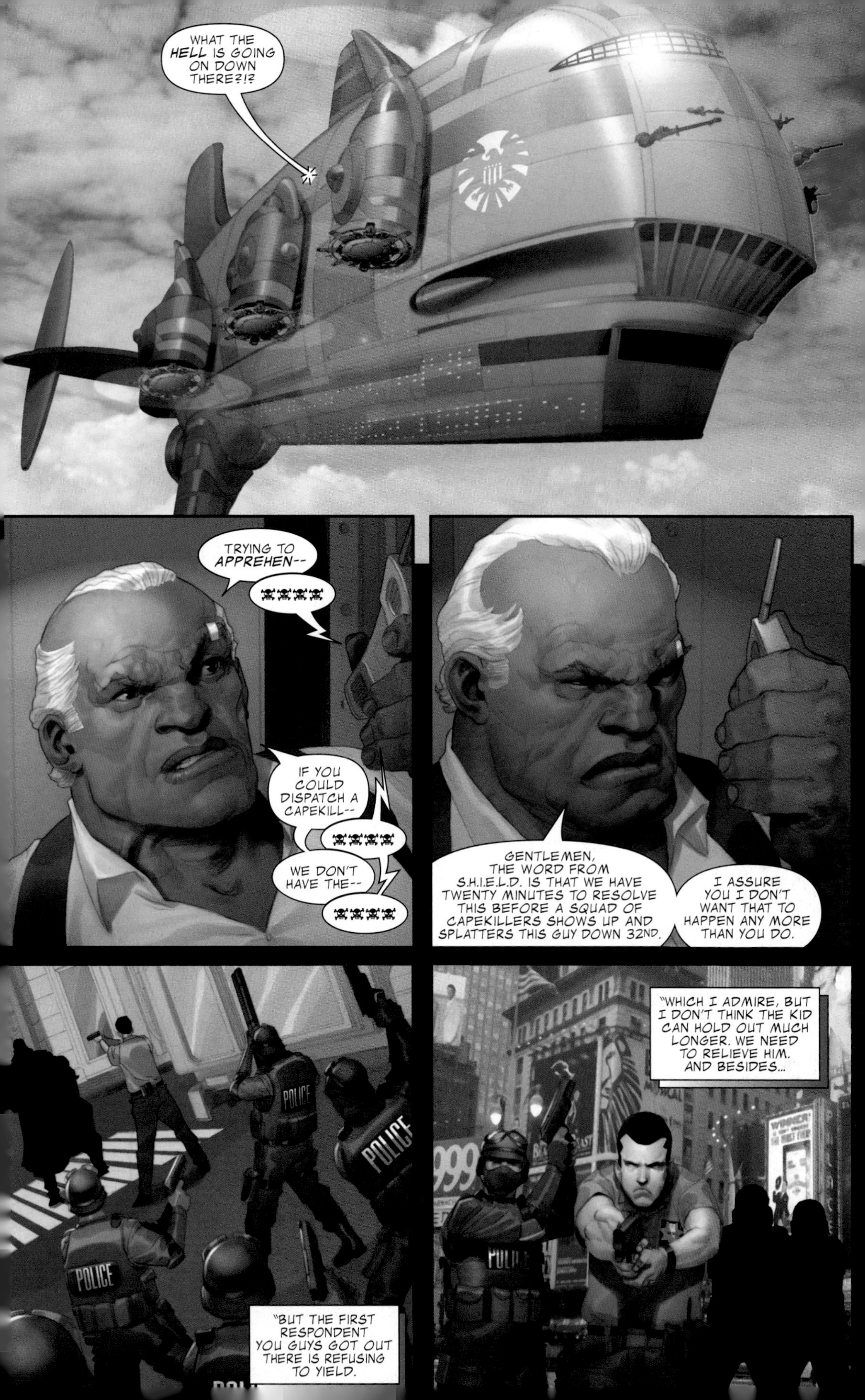
WHAT THE HELL IS GOING ON DOWN THERE?!?
TRYING TO APPREHEN--
IF YOU COULD DISPATCH A CAPEKILL--
WE DON'T HAVE THE--
GENTLEMEN, THE WORD FROM S.H.I.E.L.D. IS THAT WE HAVE TWENTY MINUTES TO RESOLVE THIS BEFORE A SQUAD OF CAPEKILLERS SHOWS UP AND SPLATTERS THIS GUY DOWN 32ND.
I ASSURE YOU I DON'T WANT THAT TO HAPPEN ANY MORE THAN YOU DO.
"BUT THE FIRST RESPONDENT YOU GUYS GOT OUT THERE IS REFUSING TO YIELD.
"WHICH I ADMIRE, BUT I DON'T THINK THE KID CAN HOLD OUT MUCH LONGER. WE NEED TO RELIEVE HIM. AND BESIDES...
POLICE
POLICE
POLICE

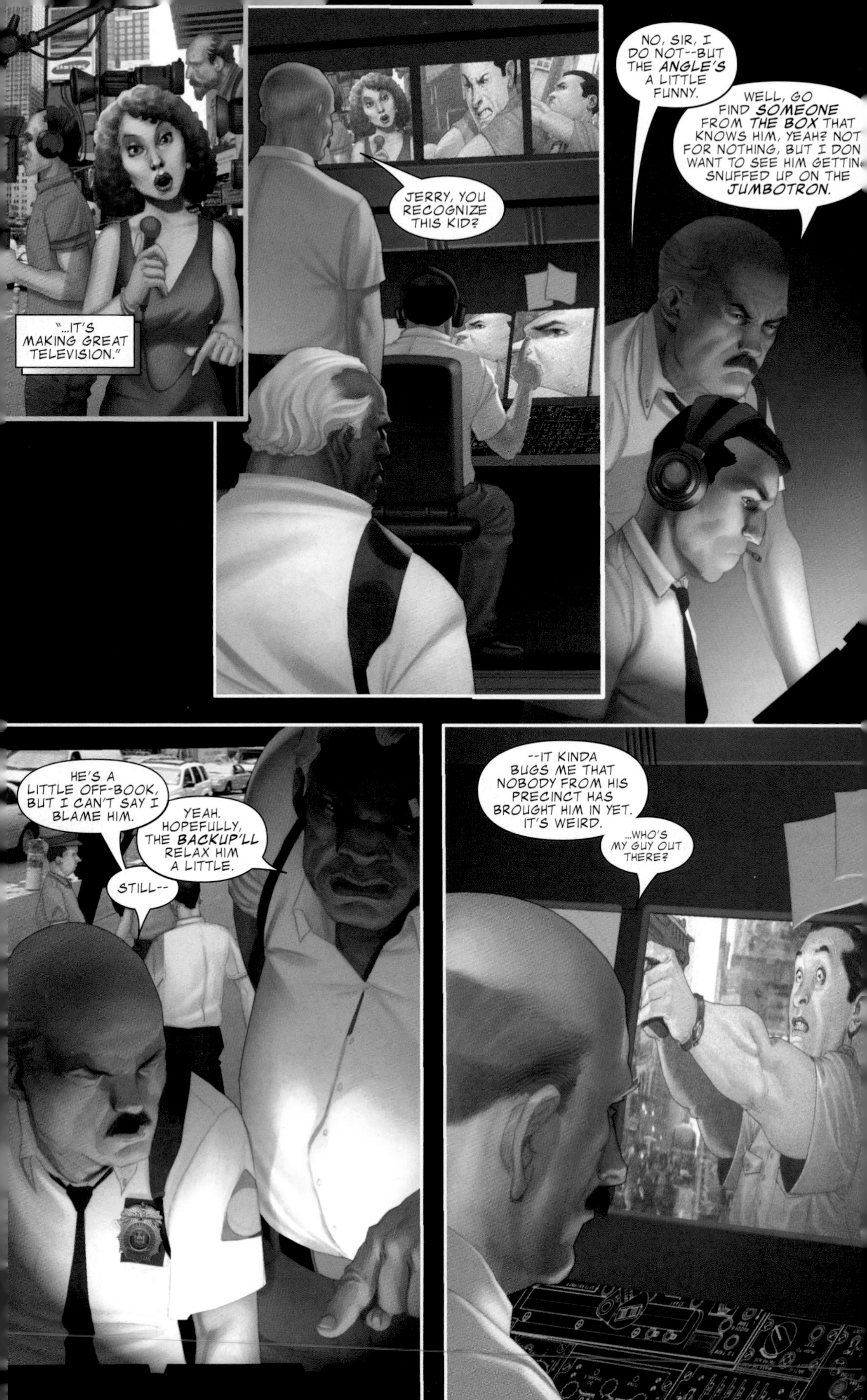
"...IT'S MAKING GREAT TELEVISION."
JERRY, YOU RECOGNIZE THIS KID?
NO, SIR, I DO NOT--BUT THE ANGLE'S A LITTLE FUNNY.
WELL, GO FIND SOMEONE FROM THE BOX THAT KNOWS HIM, YEAH? NOT FOR NOTHING, BUT I DON WANT TO SEE HIM GETTIN SNUFFED UP ON THE JUMBOTRON.
HE'S A LITTLE OFF-BOOK, BUT I CAN'T SAY I BLAME HIM.
YEAH. HOPEFULLY, THE BACKUP'LL RELAX HIM A LITTLE.
STILL--
--IT KINDA BUGS ME THAT NOBODY FROM HIS PRECINCT HAS BROUGHT HIM IN YET. IT'S WEIRD.
...WHO'S MY GUY OUT THERE?

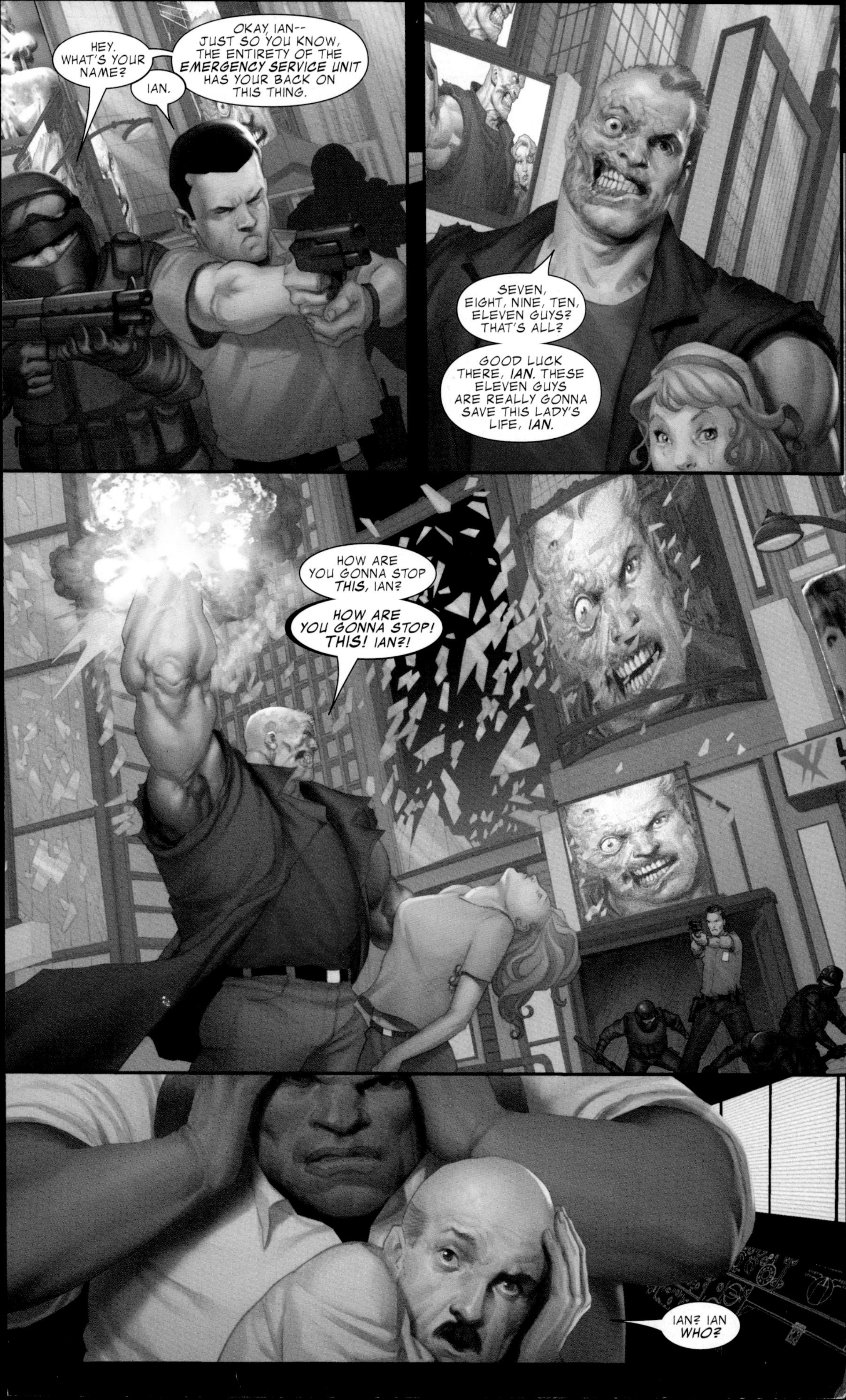
HEY. WHAT'S YOUR NAME?
IAN.
OKAY, IAN-- JUST SO YOU KNOW, THE ENTIRETY OF THE EMERGENCY SERVICE UNIT HAS YOUR BACK ON THIS THING.
SEVEN, EIGHT, NINE, TEN, ELEVEN GUYS? THAT'S ALL?
GOOD LUCK THERE, IAN. THESE ELEVEN GUYS ARE REALLY GONNA SAVE THIS LADY'S LIFE, IAN.
HOW ARE YOU GONNA STOP THIS, IAN?
HOW ARE YOU GONNA STOP! THIS! IAN?!
IAN? IAN WHO?

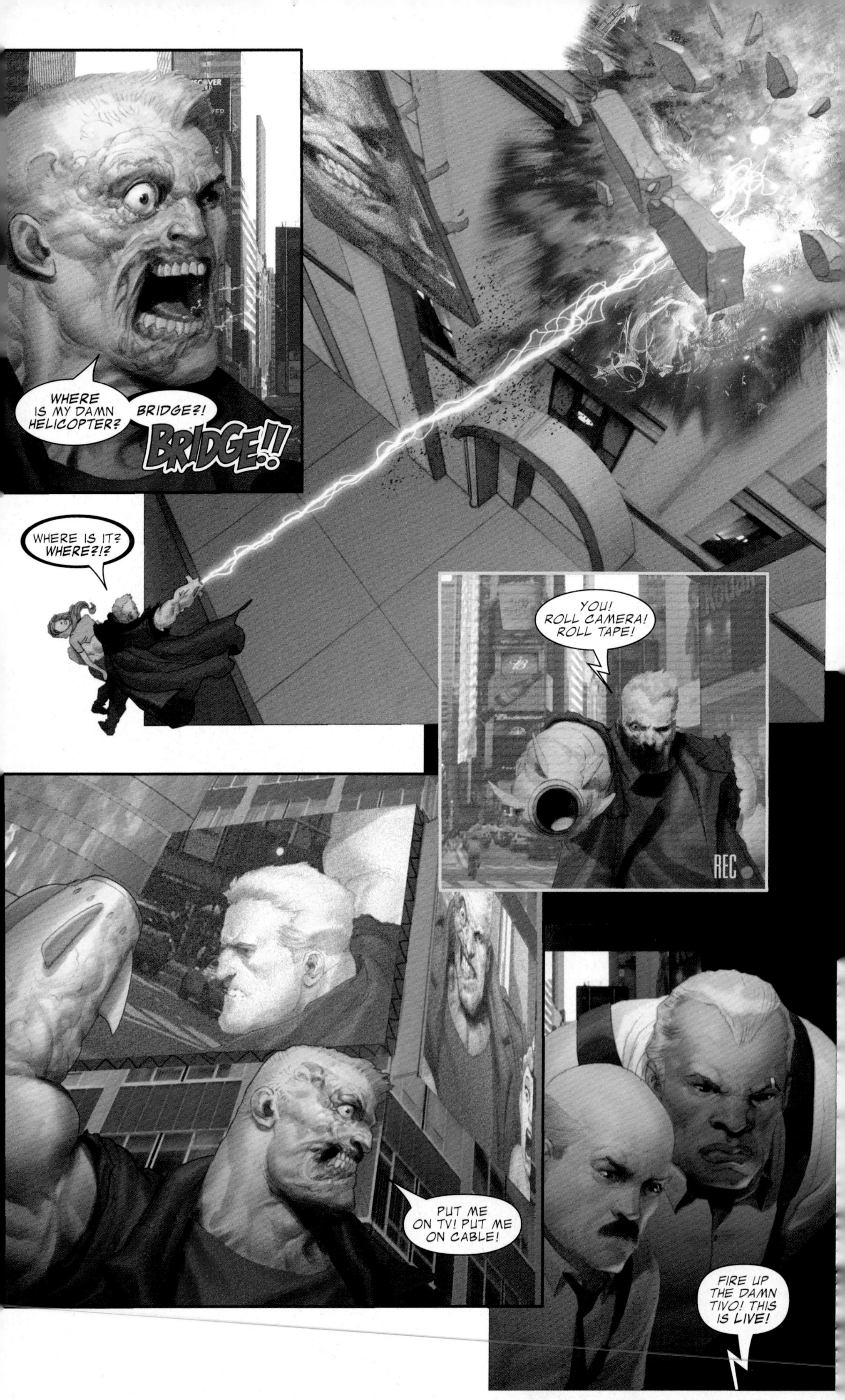
WHERE IS MY DAMN HELICOPTER?
BRIDGE?!
BRIDGE!!
WHERE IS IT? WHERE?!?
YOU! ROLL CAMERA! ROLL TAPE!
REC
PUT ME ON TV! PUT ME ON CABLE!
FIRE UP THE DAMN TIVO! THIS IS LIVE!

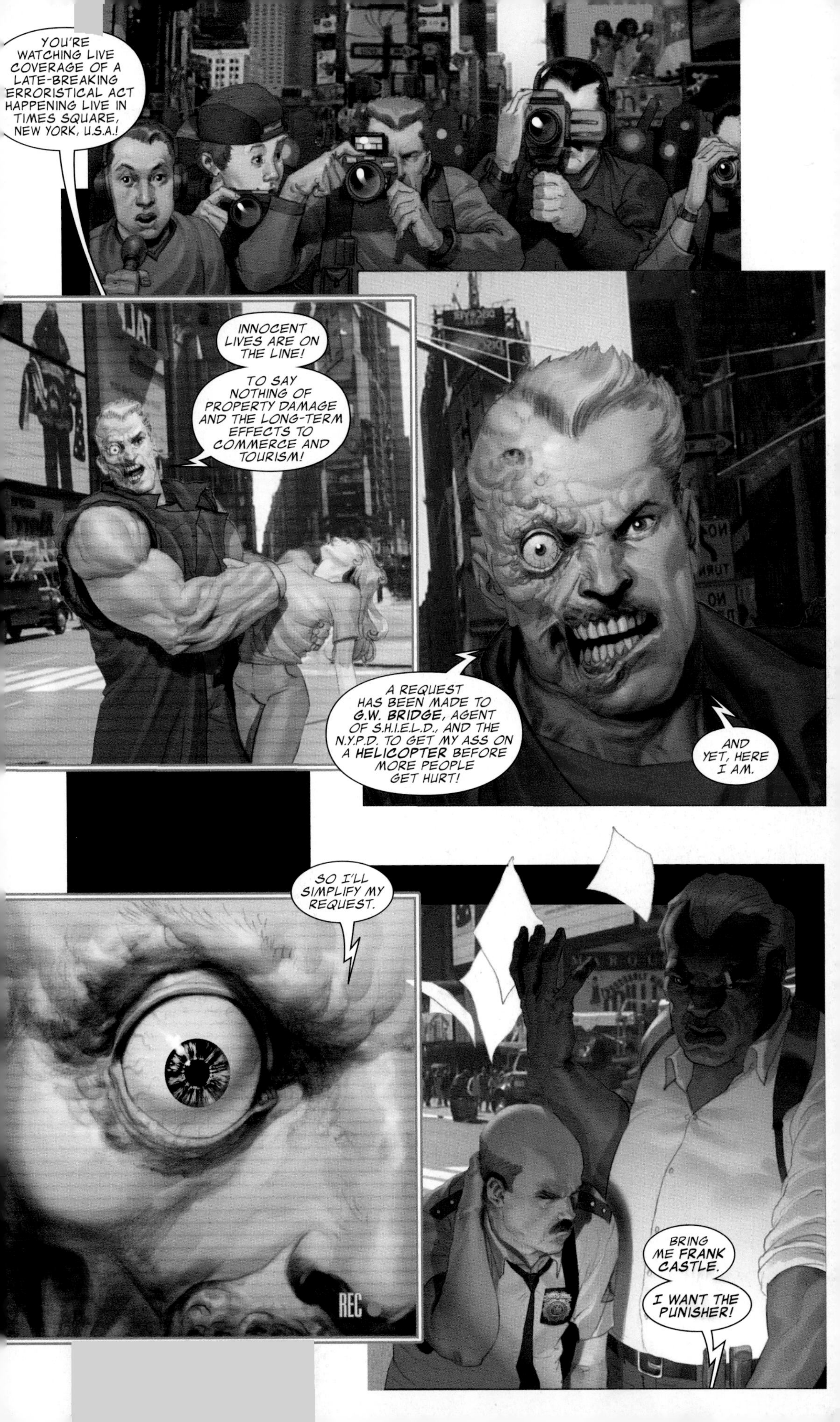
YOU'RE WATCHING LIVE COVERAGE OF A LATE-BREAKING ERRORISTICAL ACT HAPPENING LIVE IN TIMES SQUARE, NEW YORK, U.S.A.!
INNOCENT LIVES ARE ON THE LINE!
TO SAY NOTHING OF PROPERTY DAMAGE AND THE LONG-TERM EFFECTS TO COMMERCE AND TOURISM!
A REQUEST HAS BEEN MADE TO G.W. BRIDGE, AGENT OF S.H.I.E.L.D., AND THE N.Y.P.D. TO GET MY ASS ON A HELICOPTER BEFORE MORE PEOPLE GET HURT!
AND YET, HERE I AM.
SO I'LL SIMPLIFY MY REQUEST.
REC
BRING ME FRANK CASTLE.
I WANT THE PUNISHER!

WHADDAYA THINK, *IAN?* THE GIRL FOR THE PUNISHER? SURELY THE PUNISHER IS EASIER TO PRODUCE THAN A *HELICOPTER.*

I GIVE IT *TEN MINUTES* BEFORE WE ALL GET *MESSY.*

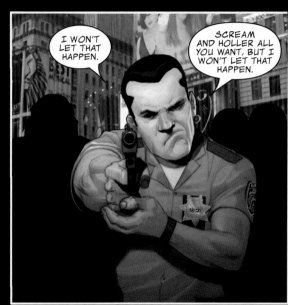

I WON'T LET THAT HAPPEN.

SCREAM AND HOLLER ALL YOU WANT, BUT I WON'T LET THAT HAPPEN.

WE'LL SEE, LITTLE MAN.

WE'LL SEE...

HEY, NOW. BOB RANKS. I'M THE *PATROL SERGEANT* OUT OF *MIDTOWN SOUTH.*

BOB, I'M PHIL JAMES, E.S.U. THIS HERE IS--

BRIDGE. I'VE GOT S.H.I.E.L.D. JURISDICTION HERE, AND I GUARANTEE YOU I WANT OUT OF HERE AS BAD AS YOU *WANT* ME OUT OF HERE.

I GOTTA TAKE *YOUR GUY* OFF THE BOARD FOR THAT TO HAPPEN.

HE SAYS HIS NAME IS IAN, AND HE REFUSES TO STAND DOW--

WAITAMINUTE-- IAN?

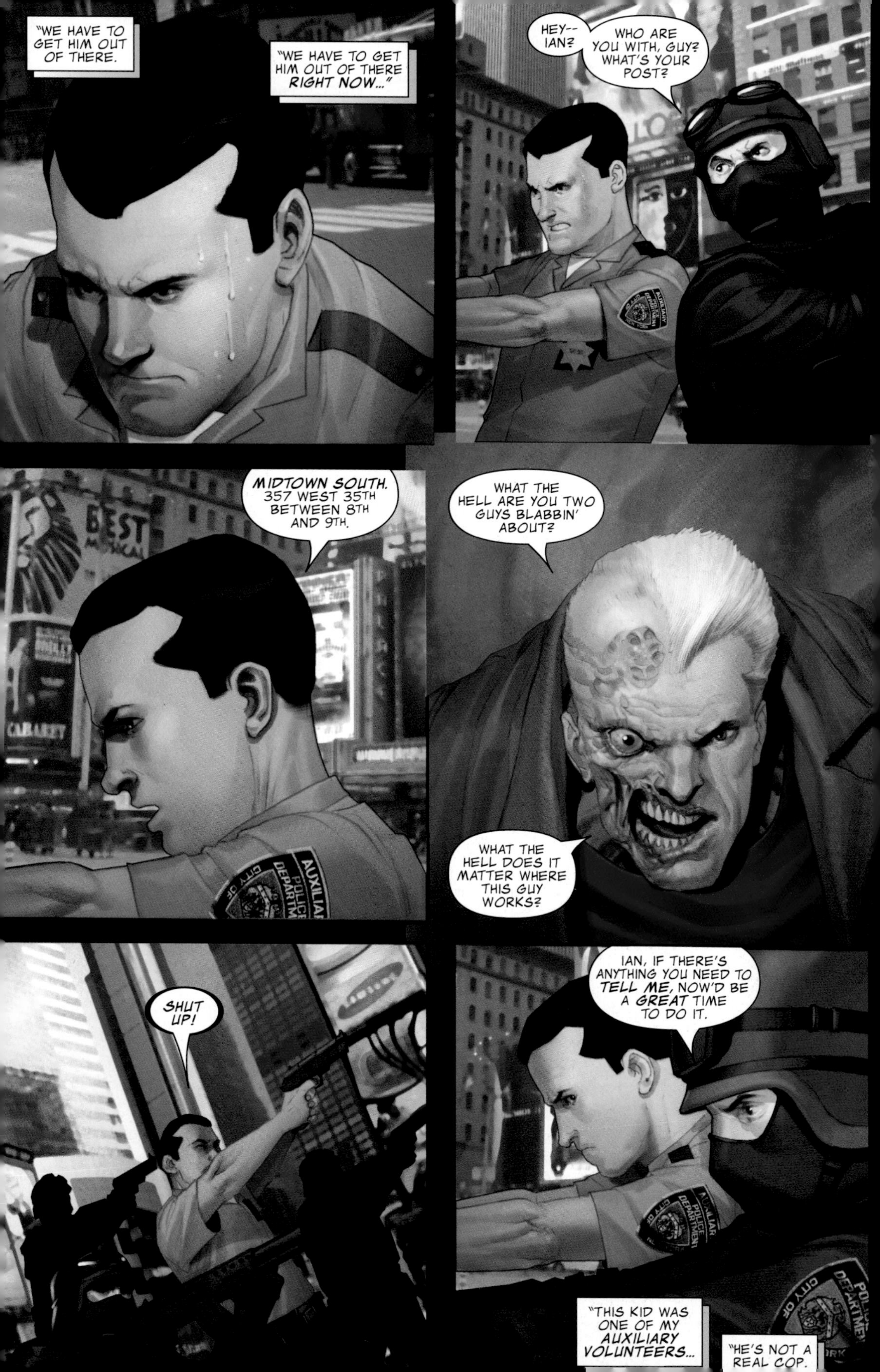
"WE HAVE TO GET HIM OUT OF THERE.
"WE HAVE TO GET HIM OUT OF THERE RIGHT NOW..."
HEY-- IAN?
WHO ARE YOU WITH, GUY? WHAT'S YOUR POST?
MIDTOWN SOUTH. 357 WEST 35TH BETWEEN 8TH AND 9TH.
WHAT THE HELL ARE YOU TWO GUYS BLABBIN' ABOUT?
WHAT THE HELL DOES IT MATTER WHERE THIS GUY WORKS?
SHUT UP!
IAN, IF THERE'S ANYTHING YOU NEED TO TELL ME, NOW'D BE A GREAT TIME TO DO IT.
"THIS KID WAS ONE OF MY AUXILIARY VOLUNTEERS...
"HE'S NOT A REAL COP.

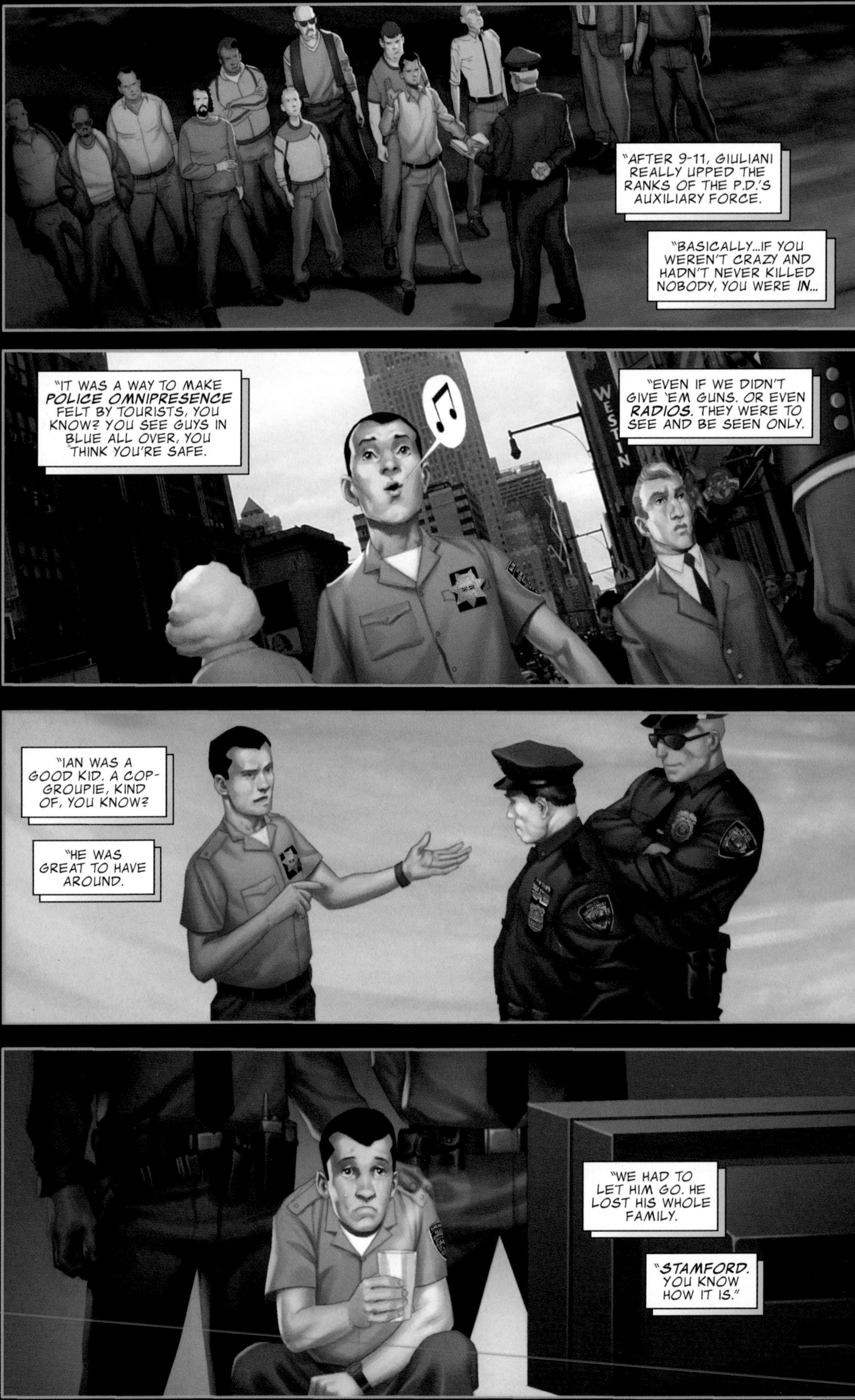
"AFTER 9-11, GIULIANI REALLY UPPED THE RANKS OF THE P.D.'S AUXILIARY FORCE.
"BASICALLY...IF YOU WEREN'T CRAZY AND HADN'T NEVER KILLED NOBODY, YOU WERE IN...
"IT WAS A WAY TO MAKE POLICE OMNIPRESENCE FELT BY TOURISTS, YOU KNOW? YOU SEE GUYS IN BLUE ALL OVER, YOU THINK YOU'RE SAFE.
"EVEN IF WE DIDN'T GIVE 'EM GUNS. OR EVEN RADIOS. THEY WERE TO SEE AND BE SEEN ONLY.
WESTIN
"IAN WAS A GOOD KID. A COP-GROUPIE, KIND OF, YOU KNOW?
"HE WAS GREAT TO HAVE AROUND.
"WE HAD TO LET HIM GO. HE LOST HIS WHOLE FAMILY.
"STAMFORD. YOU KNOW HOW IT IS."

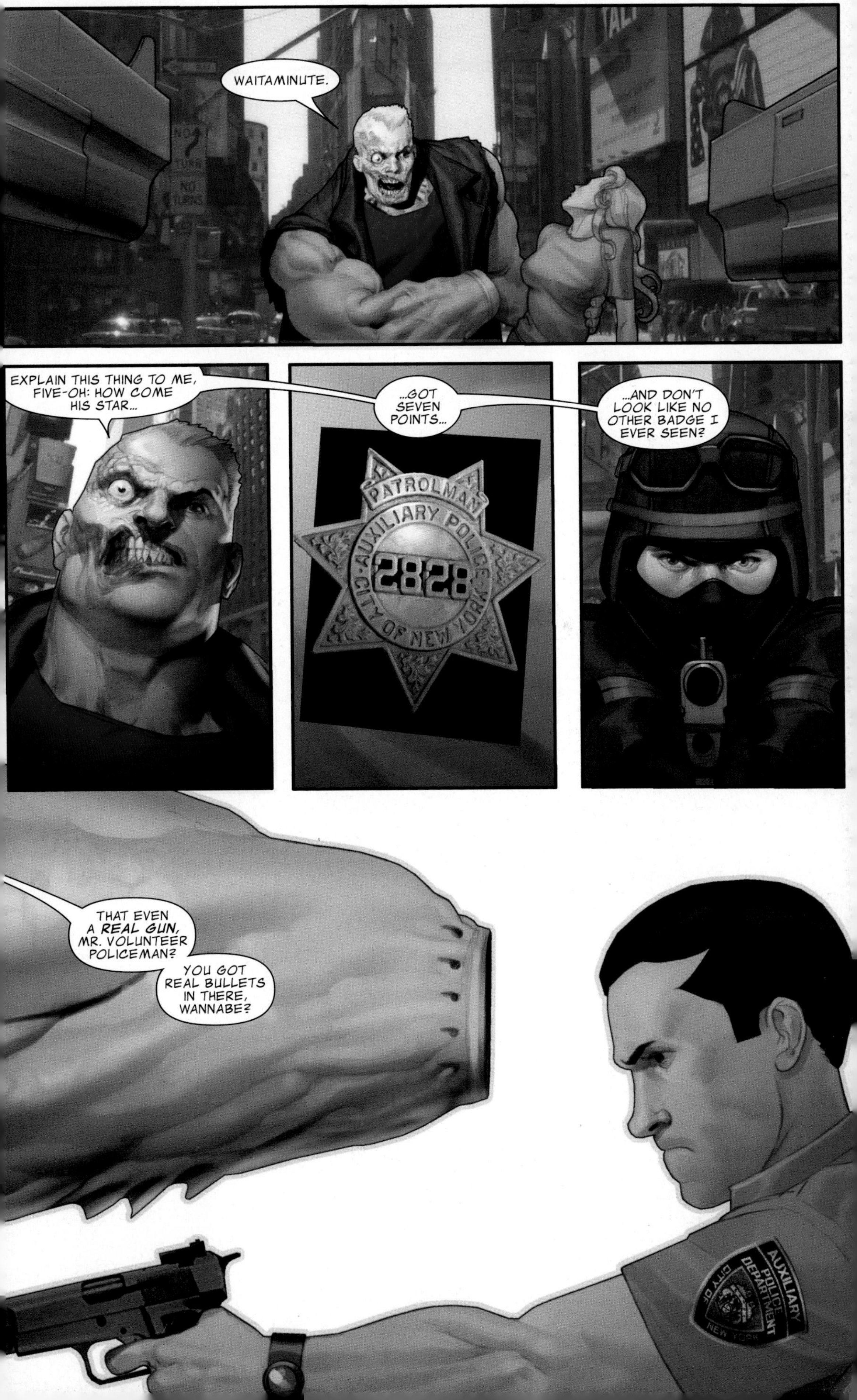
WAITAMINUTE.
EXPLAIN THIS THING TO ME, FIVE-OH: HOW COME HIS STAR...
...GOT SEVEN POINTS...
...AND DON'T LOOK LIKE NO OTHER BADGE I EVER SEEN?
PATROLMAN
AUXILIARY POLICE
2828
CITY OF NEW YORK
THAT EVEN A *REAL GUN*, MR. VOLUNTEER POLICEMAN?
YOU GOT REAL BULLETS IN THERE, WANNABE?
AUXILIARY POLICE DEPARTMENT
CITY OF NEW YORK

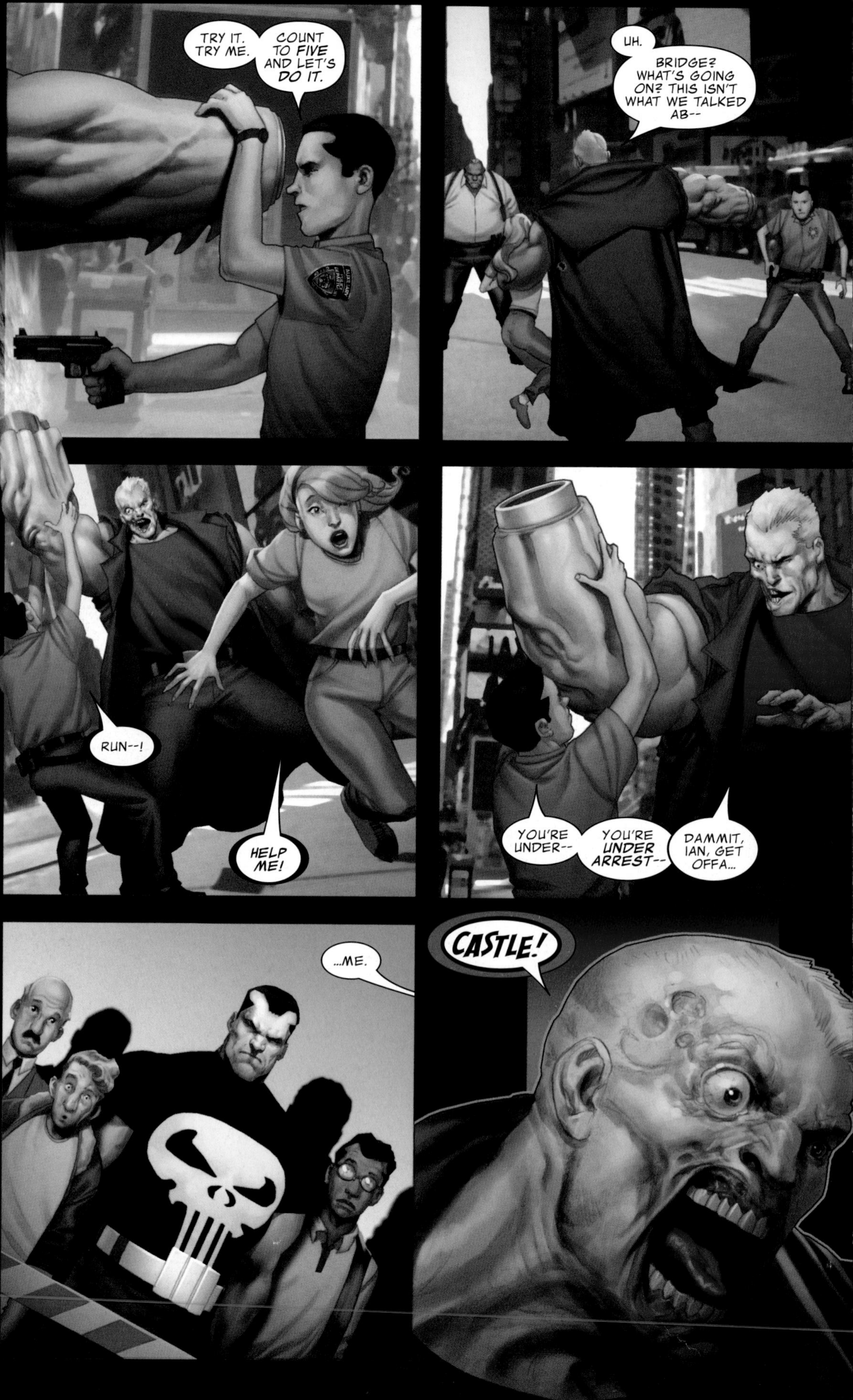
TRY IT. TRY ME.
COUNT TO FIVE AND LET'S DO IT.
UH.
BRIDGE? WHAT'S GOING ON? THIS ISN'T WHAT WE TALKED AB--
RUN--!
HELP ME!
YOU'RE UNDER--
YOU'RE UNDER ARREST--
DAMMIT, IAN, GET OFFA...
...ME.
CASTLE!

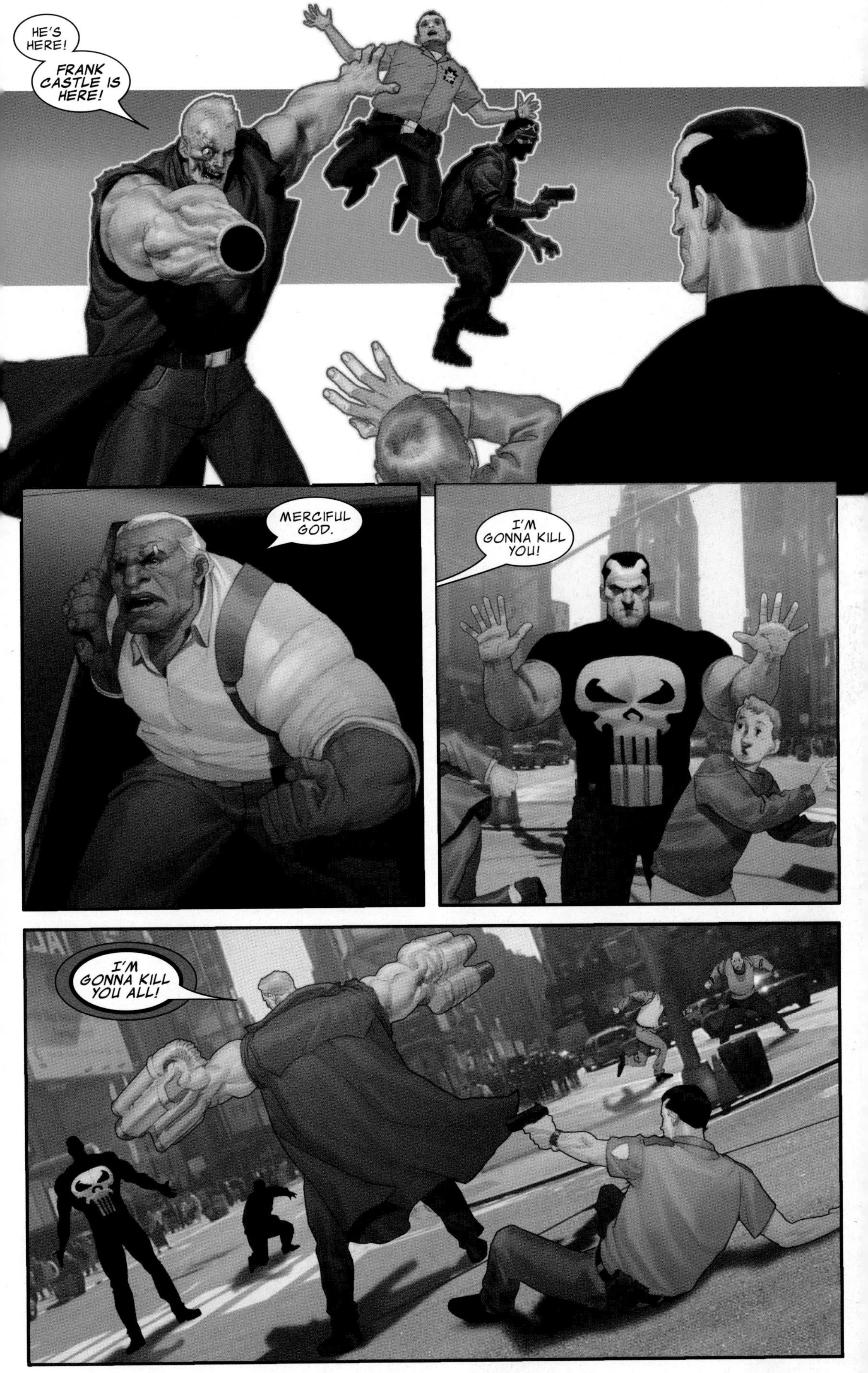
HE'S HERE! FRANK CASTLE IS HERE!
MERCIFUL GOD.
I'M GONNA KILL YOU!
I'M GONNA KILL YOU ALL!

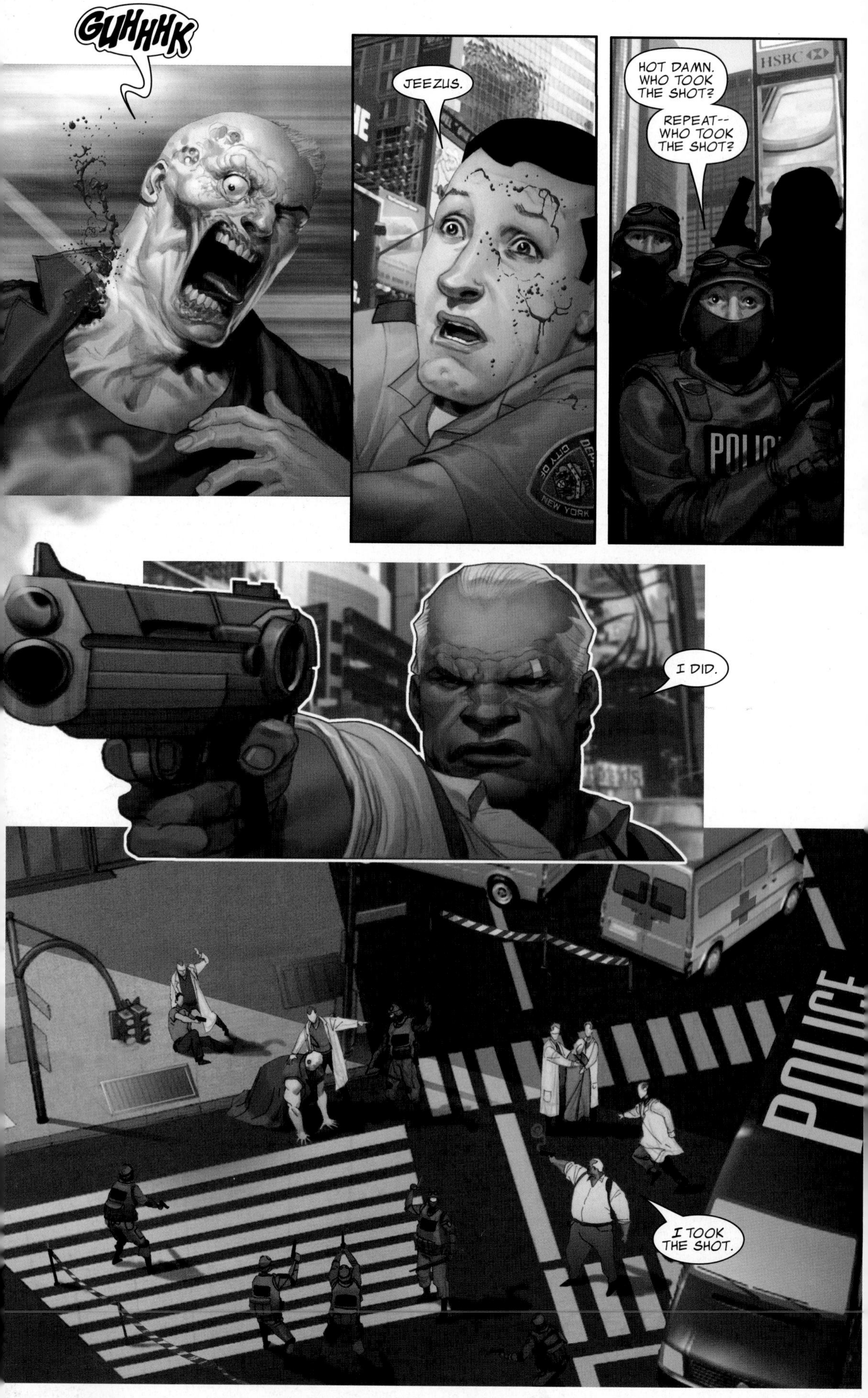
GUHHHK
JEEZUS.
HOT DAMN. WHO TOOK THE SHOT?
REPEAT-- WHO TOOK THE SHOT?
HSBC
POLICE
I DID.
POLICE
I TOOK THE SHOT.

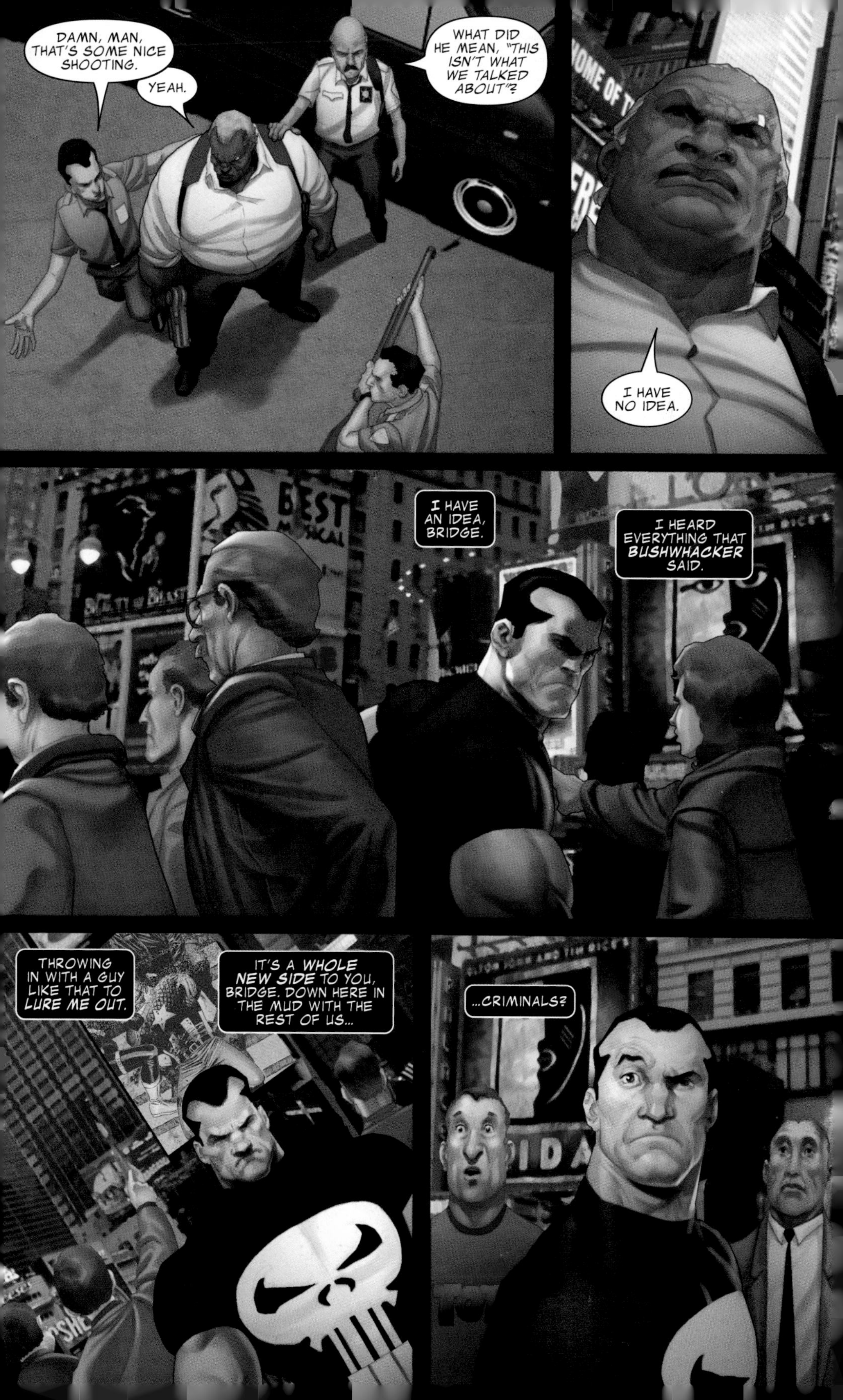
DAMN, MAN, THAT'S SOME NICE SHOOTING.
YEAH.
WHAT DID HE MEAN, "THIS ISN'T WHAT WE TALKED ABOUT"?
I HAVE NO IDEA.
I HAVE AN IDEA, BRIDGE.
I HEARD EVERYTHING THAT BUSHWHACKER SAID.
THROWING IN WITH A GUY LIKE THAT TO LURE ME OUT.
IT'S A WHOLE NEW SIDE TO YOU, BRIDGE. DOWN HERE IN THE MUD WITH THE REST OF US...
...CRIMINALS?

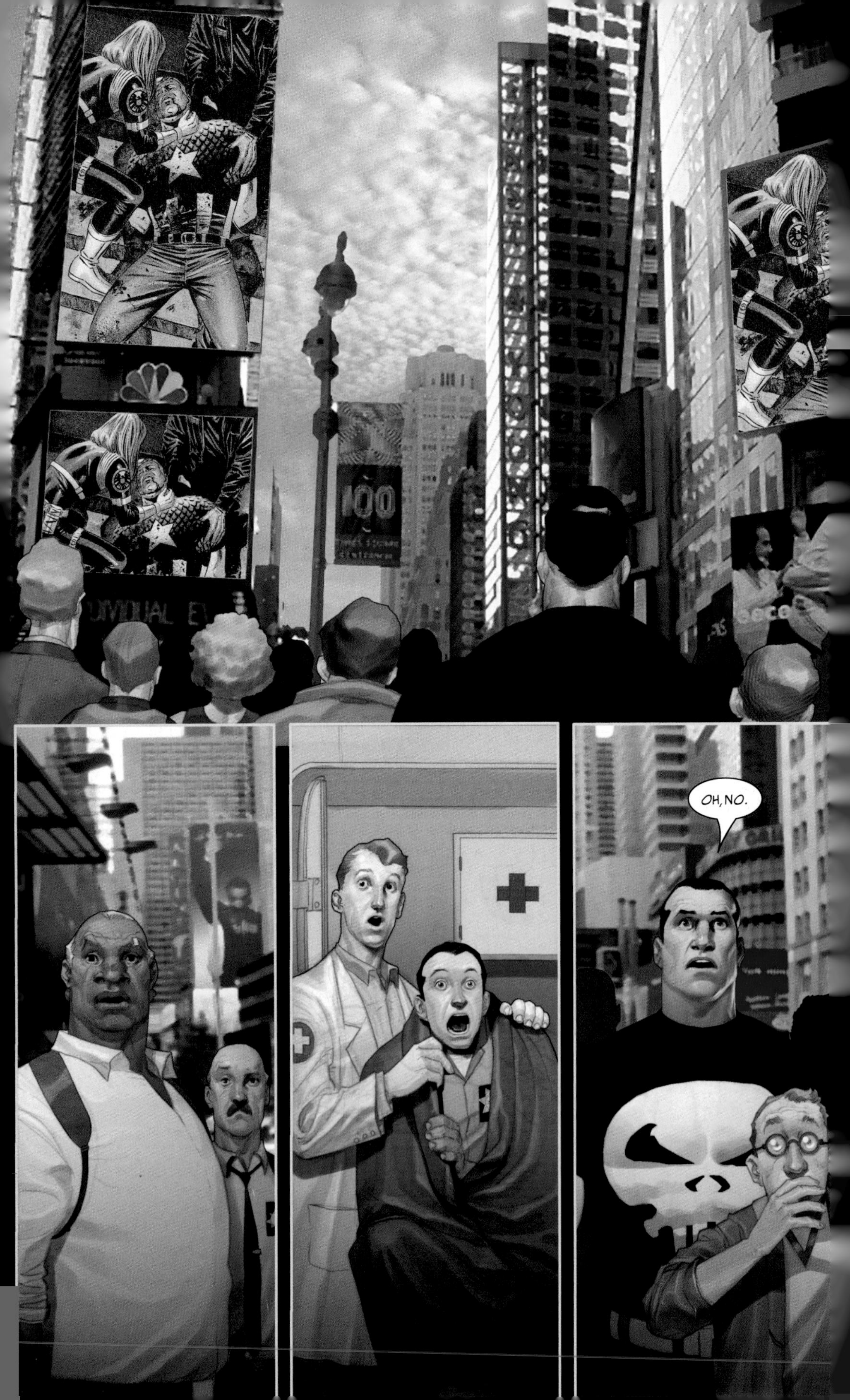
OH, NO.

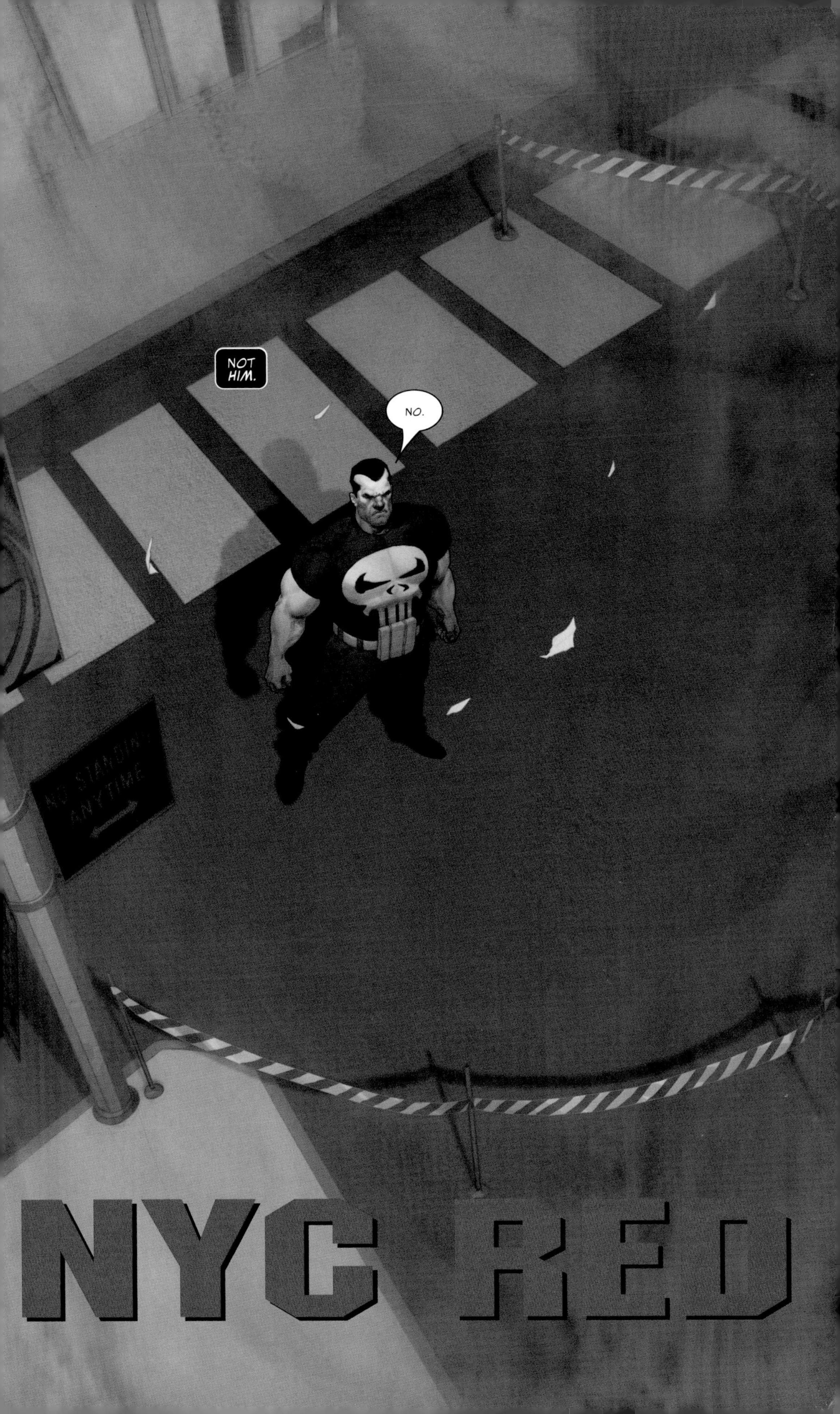
NOT HIM.
NO.
NYC RED

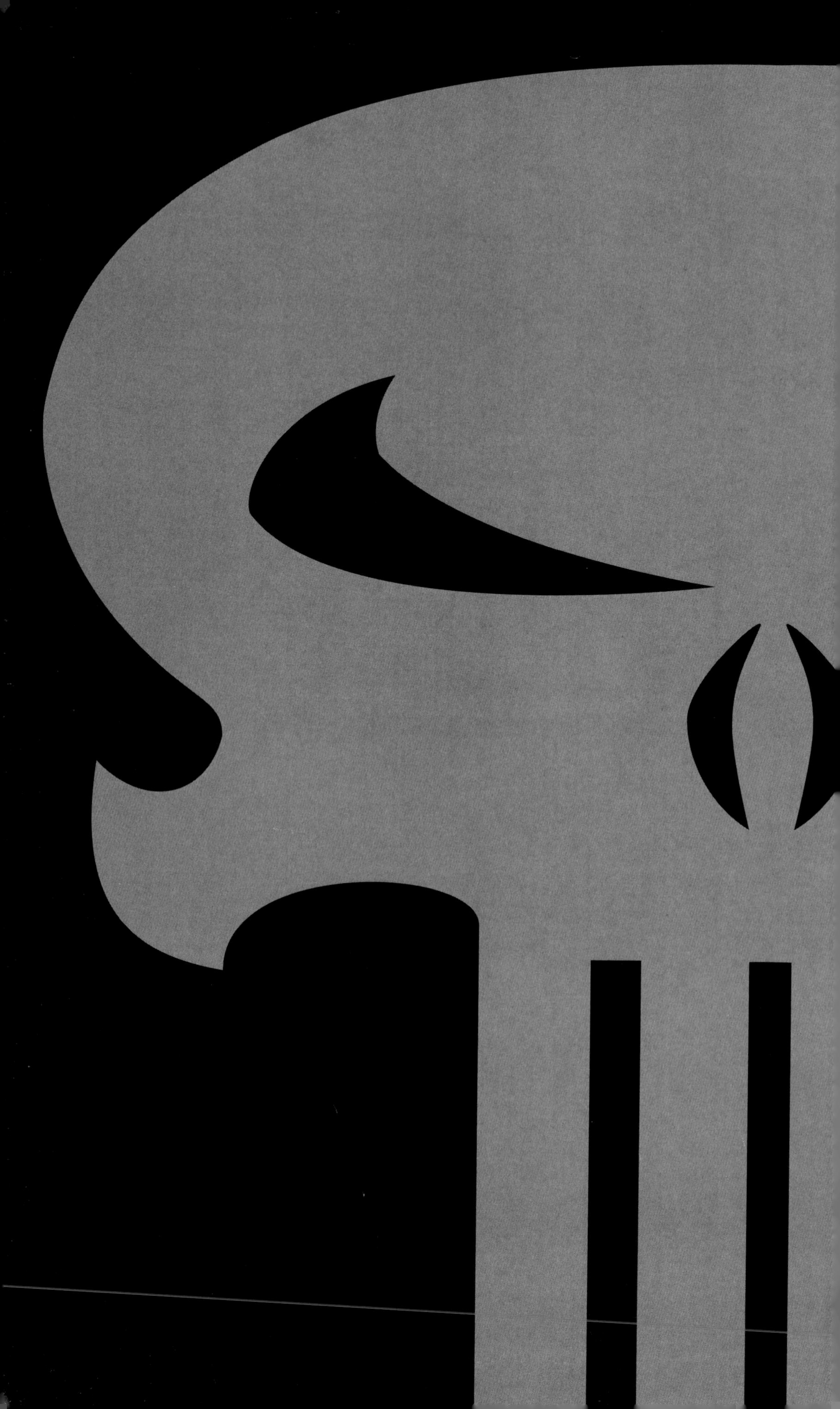

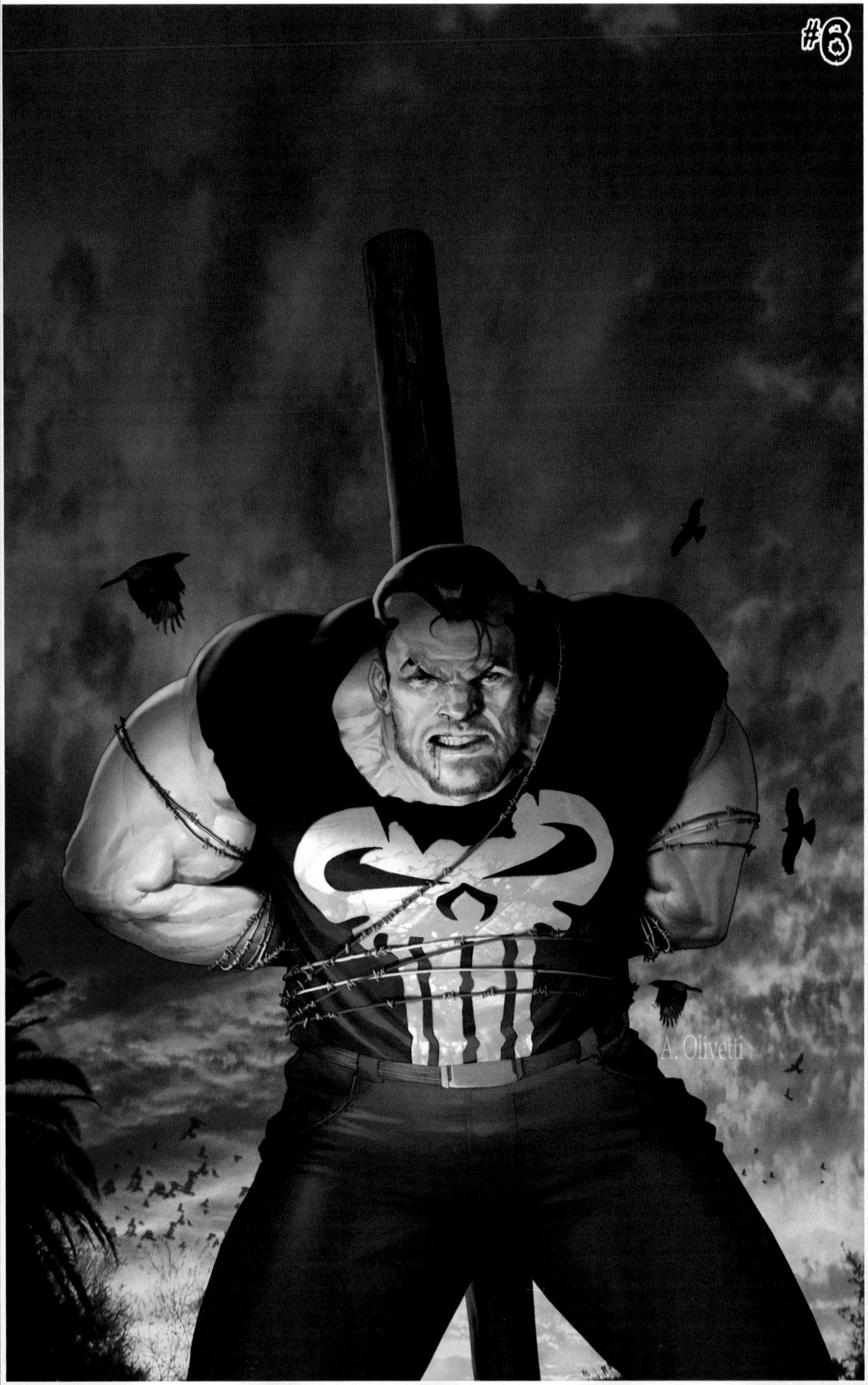
#6
A. Olivetti

GOIN' OUT WEST

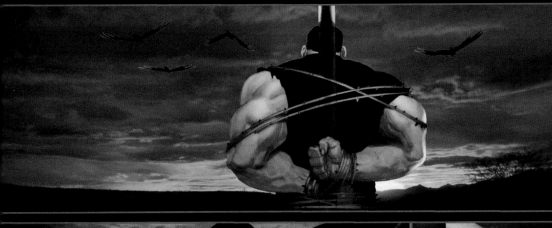

I'M GONNA DIE OUT HERE.

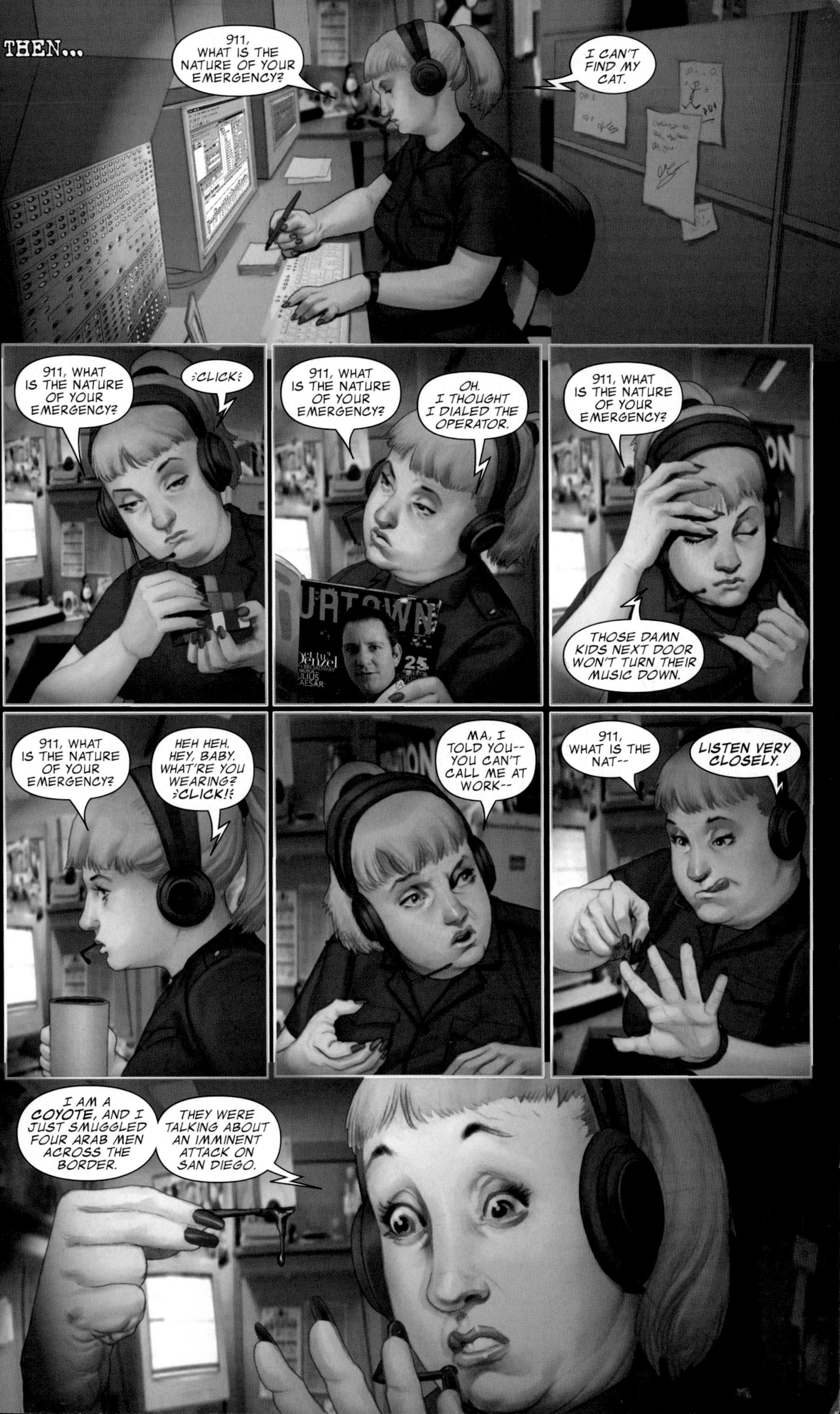
THEN...
911, WHAT IS THE NATURE OF YOUR EMERGENCY?
I CAN'T FIND MY CAT.
911, WHAT IS THE NATURE OF YOUR EMERGENCY?
CLICK
911, WHAT IS THE NATURE OF YOUR EMERGENCY?
OH. I THOUGHT I DIALED THE OPERATOR.
911, WHAT IS THE NATURE OF YOUR EMERGENCY?
THOSE DAMN KIDS NEXT DOOR WON'T TURN THEIR MUSIC DOWN.
911, WHAT IS THE NATURE OF YOUR EMERGENCY?
HEH HEH. HEY, BABY. WHAT'RE YOU WEARING? CLICK!
MA, I TOLD YOU-- YOU CAN'T CALL ME AT WORK--
911, WHAT IS THE NAT--
LISTEN VERY CLOSELY.
I AM A COYOTE, AND I JUST SMUGGLED FOUR ARAB MEN ACROSS THE BORDER.
THEY WERE TALKING ABOUT AN IMMINENT ATTACK ON SAN DIEGO.

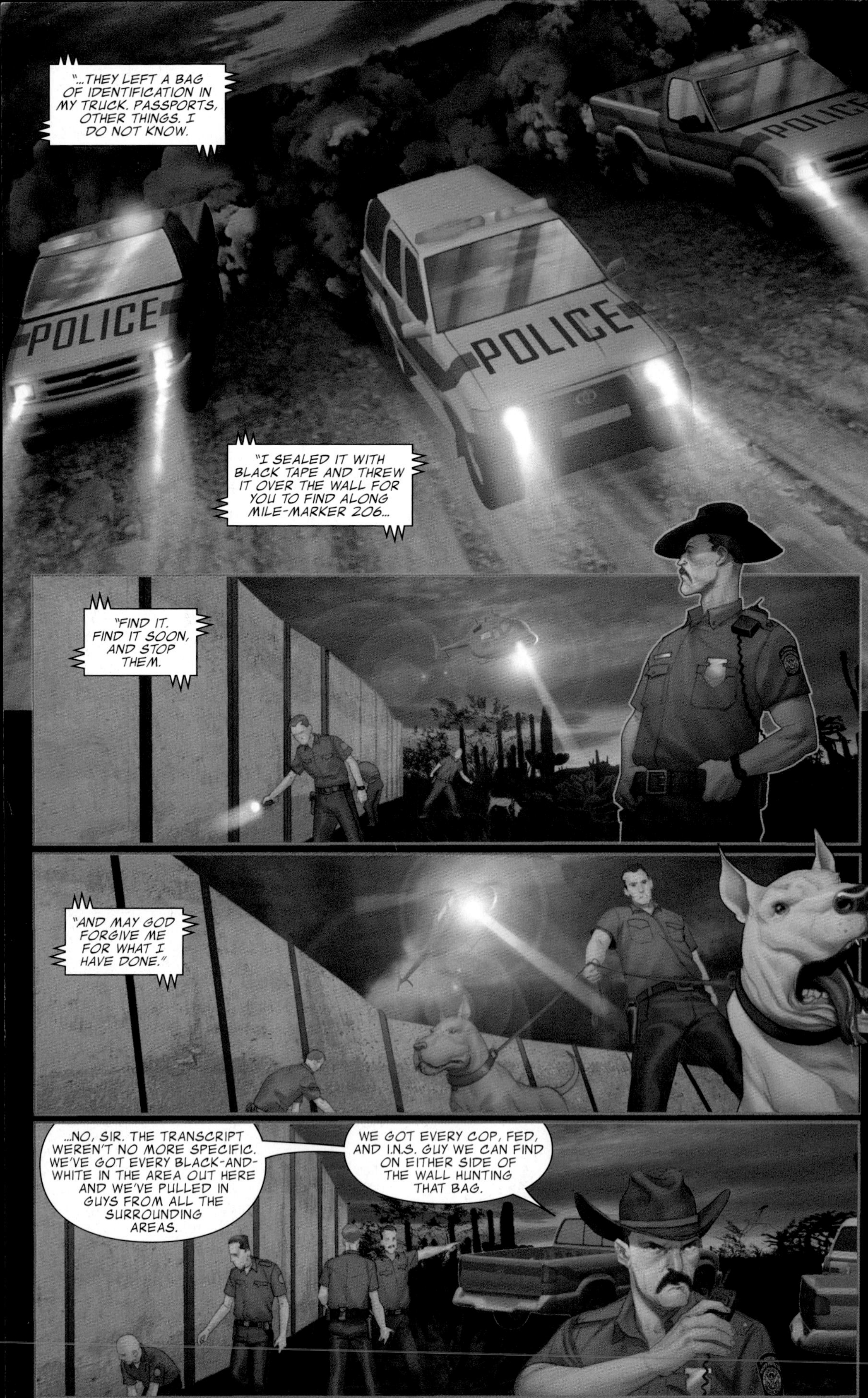
"...THEY LEFT A BAG OF IDENTIFICATION IN MY TRUCK. PASSPORTS, OTHER THINGS. I DO NOT KNOW.
POLICE
POLICE
POLICE
"I SEALED IT WITH BLACK TAPE AND THREW IT OVER THE WALL FOR YOU TO FIND ALONG MILE-MARKER 206...
"FIND IT. FIND IT SOON, AND STOP THEM.
"AND MAY GOD FORGIVE ME FOR WHAT I HAVE DONE."
...NO, SIR. THE TRANSCRIPT WEREN'T NO MORE SPECIFIC. WE'VE GOT EVERY BLACK-AND-WHITE IN THE AREA OUT HERE AND WE'VE PULLED IN GUYS FROM ALL THE SURROUNDING AREAS.
WE GOT EVERY COP, FED, AND I.N.S. GUY WE CAN FIND ON EITHER SIDE OF THE WALL HUNTING THAT BAG.

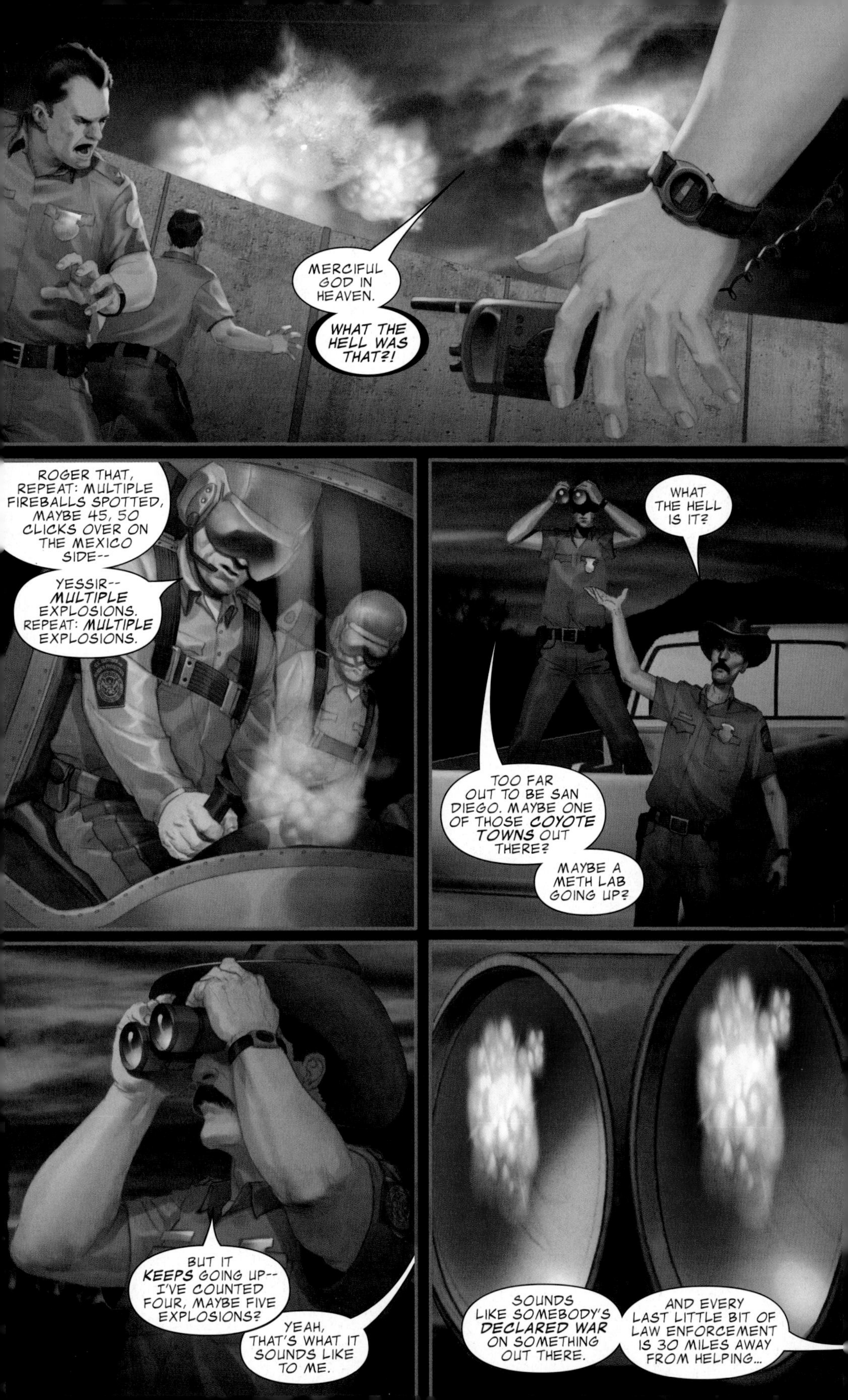
MERCIFUL GOD IN HEAVEN.
WHAT THE HELL WAS THAT?!
ROGER THAT, REPEAT: MULTIPLE FIREBALLS SPOTTED, MAYBE 45, 50 CLICKS OVER ON THE MEXICO SIDE--
YESSIR-- MULTIPLE EXPLOSIONS. REPEAT: MULTIPLE EXPLOSIONS.
WHAT THE HELL IS IT?
TOO FAR OUT TO BE SAN DIEGO. MAYBE ONE OF THOSE COYOTE TOWNS OUT THERE?
MAYBE A METH LAB GOING UP?
BUT IT KEEPS GOING UP-- I'VE COUNTED FOUR, MAYBE FIVE EXPLOSIONS?
YEAH, THAT'S WHAT IT SOUNDS LIKE TO ME.
SOUNDS LIKE SOMEBODY'S DECLARED WAR ON SOMETHING OUT THERE.
AND EVERY LAST LITTLE BIT OF LAW ENFORCEMENT IS 30 MILES AWAY FROM HELPING...

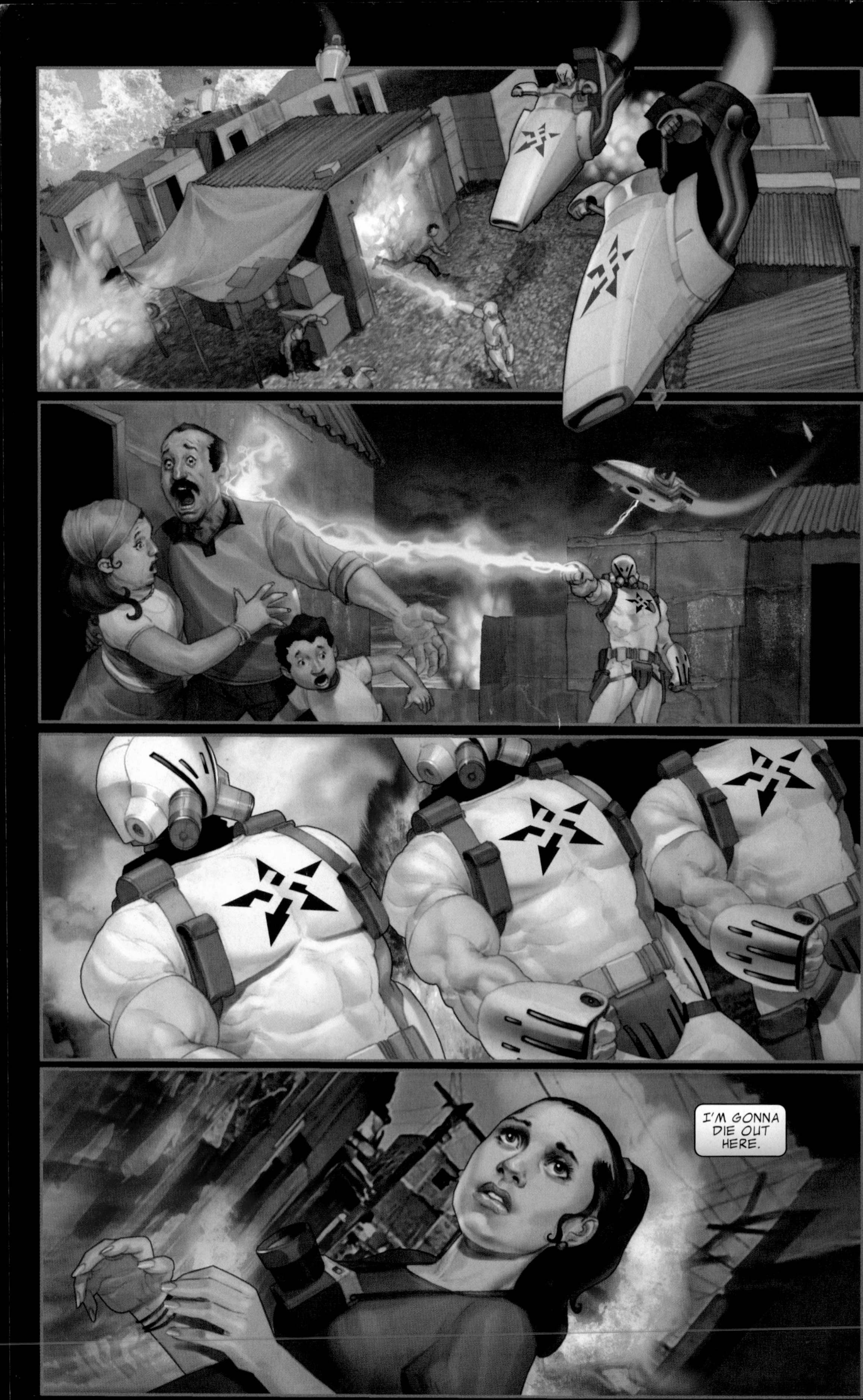
I'M GONNA DIE OUT HERE.

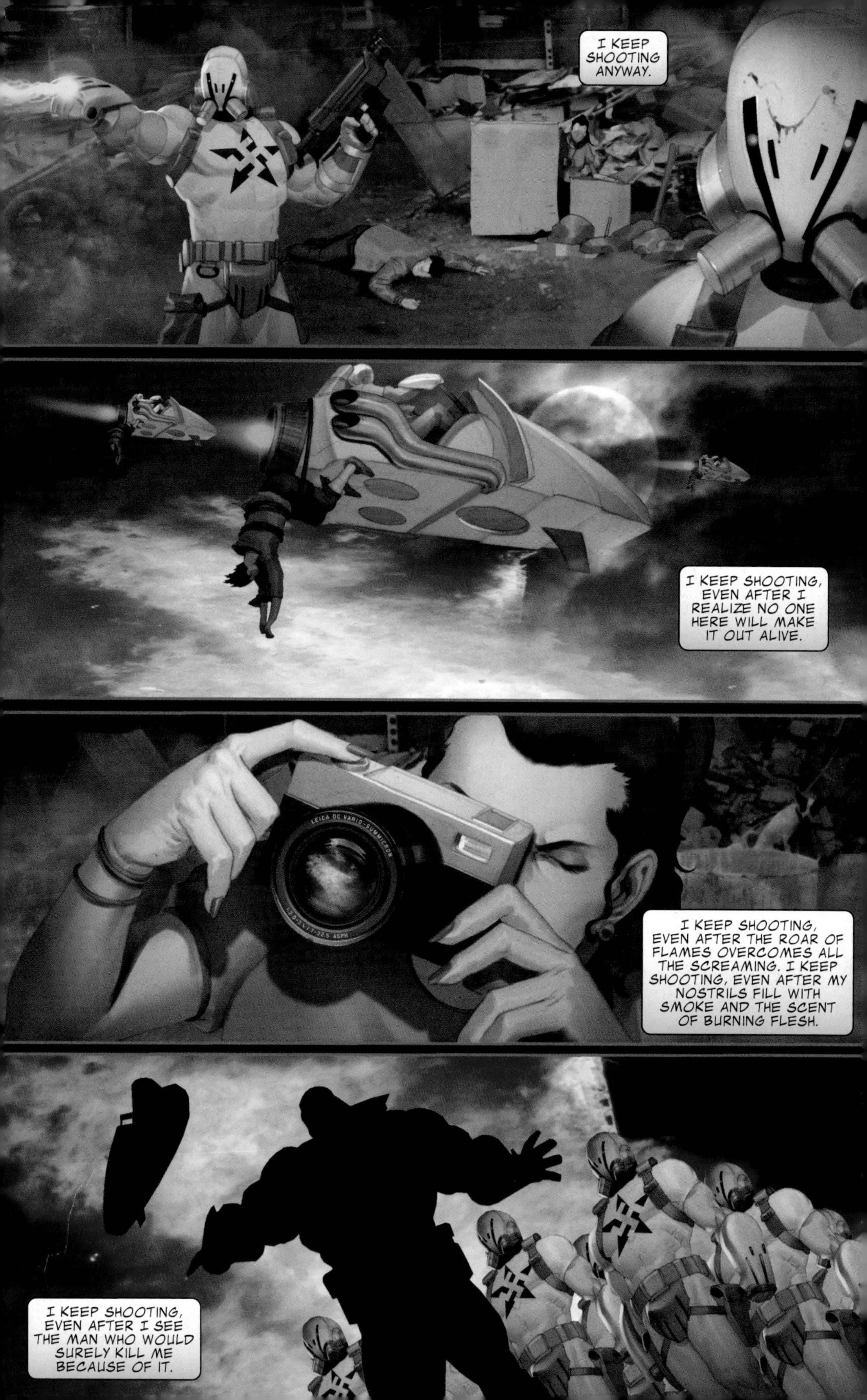
I KEEP SHOOTING ANYWAY.
I KEEP SHOOTING, EVEN AFTER I REALIZE NO ONE HERE WILL MAKE IT OUT ALIVE.
I KEEP SHOOTING, EVEN AFTER THE ROAR OF FLAMES OVERCOMES ALL THE SCREAMING. I KEEP SHOOTING, EVEN AFTER MY NOSTRILS FILL WITH SMOKE AND THE SCENT OF BURNING FLESH.
I KEEP SHOOTING, EVEN AFTER I SEE THE MAN WHO WOULD SURELY KILL ME BECAUSE OF IT.

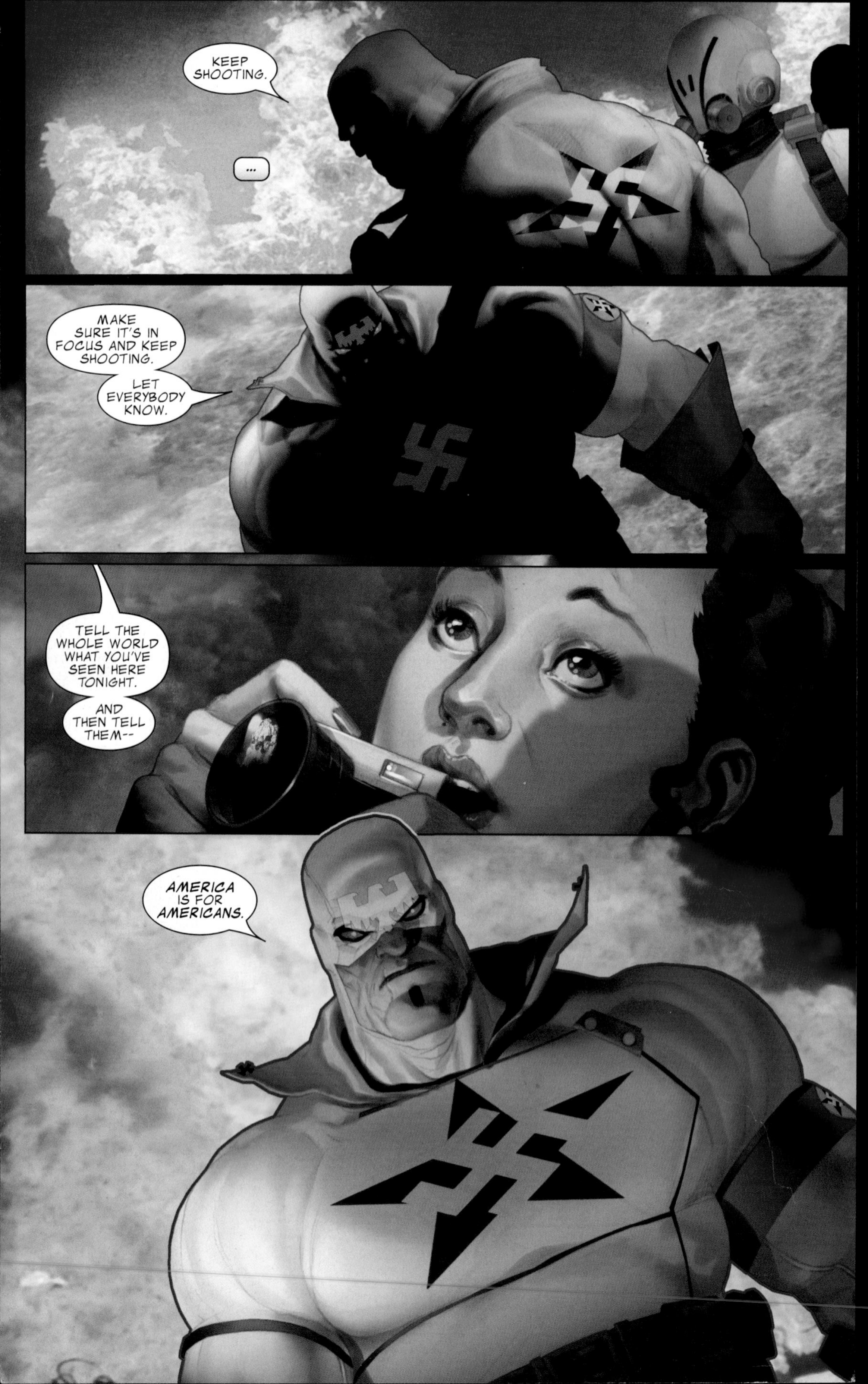
KEEP SHOOTING.
...
MAKE SURE IT'S IN FOCUS AND KEEP SHOOTING.
LET EVERYBODY KNOW.
TELL THE WHOLE WORLD WHAT YOU'VE SEEN HERE TONIGHT.
AND THEN TELL THEM--
AMERICA IS FOR AMERICANS.

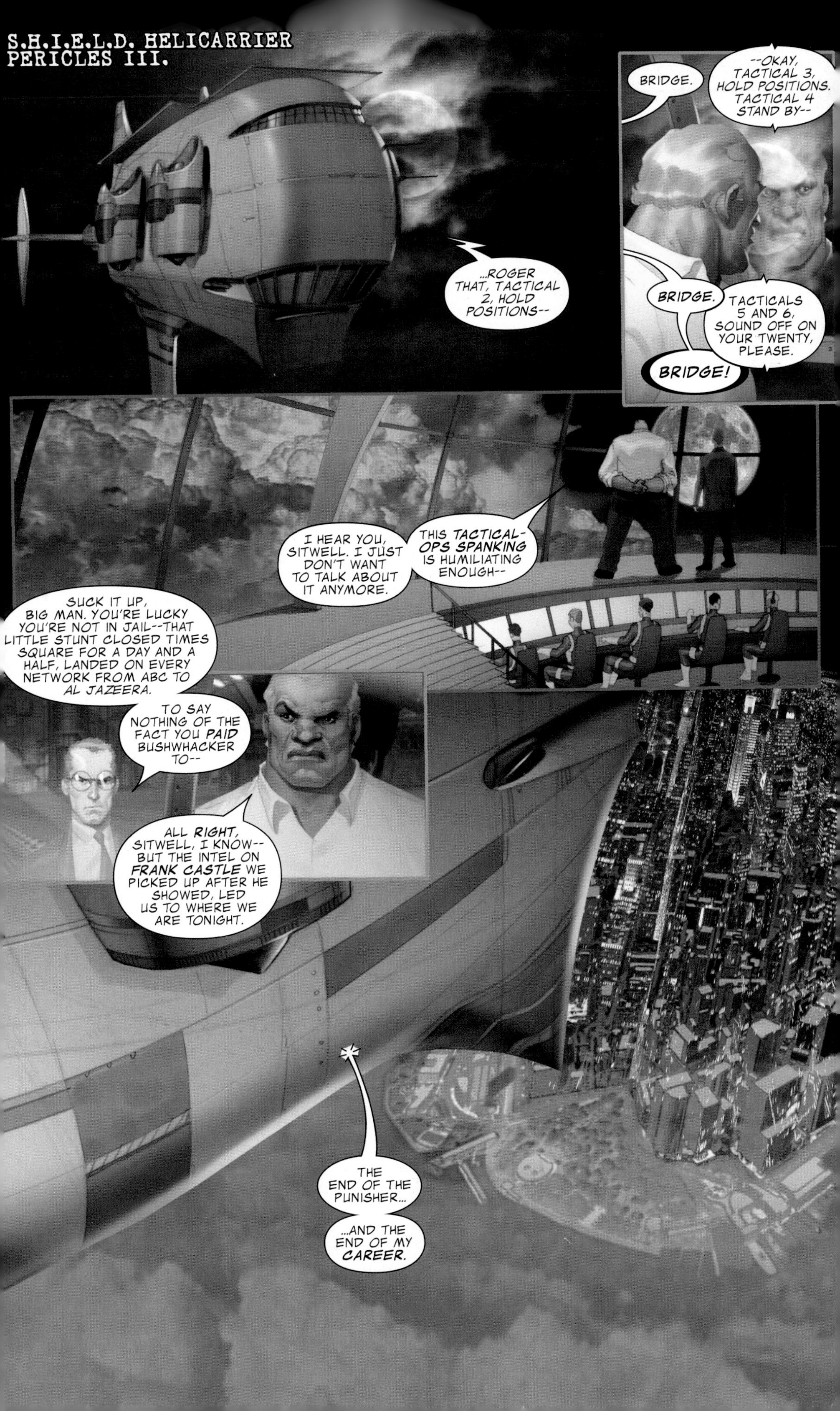
S.H.I.E.L.D. HELICARRIER PERICLES III.
...ROGER THAT, TACTICAL 2, HOLD POSITIONS--
BRIDGE.
--OKAY, TACTICAL 3, HOLD POSITIONS. TACTICAL 4 STAND BY--
BRIDGE.
TACTICALS 5 AND 6, SOUND OFF ON YOUR TWENTY, PLEASE.
BRIDGE!
THIS TACTICAL-OPS SPANKING IS HUMILIATING ENOUGH--
I HEAR YOU, SITWELL. I JUST DON'T WANT TO TALK ABOUT IT ANYMORE.
SUCK IT UP, BIG MAN. YOU'RE LUCKY YOU'RE NOT IN JAIL--THAT LITTLE STUNT CLOSED TIMES SQUARE FOR A DAY AND A HALF, LANDED ON EVERY NETWORK FROM ABC TO AL JAZEERA.
TO SAY NOTHING OF THE FACT YOU PAID BUSHWHACKER TO--
ALL RIGHT, SITWELL, I KNOW--BUT THE INTEL ON FRANK CASTLE WE PICKED UP AFTER HE SHOWED, LED US TO WHERE WE ARE TONIGHT.
THE END OF THE PUNISHER...
...AND THE END OF MY CAREER.

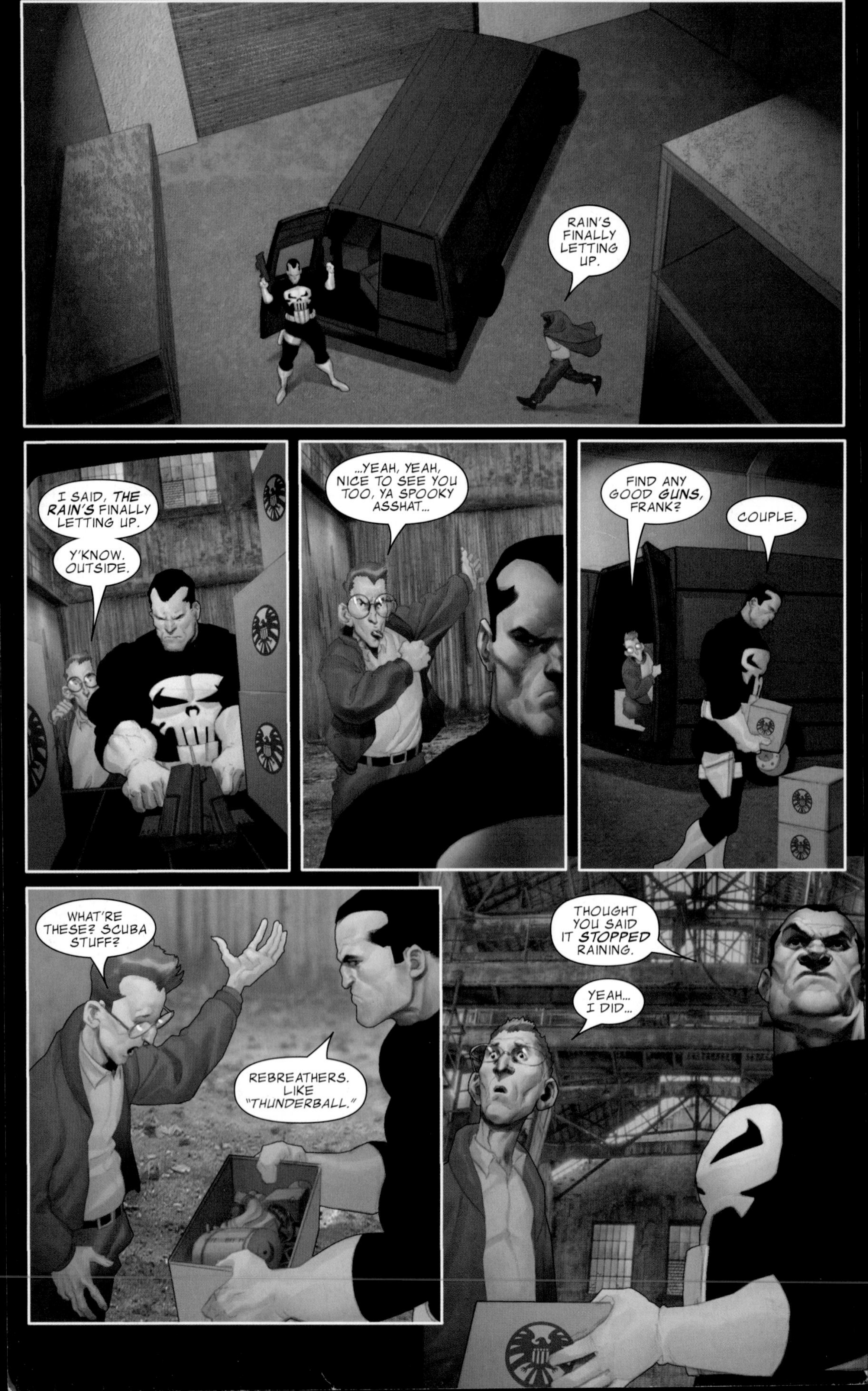
RAIN'S FINALLY LETTING UP.
I SAID, THE RAIN'S FINALLY LETTING UP.
Y'KNOW. OUTSIDE.
...YEAH, YEAH, NICE TO SEE YOU TOO, YA SPOOKY ASSHAT...
FIND ANY GOOD GUNS, FRANK?
COUPLE.
WHAT'RE THESE? SCUBA STUFF?
REBREATHERS. LIKE "THUNDERBALL."
THOUGHT YOU SAID IT STOPPED RAINING.
YEAH... I DID...

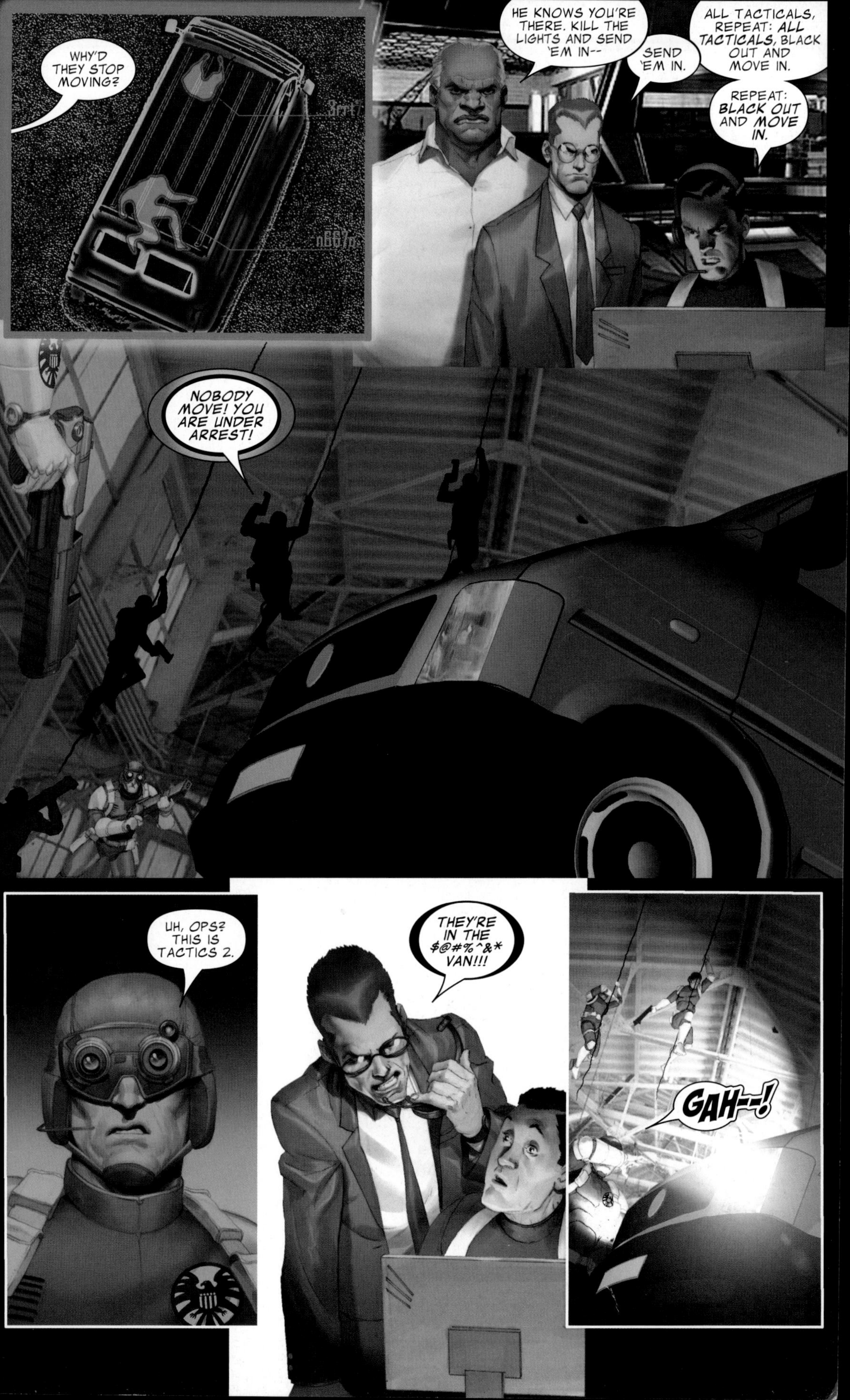
WHY'D THEY STOP MOVING?
HE KNOWS YOU'RE THERE. KILL THE LIGHTS AND SEND 'EM IN--
SEND 'EM IN.
ALL TACTICALS, REPEAT: ALL TACTICALS, BLACK OUT AND MOVE IN.
REPEAT: BLACK OUT AND MOVE IN.
NOBODY MOVE! YOU ARE UNDER ARREST!
UH, OPS? THIS IS TACTICS 2.
THEY'RE IN THE $@#%^&* VAN!!!
GAH--!

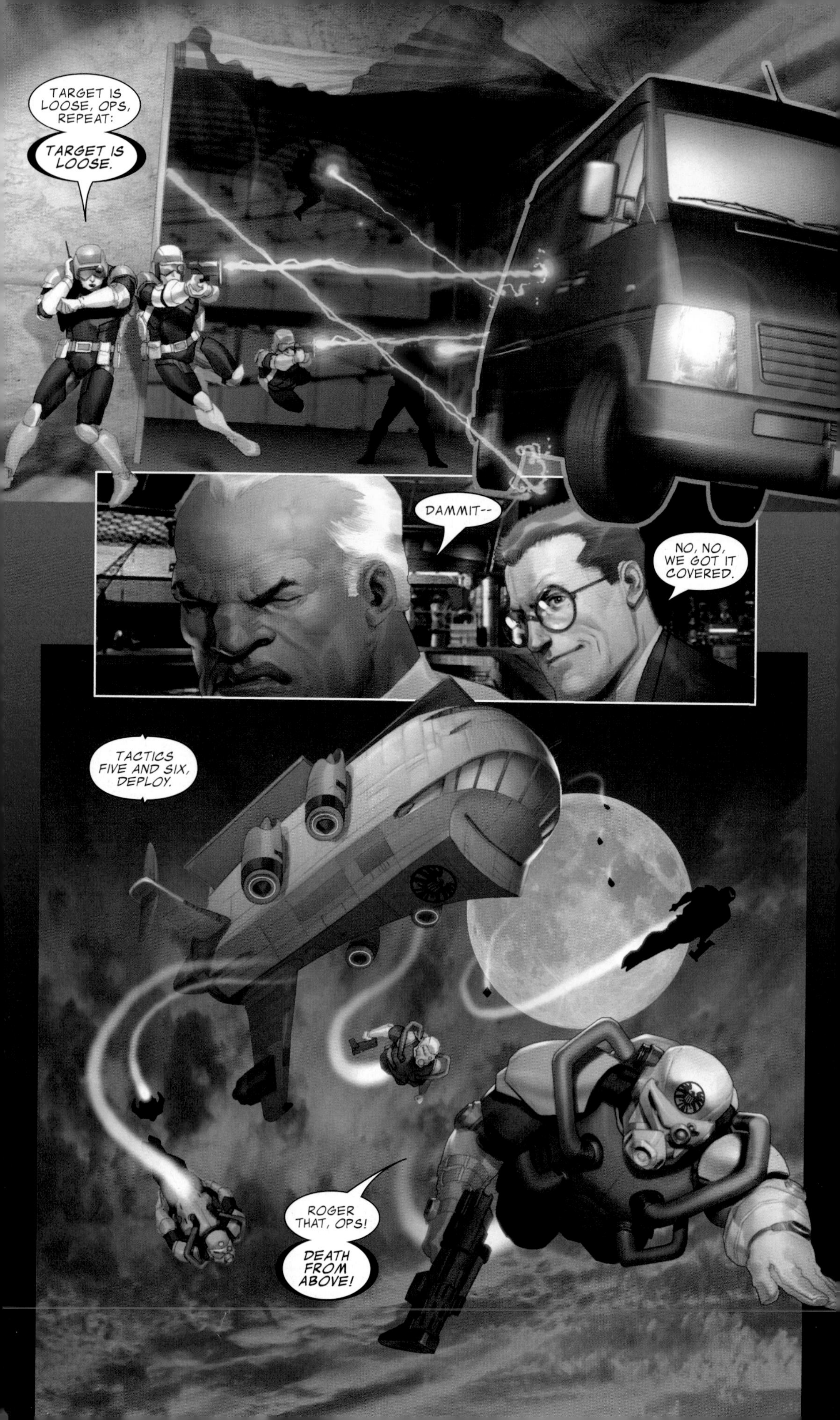
TARGET IS LOOSE, OPS, REPEAT:
TARGET IS LOOSE.
DAMMIT--
NO, NO, WE GOT IT COVERED.
TACTICS FIVE AND SIX, DEPLOY.
ROGER THAT, OPS!
DEATH FROM ABOVE!

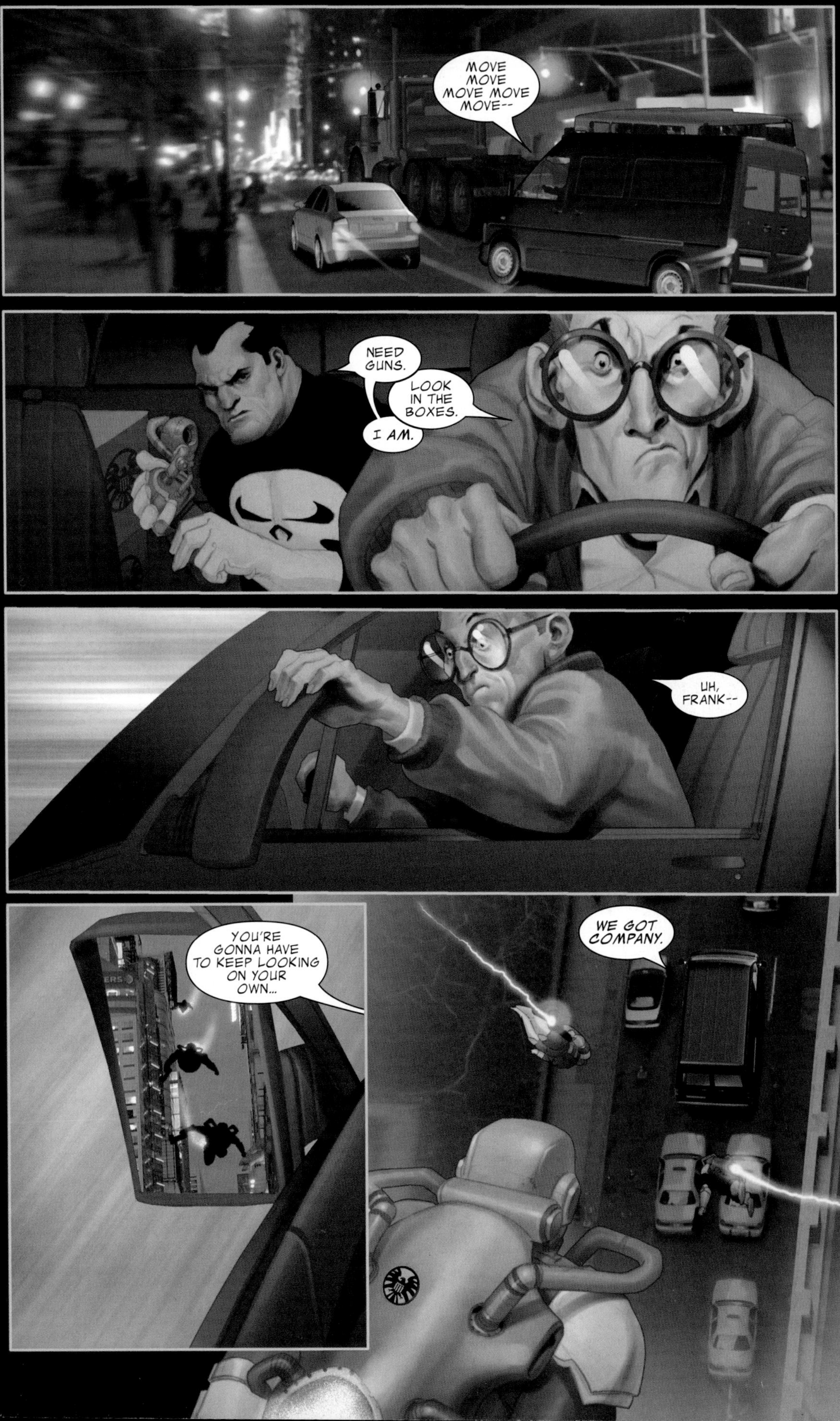
MOVE MOVE MOVE MOVE MOVE--
NEED GUNS.
LOOK IN THE BOXES.
I AM.
UH, FRANK--
YOU'RE GONNA HAVE TO KEEP LOOKING ON YOUR OWN...
WE GOT COMPANY.

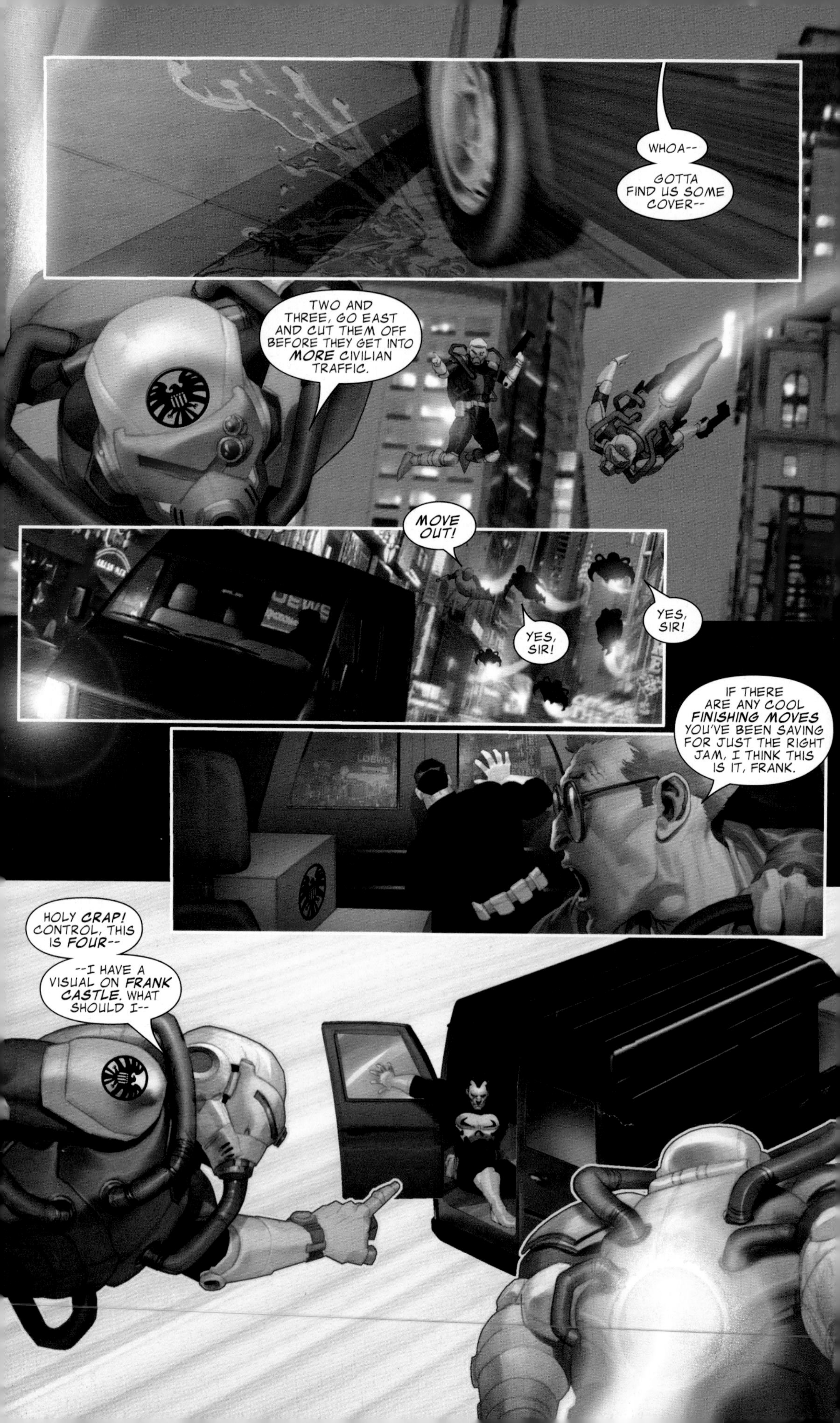
WHOA--
GOTTA FIND US SOME COVER--
TWO AND THREE, GO EAST AND CUT THEM OFF BEFORE THEY GET INTO MORE CIVILIAN TRAFFIC.
MOVE OUT!
YES, SIR!
YES, SIR!
IF THERE ARE ANY COOL FINISHING MOVES YOU'VE BEEN SAVING FOR JUST THE RIGHT JAM, I THINK THIS IS IT, FRANK.
HOLY CRAP! CONTROL, THIS IS FOUR--
--I HAVE A VISUAL ON FRANK CASTLE. WHAT SHOULD I--

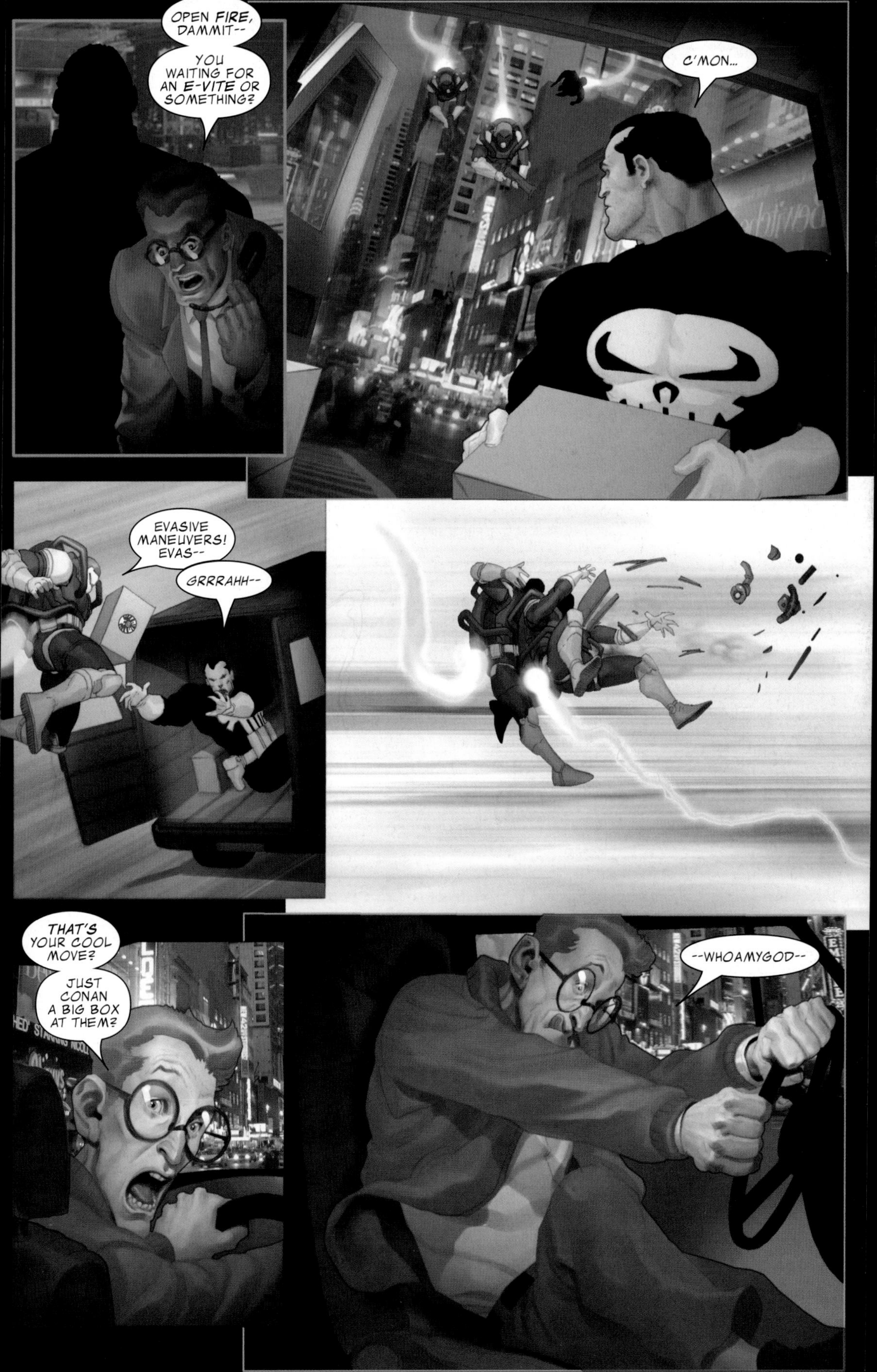
OPEN FIRE, DAMMIT--
YOU WAITING FOR AN E-VITE OR SOMETHING?
C'MON...
EVASIVE MANEUVERS! EVAS--
GRRRAHH--
THAT'S YOUR COOL MOVE?
JUST CONAN A BIG BOX AT THEM?
--WHOAMYGOD--

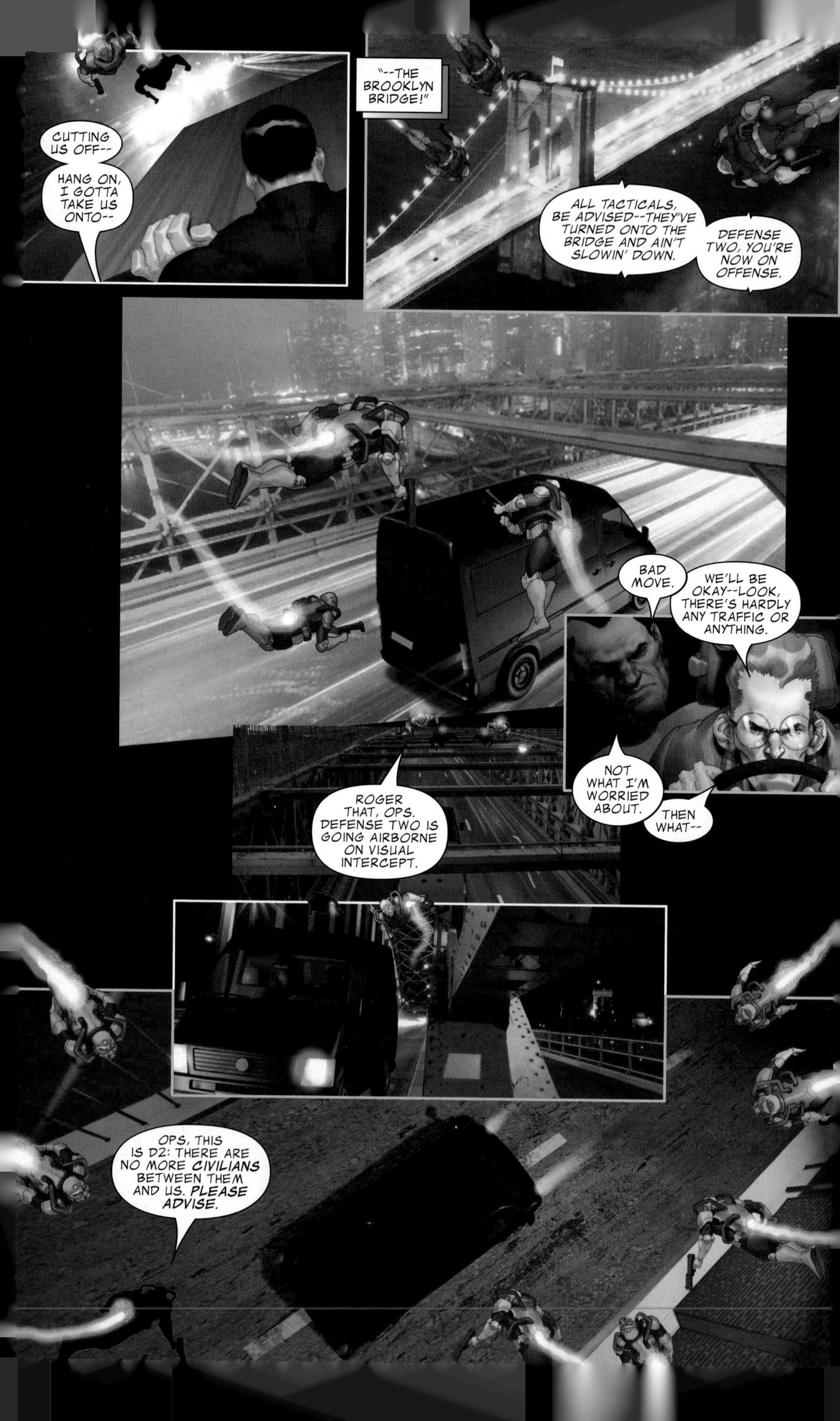
CUTTING US OFF--
HANG ON, I GOTTA TAKE US ONTO--
"--THE BROOKLYN BRIDGE!"
ALL TACTICALS, BE ADVISED--THEY'VE TURNED ONTO THE BRIDGE AND AIN'T SLOWIN' DOWN.
DEFENSE TWO, YOU'RE NOW ON OFFENSE.
BAD MOVE.
WE'LL BE OKAY--LOOK, THERE'S HARDLY ANY TRAFFIC OR ANYTHING.
NOT WHAT I'M WORRIED ABOUT.
THEN WHAT--
ROGER THAT, OPS. DEFENSE TWO IS GOING AIRBORNE ON VISUAL INTERCEPT.
OPS, THIS IS D2: THERE ARE NO MORE CIVILIANS BETWEEN THEM AND US. PLEASE ADVISE.

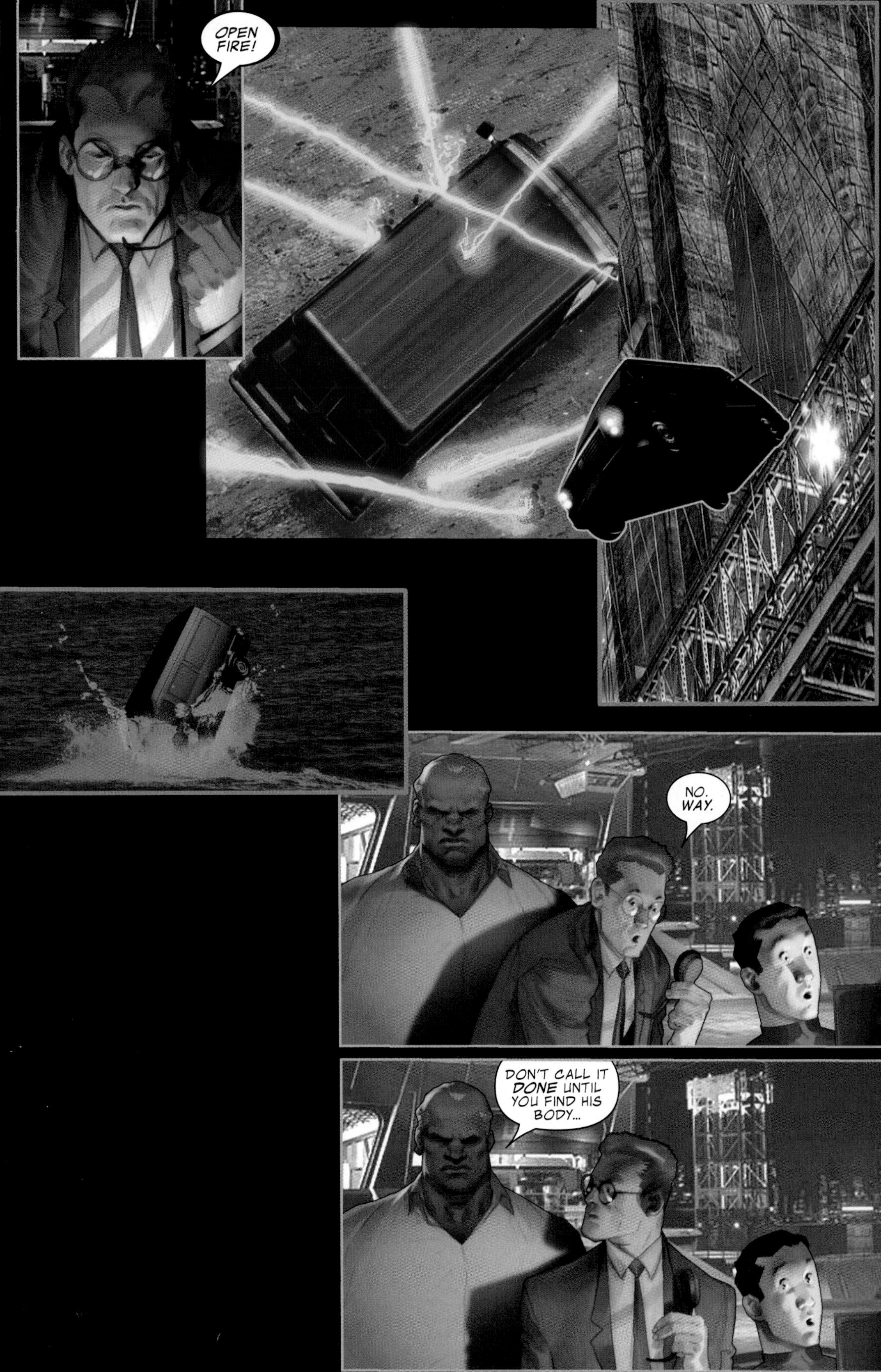
OPEN FIRE!
NO. WAY.
DON'T CALL IT DONE UNTIL YOU FIND HIS BODY...

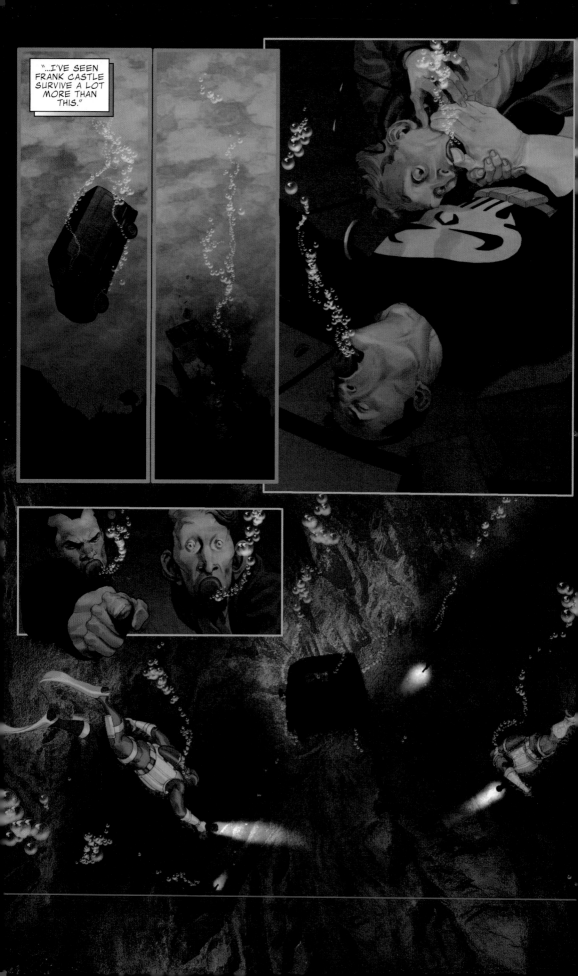

"...I'VE SEEN FRANK CASTLE SURVIVE A LOT MORE THAN THIS."

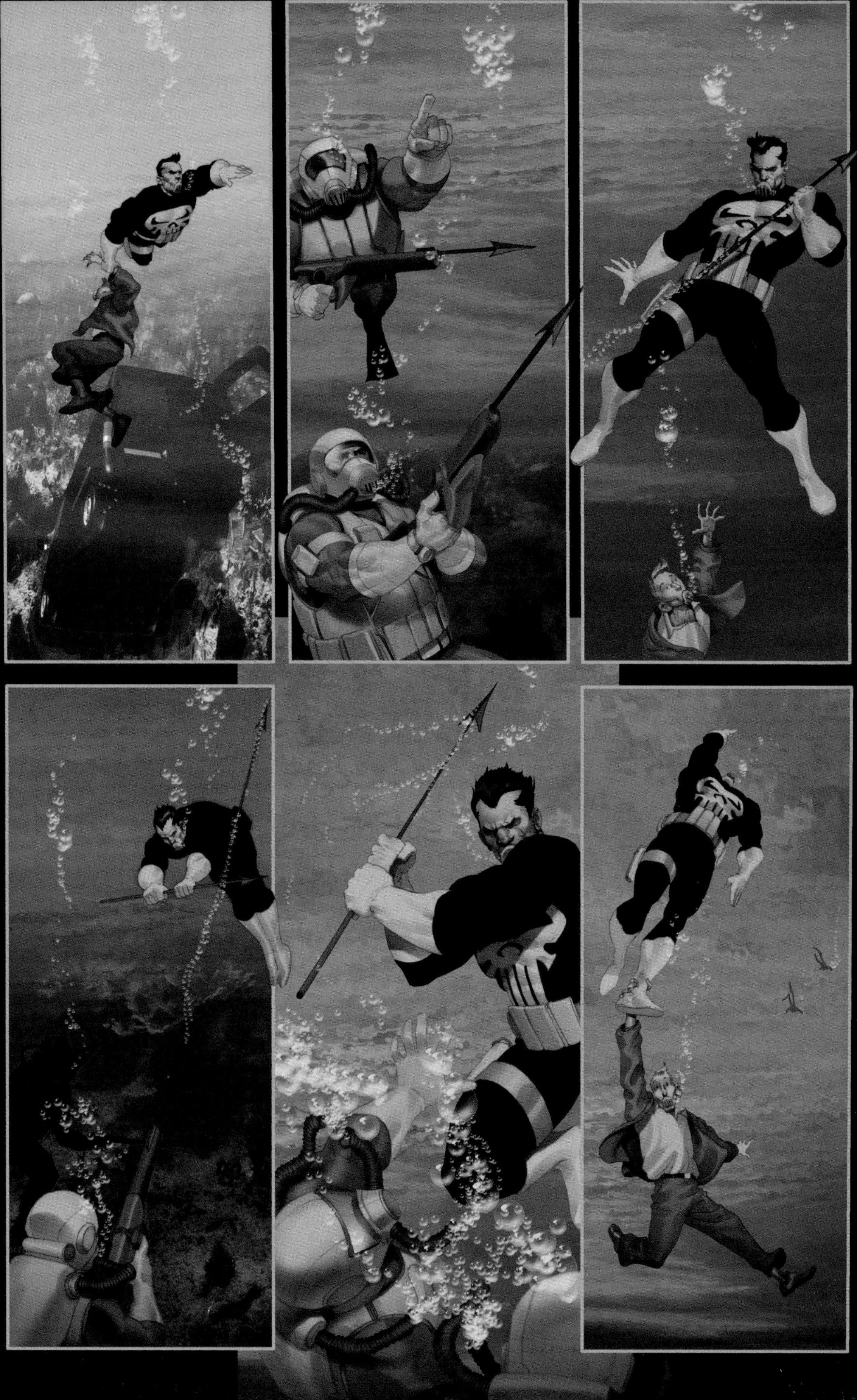

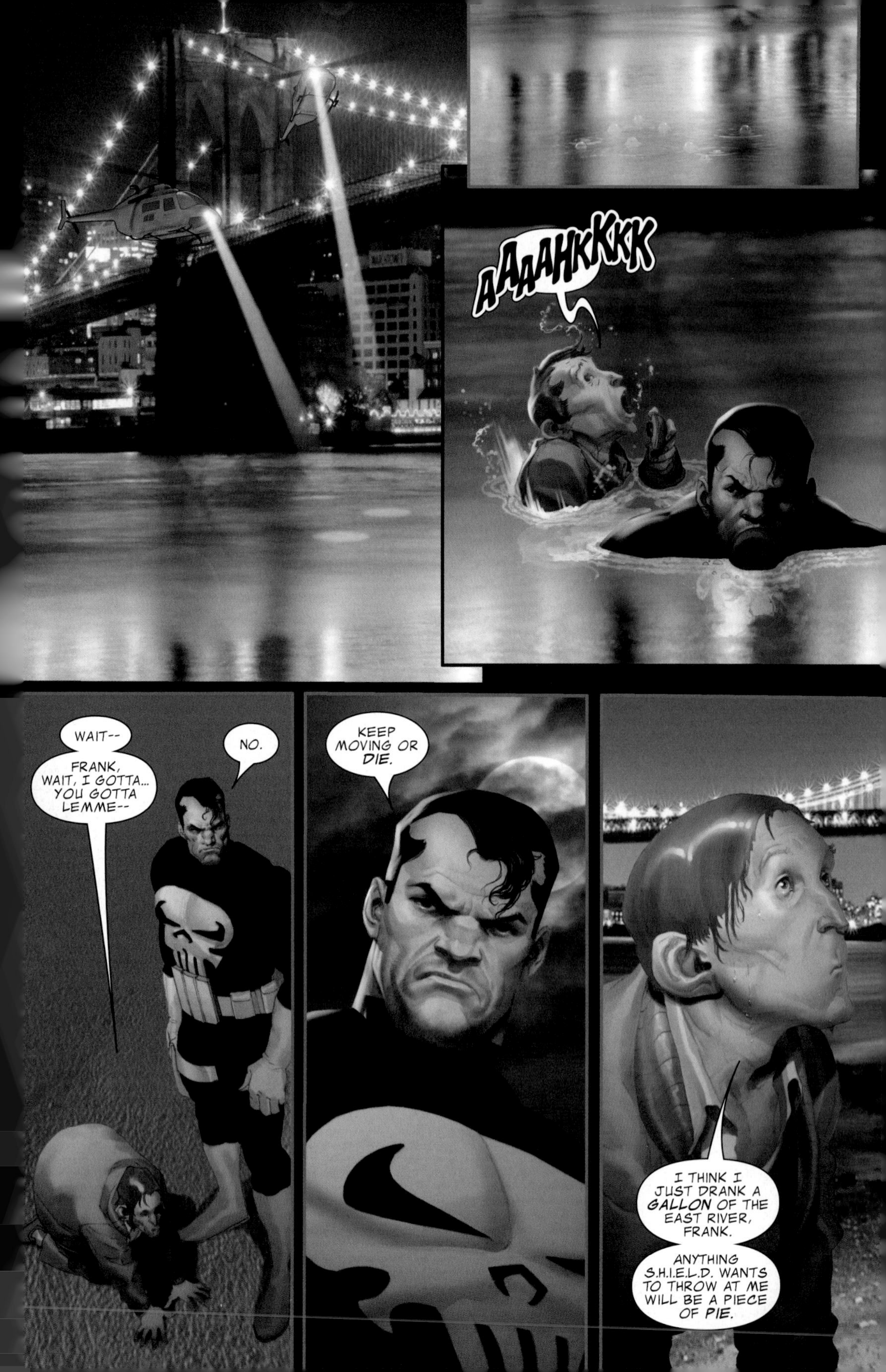
AAAAHKKKK
WAIT--
FRANK, WAIT, I GOTTA... YOU GOTTA LEMME--
NO.
KEEP MOVING OR DIE.
I THINK I JUST DRANK A GALLON OF THE EAST RIVER, FRANK.
ANYTHING S.H.I.E.L.D. WANTS TO THROW AT ME WILL BE A PIECE OF PIE.

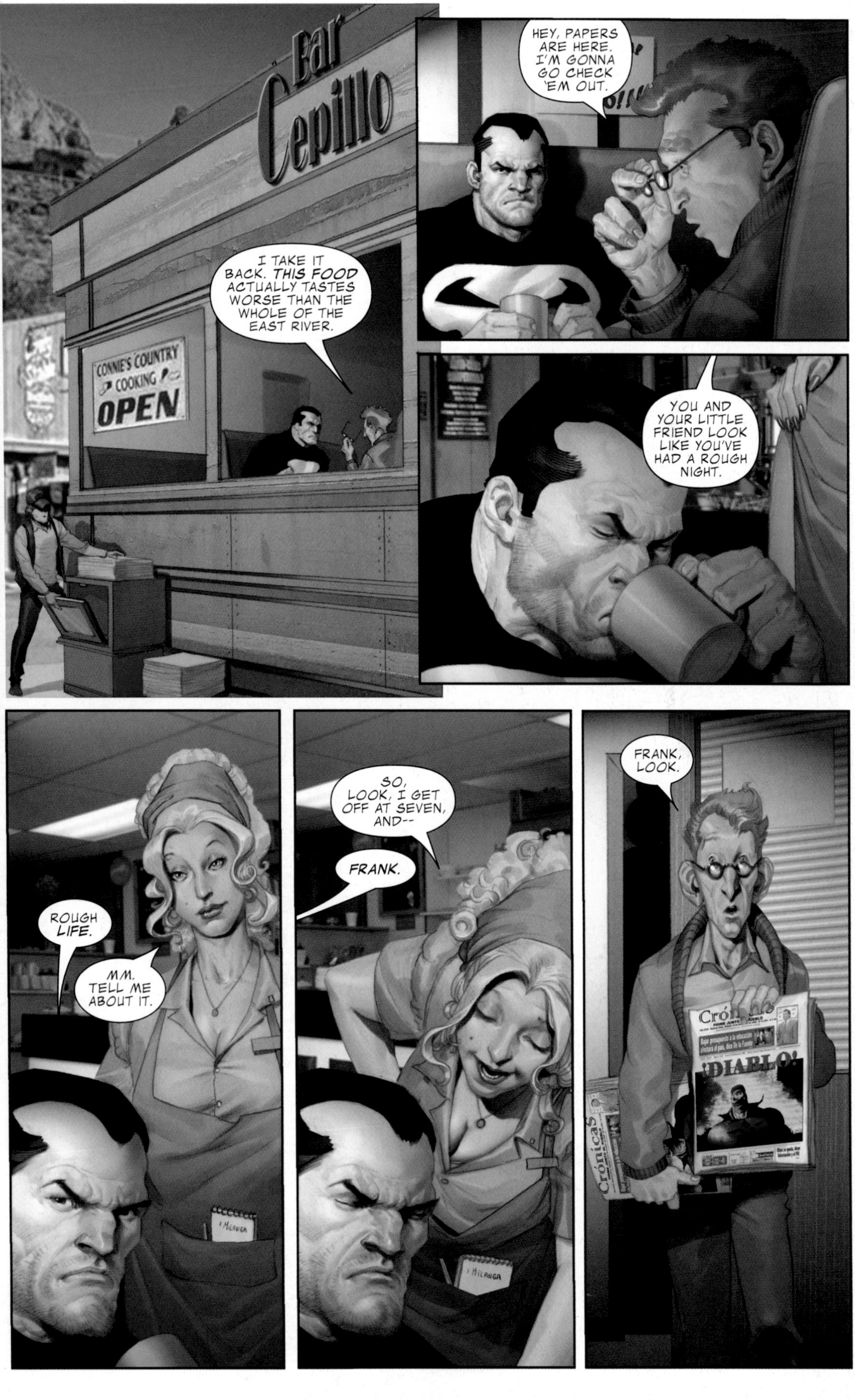
Bar Cepillo
CONNIE'S COUNTRY COOKING OPEN
I TAKE IT BACK. THIS FOOD ACTUALLY TASTES WORSE THAN THE WHOLE OF THE EAST RIVER.
HEY, PAPERS ARE HERE. I'M GONNA GO CHECK 'EM OUT.
YOU AND YOUR LITTLE FRIEND LOOK LIKE YOU'VE HAD A ROUGH NIGHT.
ROUGH LIFE.
MM. TELL ME ABOUT IT.
SO, LOOK, I GET OFF AT SEVEN, AND--
FRANK.
FRANK, LOOK.
¡DIABLO!

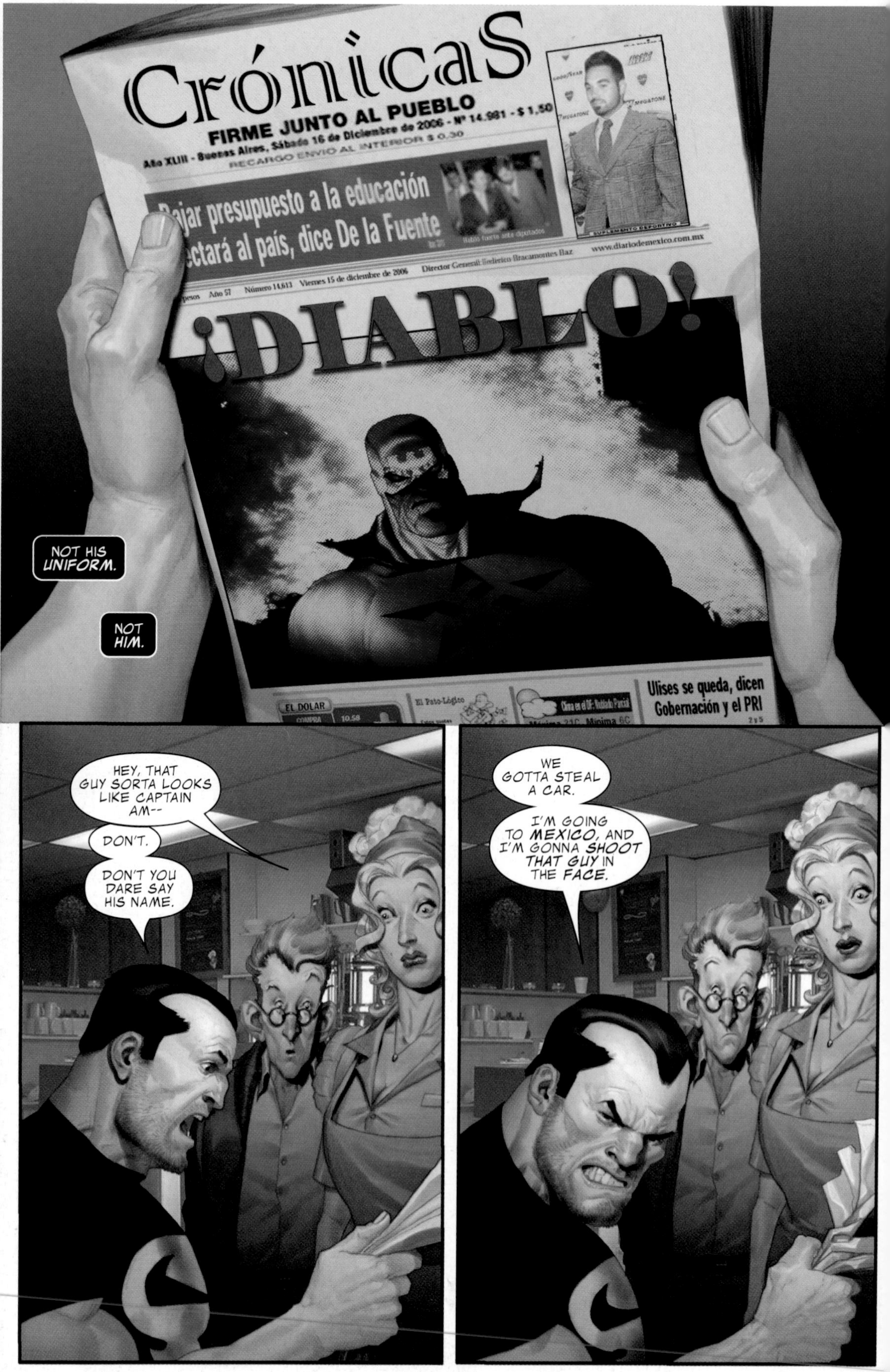

Crónicas
FIRME JUNTO AL PUEBLO
Año XLIII - Buenos Aires, Sábado 16 de Diciembre de 2006 - Nº 14.981 - $ 1,50
RECARGO ENVIO AL INTERIOR $ 0,30
ajar presupuesto a la educación
ectará al país, dice De la Fuente
SUPLEMENTO DEPORTIVO
www.diariodemexico.com.mx
Año 57 Número 14,613 Viernes 15 de diciembre de 2006
¡DIABLO!
Ulises se queda, dicen Gobernación y el PRI
EL DOLAR
NOT HIS UNIFORM.
NOT HIM.
HEY, THAT GUY SORTA LOOKS LIKE CAPTAIN AM--
DON'T.
DON'T YOU DARE SAY HIS NAME.
WE GOTTA STEAL A CAR.
I'M GOING TO MEXICO, AND I'M GONNA SHOOT THAT GUY IN THE FACE.

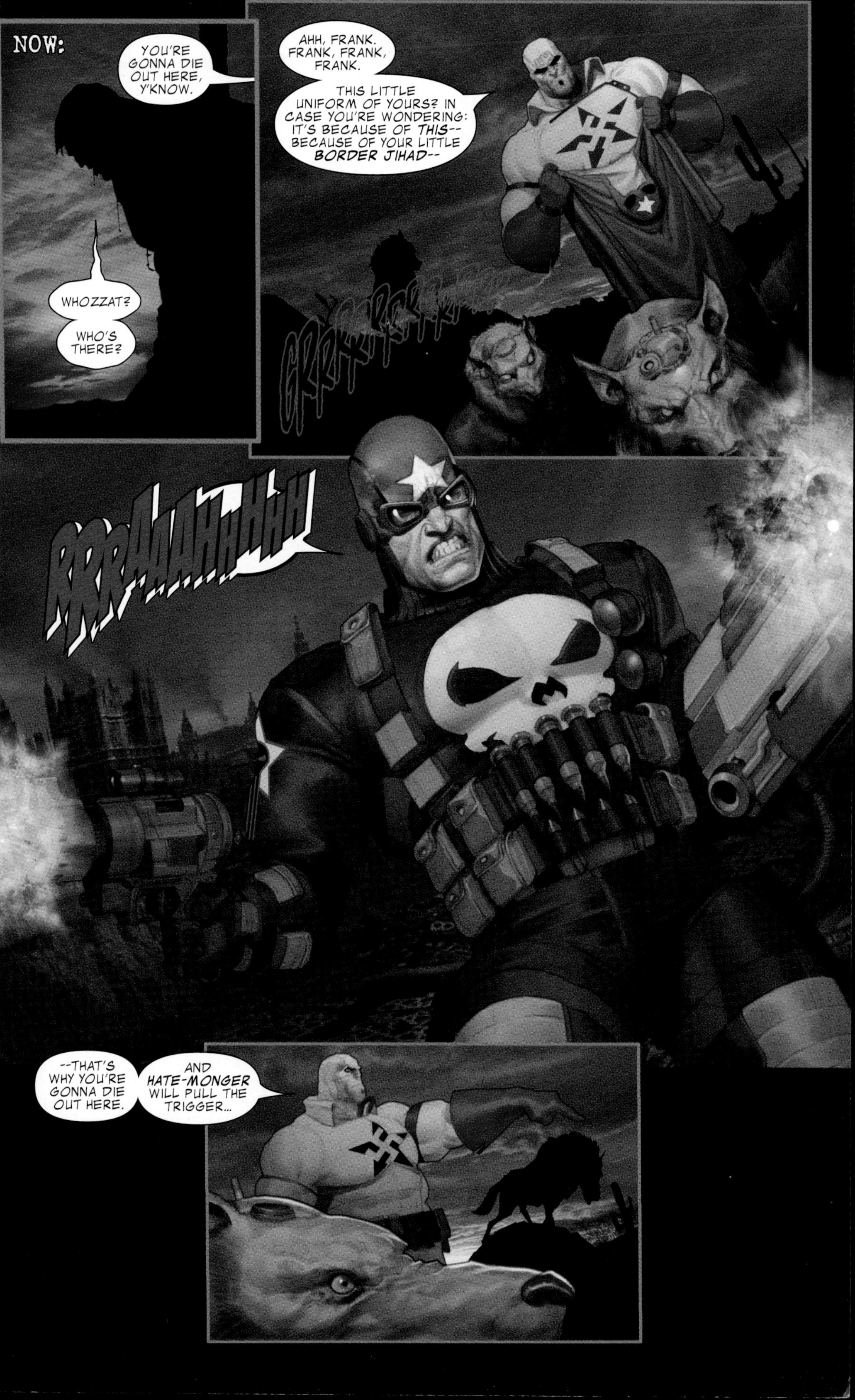
NOW:
YOU'RE GONNA DIE OUT HERE, Y'KNOW.
WHOZZAT?
WHO'S THERE?
AHH, FRANK. FRANK, FRANK, FRANK.
THIS LITTLE UNIFORM OF YOURS? IN CASE YOU'RE WONDERING: IT'S BECAUSE OF THIS-- BECAUSE OF YOUR LITTLE BORDER JIHAD--
GRRRRRRRRRRR
RRRAAAHHHHHH
--THAT'S WHY YOU'RE GONNA DIE OUT HERE.
AND HATE-MONGER WILL PULL THE TRIGGER...

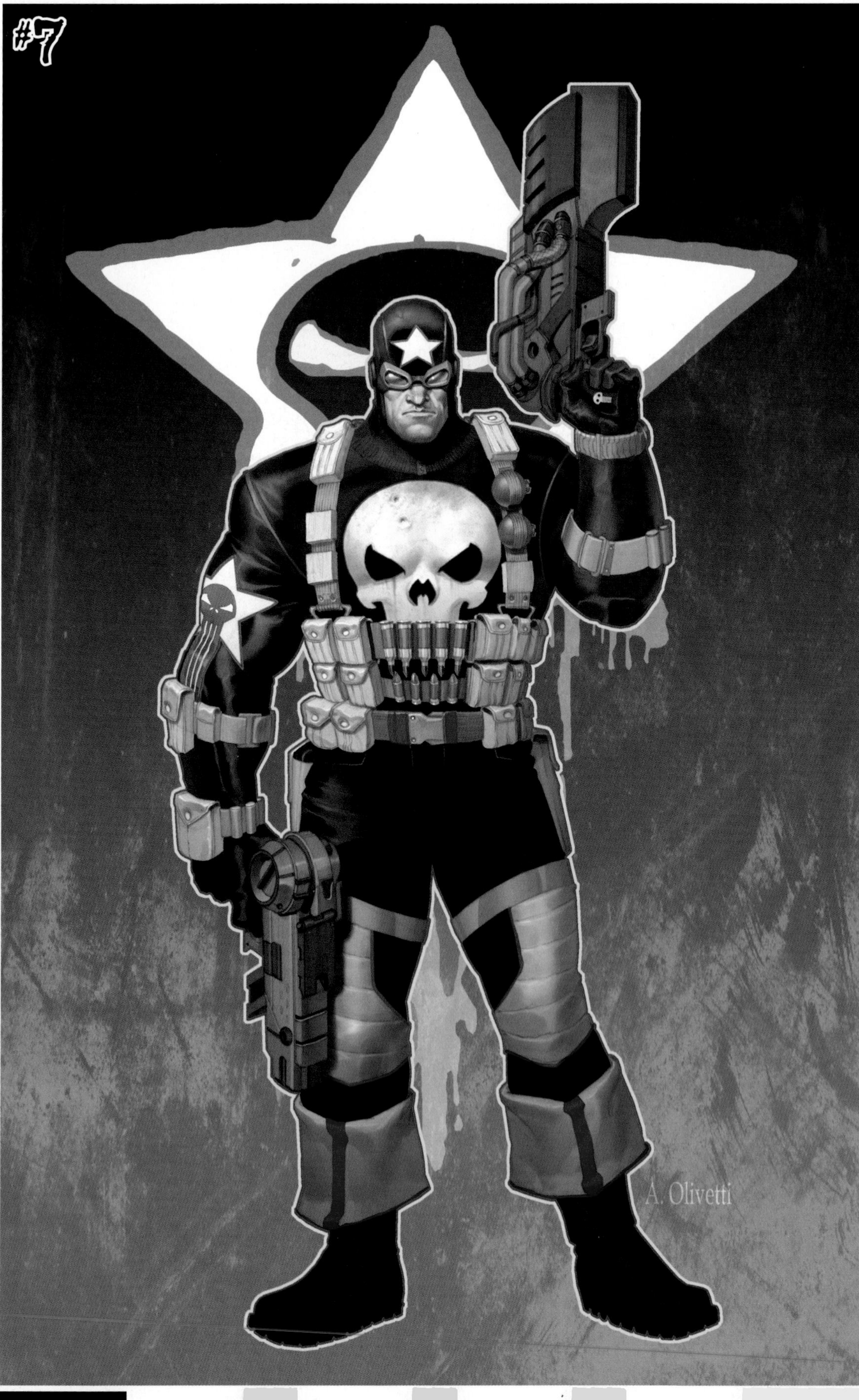
#7
A. Olivetti

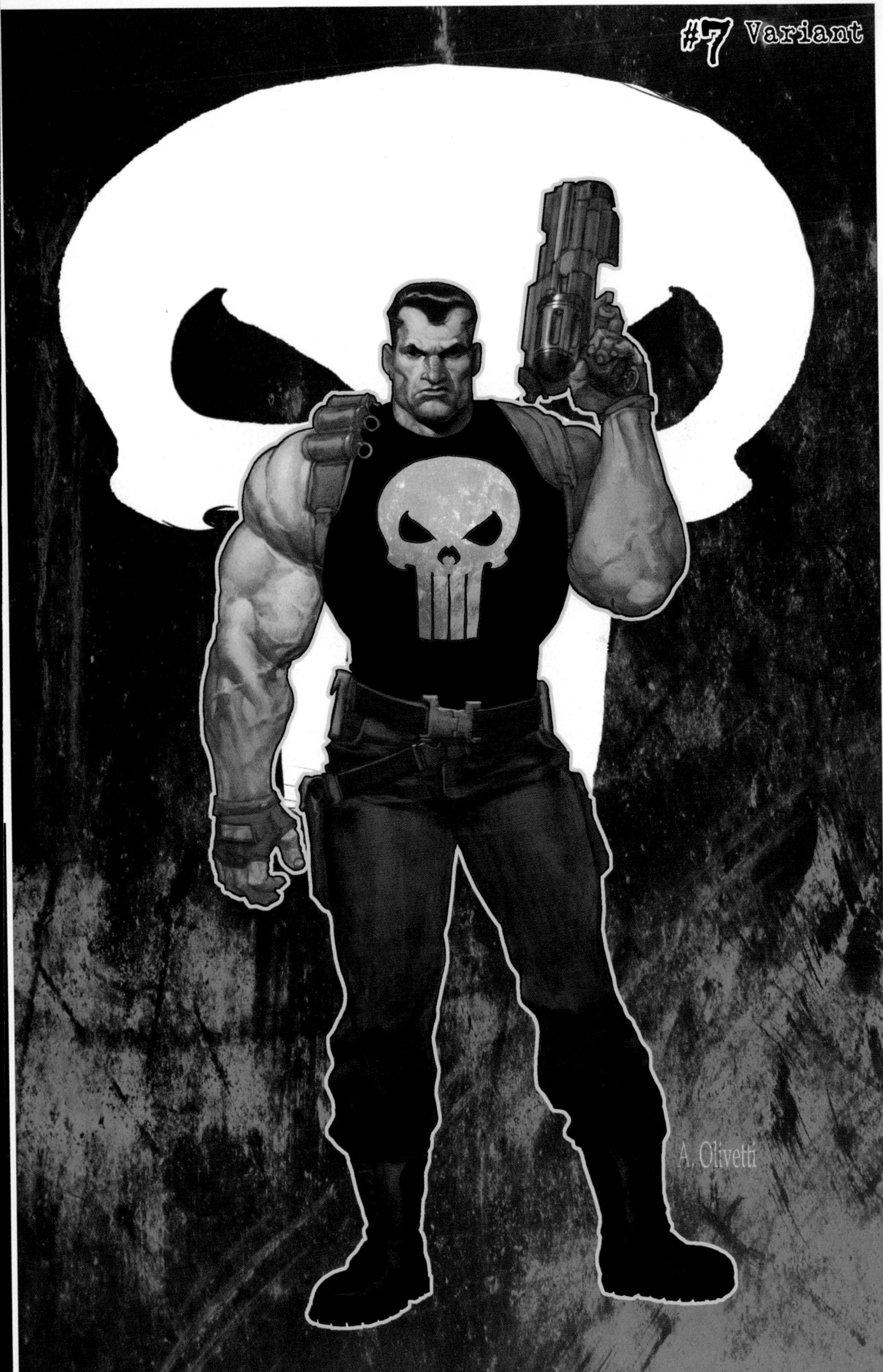
#7 Variant
A. Olivetti

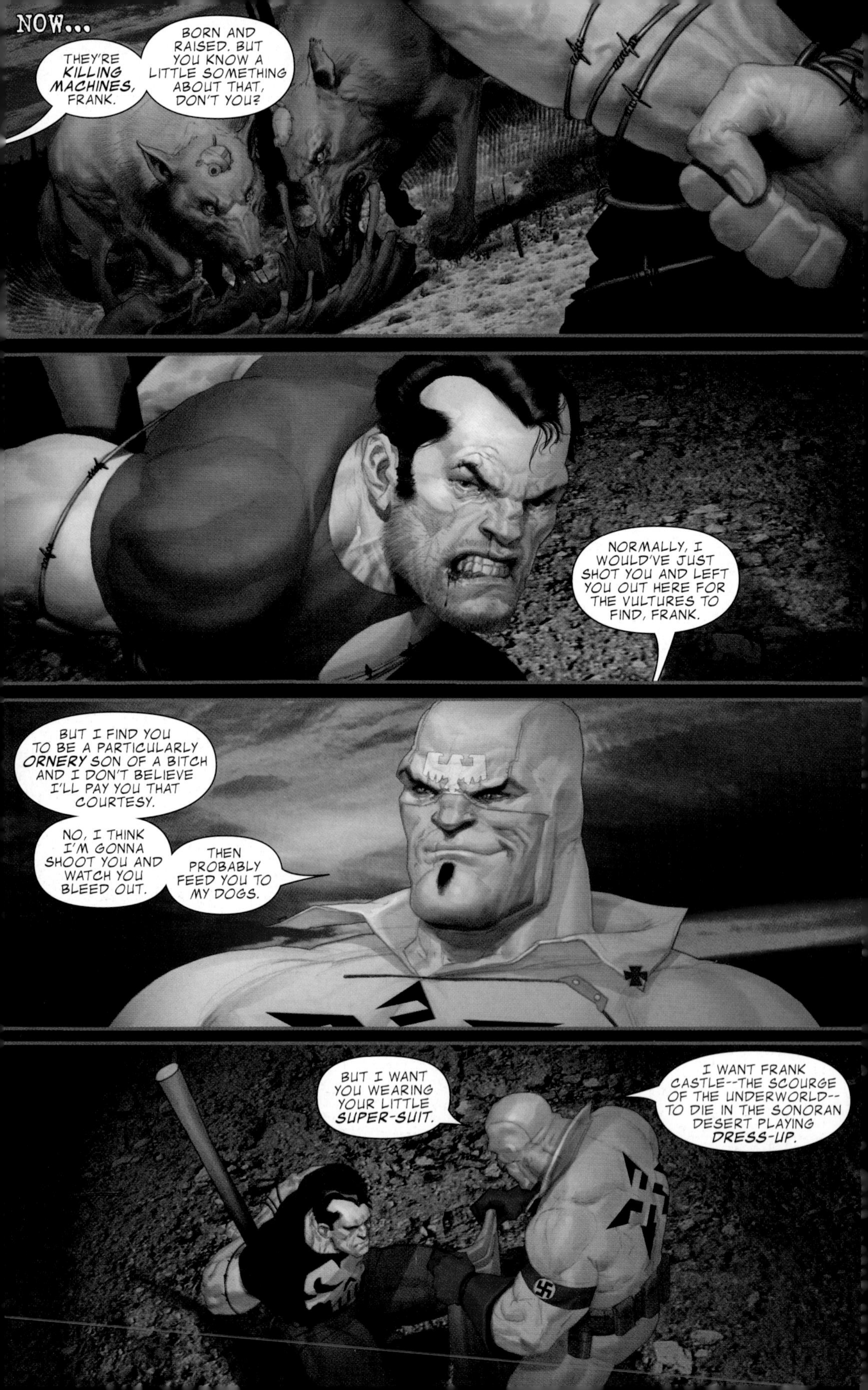
NOW...
THEY'RE KILLING MACHINES, FRANK.
BORN AND RAISED. BUT YOU KNOW A LITTLE SOMETHING ABOUT THAT, DON'T YOU?
NORMALLY, I WOULD'VE JUST SHOT YOU AND LEFT YOU OUT HERE FOR THE VULTURES TO FIND, FRANK.
BUT I FIND YOU TO BE A PARTICULARLY ORNERY SON OF A BITCH AND I DON'T BELIEVE I'LL PAY YOU THAT COURTESY.
NO, I THINK I'M GONNA SHOOT YOU AND WATCH YOU BLEED OUT.
THEN PROBABLY FEED YOU TO MY DOGS.
BUT I WANT YOU WEARING YOUR LITTLE SUPER-SUIT.
I WANT FRANK CASTLE--THE SCOURGE OF THE UNDERWORLD--TO DIE IN THE SONORAN DESERT PLAYING DRESS-UP.

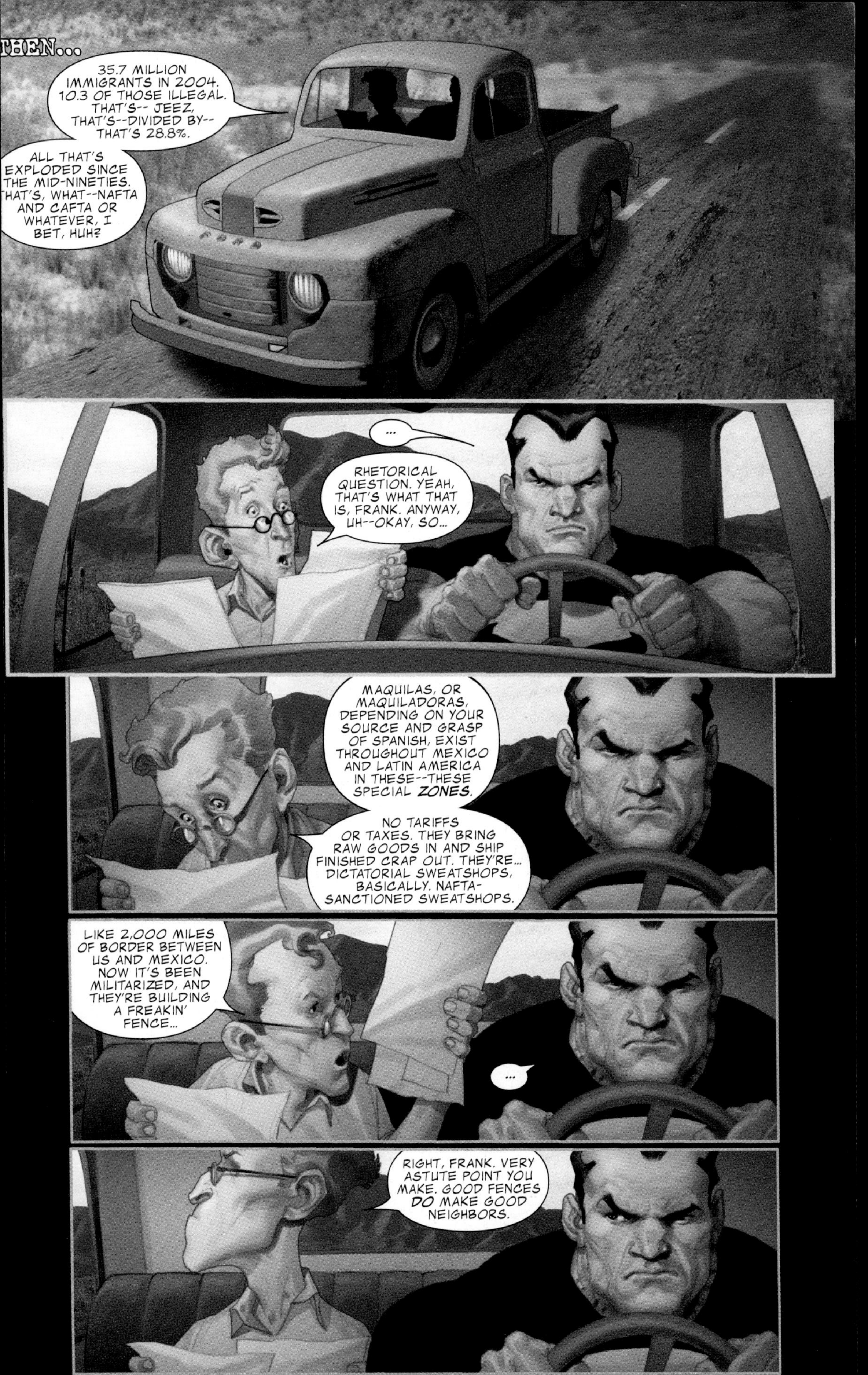
THEN...
35.7 MILLION IMMIGRANTS IN 2004. 10.3 OF THOSE ILLEGAL. THAT'S-- JEEZ, THAT'S--DIVIDED BY-- THAT'S 28.8%.
ALL THAT'S EXPLODED SINCE THE MID-NINETIES. THAT'S, WHAT--NAFTA AND CAFTA OR WHATEVER, I BET, HUH?
...
RHETORICAL QUESTION. YEAH, THAT'S WHAT THAT IS, FRANK. ANYWAY, UH--OKAY, SO...
MAQUILAS, OR MAQUILADORAS, DEPENDING ON YOUR SOURCE AND GRASP OF SPANISH, EXIST THROUGHOUT MEXICO AND LATIN AMERICA IN THESE--THESE SPECIAL ZONES.
NO TARIFFS OR TAXES. THEY BRING RAW GOODS IN AND SHIP FINISHED CRAP OUT. THEY'RE... DICTATORIAL SWEATSHOPS, BASICALLY. NAFTA-SANCTIONED SWEATSHOPS.
LIKE 2,000 MILES OF BORDER BETWEEN US AND MEXICO. NOW IT'S BEEN MILITARIZED, AND THEY'RE BUILDING A FREAKIN' FENCE...
...
RIGHT, FRANK. VERY ASTUTE POINT YOU MAKE. GOOD FENCES DO MAKE GOOD NEIGHBORS.

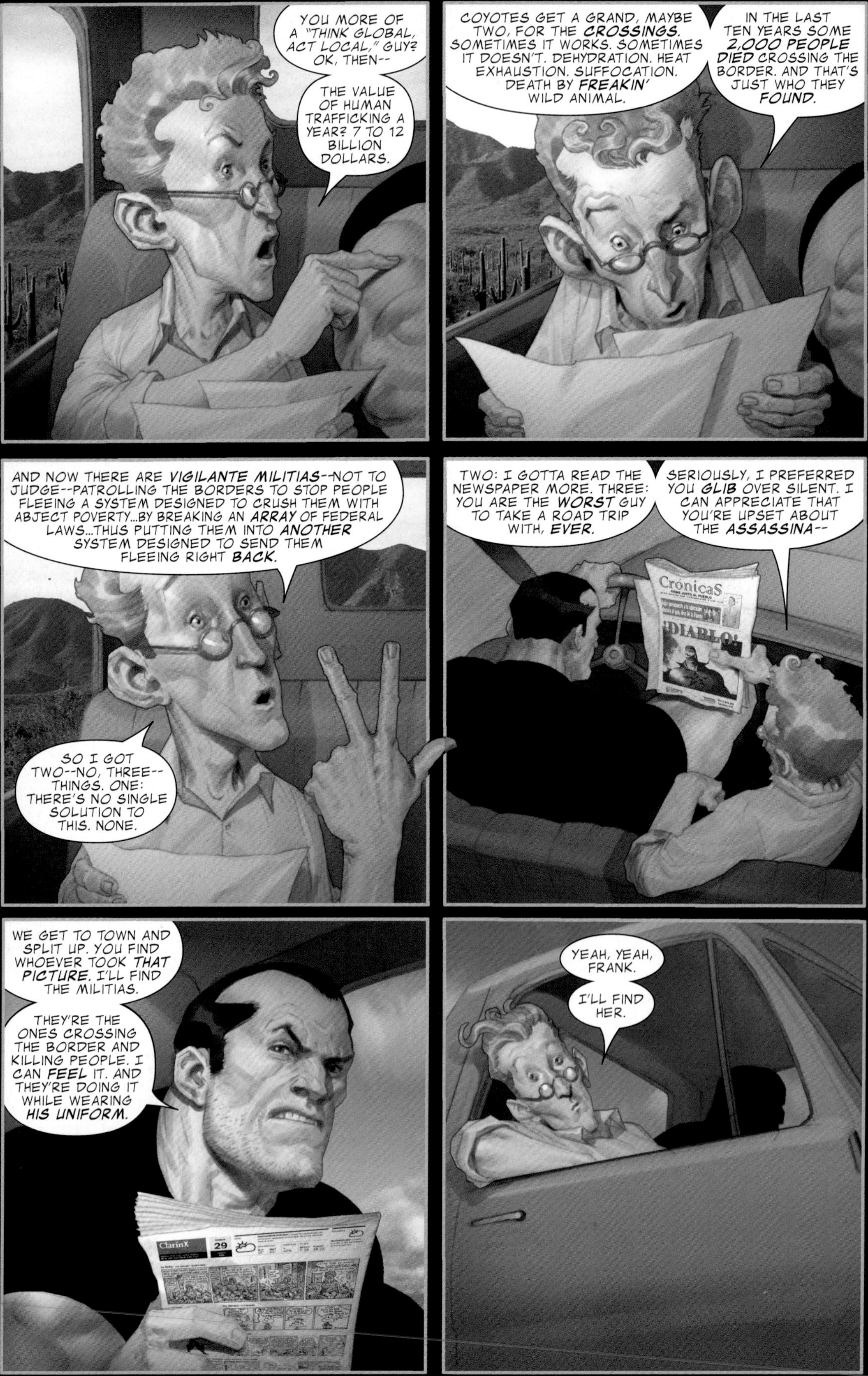

YOU MORE OF A "THINK GLOBAL, ACT LOCAL," GUY? OK, THEN--
THE VALUE OF HUMAN TRAFFICKING A YEAR? 7 TO 12 BILLION DOLLARS.
COYOTES GET A GRAND, MAYBE TWO, FOR THE CROSSINGS. SOMETIMES IT WORKS. SOMETIMES IT DOESN'T. DEHYDRATION. HEAT EXHAUSTION. SUFFOCATION. DEATH BY FREAKIN' WILD ANIMAL.
IN THE LAST TEN YEARS SOME 2,000 PEOPLE DIED CROSSING THE BORDER. AND THAT'S JUST WHO THEY FOUND.
AND NOW THERE ARE VIGILANTE MILITIAS--NOT TO JUDGE--PATROLLING THE BORDERS TO STOP PEOPLE FLEEING A SYSTEM DESIGNED TO CRUSH THEM WITH ABJECT POVERTY...BY BREAKING AN ARRAY OF FEDERAL LAWS...THUS PUTTING THEM INTO ANOTHER SYSTEM DESIGNED TO SEND THEM FLEEING RIGHT BACK.
SO I GOT TWO--NO, THREE--THINGS. ONE: THERE'S NO SINGLE SOLUTION TO THIS. NONE.
TWO: I GOTTA READ THE NEWSPAPER MORE. THREE: YOU ARE THE WORST GUY TO TAKE A ROAD TRIP WITH, EVER.
SERIOUSLY, I PREFERRED YOU GLIB OVER SILENT. I CAN APPRECIATE THAT YOU'RE UPSET ABOUT THE ASSASSINA--
Crónicas
¡DIABLO!
WE GET TO TOWN AND SPLIT UP. YOU FIND WHOEVER TOOK THAT PICTURE. I'LL FIND THE MILITIAS.
THEY'RE THE ONES CROSSING THE BORDER AND KILLING PEOPLE. I CAN FEEL IT. AND THEY'RE DOING IT WHILE WEARING HIS UNIFORM.
Clarín
29
YEAH, YEAH, FRANK.
I'LL FIND HER.

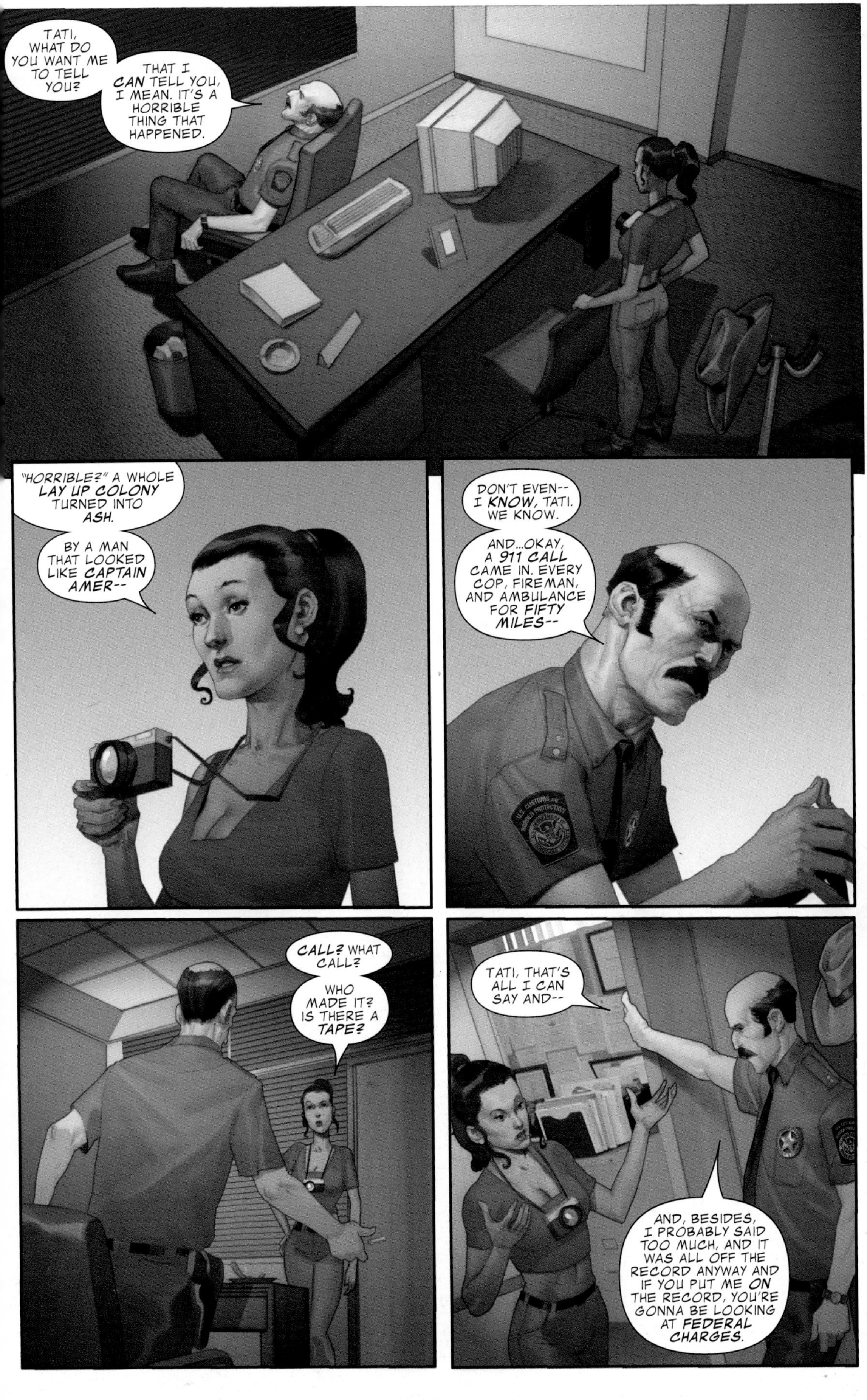
TATI, WHAT DO YOU WANT ME TO TELL YOU?
THAT I CAN TELL YOU, I MEAN. IT'S A HORRIBLE THING THAT HAPPENED.
"HORRIBLE?" A WHOLE LAY UP COLONY TURNED INTO ASH.
BY A MAN THAT LOOKED LIKE CAPTAIN AMER--
DON'T EVEN-- I KNOW, TATI. WE KNOW.
AND...OKAY, A 911 CALL CAME IN. EVERY COP, FIREMAN, AND AMBULANCE FOR FIFTY MILES--
CALL? WHAT CALL?
WHO MADE IT? IS THERE A TAPE?
TATI, THAT'S ALL I CAN SAY AND--
AND, BESIDES, I PROBABLY SAID TOO MUCH, AND IT WAS ALL OFF THE RECORD ANYWAY AND IF YOU PUT ME ON THE RECORD, YOU'RE GONNA BE LOOKING AT FEDERAL CHARGES.

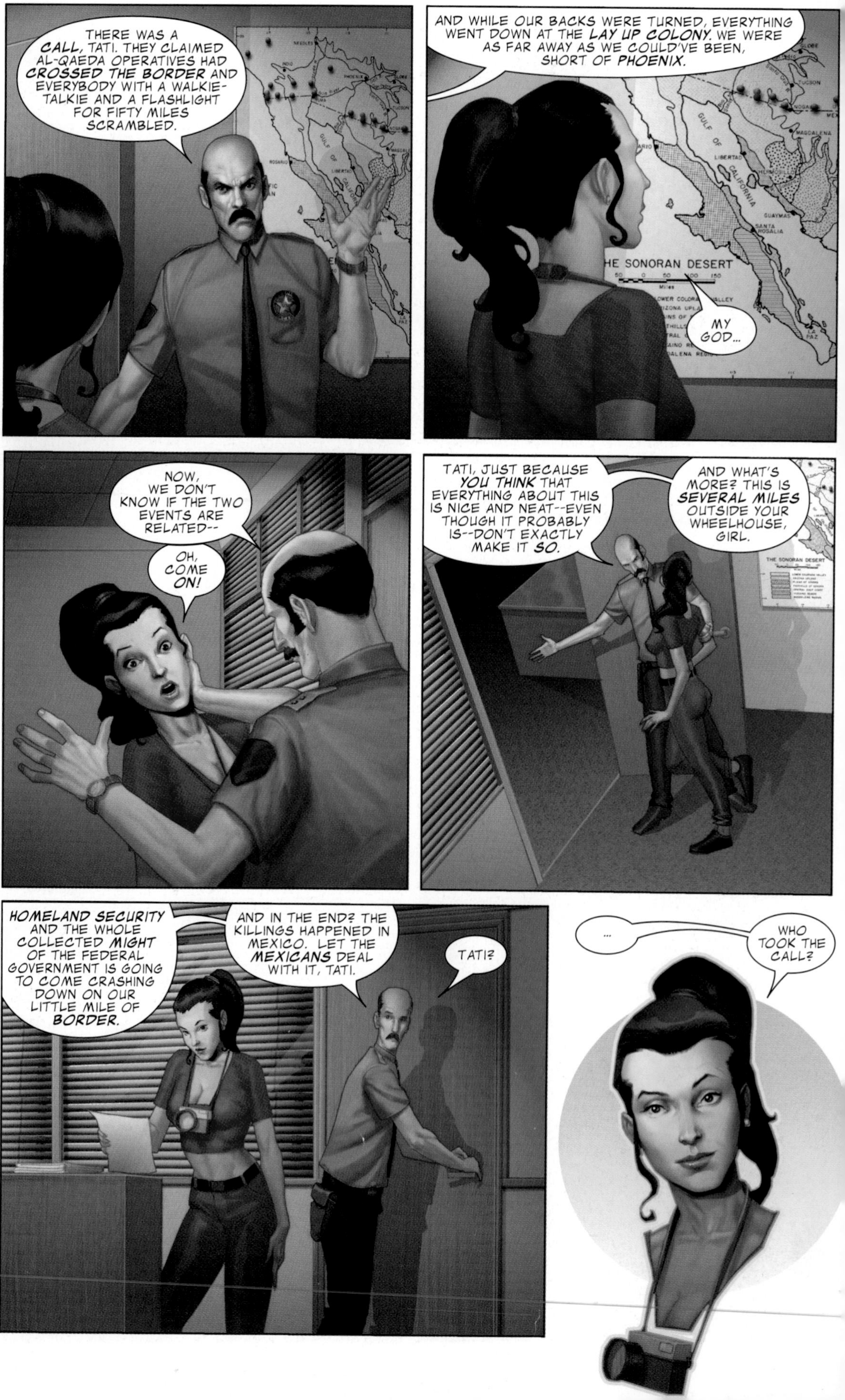
THERE WAS A CALL, TATI. THEY CLAIMED AL-QAEDA OPERATIVES HAD CROSSED THE BORDER AND EVERYBODY WITH A WALKIE-TALKIE AND A FLASHLIGHT FOR FIFTY MILES SCRAMBLED.
AND WHILE OUR BACKS WERE TURNED, EVERYTHING WENT DOWN AT THE LAY UP COLONY. WE WERE AS FAR AWAY AS WE COULD'VE BEEN, SHORT OF PHOENIX.
THE SONORAN DESERT
MY GOD...
NOW, WE DON'T KNOW IF THE TWO EVENTS ARE RELATED--
OH, COME ON!
TATI, JUST BECAUSE YOU THINK THAT EVERYTHING ABOUT THIS IS NICE AND NEAT--EVEN THOUGH IT PROBABLY IS--DON'T EXACTLY MAKE IT SO.
AND WHAT'S MORE? THIS IS SEVERAL MILES OUTSIDE YOUR WHEELHOUSE, GIRL.
HOMELAND SECURITY AND THE WHOLE COLLECTED MIGHT OF THE FEDERAL GOVERNMENT IS GOING TO COME CRASHING DOWN ON OUR LITTLE MILE OF BORDER.
AND IN THE END? THE KILLINGS HAPPENED IN MEXICO. LET THE MEXICANS DEAL WITH IT, TATI.
TATI?
...
WHO TOOK THE CALL?

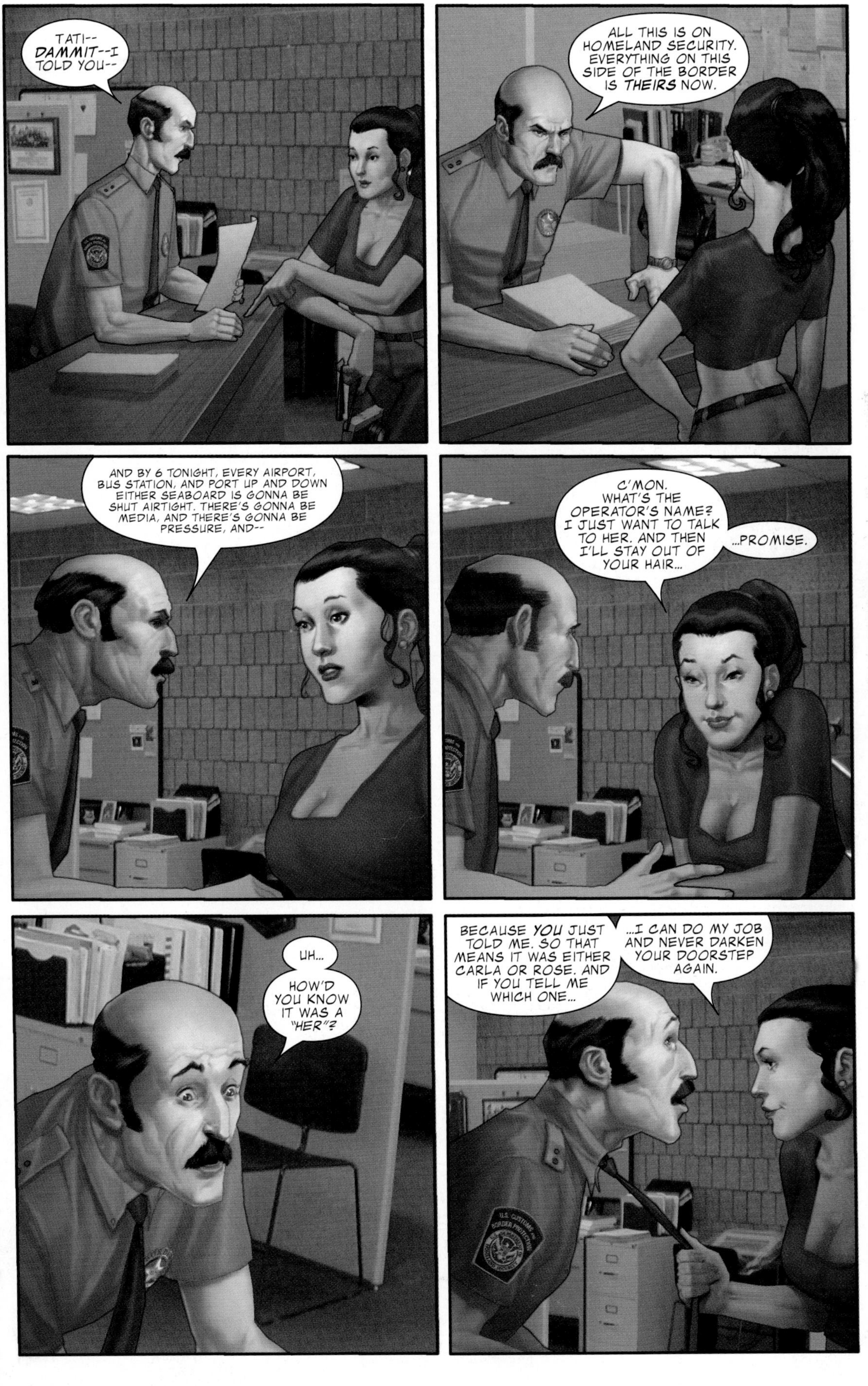

TATI-- DAMMIT--I TOLD YOU--
ALL THIS IS ON HOMELAND SECURITY. EVERYTHING ON THIS SIDE OF THE BORDER IS THEIRS NOW.
AND BY 6 TONIGHT, EVERY AIRPORT, BUS STATION, AND PORT UP AND DOWN EITHER SEABOARD IS GONNA BE SHUT AIRTIGHT. THERE'S GONNA BE MEDIA, AND THERE'S GONNA BE PRESSURE, AND--
C'MON. WHAT'S THE OPERATOR'S NAME? I JUST WANT TO TALK TO HER. AND THEN I'LL STAY OUT OF YOUR HAIR...
...PROMISE.
UH...
HOW'D YOU KNOW IT WAS A "HER"?
BECAUSE YOU JUST TOLD ME. SO THAT MEANS IT WAS EITHER CARLA OR ROSE. AND IF YOU TELL ME WHICH ONE...
...I CAN DO MY JOB AND NEVER DARKEN YOUR DOORSTEP AGAIN.

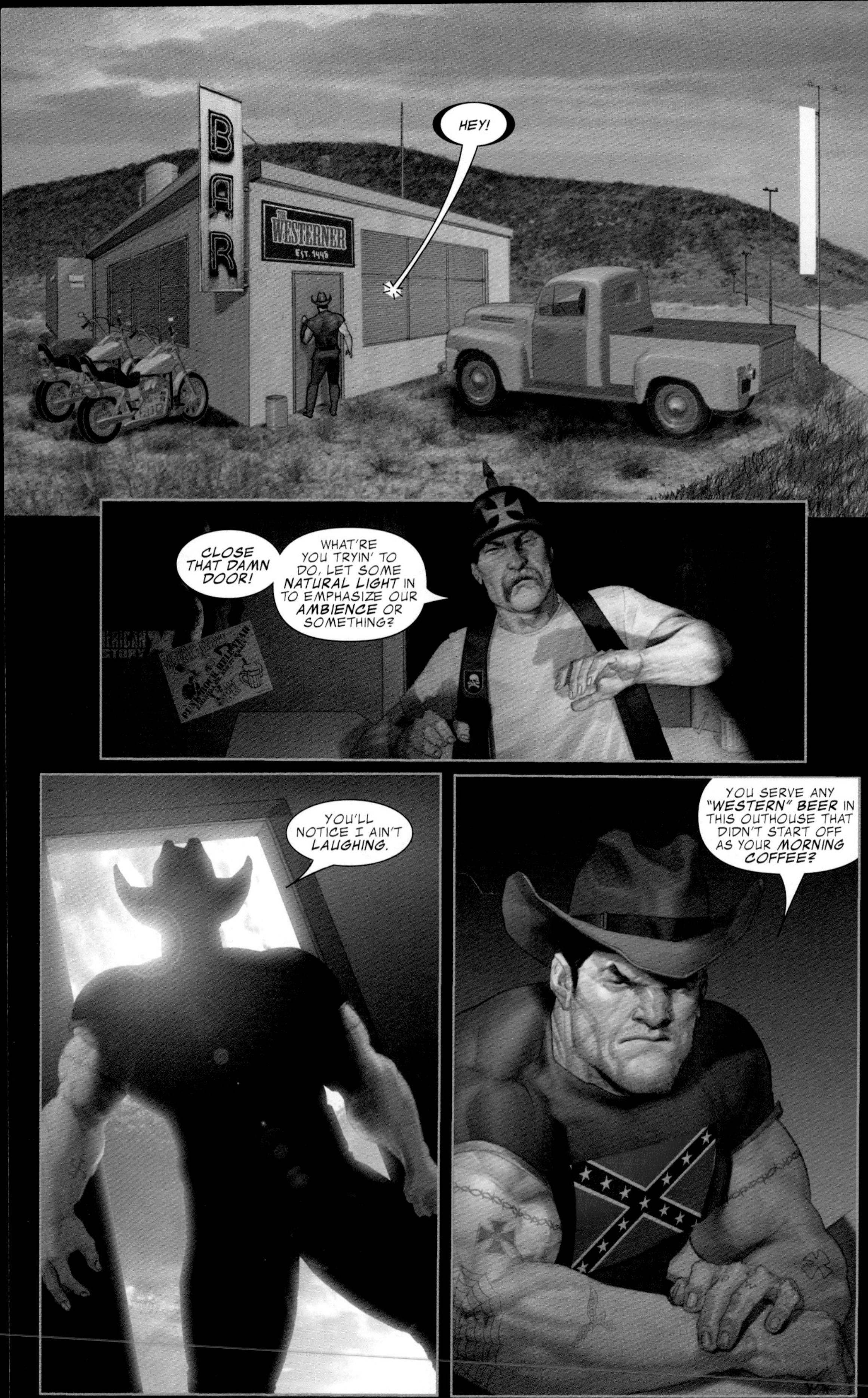

BAR
THE WESTERNER
HEY!
CLOSE THAT DAMN DOOR!
WHAT'RE YOU TRYIN' TO DO, LET SOME NATURAL LIGHT IN TO EMPHASIZE OUR AMBIENCE OR SOMETHING?
YOU'LL NOTICE I AIN'T LAUGHING.
YOU SERVE ANY "WESTERN" BEER IN THIS OUTHOUSE THAT DIDN'T START OFF AS YOUR MORNING COFFEE?

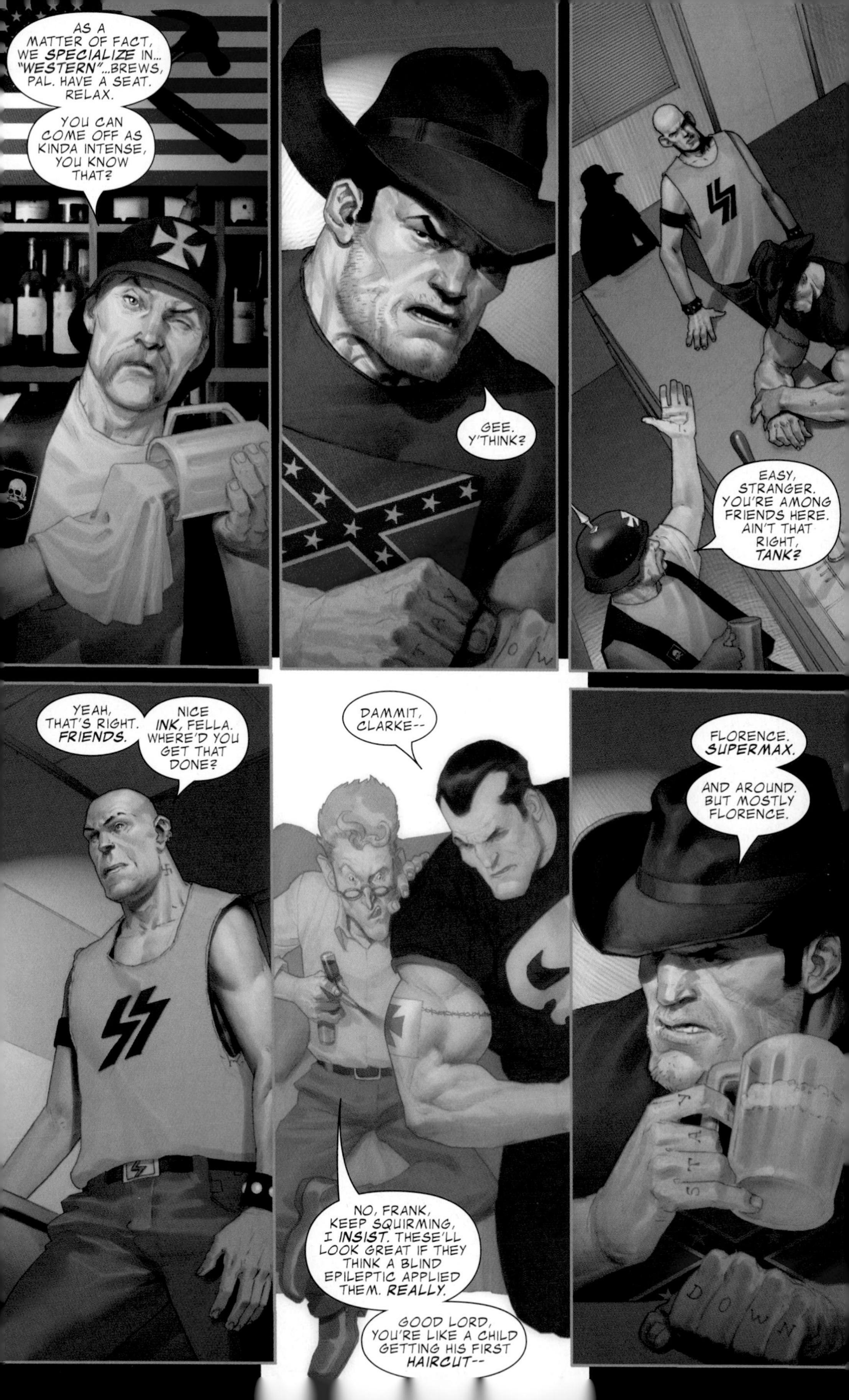

AS A MATTER OF FACT, WE SPECIALIZE IN... "WESTERN"...BREWS, PAL. HAVE A SEAT. RELAX.
YOU CAN COME OFF AS KINDA INTENSE, YOU KNOW THAT?
GEE. Y'THINK?
EASY, STRANGER. YOU'RE AMONG FRIENDS HERE. AIN'T THAT RIGHT, TANK?
YEAH, THAT'S RIGHT. FRIENDS.
NICE INK, FELLA. WHERE'D YOU GET THAT DONE?
DAMMIT, CLARKE--
NO, FRANK, KEEP SQUIRMING, I INSIST. THESE'LL LOOK GREAT IF THEY THINK A BLIND EPILEPTIC APPLIED THEM. REALLY.
GOOD LORD, YOU'RE LIKE A CHILD GETTING HIS FIRST HAIRCUT--
FLORENCE. SUPERMAX.
AND AROUND. BUT MOSTLY FLORENCE.

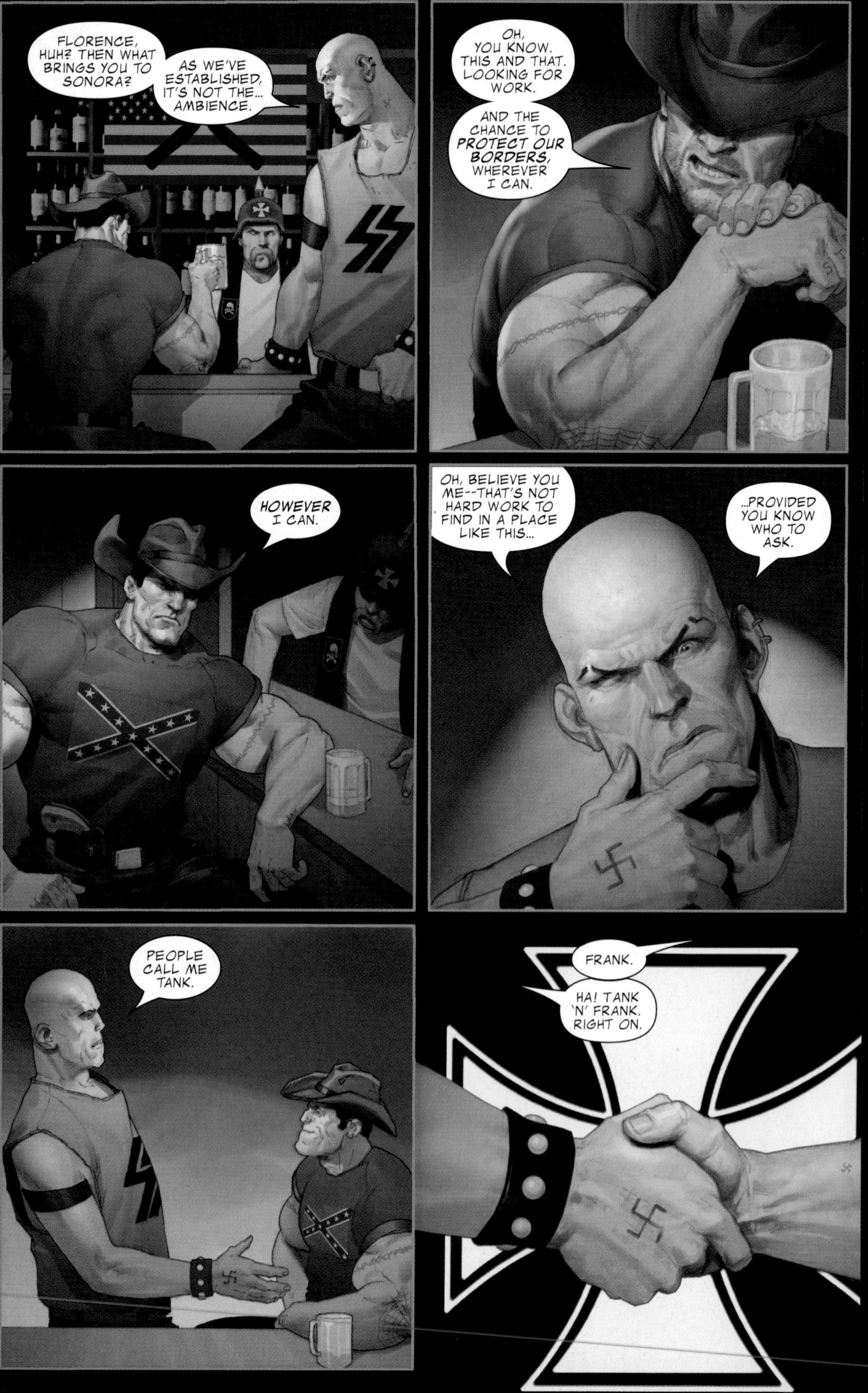
FLORENCE, HUH? THEN WHAT BRINGS YOU TO SONORA?
AS WE'VE ESTABLISHED, IT'S NOT THE... AMBIENCE.
OH, YOU KNOW. THIS AND THAT. LOOKING FOR WORK.
AND THE CHANCE TO PROTECT OUR BORDERS, WHEREVER I CAN.
HOWEVER I CAN.
OH, BELIEVE YOU ME--THAT'S NOT HARD WORK TO FIND IN A PLACE LIKE THIS...
...PROVIDED YOU KNOW WHO TO ASK.
PEOPLE CALL ME TANK.
FRANK.
HA! TANK 'N' FRANK. RIGHT ON.

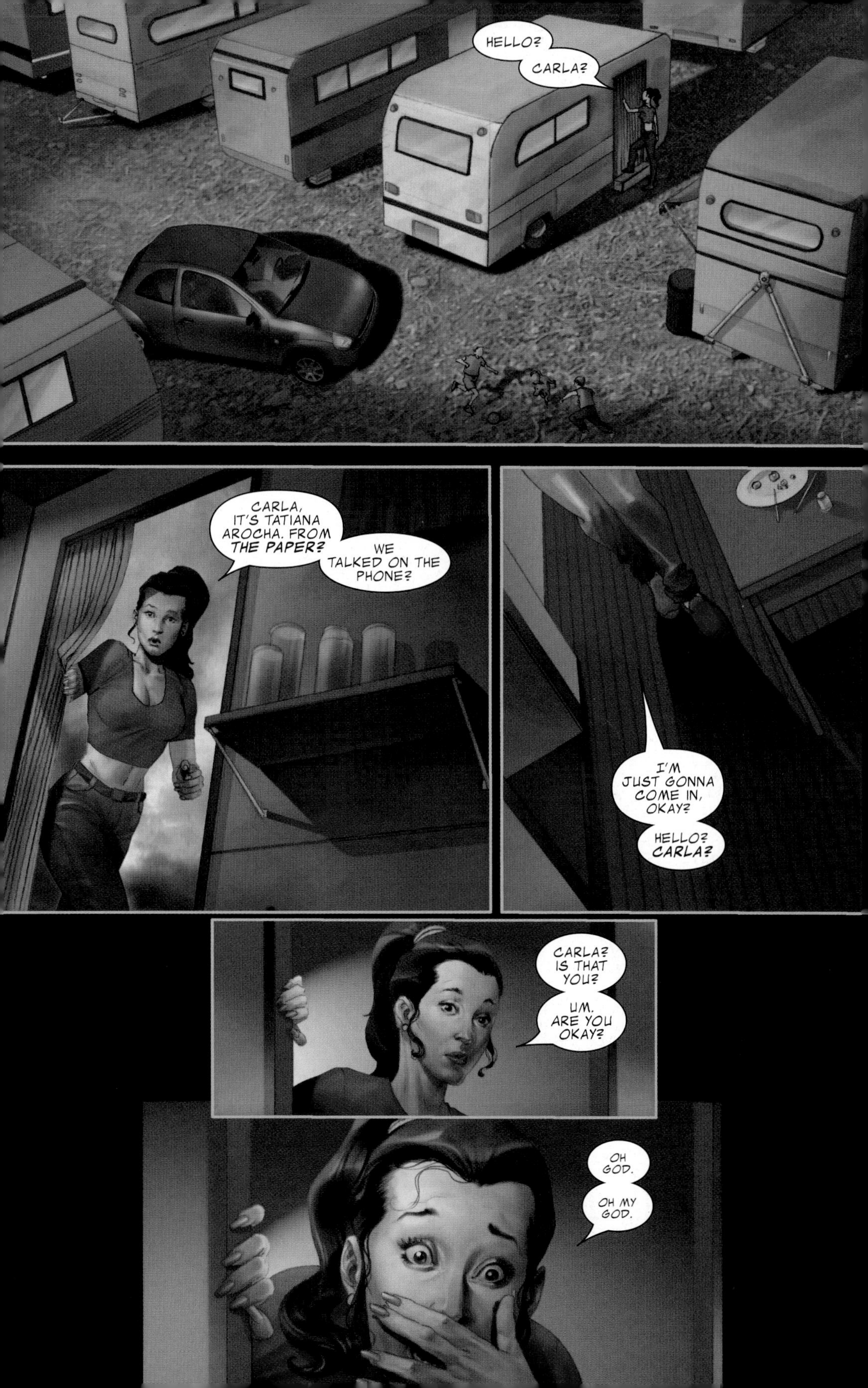
HELLO?
CARLA?
CARLA, IT'S TATIANA AROCHA. FROM *THE PAPER?*
WE TALKED ON THE PHONE?
I'M JUST GONNA COME IN, OKAY?
HELLO? *CARLA?*
CARLA? IS THAT YOU?
UM. ARE YOU OKAY?
OH GOD.
OH MY GOD.

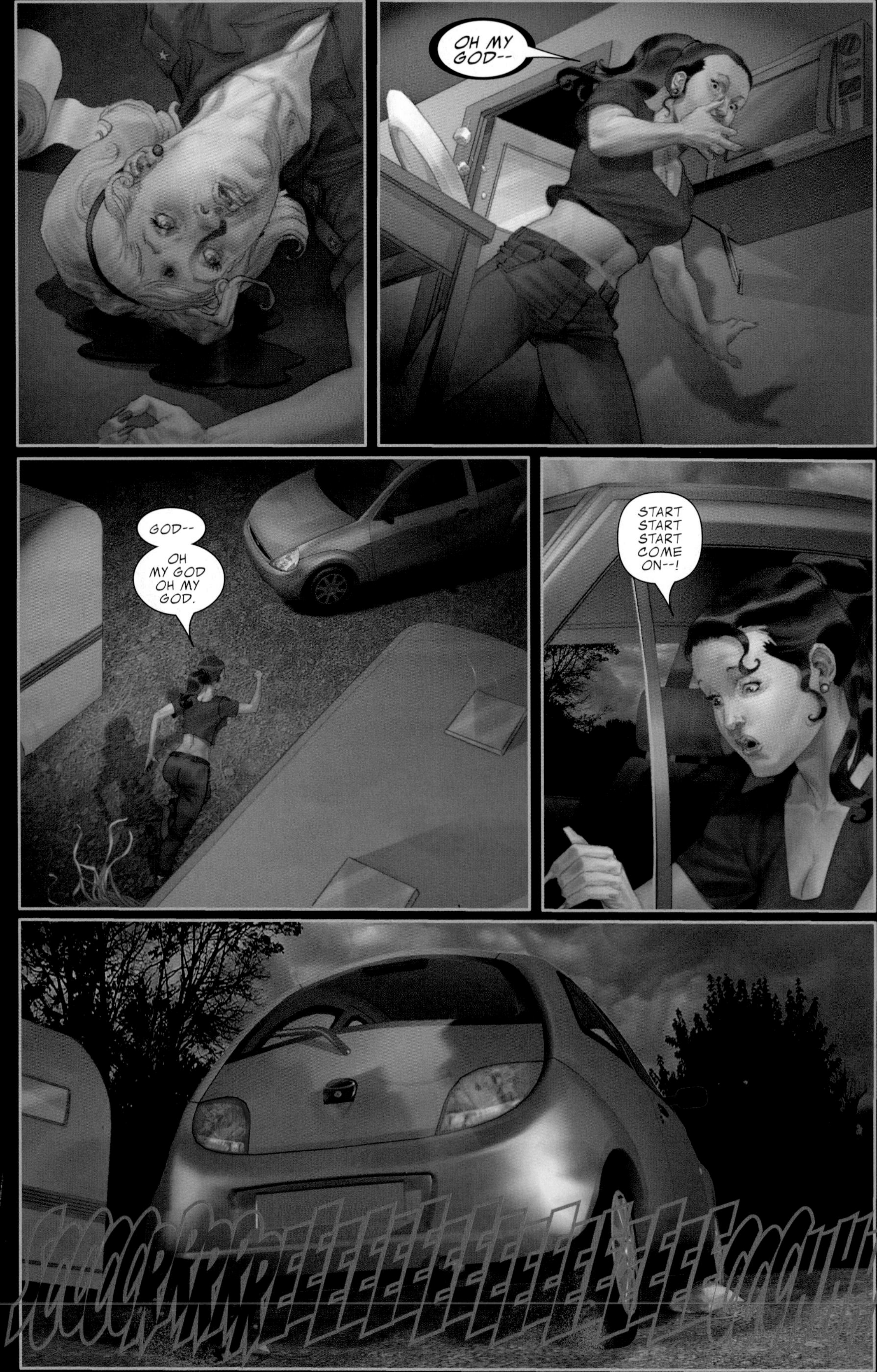
OH MY GOD--
GOD--
OH MY GOD OH MY GOD.
START START START COME ON--!

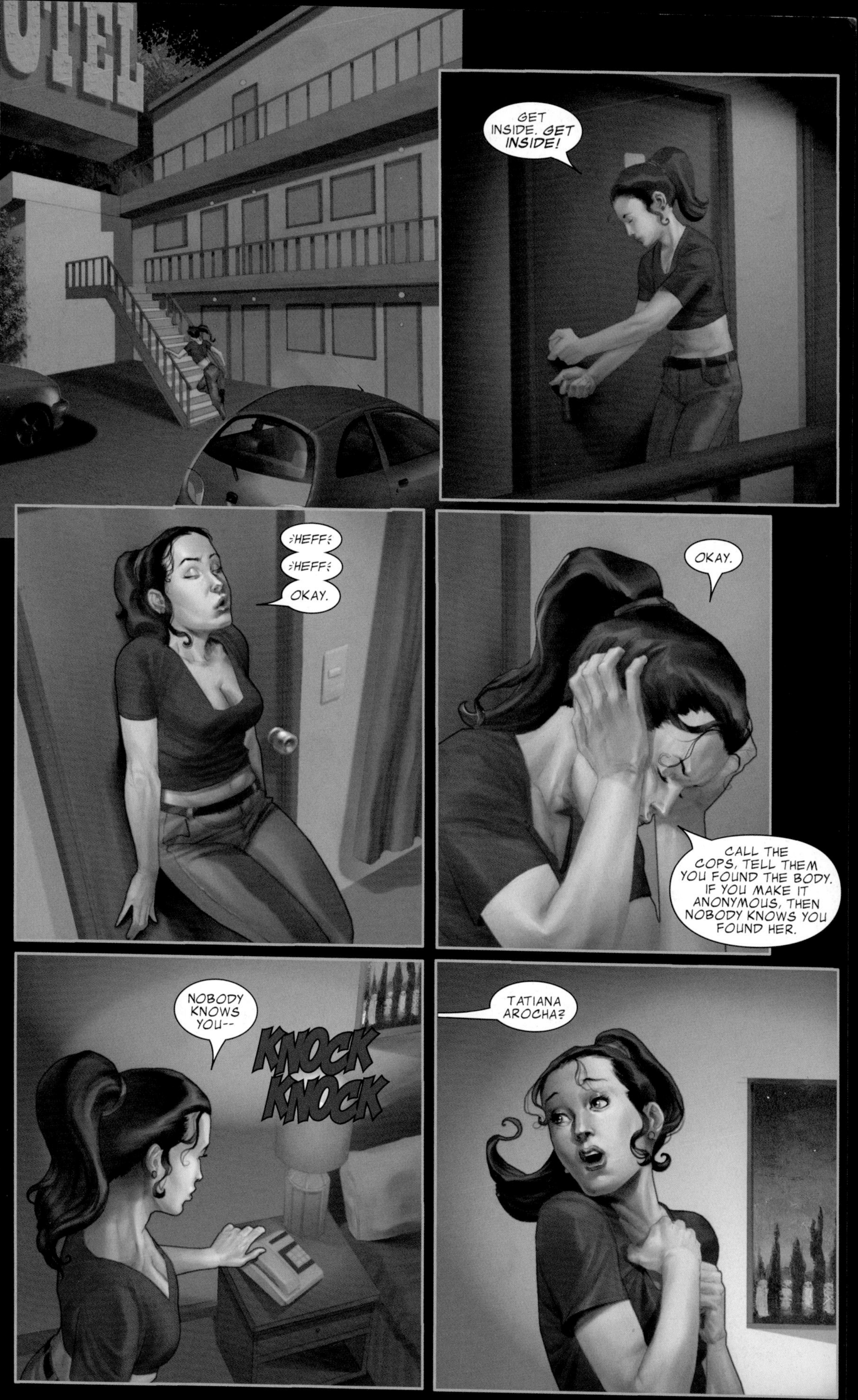
GET INSIDE. GET INSIDE!
HEFF
HEFF
OKAY.
OKAY.
CALL THE COPS, TELL THEM YOU FOUND THE BODY. IF YOU MAKE IT ANONYMOUS, THEN NOBODY KNOWS YOU FOUND HER.
NOBODY KNOWS YOU--
KNOCK KNOCK
TATIANA AROCHA?

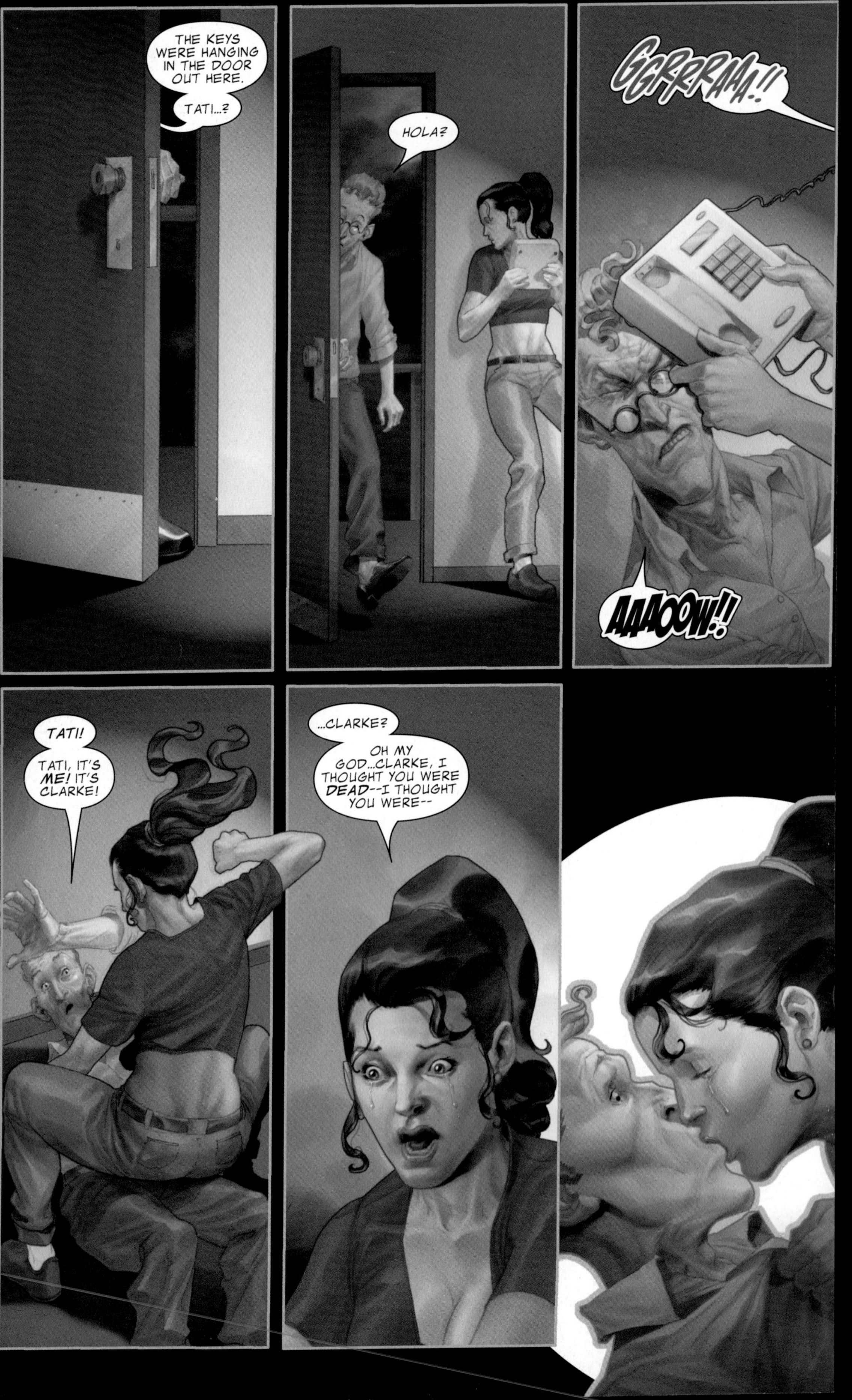
THE KEYS WERE HANGING IN THE DOOR OUT HERE.
TATI...?
HOLA?
GGRRRAAA!!
AAAOOW!!
TATI!
TATI, IT'S **ME!** IT'S CLARKE!
...CLARKE?
OH MY GOD...CLARKE, I THOUGHT YOU WERE **DEAD**--I THOUGHT YOU WERE--

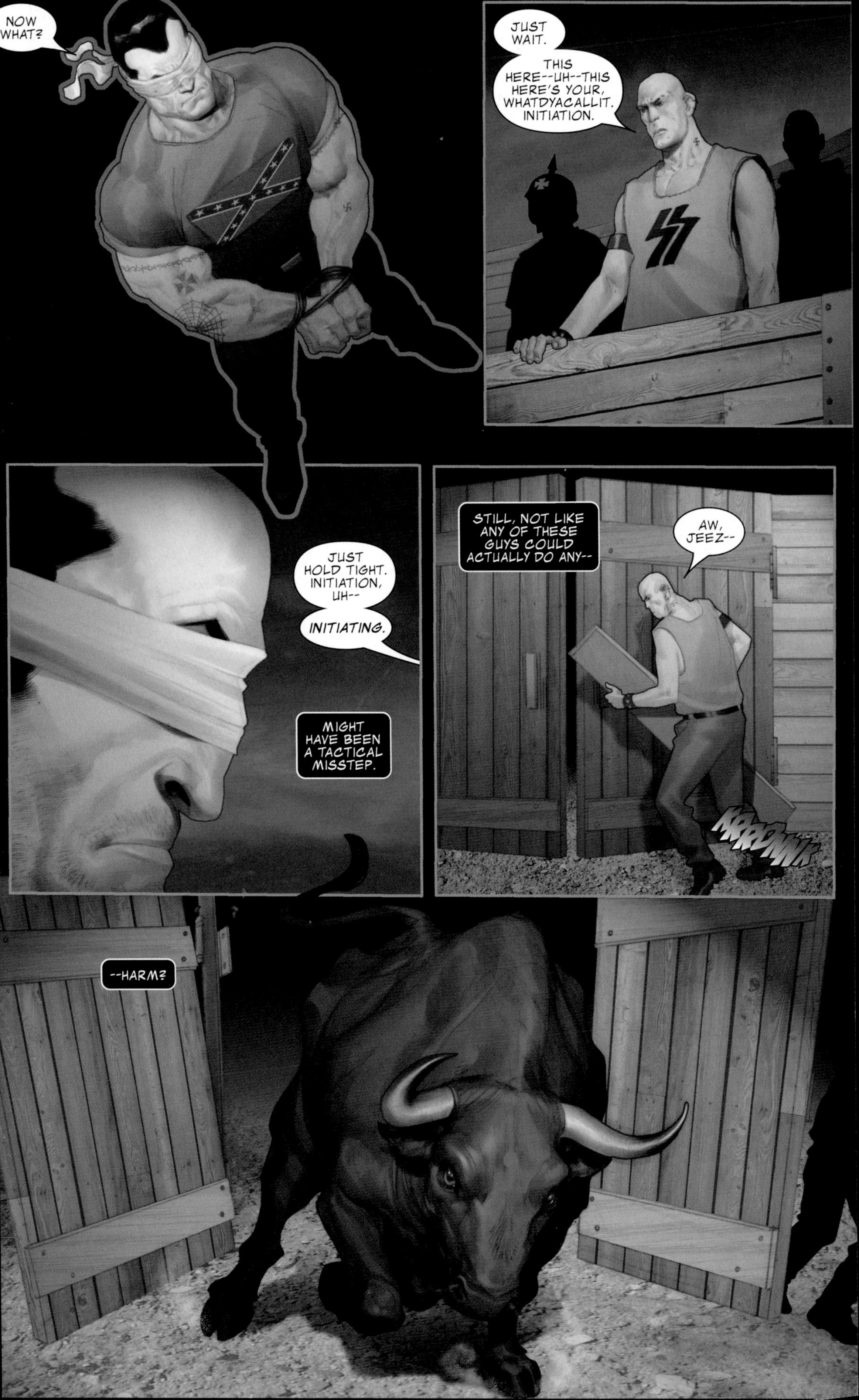
NOW WHAT?
JUST WAIT.
THIS HERE--UH--THIS HERE'S YOUR, WHATDYACALLIT. INITIATION.
JUST HOLD TIGHT. INITIATION, UH--
INITIATING.
MIGHT HAVE BEEN A TACTICAL MISSTEP.
STILL, NOT LIKE ANY OF THESE GUYS COULD ACTUALLY DO ANY--
AW, JEEZ--
KRRONNK
--HARM?

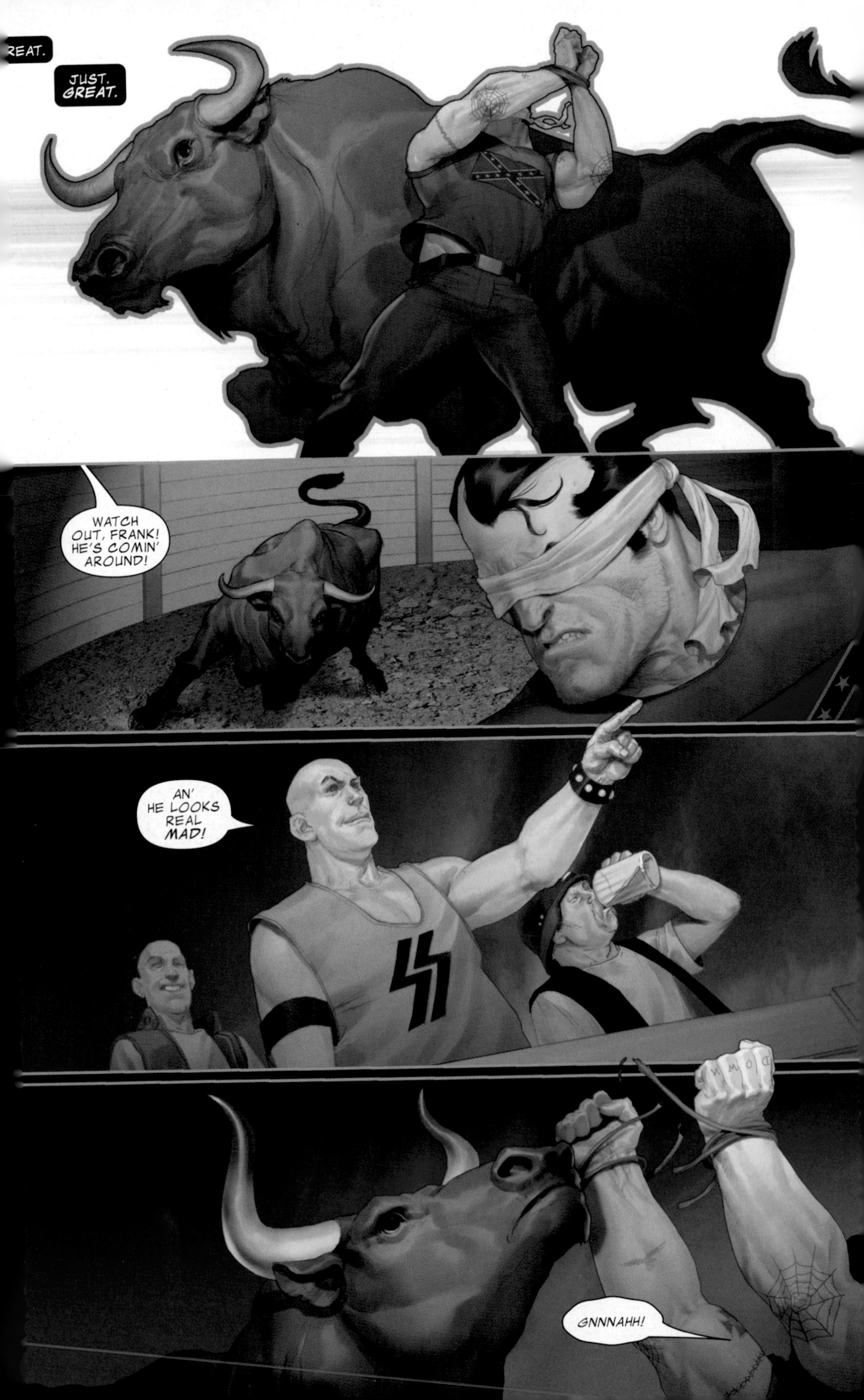

REAT.
JUST. GREAT.
WATCH OUT, FRANK! HE'S COMIN' AROUND!
AN' HE LOOKS REAL MAD!
GNNNAHH!

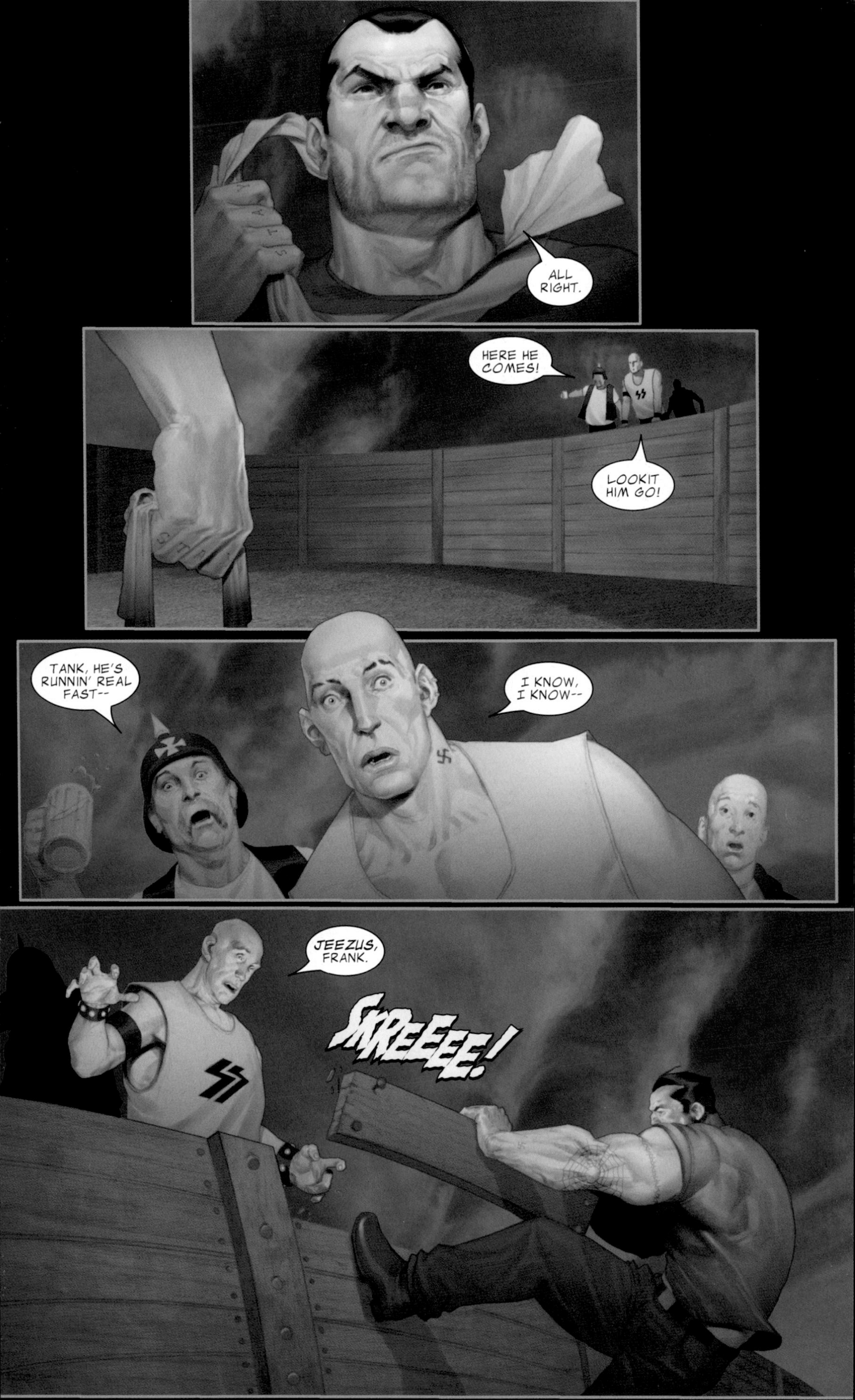
ALL RIGHT.
HERE HE COMES!
LOOKIT HIM GO!
TANK, HE'S RUNNIN' REAL FAST--
I KNOW, I KNOW--
JEEZUS, FRANK.
SKREEEEE!

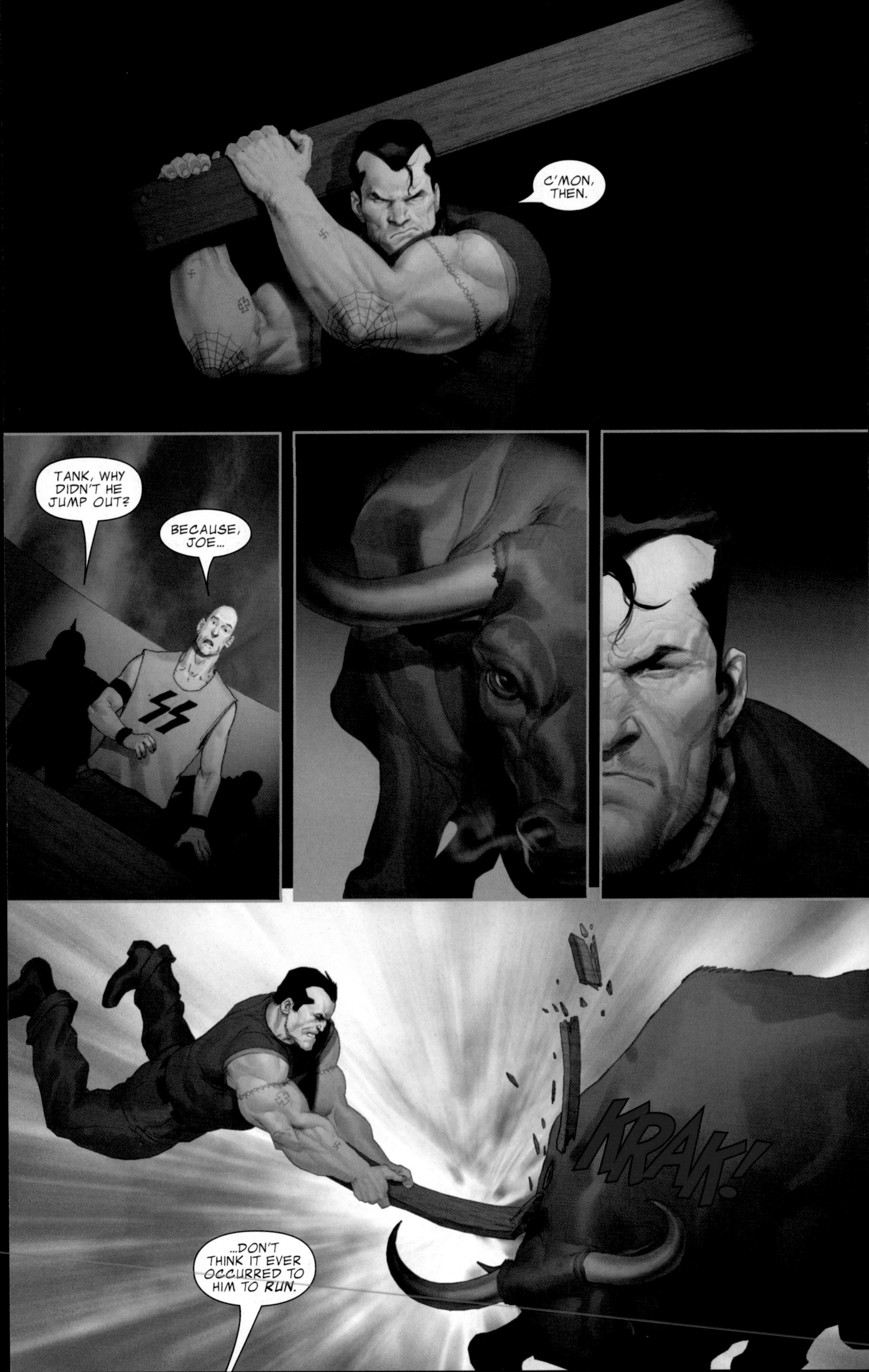
C'MON, THEN.
TANK, WHY DIDN'T HE JUMP OUT?
BECAUSE, JOE...
KRAK!
...DON'T THINK IT EVER OCCURRED TO HIM TO RUN.

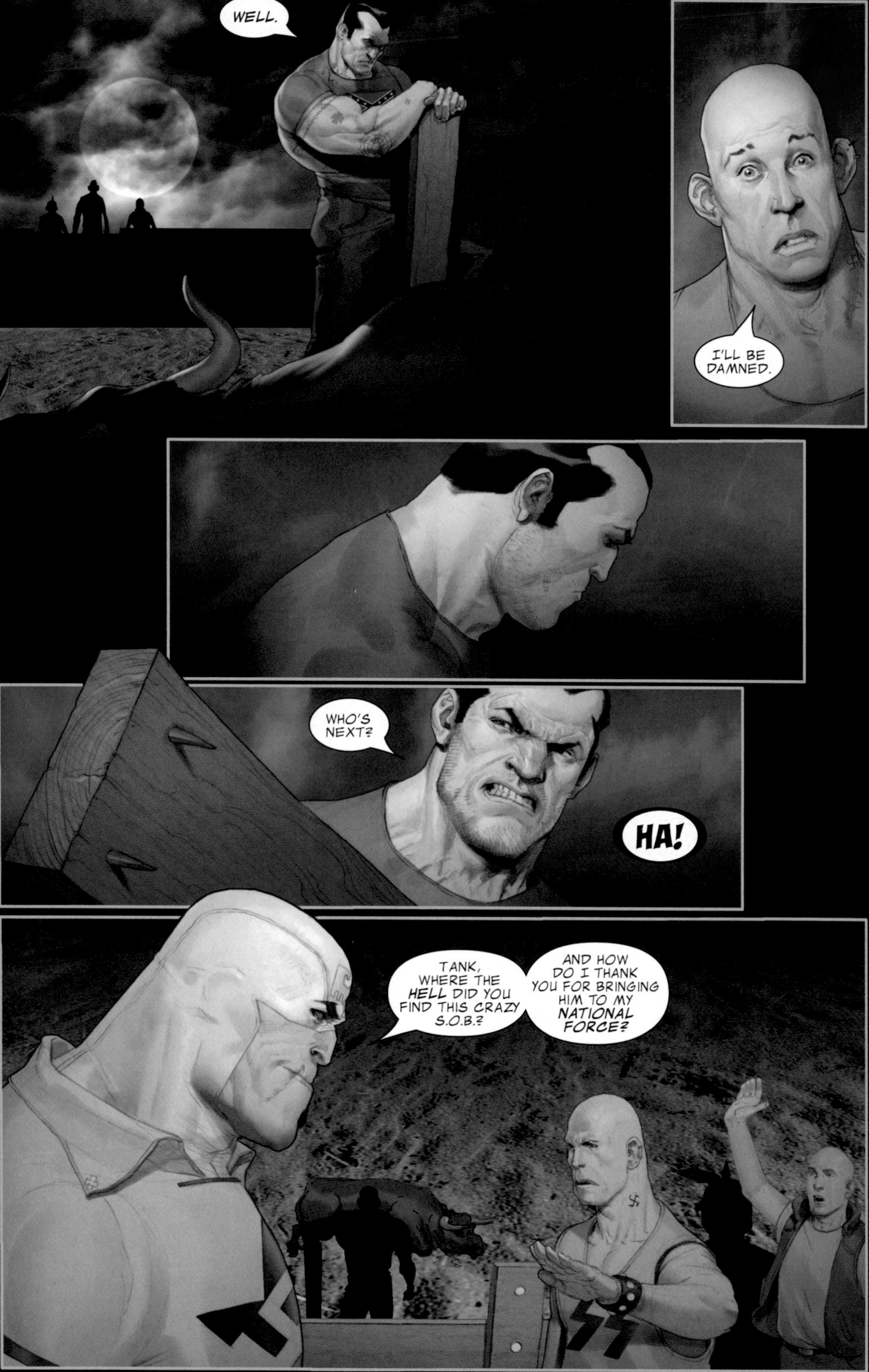
WELL.
I'LL BE DAMNED.
WHO'S NEXT?
HA!
TANK, WHERE THE HELL DID YOU FIND THIS CRAZY S.O.B.?
AND HOW DO I THANK YOU FOR BRINGING HIM TO MY NATIONAL FORCE?

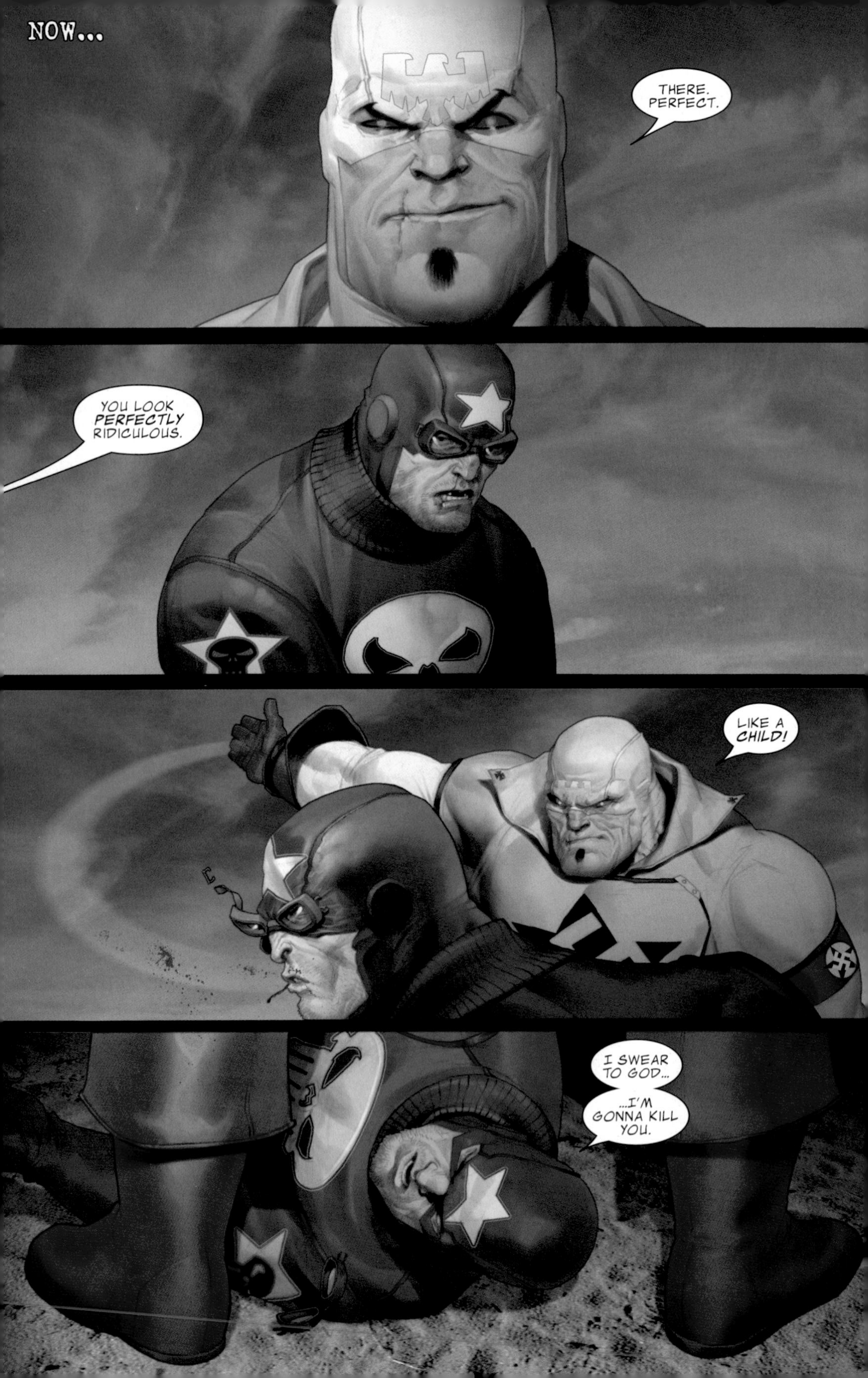
NOW...
THERE. PERFECT.
YOU LOOK PERFECTLY RIDICULOUS.
LIKE A CHILD!
I SWEAR TO GOD...
...I'M GONNA KILL YOU.

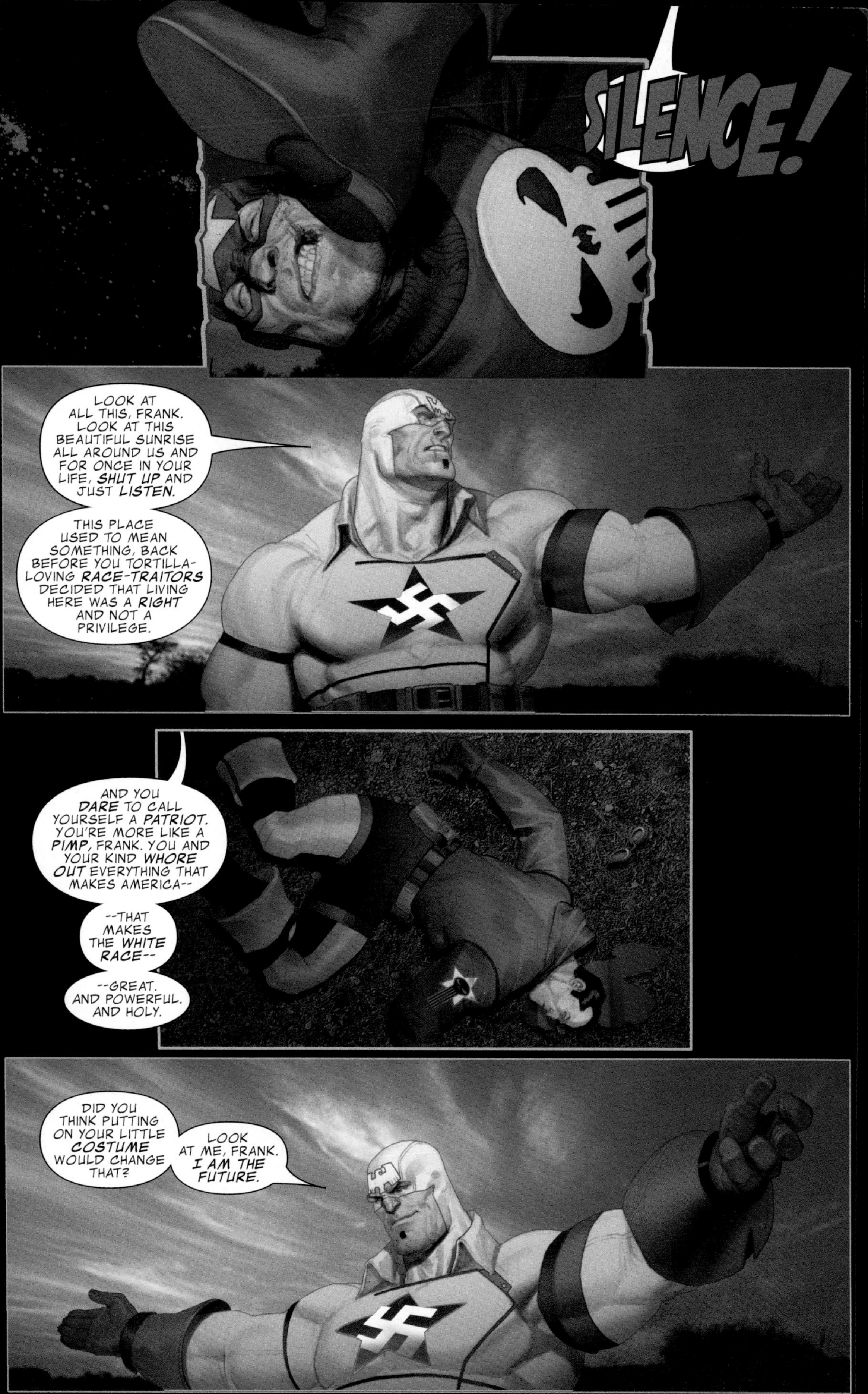
SILENCE!
LOOK AT ALL THIS, FRANK. LOOK AT THIS BEAUTIFUL SUNRISE ALL AROUND US AND FOR ONCE IN YOUR LIFE, SHUT UP AND JUST LISTEN.
THIS PLACE USED TO MEAN SOMETHING, BACK BEFORE YOU TORTILLA-LOVING RACE-TRAITORS DECIDED THAT LIVING HERE WAS A RIGHT AND NOT A PRIVILEGE.
AND YOU DARE TO CALL YOURSELF A PATRIOT. YOU'RE MORE LIKE A PIMP, FRANK. YOU AND YOUR KIND WHORE OUT EVERYTHING THAT MAKES AMERICA--
--THAT MAKES THE WHITE RACE--
--GREAT. AND POWERFUL. AND HOLY.
DID YOU THINK PUTTING ON YOUR LITTLE COSTUME WOULD CHANGE THAT?
LOOK AT ME, FRANK. I AM THE FUTURE.

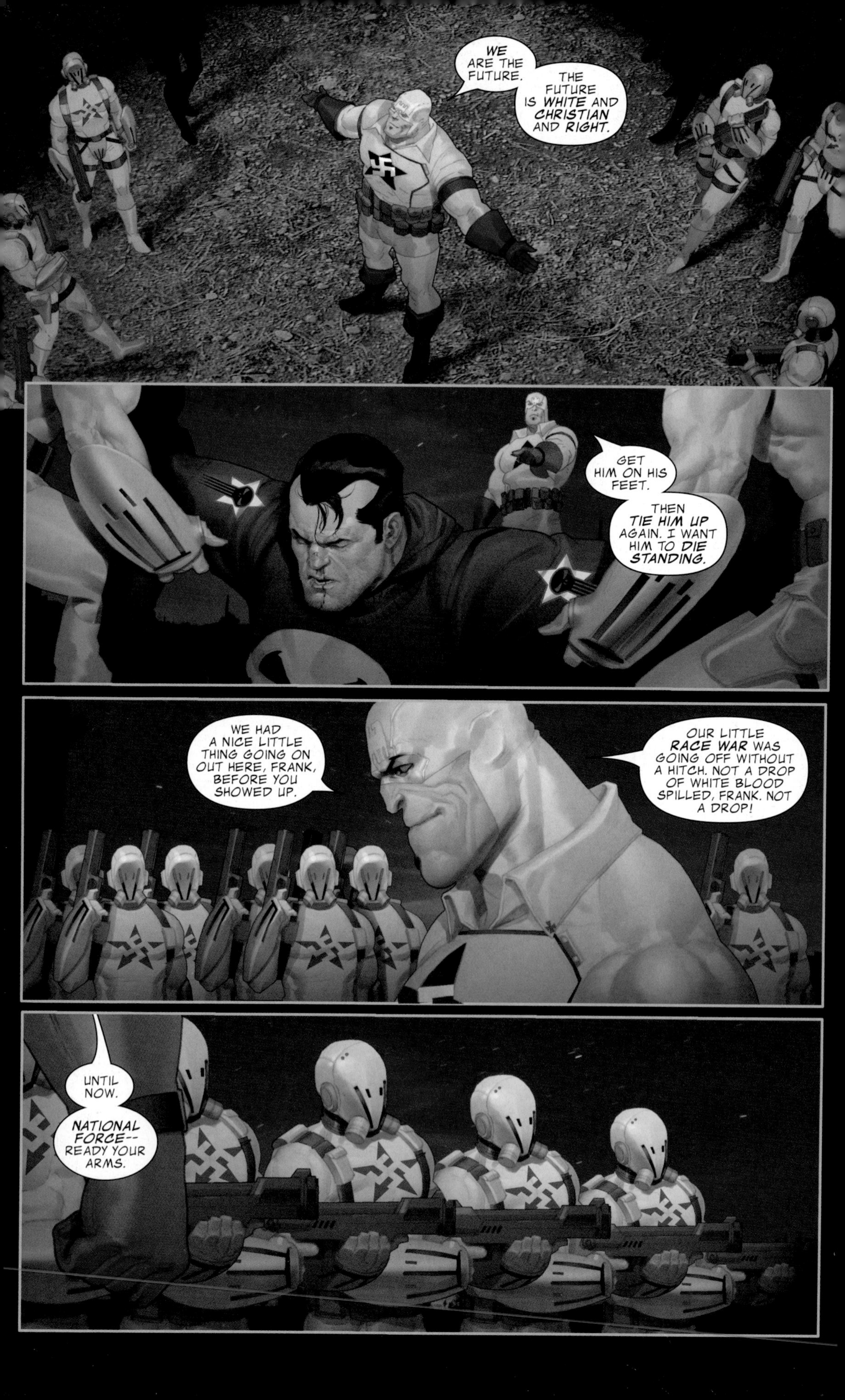

WE ARE THE FUTURE.
THE FUTURE IS WHITE AND CHRISTIAN AND RIGHT.
GET HIM ON HIS FEET.
THEN TIE HIM UP AGAIN. I WANT HIM TO DIE STANDING.
WE HAD A NICE LITTLE THING GOING ON OUT HERE, FRANK, BEFORE YOU SHOWED UP.
OUR LITTLE RACE WAR WAS GOING OFF WITHOUT A HITCH. NOT A DROP OF WHITE BLOOD SPILLED, FRANK. NOT A DROP!
UNTIL NOW.
NATIONAL FORCE-- READY YOUR ARMS.

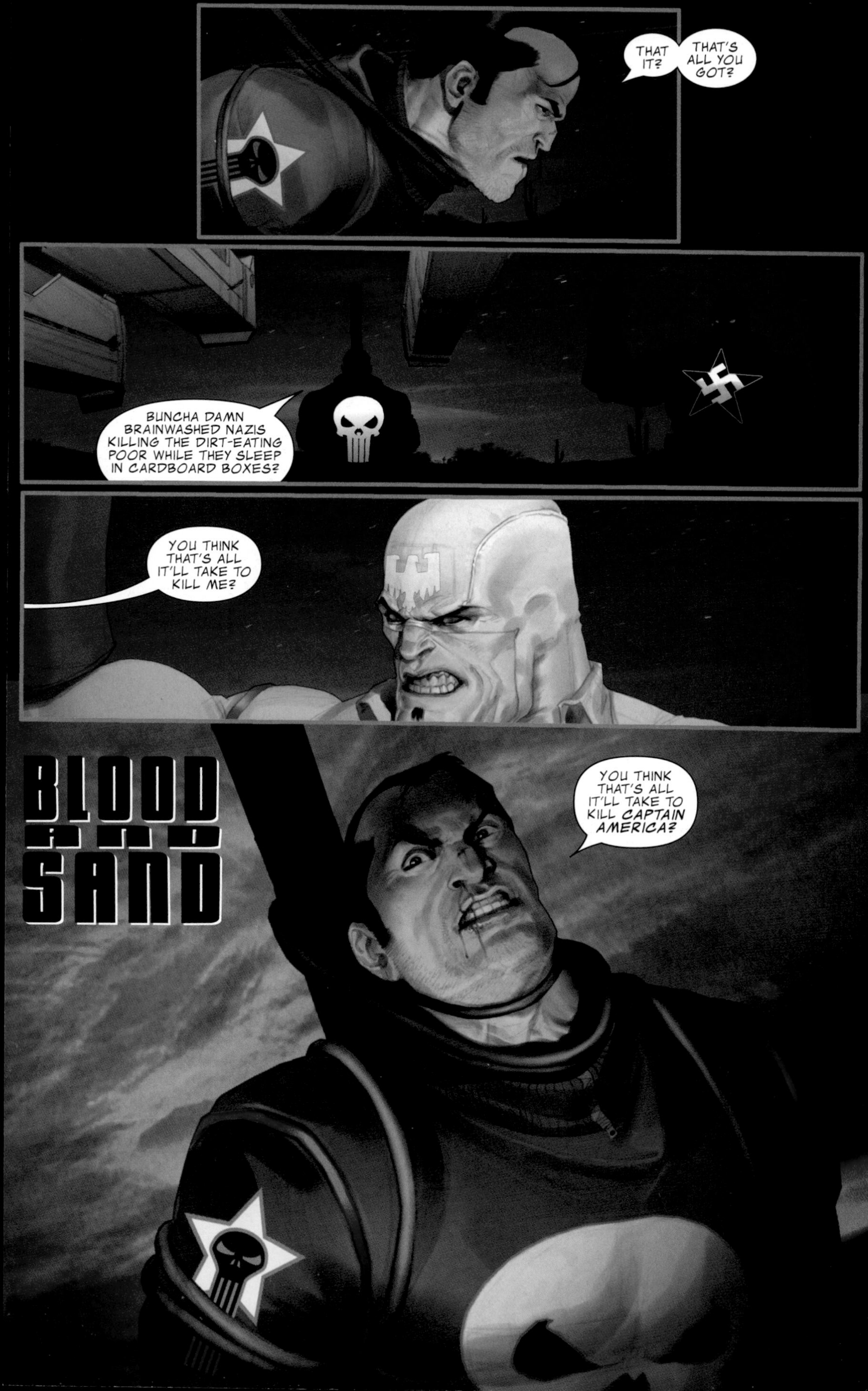
THAT IT?
THAT'S ALL YOU GOT?
BUNCHA DAMN BRAINWASHED NAZIS KILLING THE DIRT-EATING POOR WHILE THEY SLEEP IN CARDBOARD BOXES?
YOU THINK THAT'S ALL IT'LL TAKE TO KILL ME?
BLOOD AND SAND
YOU THINK THAT'S ALL IT'LL TAKE TO KILL *CAPTAIN AMERICA?*

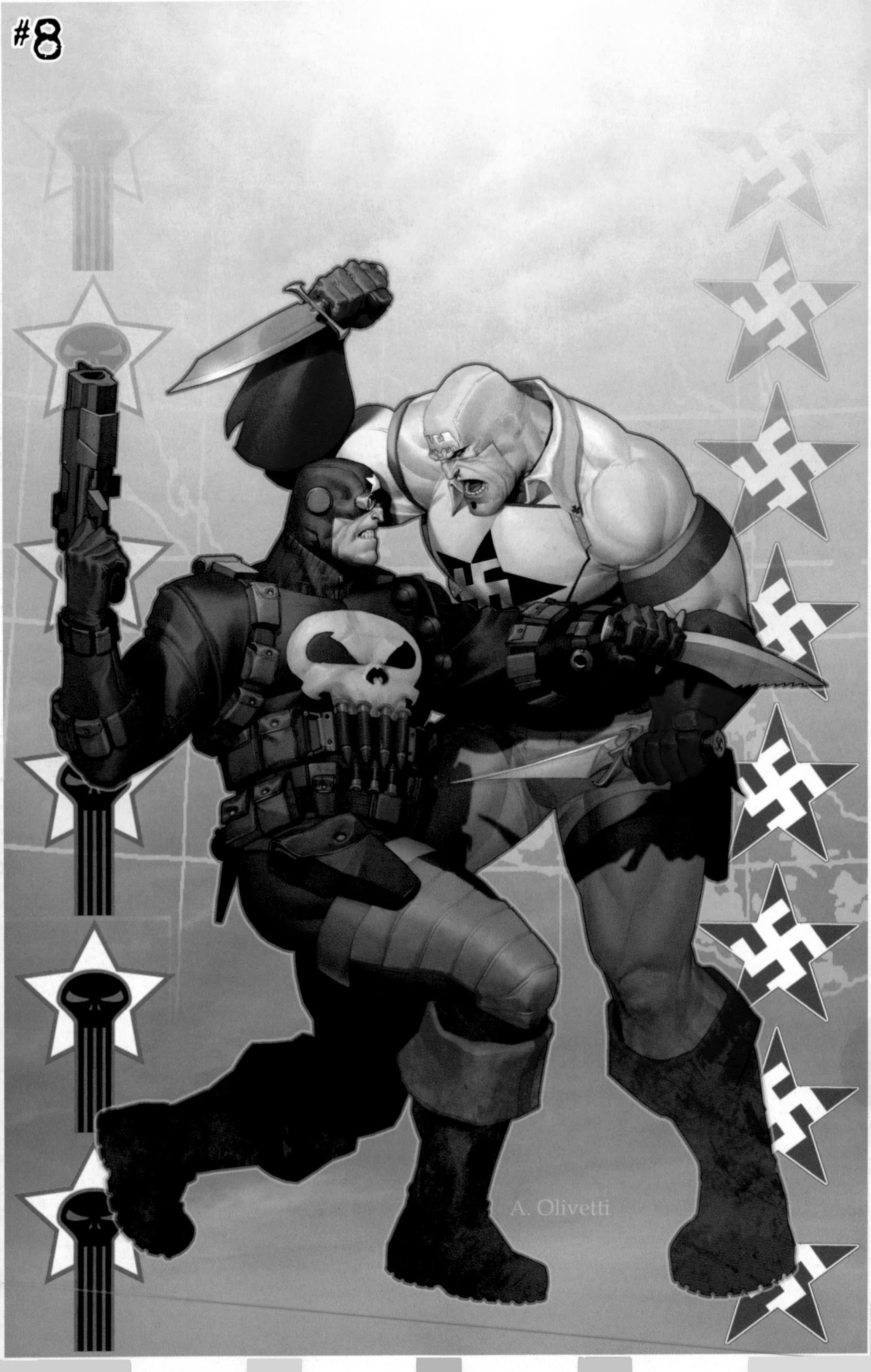
#8
A. Olivetti

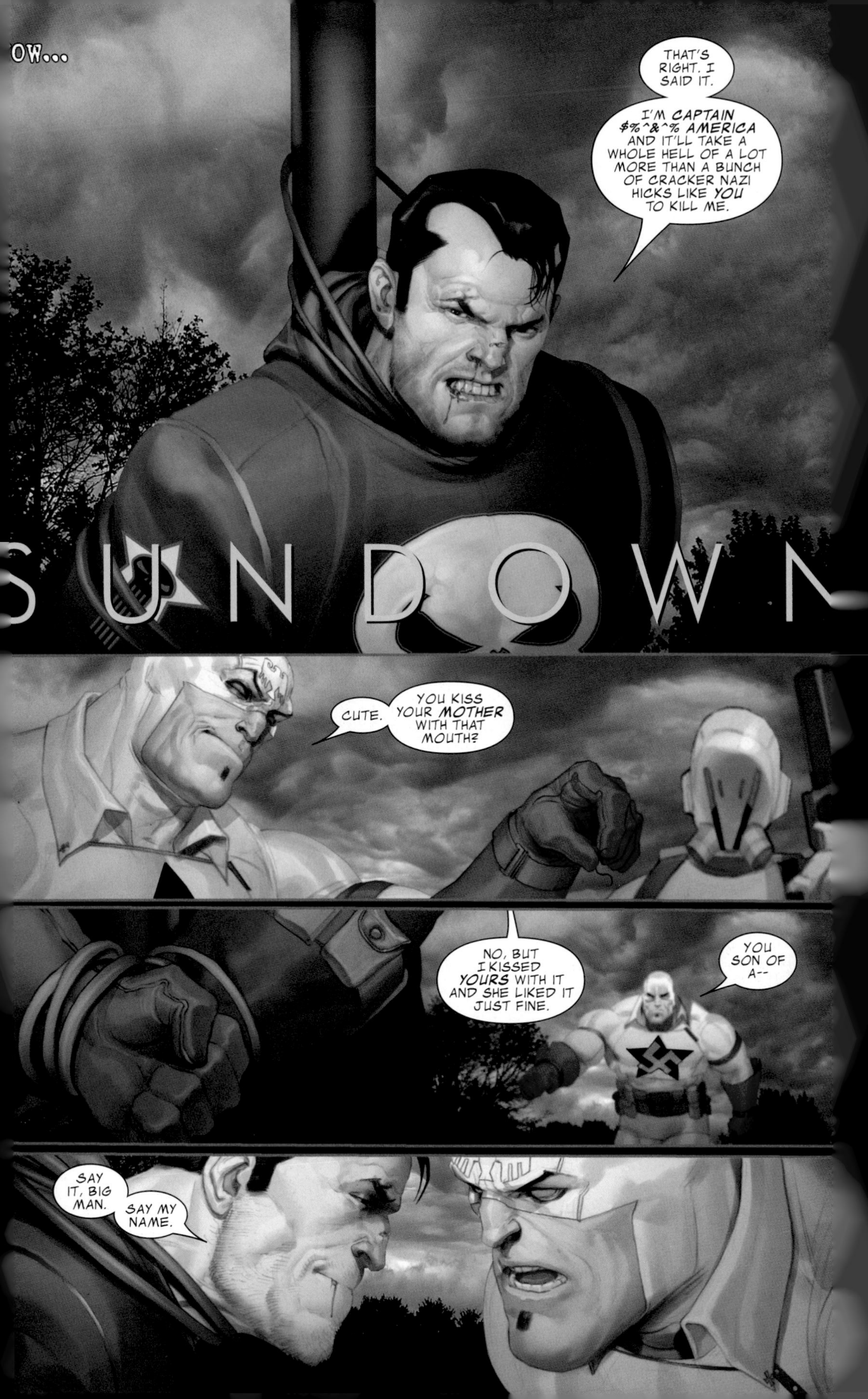
OW...
THAT'S RIGHT. I SAID IT.
I'M CAPTAIN $%^&^% AMERICA AND IT'LL TAKE A WHOLE HELL OF A LOT MORE THAN A BUNCH OF CRACKER NAZI HICKS LIKE YOU TO KILL ME.
SUNDOWN
CUTE.
YOU KISS YOUR MOTHER WITH THAT MOUTH?
NO, BUT I KISSED YOURS WITH IT AND SHE LIKED IT JUST FINE.
YOU SON OF A--
SAY IT, BIG MAN.
SAY MY NAME.

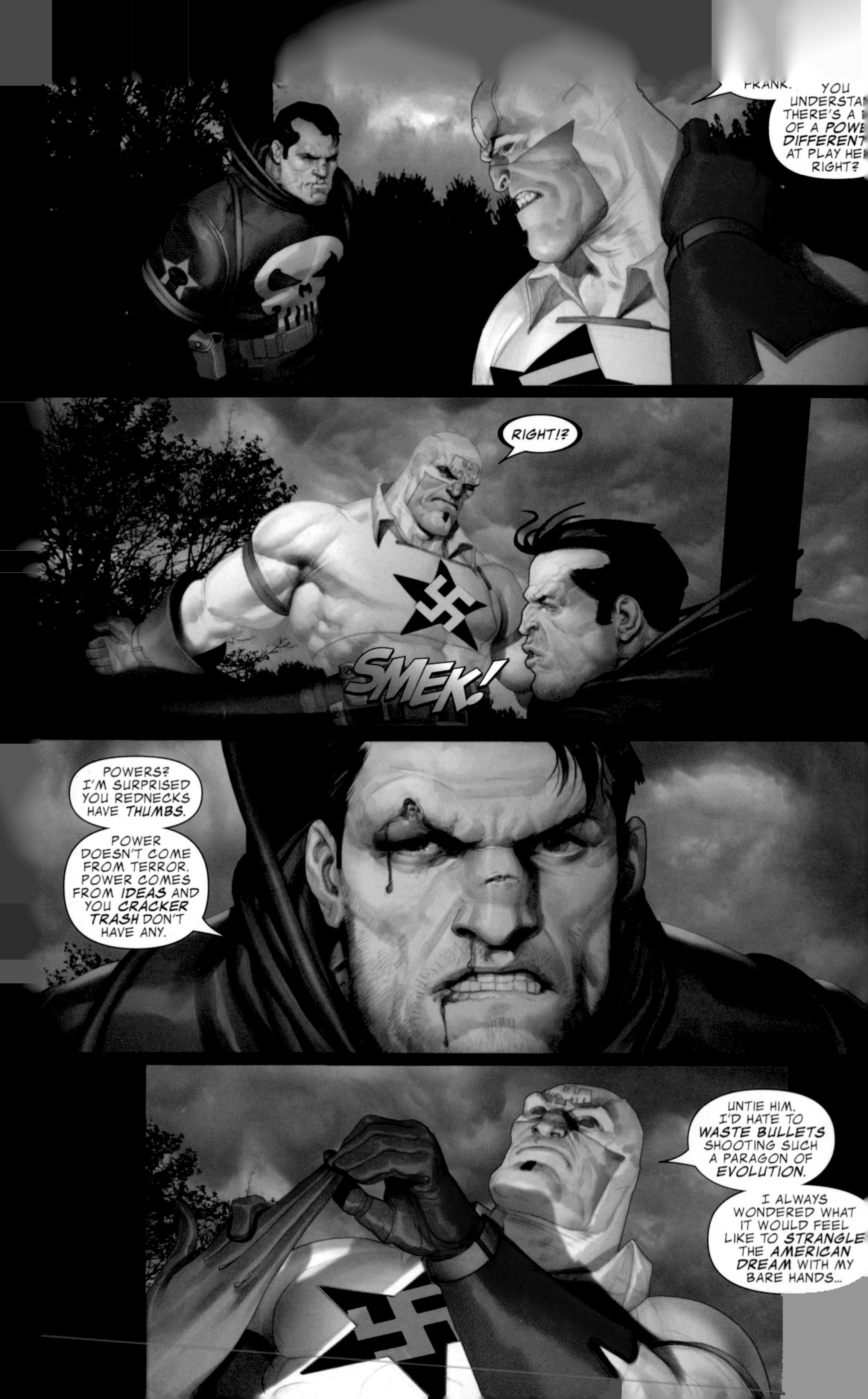
FRANK.
YOU UNDERSTAN THERE'S A OF A POWE DIFFERENT AT PLAY HE RIGHT?
RIGHT!?
SMEK!
POWERS? I'M SURPRISED YOU REDNECKS HAVE THUMBS.
POWER DOESN'T COME FROM TERROR. POWER COMES FROM IDEAS AND YOU CRACKER TRASH DON'T HAVE ANY.
UNTIE HIM. I'D HATE TO WASTE BULLETS SHOOTING SUCH A PARAGON OF EVOLUTION.
I ALWAYS WONDERED WHAT IT WOULD FEEL LIKE TO STRANGLE THE AMERICAN DREAM WITH MY BARE HANDS...

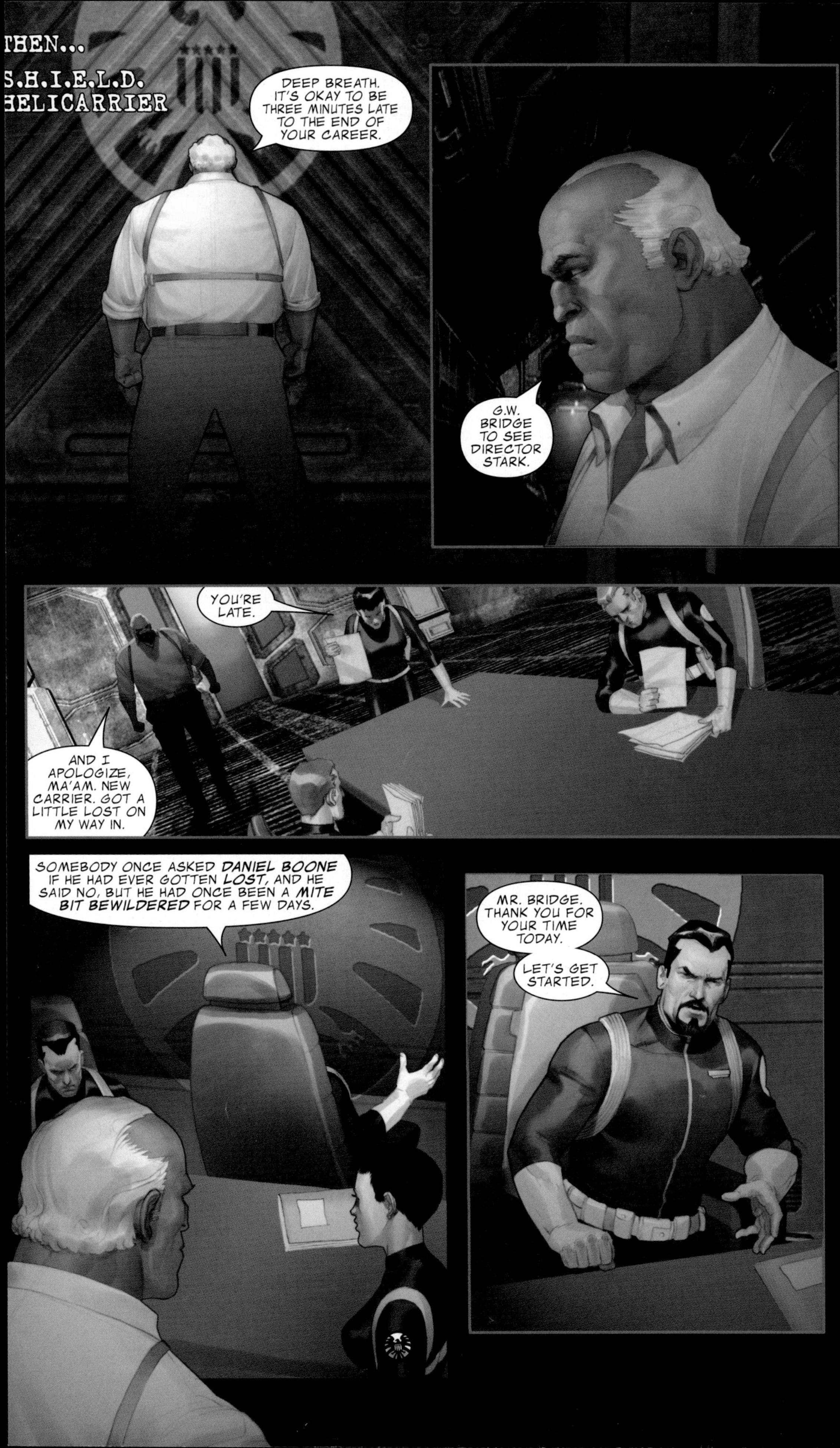
THEN...
S.H.I.E.L.D. HELICARRIER
DEEP BREATH. IT'S OKAY TO BE THREE MINUTES LATE TO THE END OF YOUR CAREER.
G.W. BRIDGE TO SEE DIRECTOR STARK.
YOU'RE LATE.
AND I APOLOGIZE, MA'AM. NEW CARRIER. GOT A LITTLE LOST ON MY WAY IN.
SOMEBODY ONCE ASKED DANIEL BOONE IF HE HAD EVER GOTTEN LOST, AND HE SAID NO, BUT HE HAD ONCE BEEN A MITE BIT BEWILDERED FOR A FEW DAYS.
MR. BRIDGE. THANK YOU FOR YOUR TIME TODAY.
LET'S GET STARTED.

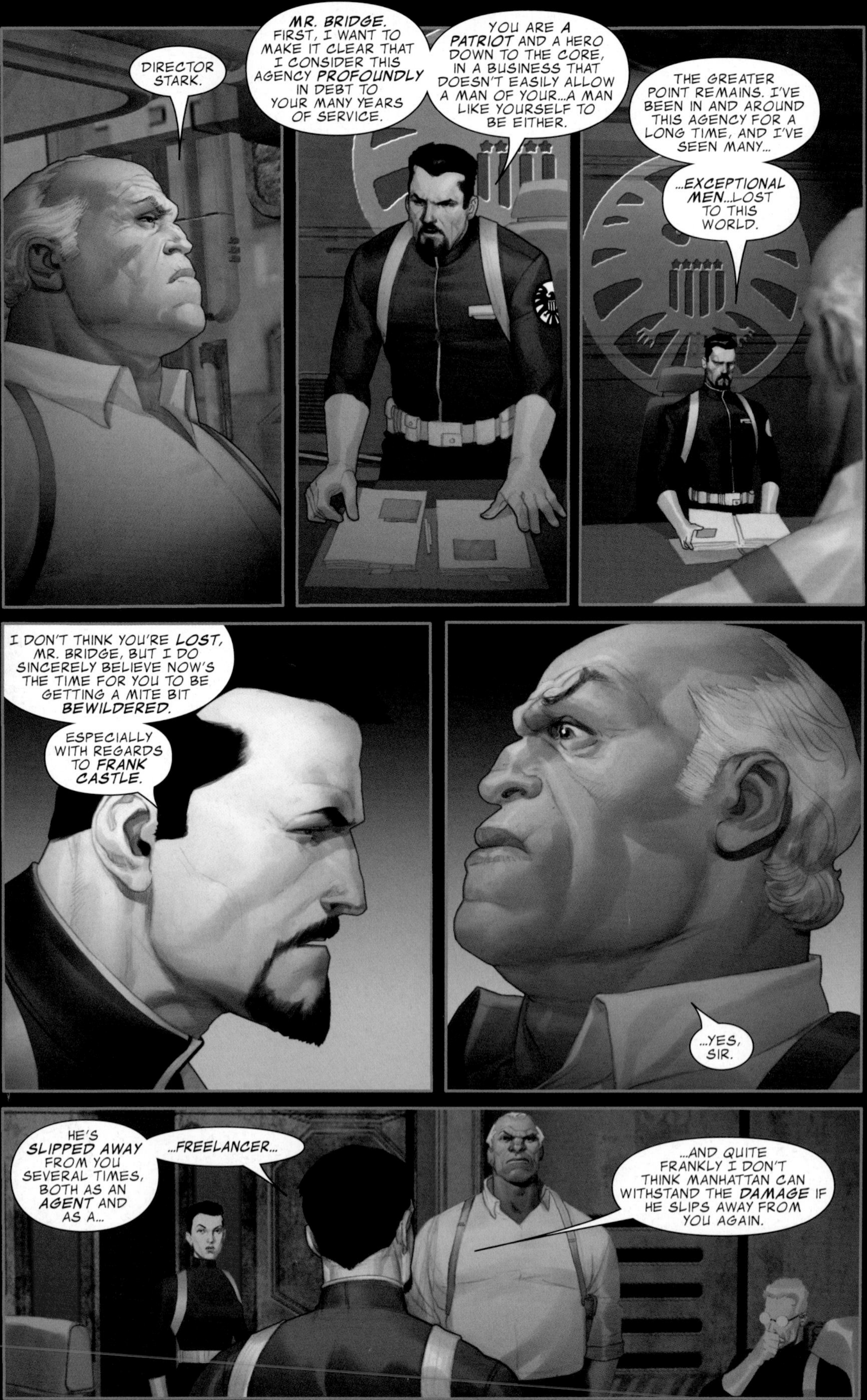
DIRECTOR STARK.
MR. BRIDGE. FIRST, I WANT TO MAKE IT CLEAR THAT I CONSIDER THIS AGENCY PROFOUNDLY IN DEBT TO YOUR MANY YEARS OF SERVICE.
YOU ARE A PATRIOT AND A HERO DOWN TO THE CORE, IN A BUSINESS THAT DOESN'T EASILY ALLOW A MAN OF YOUR...A MAN LIKE YOURSELF TO BE EITHER.
THE GREATER POINT REMAINS. I'VE BEEN IN AND AROUND THIS AGENCY FOR A LONG TIME, AND I'VE SEEN MANY...
...EXCEPTIONAL MEN...LOST TO THIS WORLD.
I DON'T THINK YOU'RE LOST, MR. BRIDGE, BUT I DO SINCERELY BELIEVE NOW'S THE TIME FOR YOU TO BE GETTING A MITE BIT BEWILDERED.
ESPECIALLY WITH REGARDS TO FRANK CASTLE.
...YES, SIR.
HE'S SLIPPED AWAY FROM YOU SEVERAL TIMES, BOTH AS AN AGENT AND AS A...
...FREELANCER...
...AND QUITE FRANKLY I DON'T THINK MANHATTAN CAN WITHSTAND THE DAMAGE IF HE SLIPS AWAY FROM YOU AGAIN.

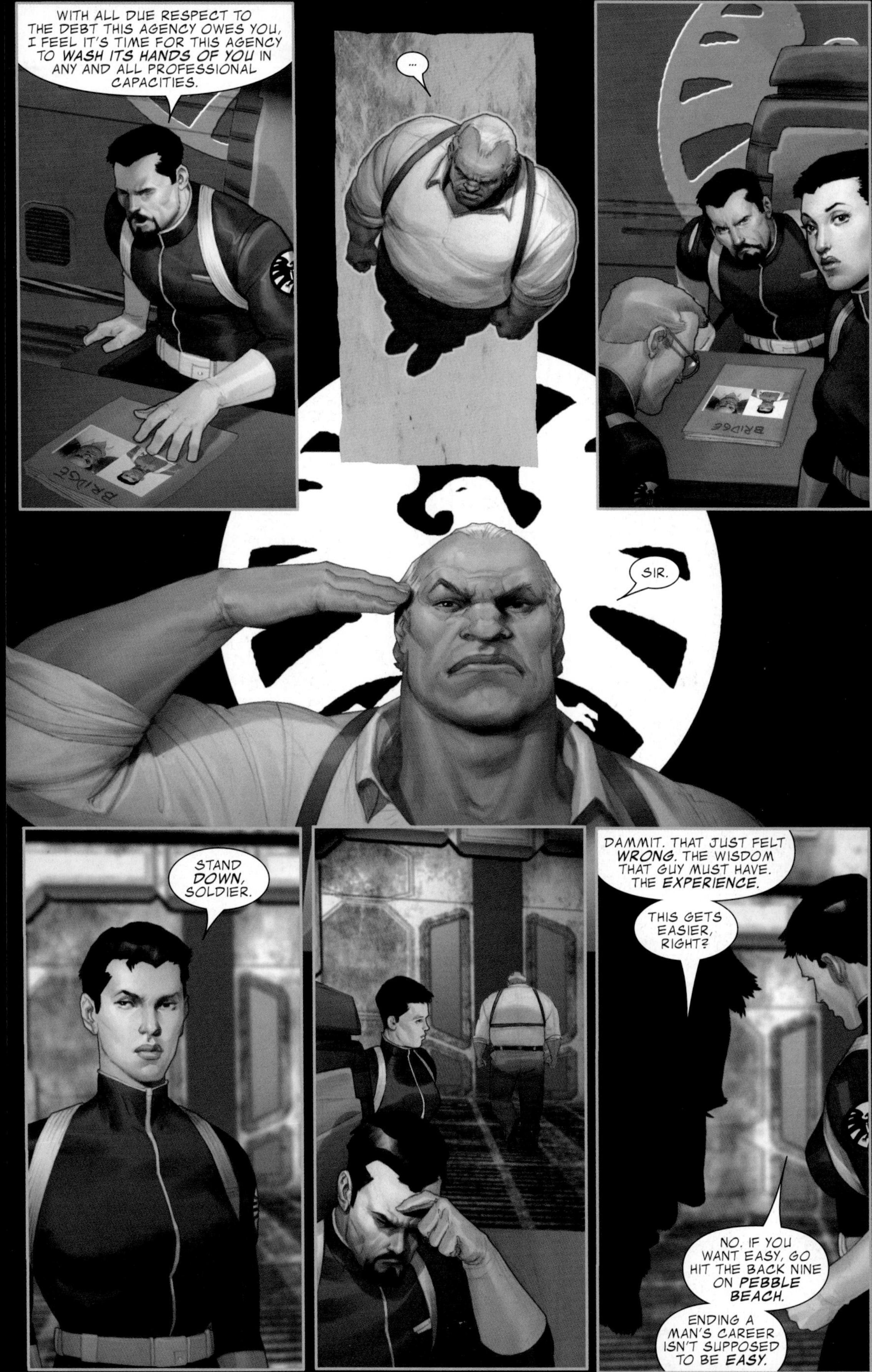
WITH ALL DUE RESPECT TO THE DEBT THIS AGENCY OWES YOU, I FEEL IT'S TIME FOR THIS AGENCY TO WASH ITS HANDS OF YOU IN ANY AND ALL PROFESSIONAL CAPACITIES.
...
BRIDGE
BRIDGE
SIR.
STAND DOWN, SOLDIER.
DAMMIT. THAT JUST FELT WRONG. THE WISDOM THAT GUY MUST HAVE. THE EXPERIENCE.
THIS GETS EASIER, RIGHT?
NO. IF YOU WANT EASY, GO HIT THE BACK NINE ON PEBBLE BEACH.
ENDING A MAN'S CAREER ISN'T SUPPOSED TO BE EASY.

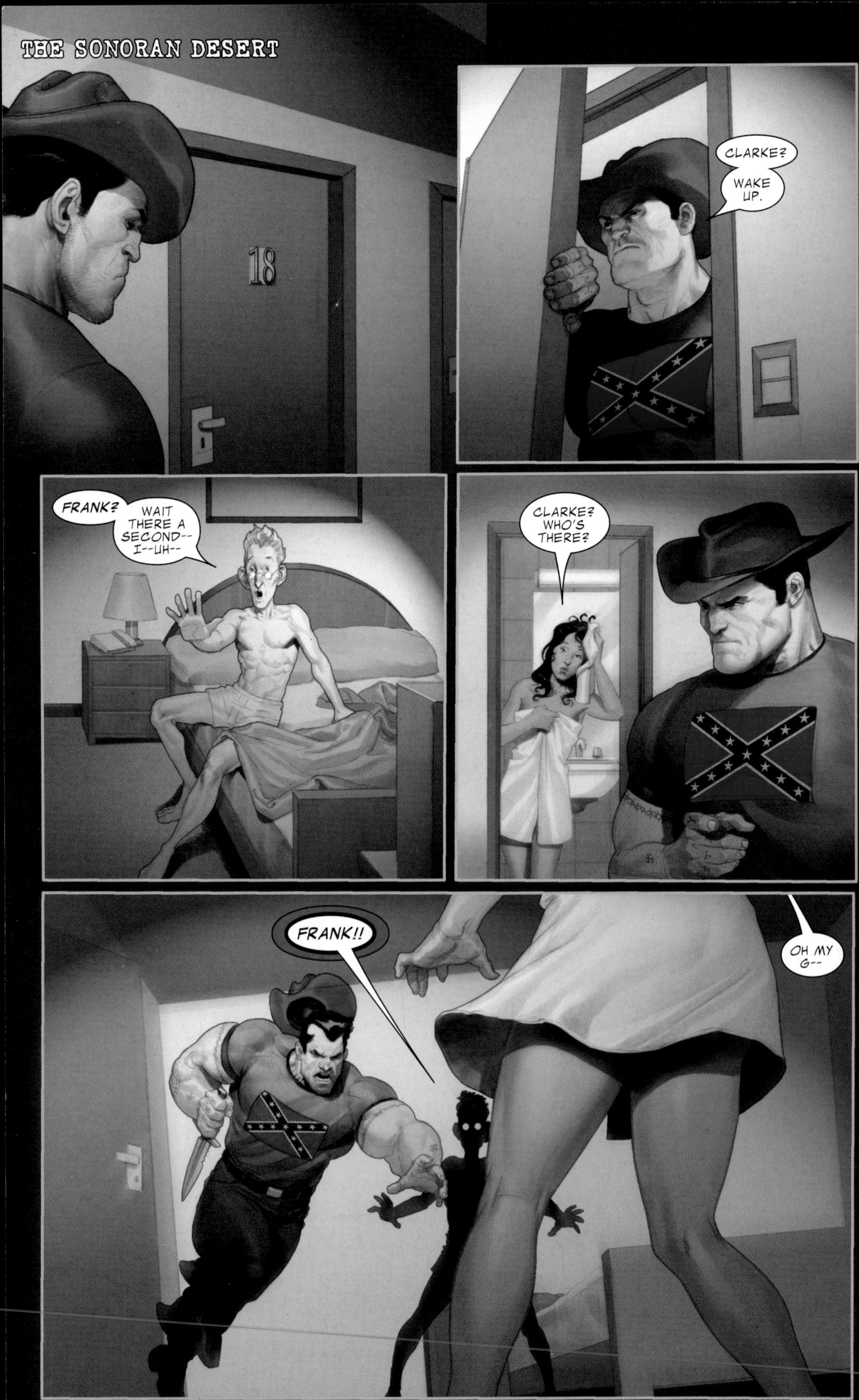
THE SONORAN DESERT
CLARKE?
WAKE UP.
FRANK?
WAIT THERE A SECOND-- I--UH--
CLARKE? WHO'S THERE?
FRANK!!
OH MY G--

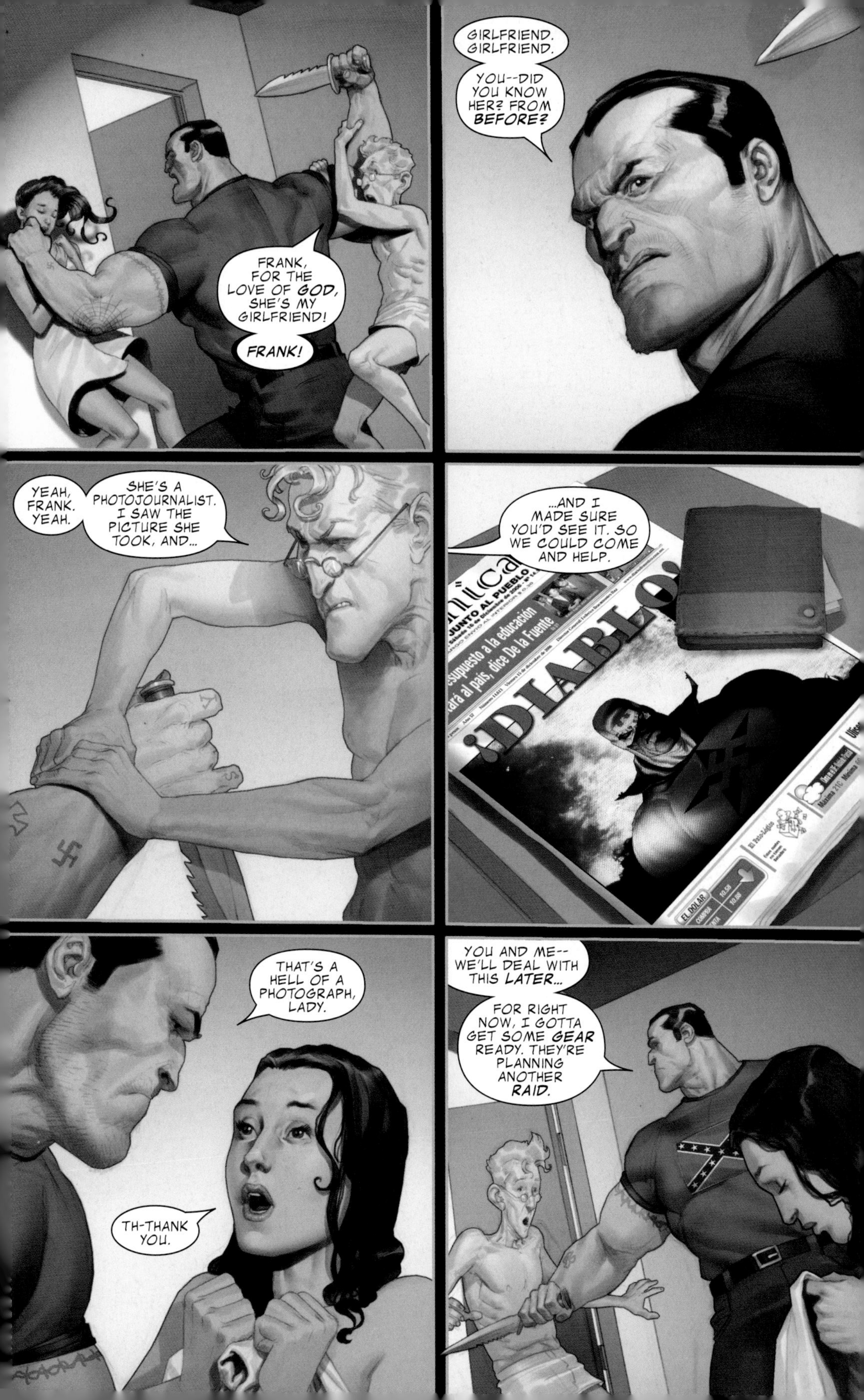
FRANK, FOR THE LOVE OF GOD, SHE'S MY GIRLFRIEND!
FRANK!
GIRLFRIEND. GIRLFRIEND.
YOU--DID YOU KNOW HER? FROM BEFORE?
YEAH, FRANK. YEAH.
SHE'S A PHOTOJOURNALIST. I SAW THE PICTURE SHE TOOK, AND...
...AND I MADE SURE YOU'D SEE IT. SO WE COULD COME AND HELP.
THAT'S A HELL OF A PHOTOGRAPH, LADY.
TH-THANK YOU.
YOU AND ME-- WE'LL DEAL WITH THIS LATER...
FOR RIGHT NOW, I GOTTA GET SOME GEAR READY. THEY'RE PLANNING ANOTHER RAID.

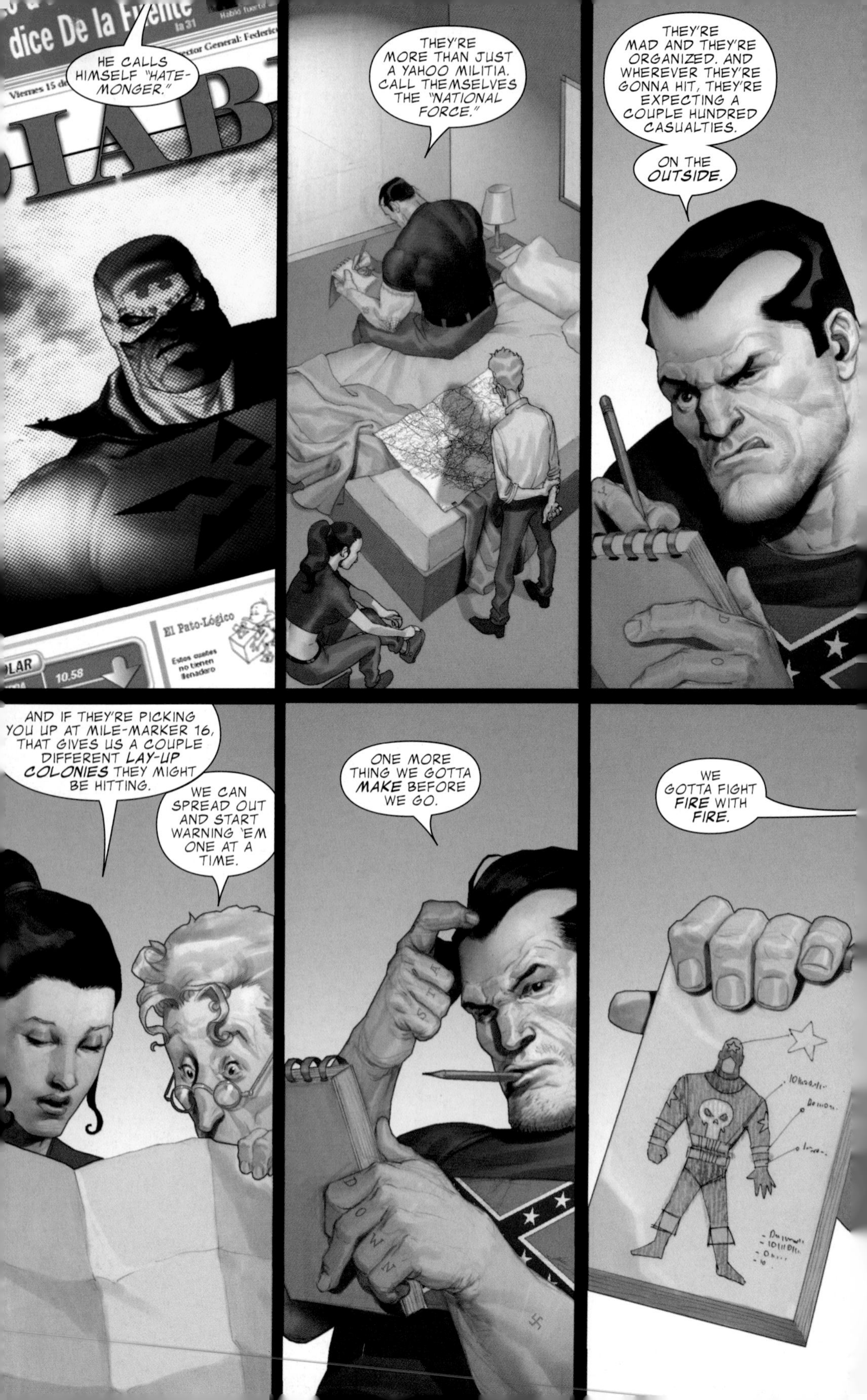
dice De la Fuente
Viernes 15 de
HE CALLS HIMSELF "HATE-MONGER."
El Pato-Lógico
Estos cuates no tienen llenadero
10.58
THEY'RE MORE THAN JUST A YAHOO MILITIA. CALL THEMSELVES THE "NATIONAL FORCE."
THEY'RE MAD AND THEY'RE ORGANIZED. AND WHEREVER THEY'RE GONNA HIT, THEY'RE EXPECTING A COUPLE HUNDRED CASUALTIES.
ON THE *OUTSIDE*.
AND IF THEY'RE PICKING YOU UP AT MILE-MARKER 16, THAT GIVES US A COUPLE DIFFERENT *LAY-UP COLONIES* THEY MIGHT BE HITTING.
WE CAN SPREAD OUT AND START WARNING 'EM ONE AT A TIME.
ONE MORE THING WE GOTTA *MAKE* BEFORE WE GO.
WE GOTTA FIGHT *FIRE* WITH *FIRE*.

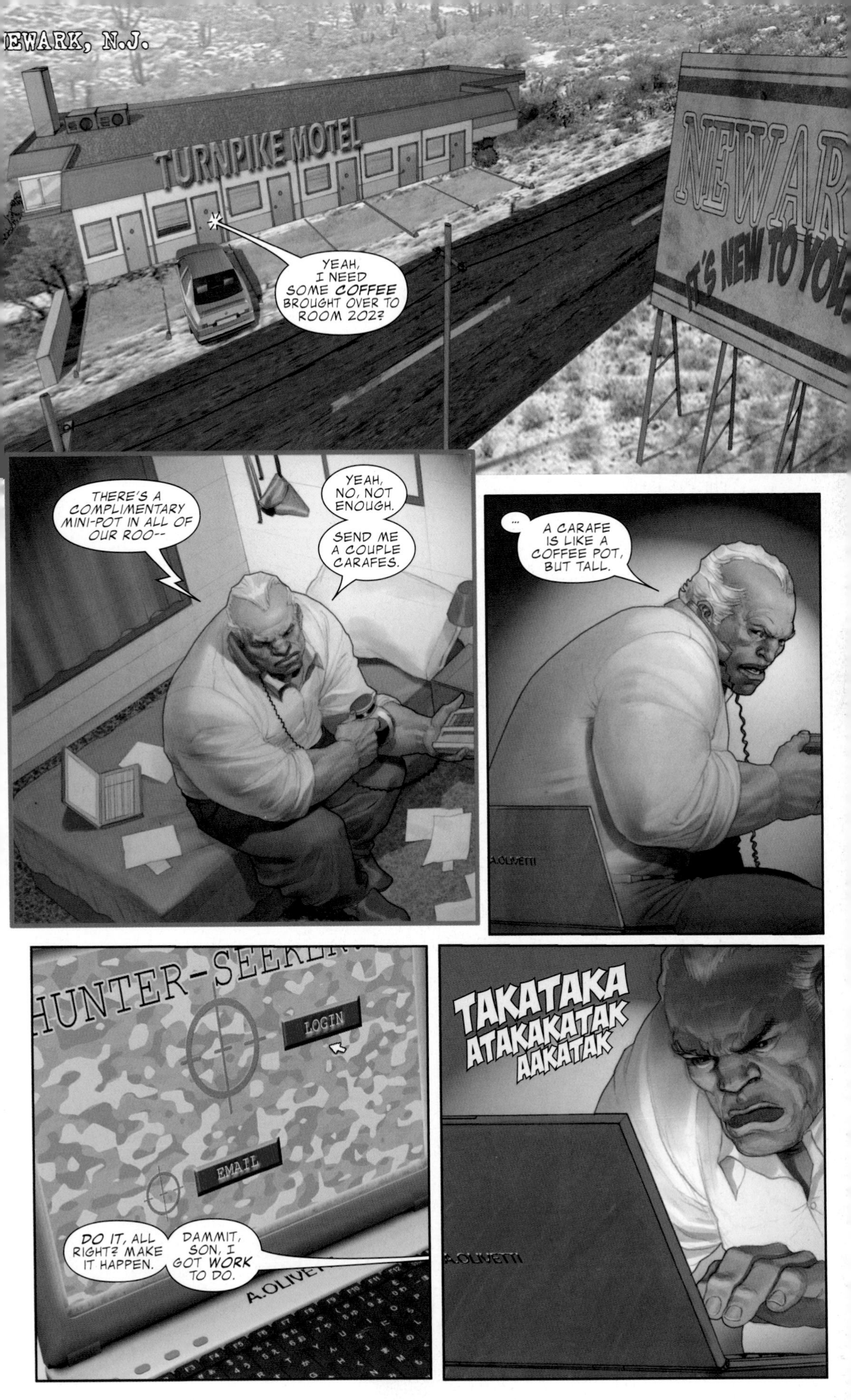
EWARK, N.J.
TURNPIKE MOTEL
NEWAR
IT'S NEW TO YOU
YEAH, I NEED SOME COFFEE BROUGHT OVER TO ROOM 202?
THERE'S A COMPLIMENTARY MINI-POT IN ALL OF OUR ROO--
YEAH, NO, NOT ENOUGH.
SEND ME A COUPLE CARAFES.
...
A CARAFE IS LIKE A COFFEE POT, BUT TALL.
A.OLIVETTI
HUNTER-SEEKER
LOGIN
EMAIL
DO IT, ALL RIGHT? MAKE IT HAPPEN.
DAMMIT, SON, I GOT WORK TO DO.
A.OLIVETTI
TAKATAKA
ATAKAKATAK
AAKATAK

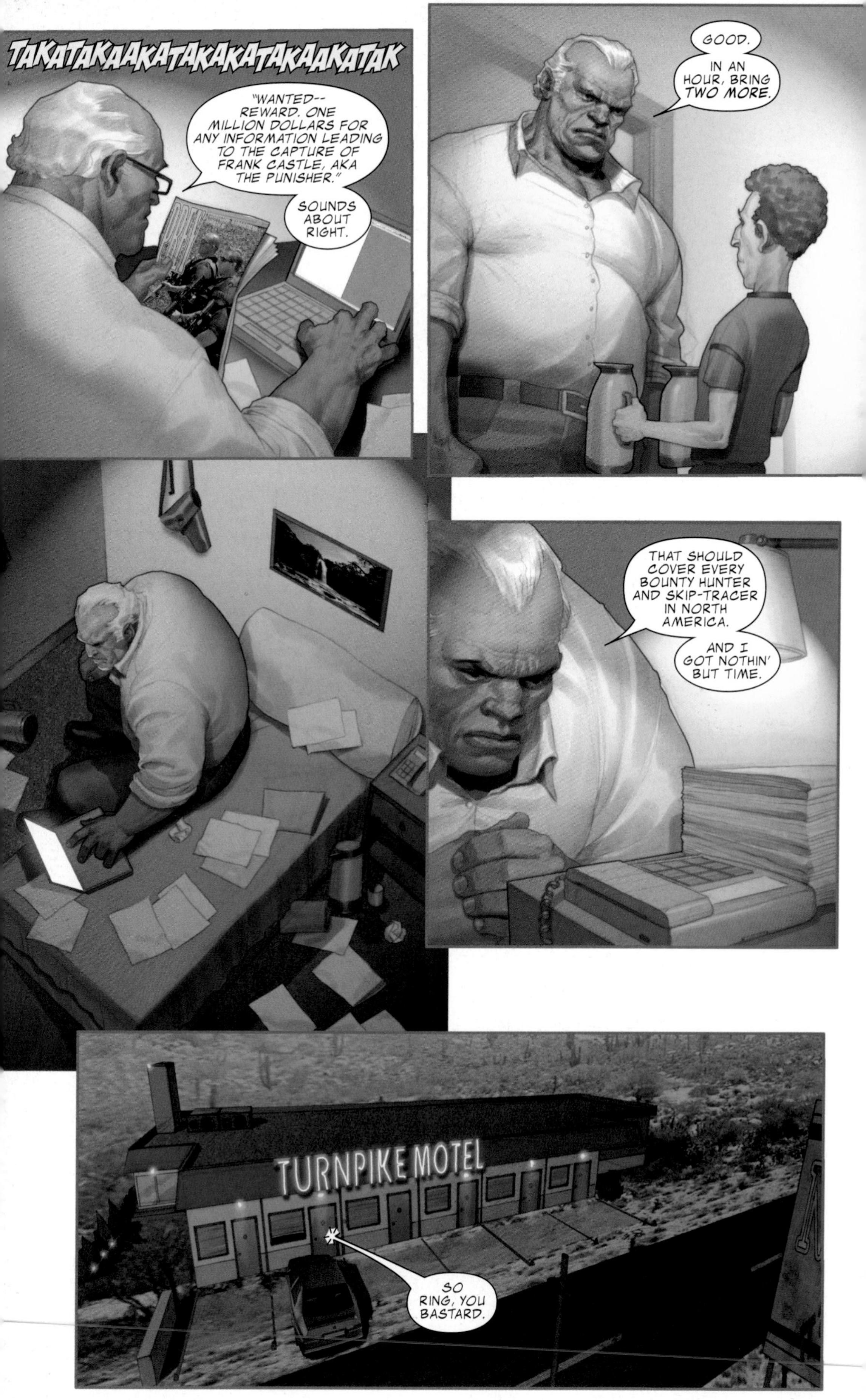
TAKATAKAAKATAKAKATAKAAKATAK
"WANTED-- REWARD. ONE MILLION DOLLARS FOR ANY INFORMATION LEADING TO THE CAPTURE OF FRANK CASTLE, AKA THE PUNISHER."
SOUNDS ABOUT RIGHT.
GOOD.
IN AN HOUR, BRING TWO MORE.
THAT SHOULD COVER EVERY BOUNTY HUNTER AND SKIP-TRACER IN NORTH AMERICA.
AND I GOT NOTHIN' BUT TIME.
TURNPIKE MOTEL
SO RING, YOU BASTARD.

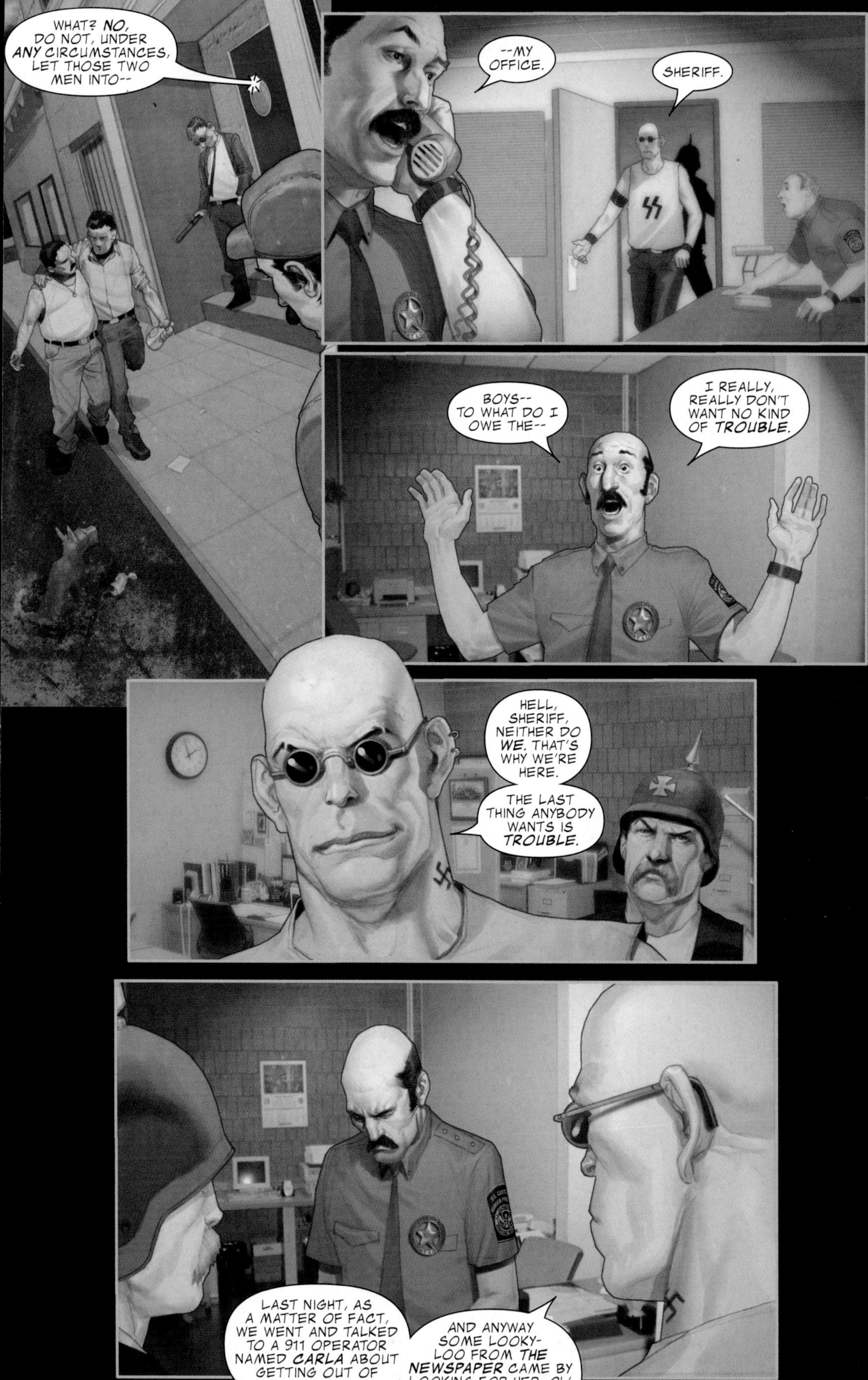

WHAT? NO, DO NOT, UNDER ANY CIRCUMSTANCES, LET THOSE TWO MEN INTO--
--MY OFFICE.
SHERIFF.
BOYS-- TO WHAT DO I OWE THE--
I REALLY, REALLY DON'T WANT NO KIND OF TROUBLE.
HELL, SHERIFF, NEITHER DO WE. THAT'S WHY WE'RE HERE.
THE LAST THING ANYBODY WANTS IS TROUBLE.
LAST NIGHT, AS A MATTER OF FACT, WE WENT AND TALKED TO A 911 OPERATOR NAMED CARLA ABOUT GETTING OUT OF
AND ANYWAY SOME LOOKY-LOO FROM THE NEWSPAPER CAME BY

WHO ON *EARTH* WOULD HAVE REASON TO COME TALK TO CARLA, SHERIFF?

WHO FROM THE NEWSPAPER WOULD HAVE HAD A SINGLE SOLITARY THING TO ASK HER?

MR. TANK...

PLEASE.

JUST A *NAME.* THAT'S ALL.

YOU'D BE SPARING YOURSELF A WHOLE LOT OF *TROUBLE,* SHERIFF...

TATIANA AROCHA.

SHE WAS THE ONE WHAT TOOK THEM PICTURES. SHE WANTED TO KNOW MORE.

TOODELOO, BOSS, AND THANKS FOR THE TIP.

AND, HEY, SHERIFF...

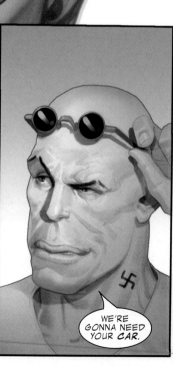

WE'RE GONNA NEED YOUR *CAR.*

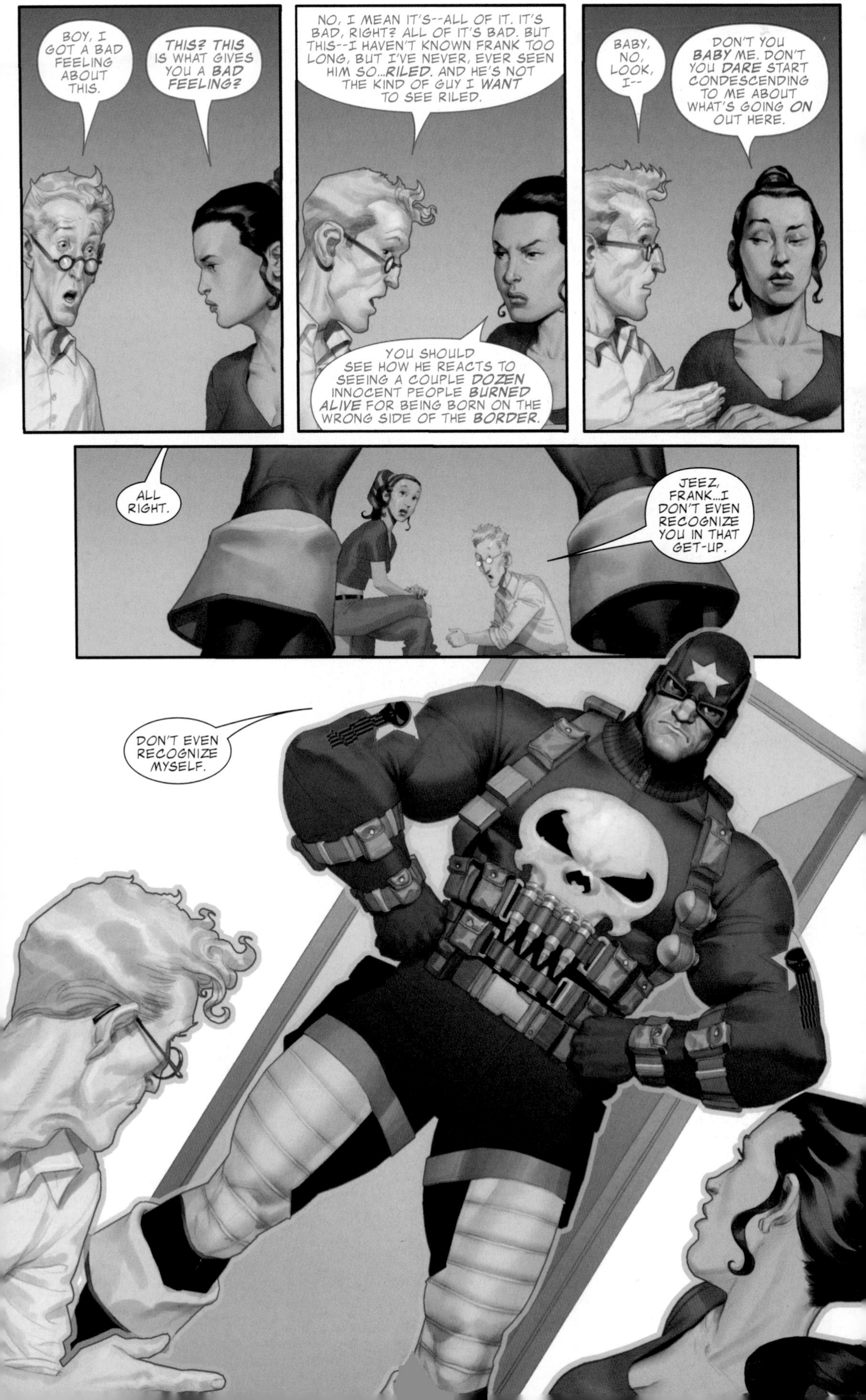
BOY, I GOT A BAD FEELING ABOUT THIS.
THIS? THIS IS WHAT GIVES YOU A BAD FEELING?
NO, I MEAN IT'S--ALL OF IT. IT'S BAD, RIGHT? ALL OF IT'S BAD. BUT THIS--I HAVEN'T KNOWN FRANK TOO LONG, BUT I'VE NEVER, EVER SEEN HIM SO...RILED. AND HE'S NOT THE KIND OF GUY I WANT TO SEE RILED.
YOU SHOULD SEE HOW HE REACTS TO SEEING A COUPLE DOZEN INNOCENT PEOPLE BURNED ALIVE FOR BEING BORN ON THE WRONG SIDE OF THE BORDER.
BABY, NO, LOOK, I--
DON'T YOU BABY ME. DON'T YOU DARE START CONDESCENDING TO ME ABOUT WHAT'S GOING ON OUT HERE.
ALL RIGHT.
JEEZ, FRANK...I DON'T EVEN RECOGNIZE YOU IN THAT GET-UP.
DON'T EVEN RECOGNIZE MYSELF.

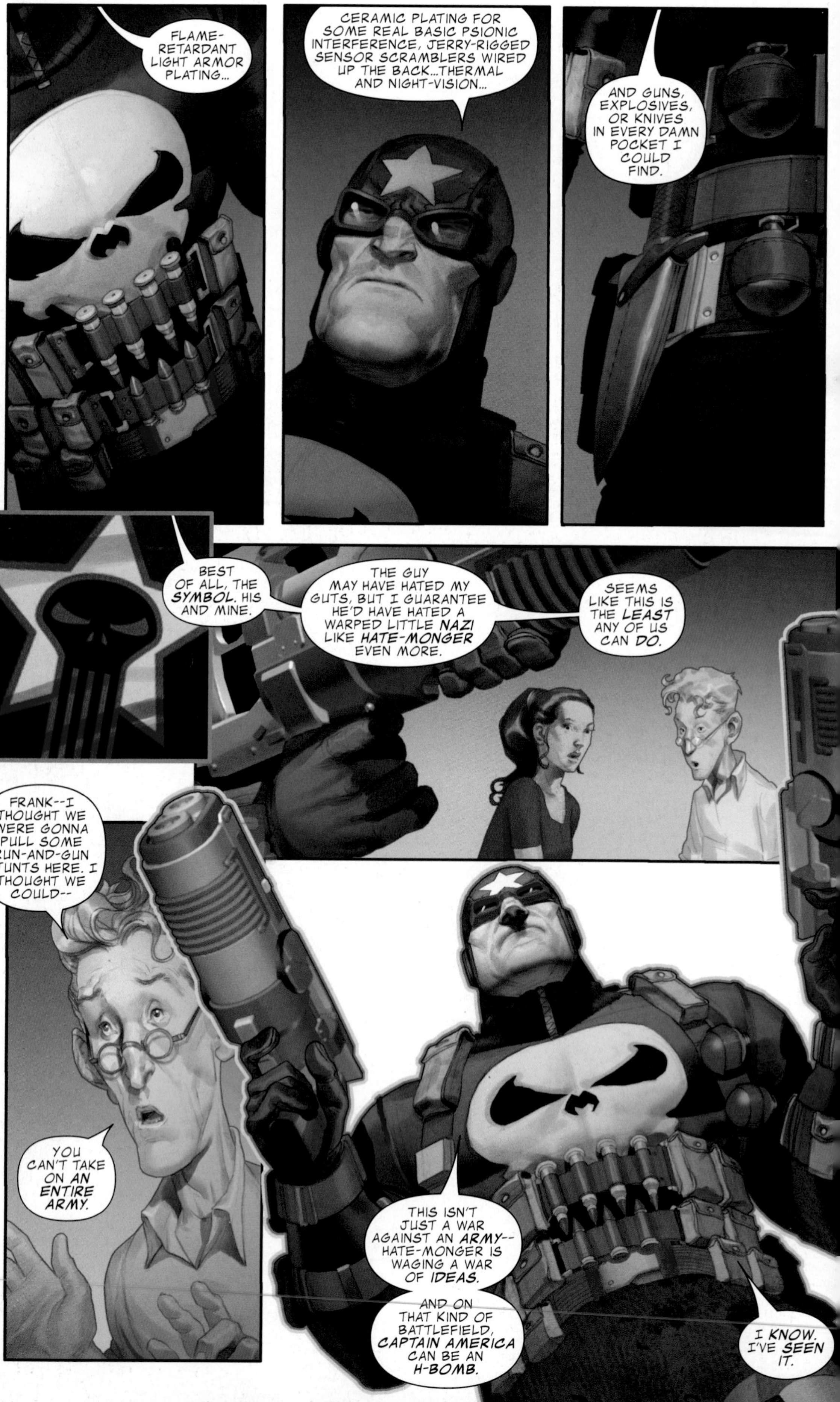

FLAME-RETARDANT LIGHT ARMOR PLATING...
CERAMIC PLATING FOR SOME REAL BASIC PSIONIC INTERFERENCE, JERRY-RIGGED SENSOR SCRAMBLERS WIRED UP THE BACK...THERMAL AND NIGHT-VISION...
AND GUNS, EXPLOSIVES, OR KNIVES IN EVERY DAMN POCKET I COULD FIND.
BEST OF ALL, THE SYMBOL. HIS AND MINE.
THE GUY MAY HAVE HATED MY GUTS, BUT I GUARANTEE HE'D HAVE HATED A WARPED LITTLE NAZI LIKE HATE-MONGER EVEN MORE.
SEEMS LIKE THIS IS THE LEAST ANY OF US CAN DO.
FRANK--I THOUGHT WE WERE GONNA PULL SOME RUN-AND-GUN STUNTS HERE. I THOUGHT WE COULD--
YOU CAN'T TAKE ON AN ENTIRE ARMY.
THIS ISN'T JUST A WAR AGAINST AN ARMY--HATE-MONGER IS WAGING A WAR OF IDEAS.
AND ON THAT KIND OF BATTLEFIELD, CAPTAIN AMERICA CAN BE AN H-BOMB.
I KNOW. I'VE SEEN IT.

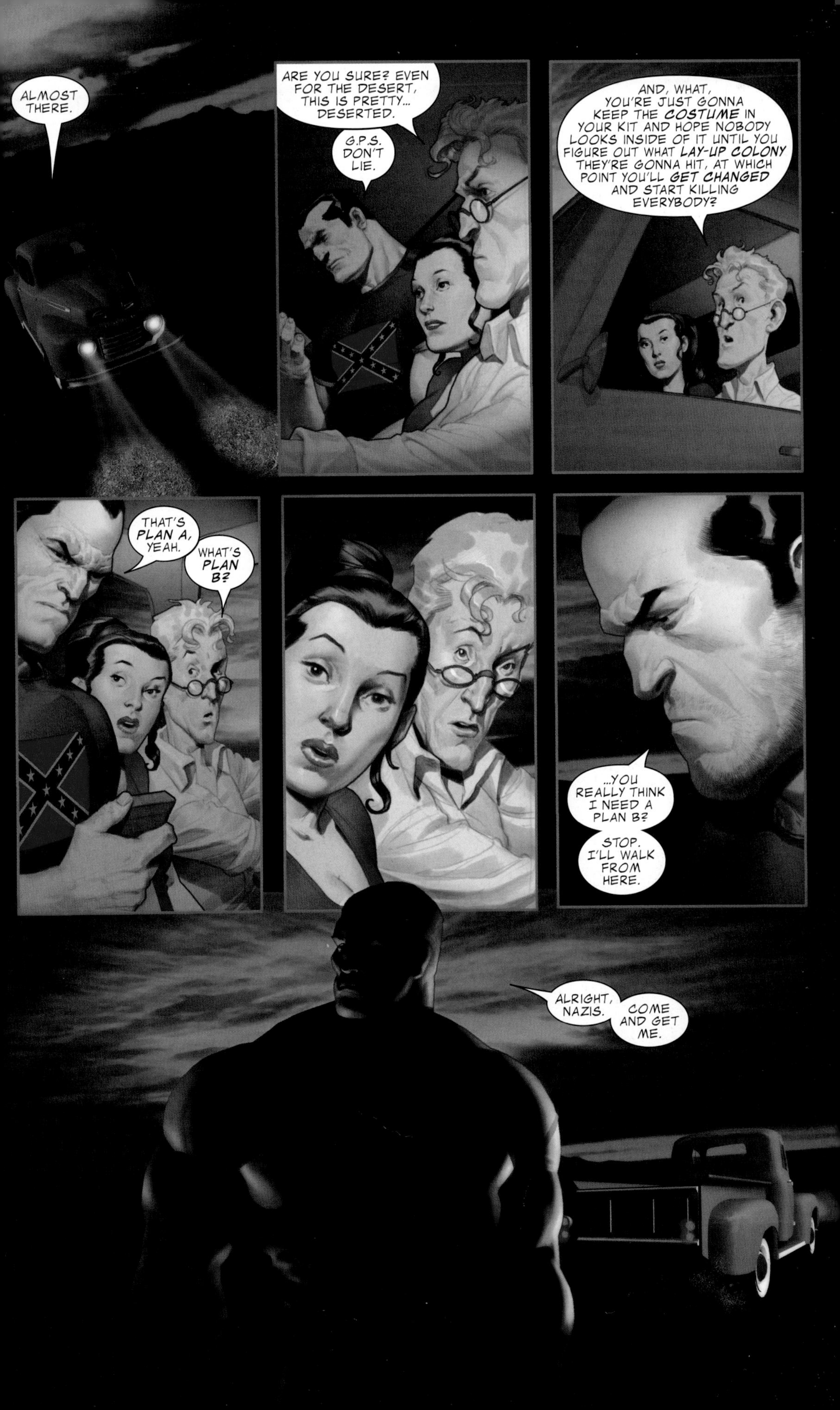
ALMOST THERE.
ARE YOU SURE? EVEN FOR THE DESERT, THIS IS PRETTY... DESERTED.
G.P.S. DON'T LIE.
AND, WHAT, YOU'RE JUST GONNA KEEP THE COSTUME IN YOUR KIT AND HOPE NOBODY LOOKS INSIDE OF IT UNTIL YOU FIGURE OUT WHAT LAY-UP COLONY THEY'RE GONNA HIT, AT WHICH POINT YOU'LL GET CHANGED AND START KILLING EVERYBODY?
THAT'S PLAN A, YEAH.
WHAT'S PLAN B?
...YOU REALLY THINK I NEED A PLAN B?
STOP. I'LL WALK FROM HERE.
ALRIGHT, NAZIS.
COME AND GET ME.

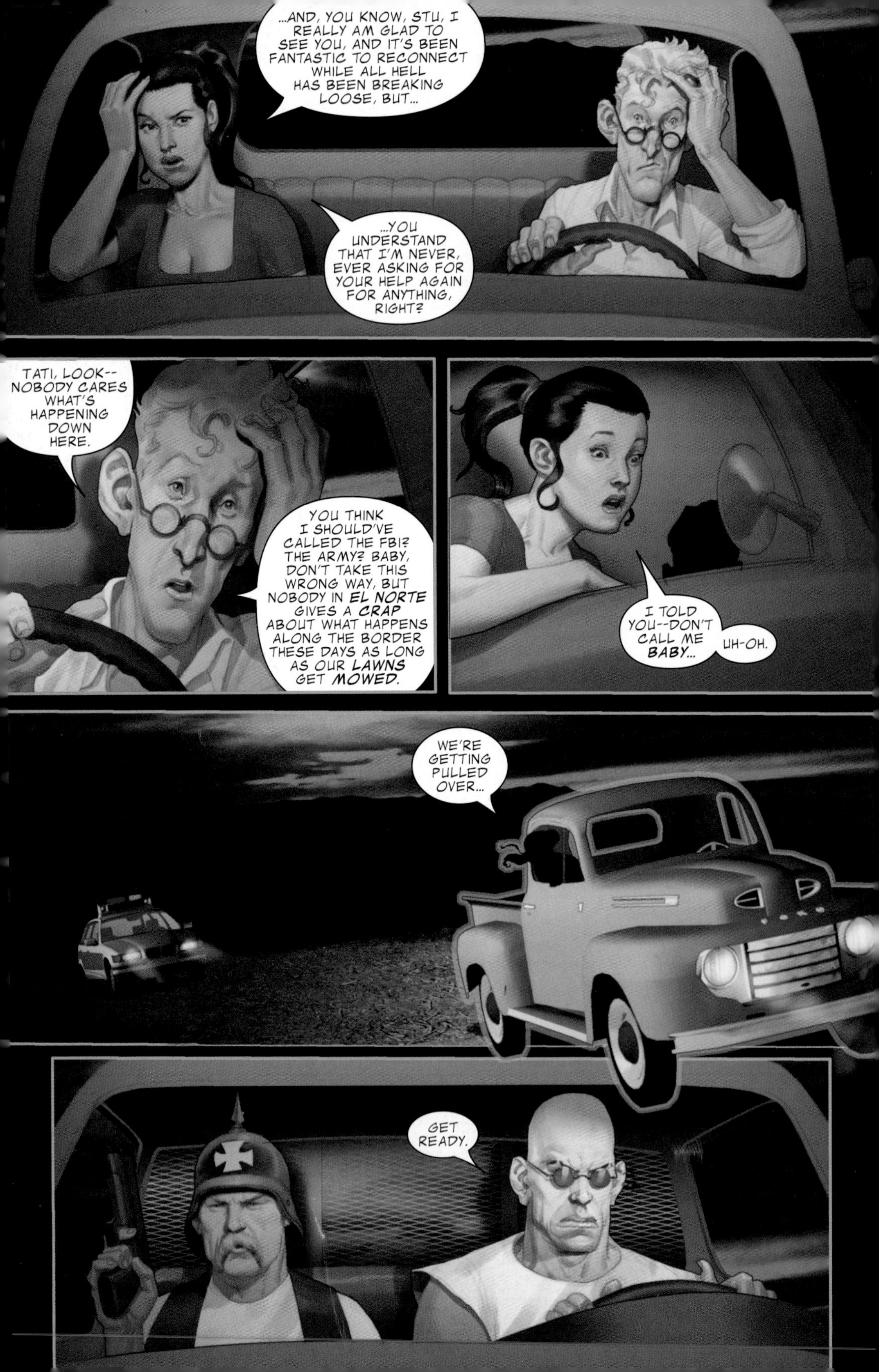
...AND, YOU KNOW, STU, I REALLY AM GLAD TO SEE YOU, AND IT'S BEEN FANTASTIC TO RECONNECT WHILE ALL HELL HAS BEEN BREAKING LOOSE, BUT...
...YOU UNDERSTAND THAT I'M NEVER, EVER ASKING FOR YOUR HELP AGAIN FOR ANYTHING, RIGHT?
TATI, LOOK-- NOBODY CARES WHAT'S HAPPENING DOWN HERE.
YOU THINK I SHOULD'VE CALLED THE FBI? THE ARMY? BABY, DON'T TAKE THIS WRONG WAY, BUT NOBODY IN EL NORTE GIVES A CRAP ABOUT WHAT HAPPENS ALONG THE BORDER THESE DAYS AS LONG AS OUR LAWNS GET MOWED.
I TOLD YOU--DON'T CALL ME BABY...
UH-OH.
WE'RE GETTING PULLED OVER...
GET READY.

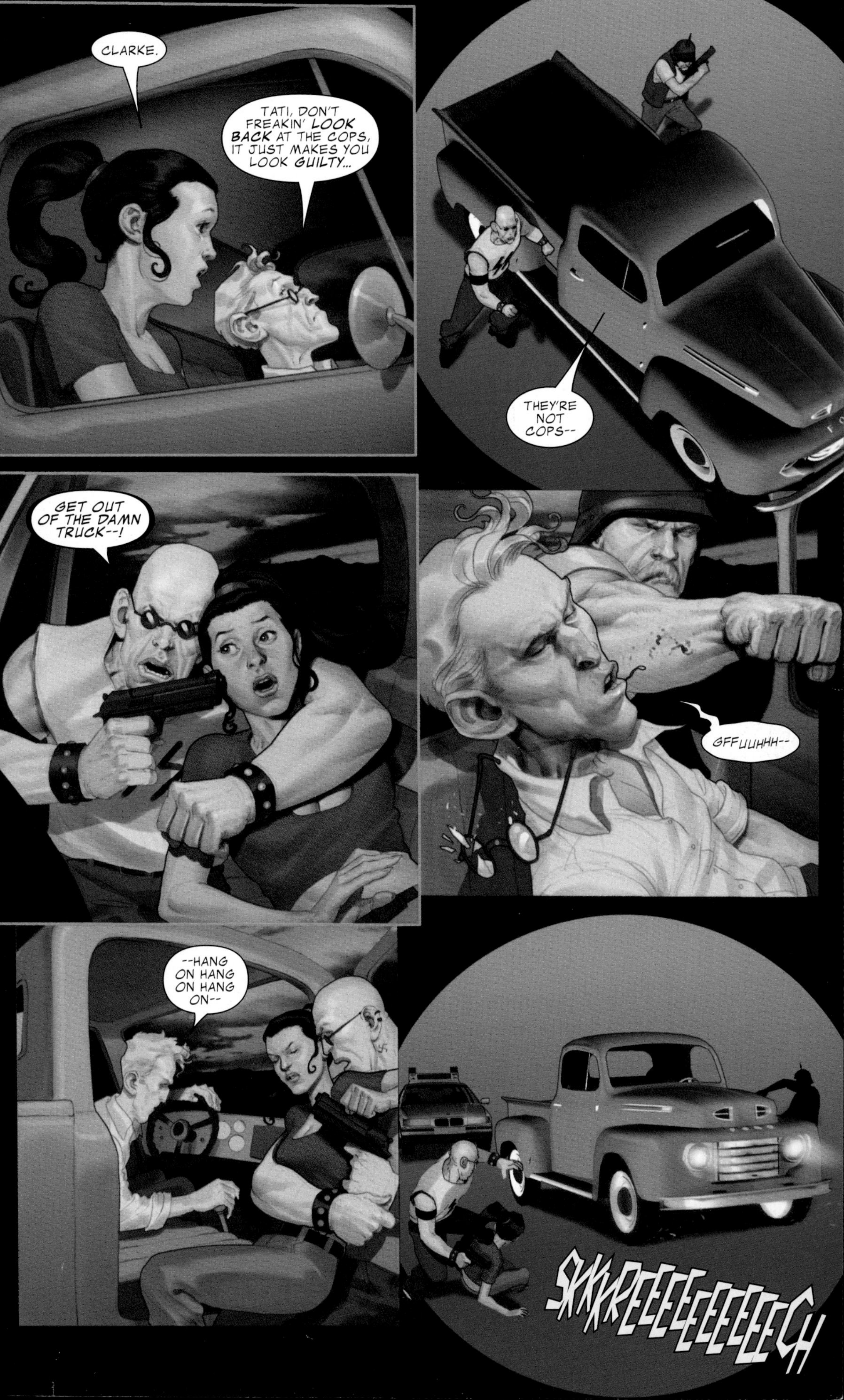
CLARKE.
TATI, DON'T FREAKIN' LOOK BACK AT THE COPS, IT JUST MAKES YOU LOOK GUILTY...
THEY'RE NOT COPS--
GET OUT OF THE DAMN TRUCK--!
GFFUUHHH--
--HANG ON HANG ON HANG ON--
SKKKREEEEEEEEEEEECH

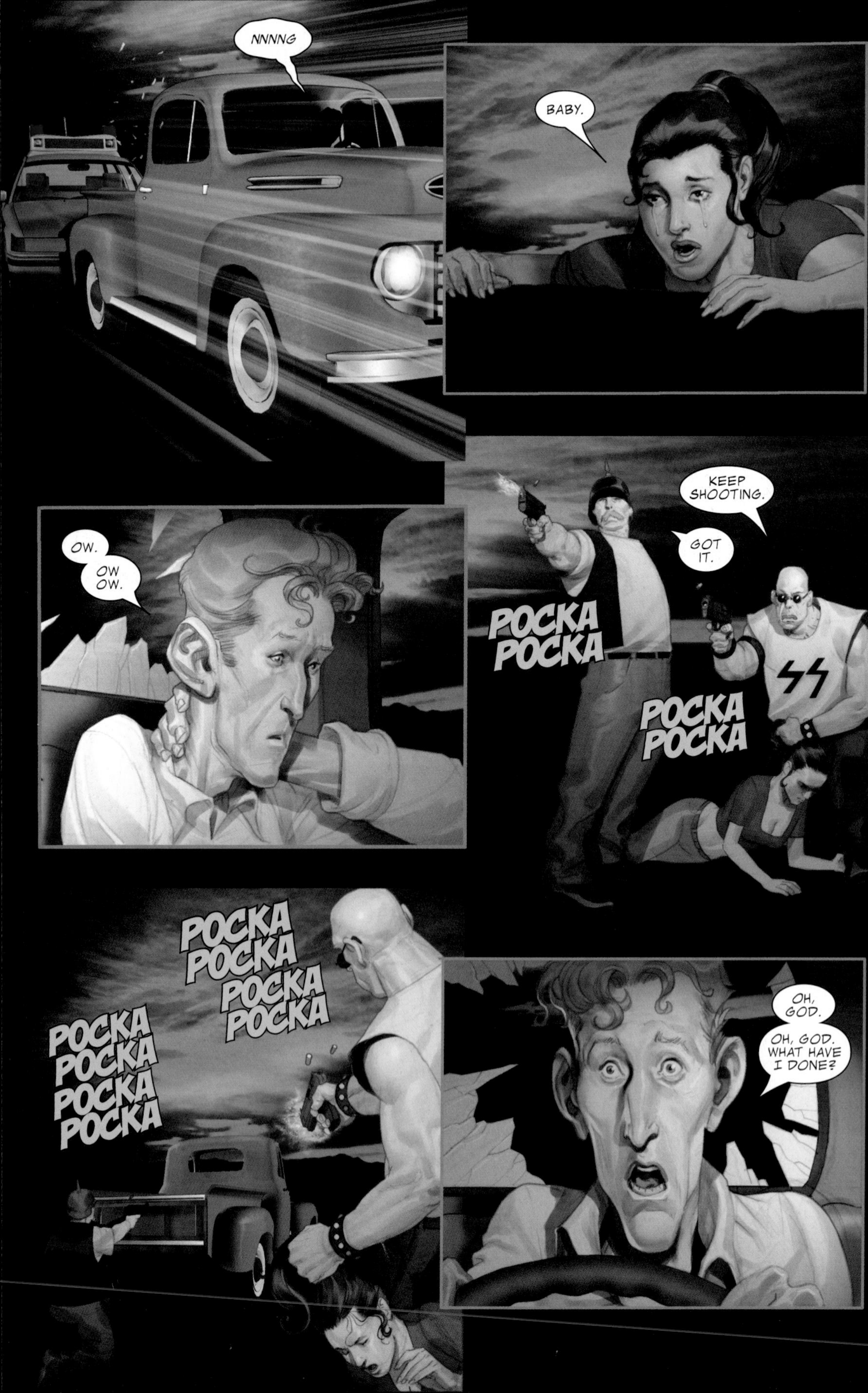
NNNNG
BABY.
OW. OW OW.
KEEP SHOOTING.
GOT IT.
POCKA POCKA
POCKA POCKA
POCKA POCKA POCKA POCKA
POCKA POCKA POCKA POCKA
OH, GOD.
OH, GOD. WHAT HAVE I DONE?

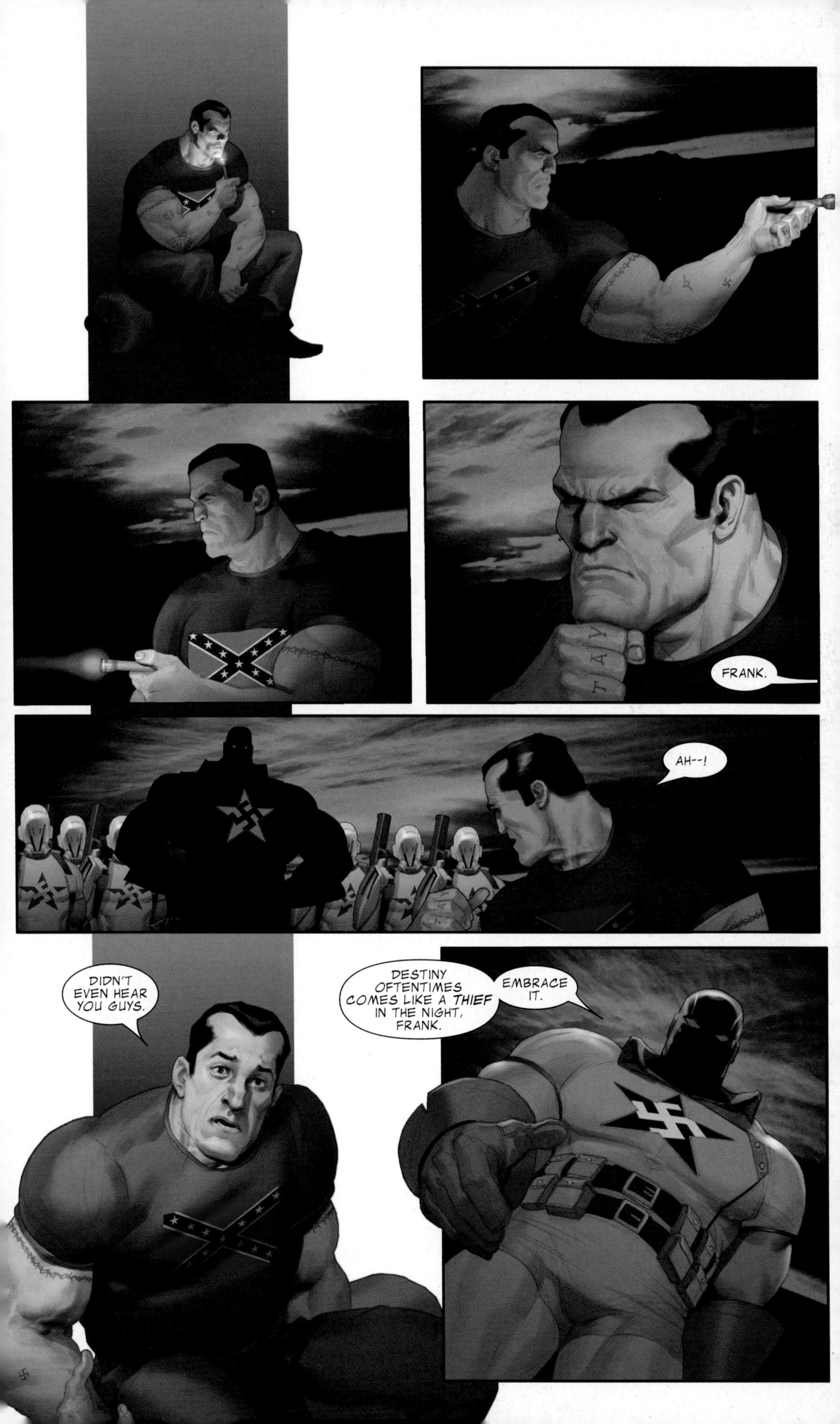
FRANK.
AH--!
DIDN'T EVEN HEAR YOU GUYS.
DESTINY OFTENTIMES COMES LIKE A THIEF IN THE NIGHT, FRANK.
EMBRACE IT.

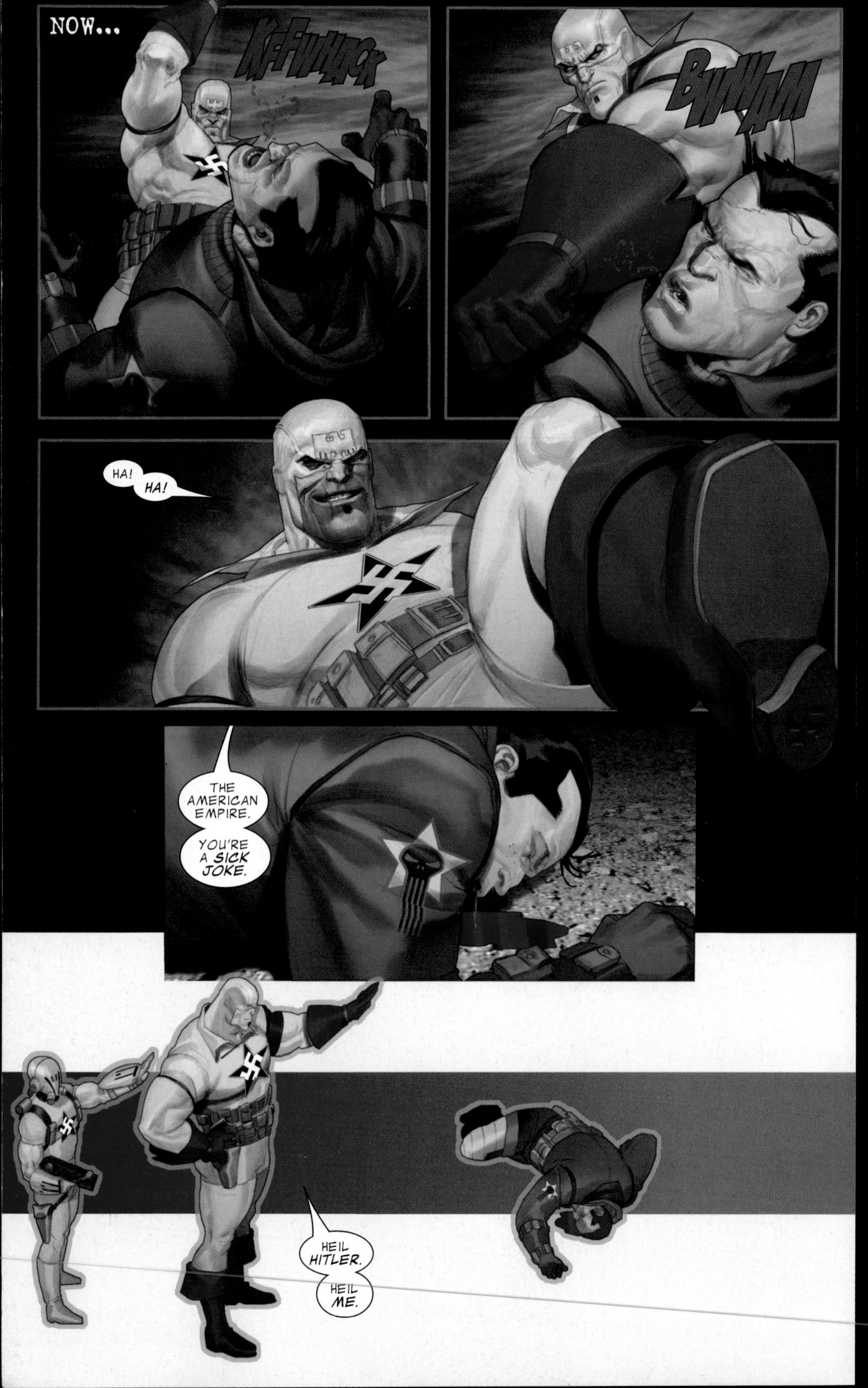
NOW...
K-FWHACK
BWHAM
HA!
HA!
THE AMERICAN EMPIRE.
YOU'RE A SICK JOKE.
HEIL HITLER.
HEIL ME.

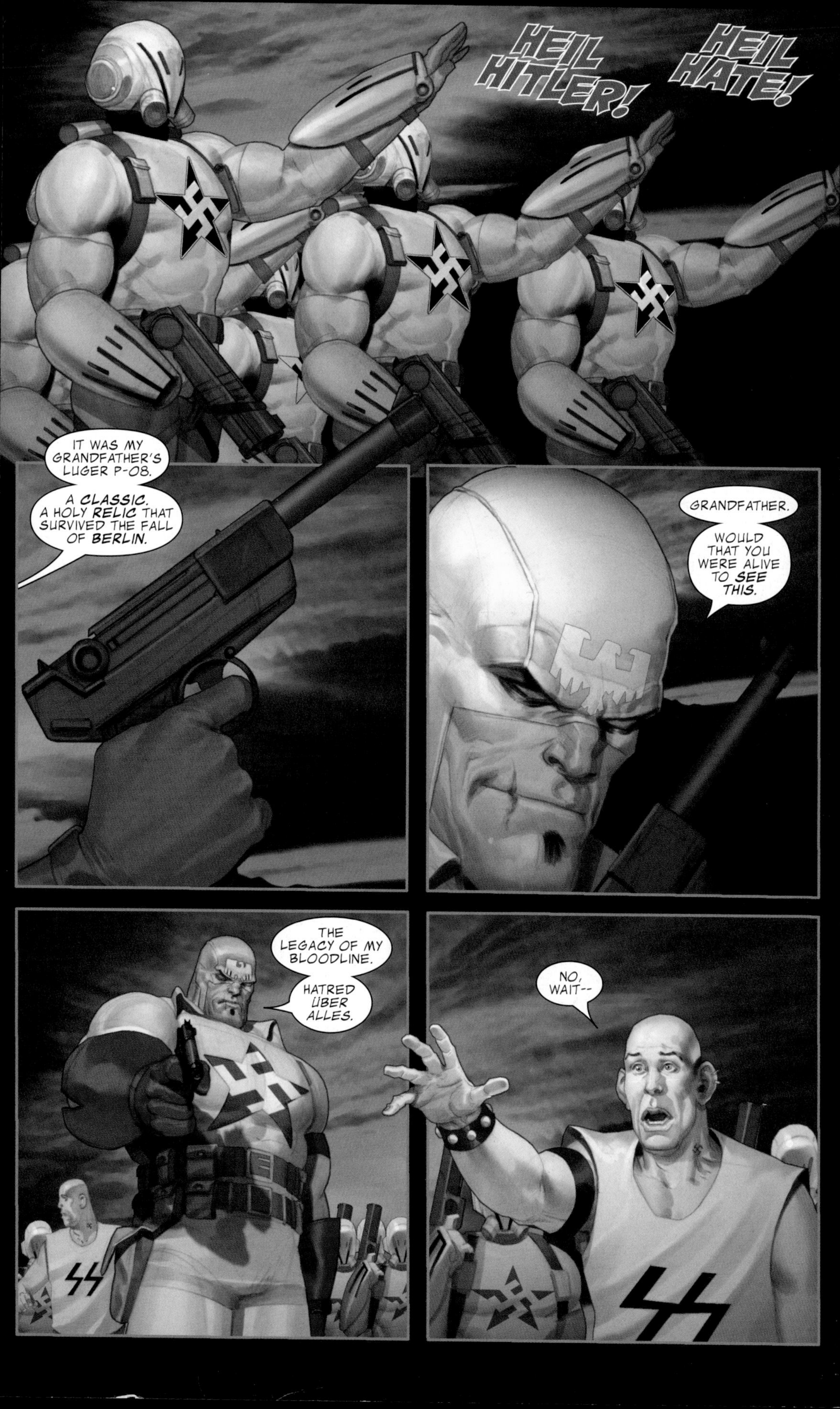

HEIL HITLER!
HEIL HATE!
IT WAS MY GRANDFATHER'S LUGER P-08.
A CLASSIC. A HOLY RELIC THAT SURVIVED THE FALL OF BERLIN.
GRANDFATHER.
WOULD THAT YOU WERE ALIVE TO SEE THIS.
THE LEGACY OF MY BLOODLINE.
HATRED ÜBER ALLES.
NO, WAIT--

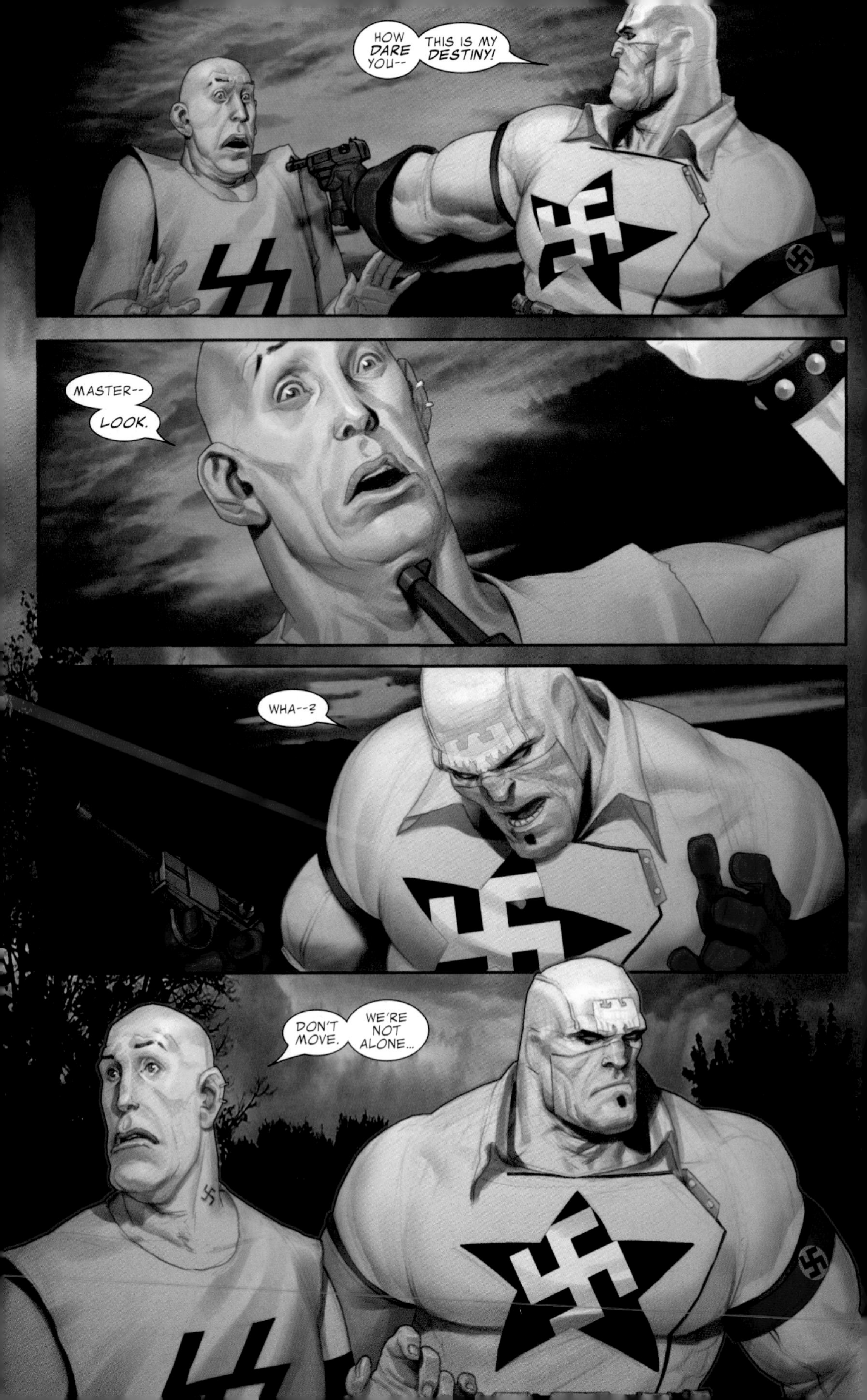
HOW DARE YOU--
THIS IS MY DESTINY!
MASTER--
LOOK.
WHA--?
DON'T MOVE.
WE'RE NOT ALONE...

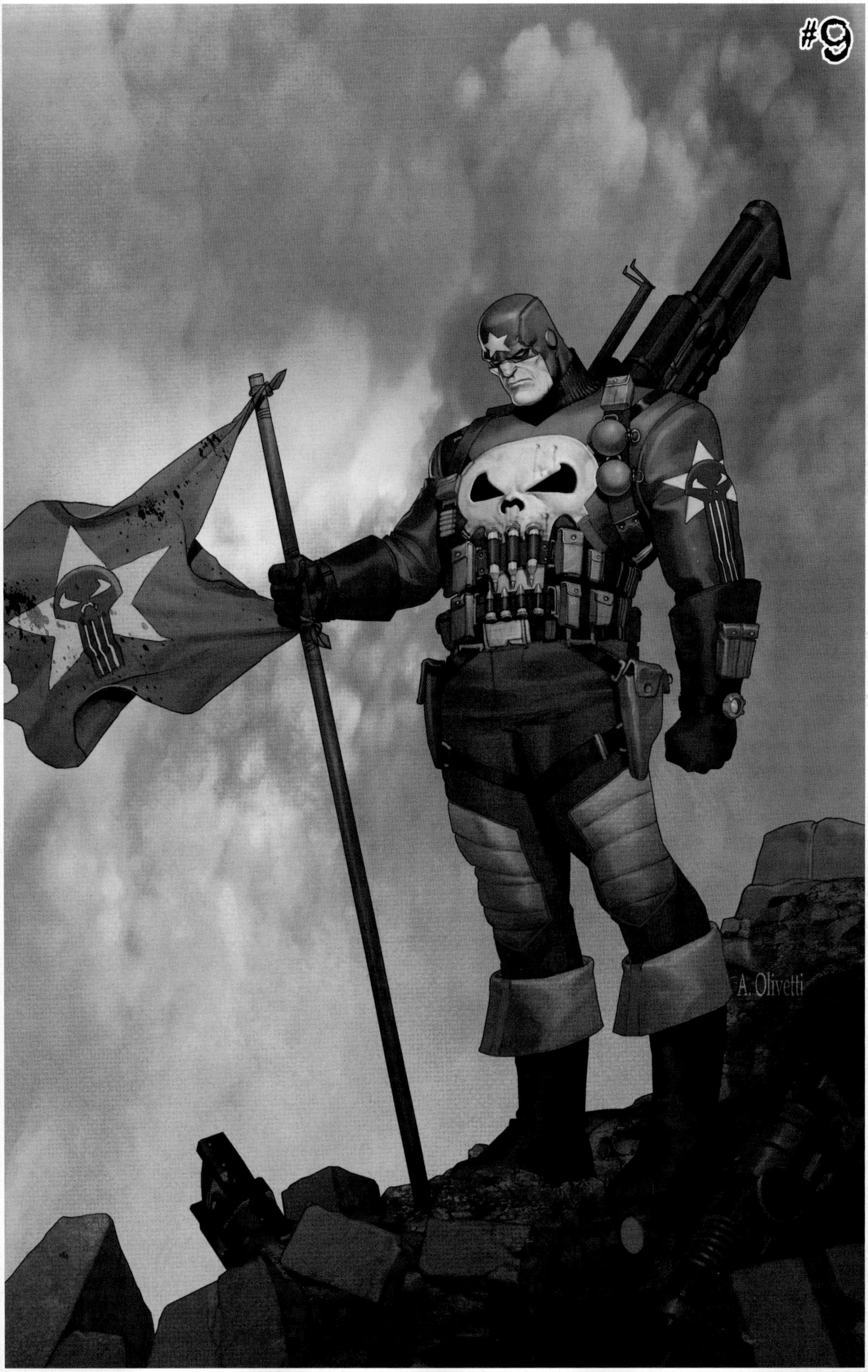
#9
A. Olivetti

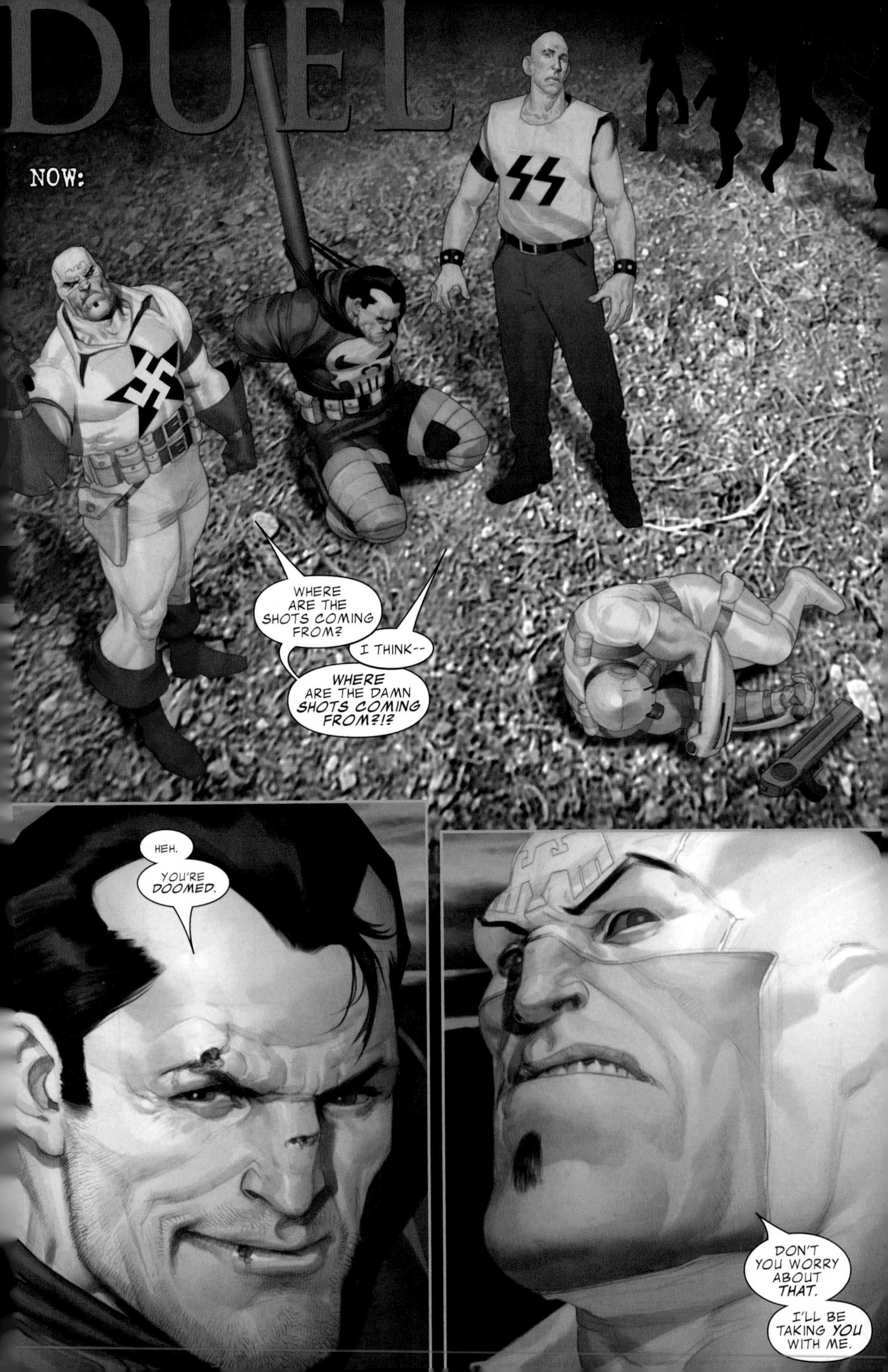
DUEL
NOW:
WHERE ARE THE SHOTS COMING FROM?
I THINK--
WHERE ARE THE DAMN SHOTS COMING FROM?!?
HEH.
YOU'RE DOOMED.
DON'T YOU WORRY ABOUT THAT.
I'LL BE TAKING YOU WITH ME.

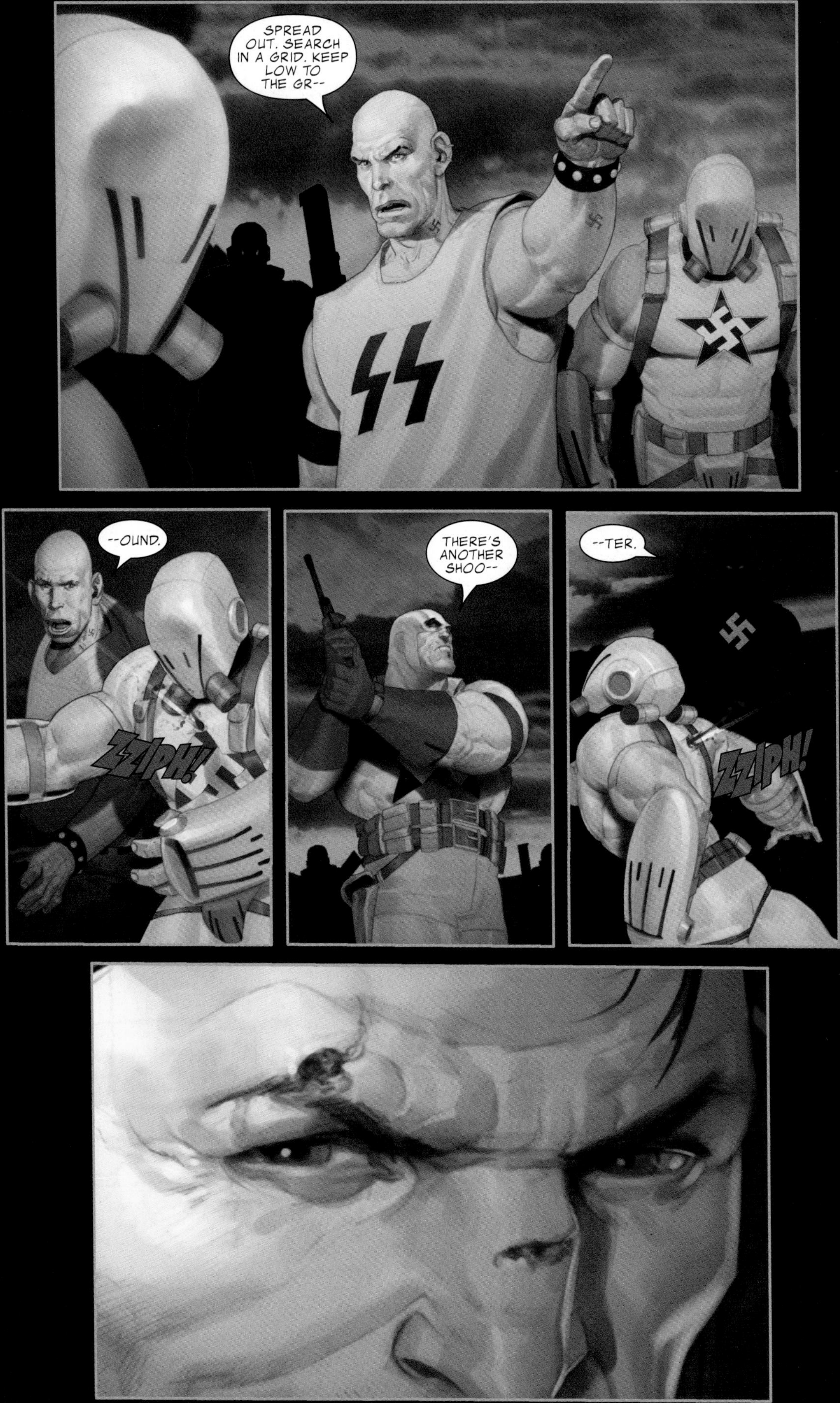

SPREAD OUT. SEARCH IN A GRID. KEEP LOW TO THE GR--
--OUND.
ZZIPH!
THERE'S ANOTHER SHOO--
--TER.
ZZIPH!

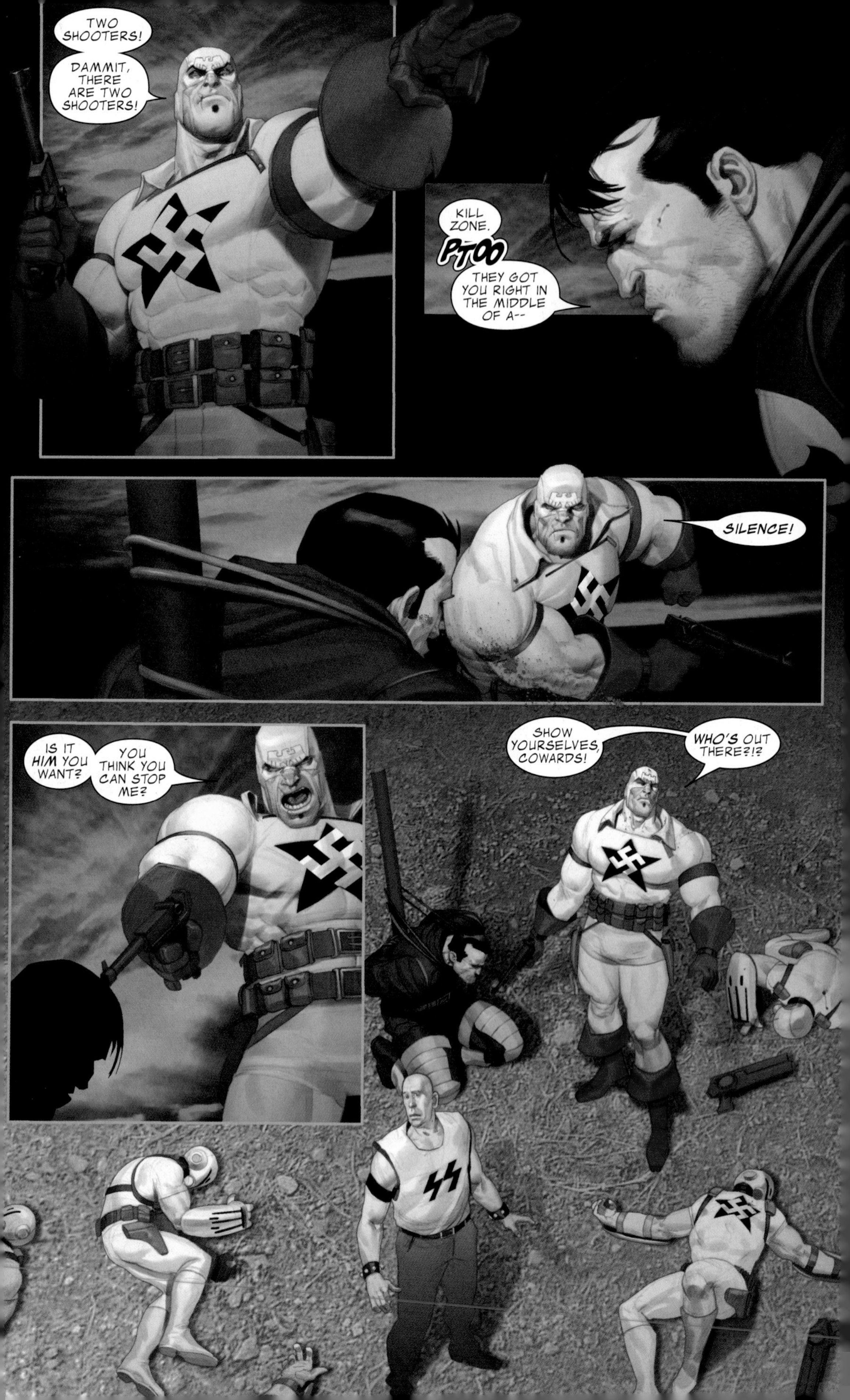
TWO SHOOTERS!
DAMMIT, THERE ARE TWO SHOOTERS!
KILL ZONE.
PTOO
THEY GOT YOU RIGHT IN THE MIDDLE OF A--
SILENCE!
IS IT HIM YOU WANT?
YOU THINK YOU CAN STOP ME?
SHOW YOURSELVES, COWARDS!
WHO'S OUT THERE?!?

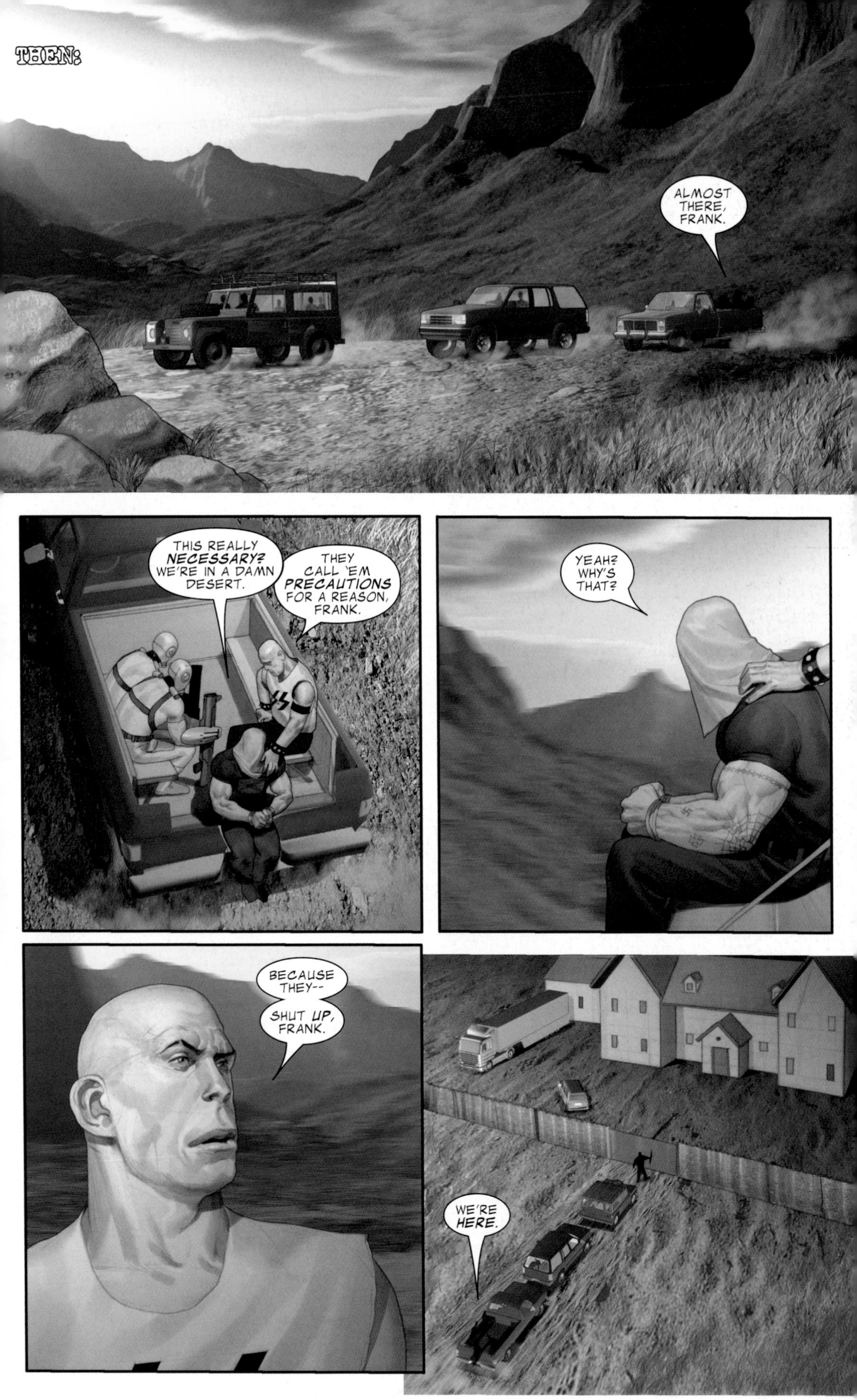
THEN:
ALMOST THERE, FRANK.
THIS REALLY NECESSARY? WE'RE IN A DAMN DESERT.
THEY CALL 'EM PRECAUTIONS FOR A REASON, FRANK.
YEAH? WHY'S THAT?
BECAUSE THEY--
SHUT UP, FRANK.
WE'RE HERE.

C'MON.

GIMME A SEC--

DID ALL THE FRAMING MYSELF.

...

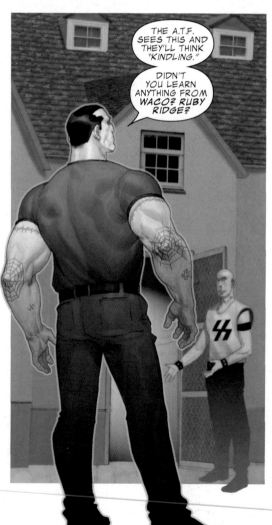

THE A.T.F. SEES THIS AND THEY'LL THINK "KINDLING."

DIDN'T YOU LEARN ANYTHING FROM WACO? RUBY RIDGE?

DON'T BE FOOLED BY OUTWARD APPEARANCES, FRANK...

...IT'S BIGGER INSIDE THAN IT LOOKS.

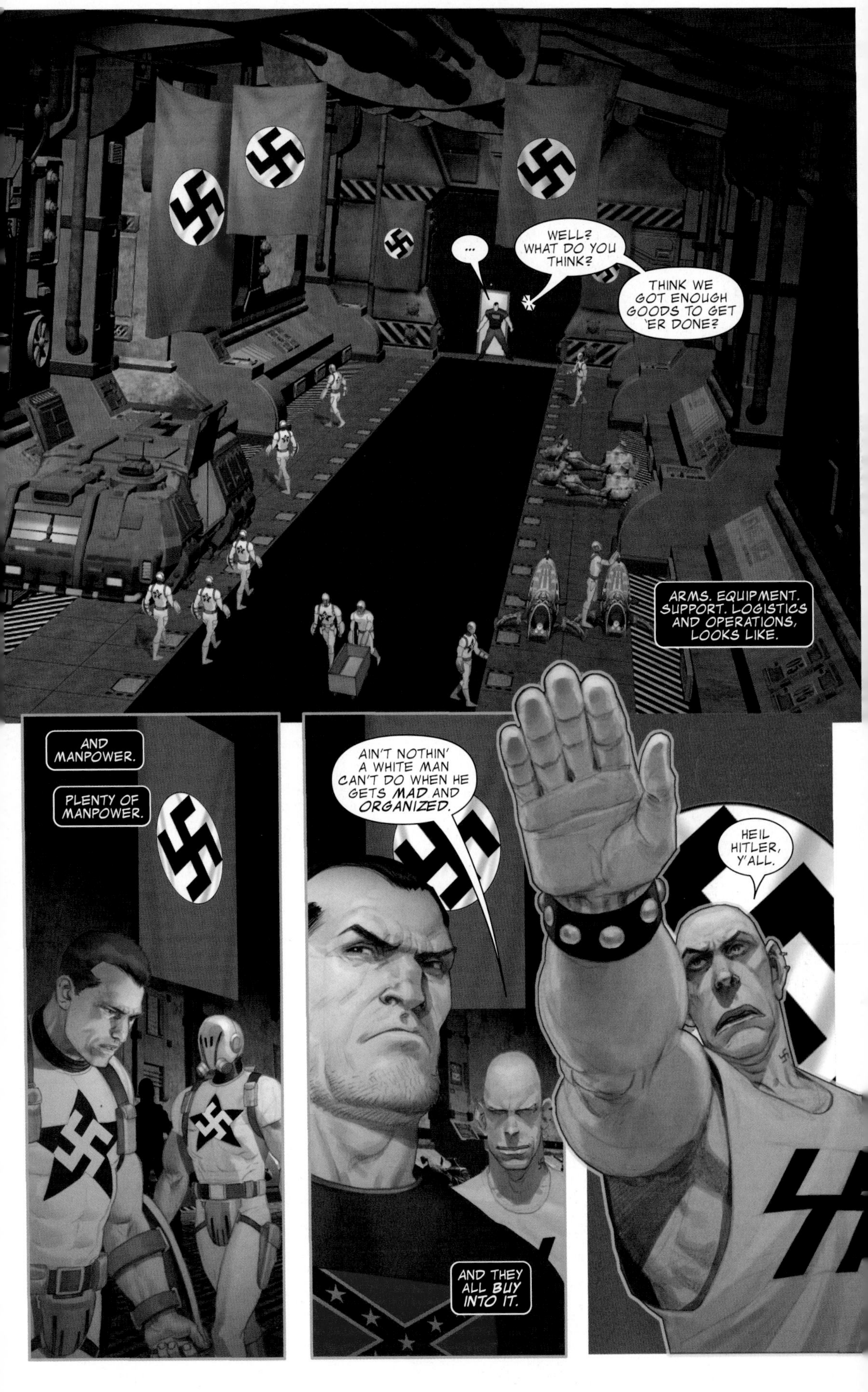
...
WELL? WHAT DO YOU THINK?
THINK WE GOT ENOUGH GOODS TO GET 'ER DONE?
ARMS. EQUIPMENT. SUPPORT. LOGISTICS AND OPERATIONS, LOOKS LIKE.
AND MANPOWER.
PLENTY OF MANPOWER.
AIN'T NOTHIN' A WHITE MAN CAN'T DO WHEN HE GETS MAD AND ORGANIZED.
AND THEY ALL BUY INTO IT.
HEIL HITLER, Y'ALL.

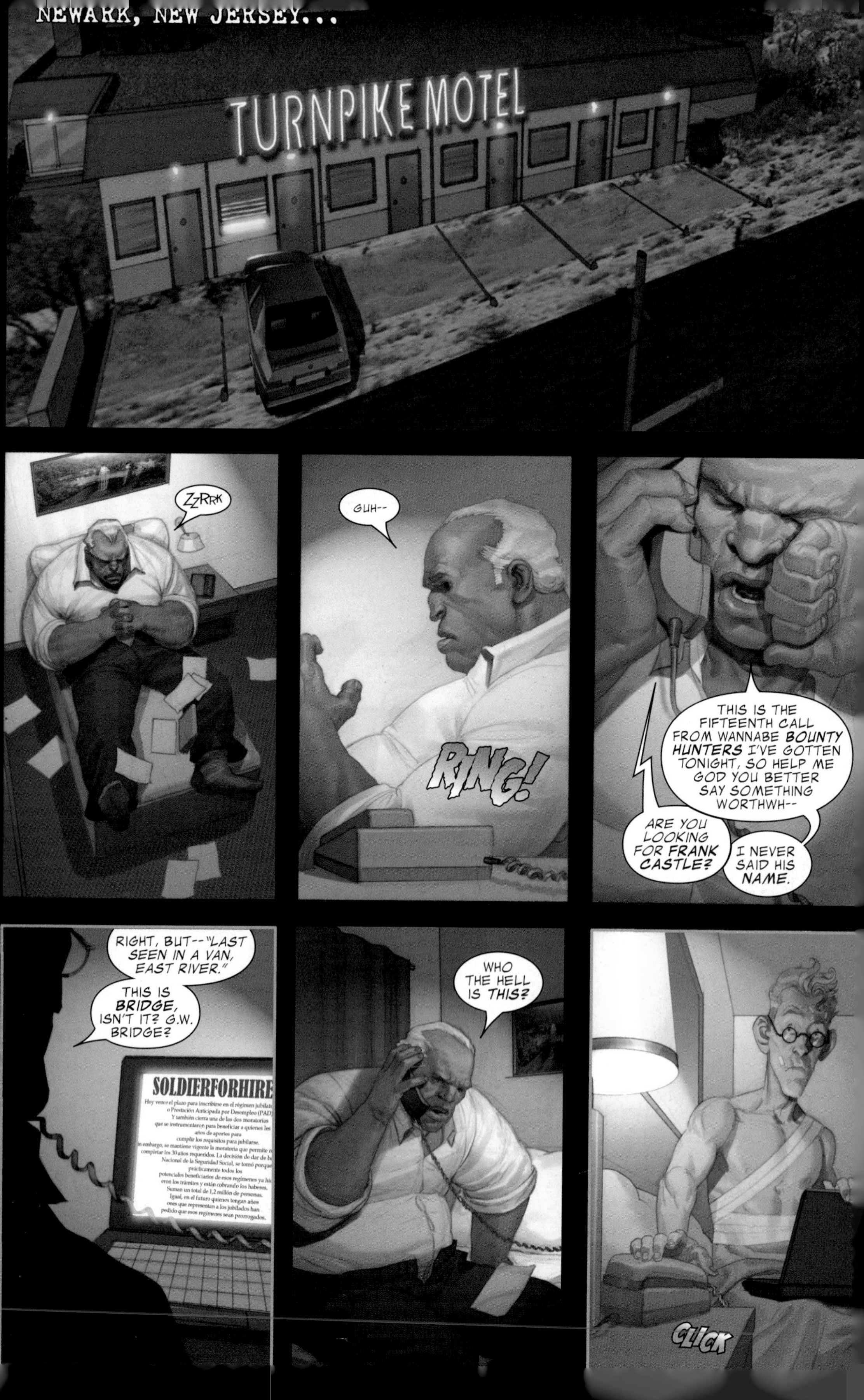
NEWARK, NEW JERSEY...
TURNPIKE MOTEL
ZZRRK
GUH--
RING!
THIS IS THE FIFTEENTH CALL FROM WANNABE BOUNTY HUNTERS I'VE GOTTEN TONIGHT, SO HELP ME GOD YOU BETTER SAY SOMETHING WORTHWH--
ARE YOU LOOKING FOR FRANK CASTLE?
I NEVER SAID HIS NAME.
RIGHT, BUT--"LAST SEEN IN A VAN, EAST RIVER."
THIS IS BRIDGE, ISN'T IT? G.W. BRIDGE?
SOLDIERFORHIRE
WHO THE HELL IS THIS?
CLICK

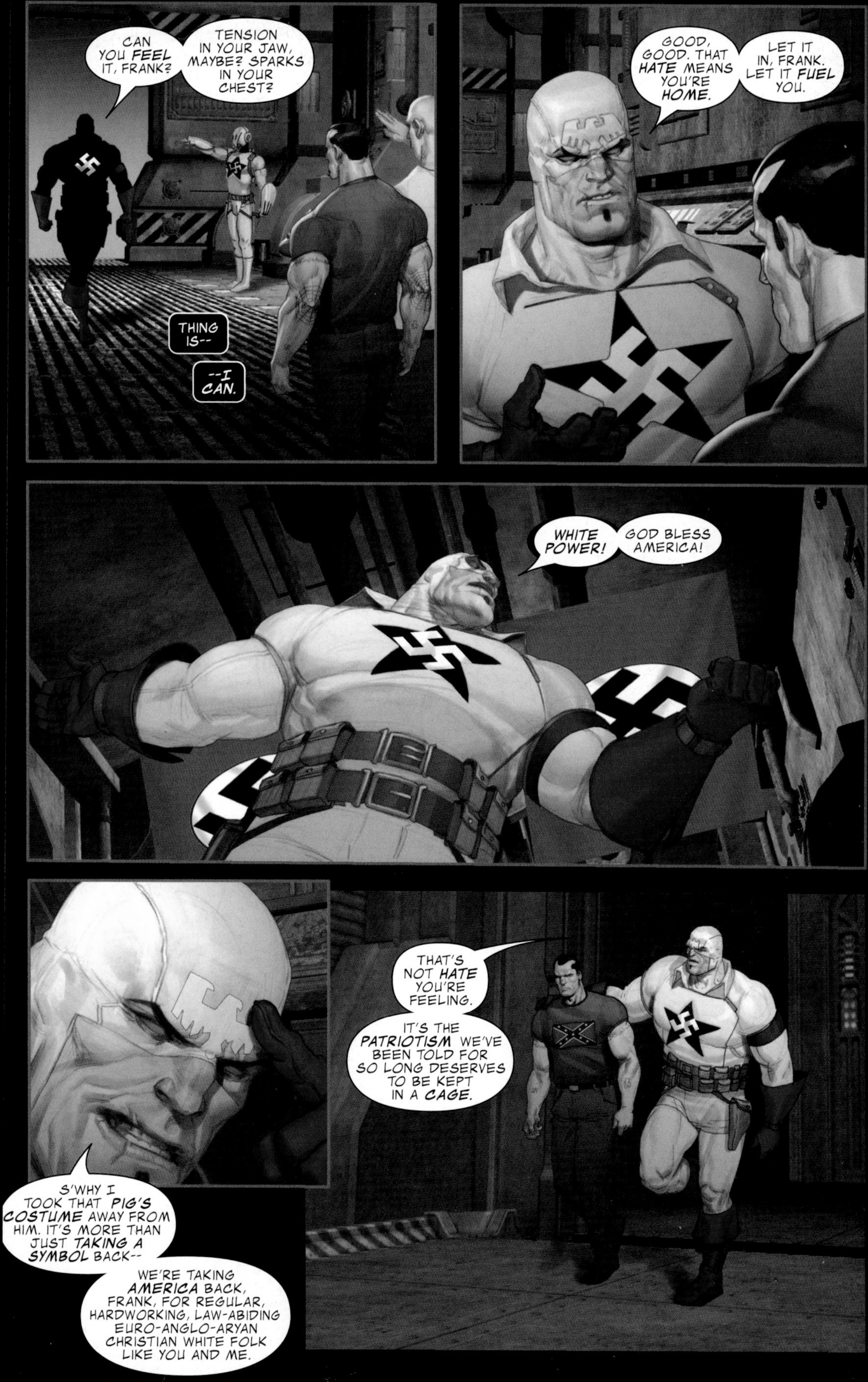
CAN YOU FEEL IT, FRANK?
TENSION IN YOUR JAW, MAYBE? SPARKS IN YOUR CHEST?
THING IS--
--I CAN.
GOOD, GOOD. THAT HATE MEANS YOU'RE HOME.
LET IT IN, FRANK. LET IT FUEL YOU.
WHITE POWER!
GOD BLESS AMERICA!
THAT'S NOT HATE YOU'RE FEELING.
IT'S THE PATRIOTISM WE'VE BEEN TOLD FOR SO LONG DESERVES TO BE KEPT IN A CAGE.
S'WHY I TOOK THAT PIG'S COSTUME AWAY FROM HIM. IT'S MORE THAN JUST TAKING A SYMBOL BACK--
WE'RE TAKING AMERICA BACK, FRANK, FOR REGULAR, HARDWORKING, LAW-ABIDING EURO-ANGLO-ARYAN CHRISTIAN WHITE FOLK LIKE YOU AND ME.

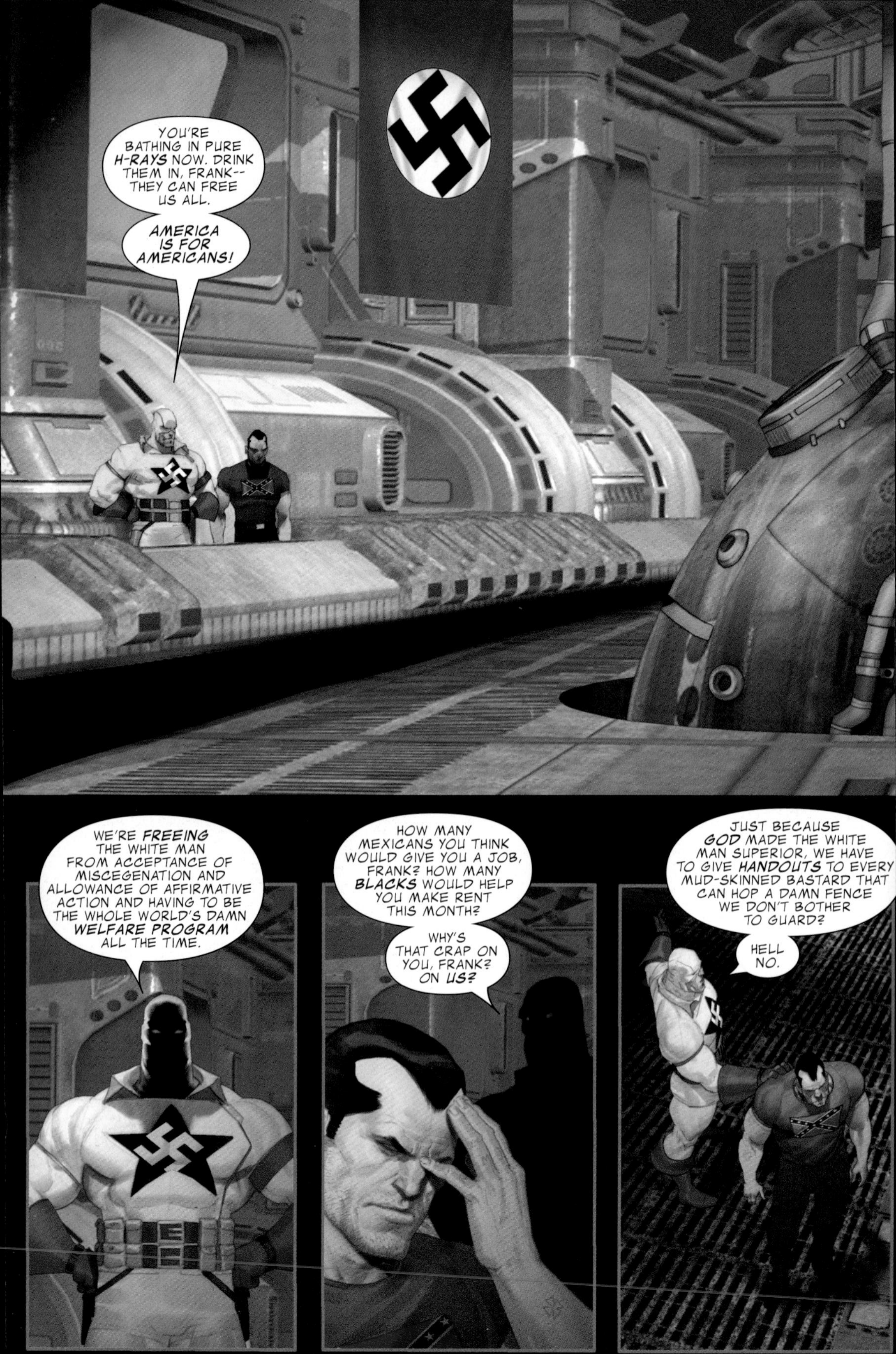
YOU'RE BATHING IN PURE H-RAYS NOW. DRINK THEM IN, FRANK-- THEY CAN FREE US ALL.
AMERICA IS FOR AMERICANS!
WE'RE FREEING THE WHITE MAN FROM ACCEPTANCE OF MISCEGENATION AND ALLOWANCE OF AFFIRMATIVE ACTION AND HAVING TO BE THE WHOLE WORLD'S DAMN WELFARE PROGRAM ALL THE TIME.
HOW MANY MEXICANS YOU THINK WOULD GIVE YOU A JOB, FRANK? HOW MANY BLACKS WOULD HELP YOU MAKE RENT THIS MONTH?
WHY'S THAT CRAP ON YOU, FRANK? ON US?
JUST BECAUSE GOD MADE THE WHITE MAN SUPERIOR, WE HAVE TO GIVE HANDOUTS TO EVERY MUD-SKINNED BASTARD THAT CAN HOP A DAMN FENCE WE DON'T BOTHER TO GUARD?
HELL NO.

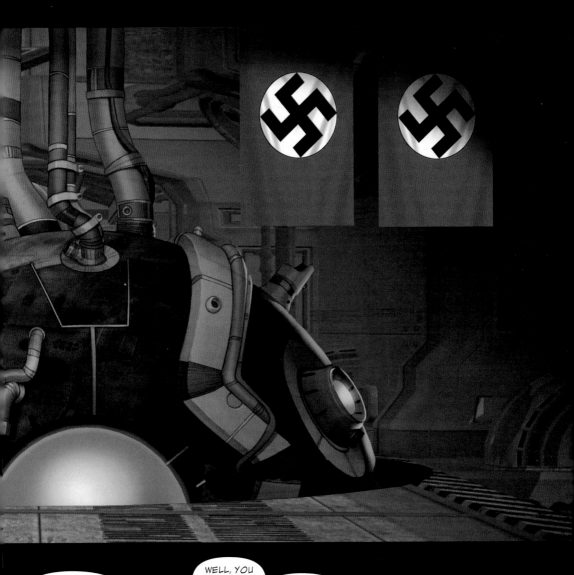

AND WE'RE NOT STOPPING *HERE*. THIS IS THE FIRST OF OUR *H-STATIONS*. WE'LL PUT ONE IN SAN DIEGO, AND LOS ANGELES, AND *CHICAGO*. BATHING THE NATION IN OUR *HATE* AND--

WELL, YOU KNOW. YOU *FEEL* IT NOW, DON'T YOU?

BLOOD IN THE CHEEKS. FIRE IN THE VEINS.

THIS PLACE.

THIS PLACE MAKES ME WANT TO *KILL*.

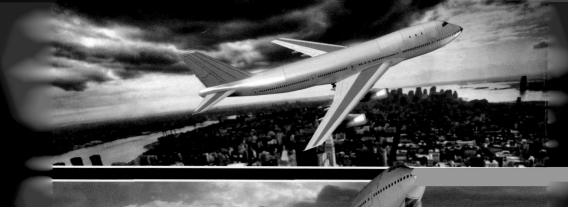

WELCOME
TO
PHOENIX

ME TO MEXICO

STOP

EVENING, SIR,
I'M GONNA NEED
TO SEE SOME
IDENTIFIC--

G.W.
BRIDGE.
AGENT OF
S.H.I.E.L.D.

DON'T
SPEND TOO
MUCH TIME AT
MY WINDOW
OR YOU'LL
COMPROMISE MY
INVESTIGATION.

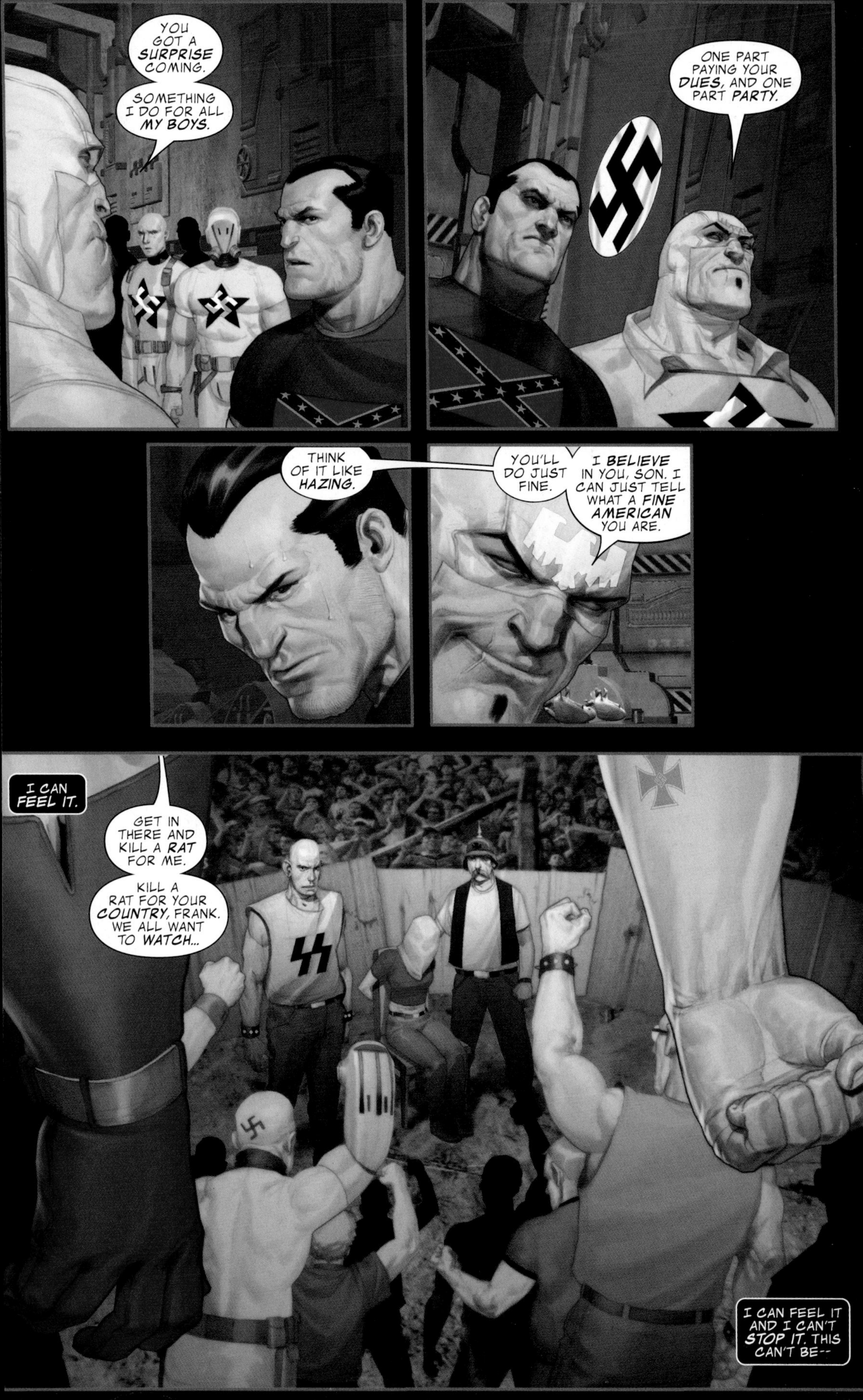
YOU GOT A SURPRISE COMING.
SOMETHING I DO FOR ALL MY BOYS.
ONE PART PAYING YOUR DUES, AND ONE PART PARTY.
THINK OF IT LIKE HAZING.
YOU'LL DO JUST FINE.
I BELIEVE IN YOU, SON. I CAN JUST TELL WHAT A FINE AMERICAN YOU ARE.
I CAN FEEL IT.
GET IN THERE AND KILL A RAT FOR ME.
KILL A RAT FOR YOUR COUNTRY, FRANK. WE ALL WANT TO WATCH...
I CAN FEEL IT AND I CAN'T STOP IT. THIS CAN'T BE--

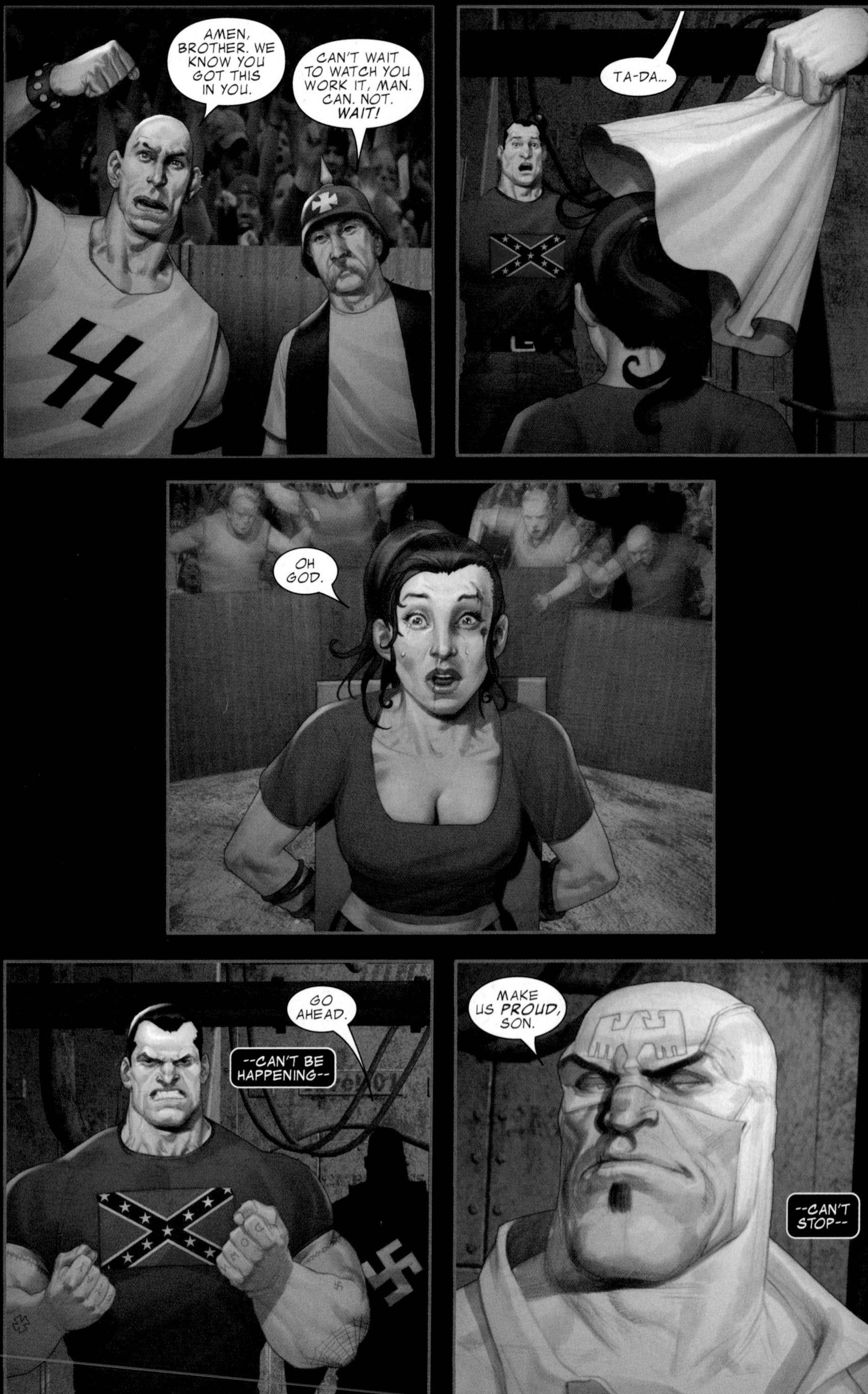
AMEN, BROTHER. WE KNOW YOU GOT THIS IN YOU.
CAN'T WAIT TO WATCH YOU WORK IT, MAN. CAN. NOT. WAIT!
TA-DA...
OH GOD.
GO AHEAD.
--CAN'T BE HAPPENING--
MAKE US PROUD, SON.
--CAN'T STOP--

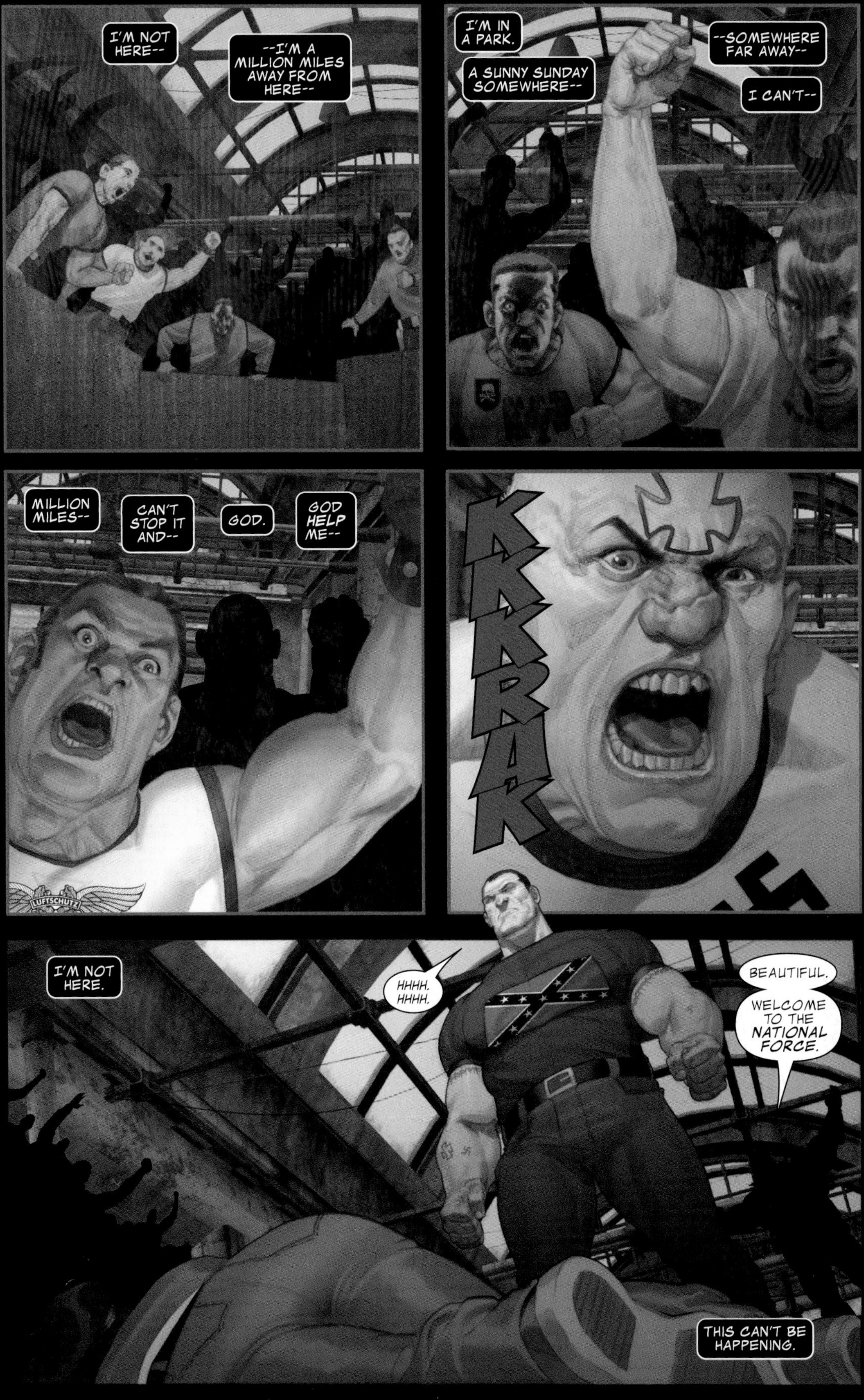
I'M NOT HERE--
--I'M A MILLION MILES AWAY FROM HERE--
I'M IN A PARK.
A SUNNY SUNDAY SOMEWHERE--
--SOMEWHERE FAR AWAY--
I CAN'T--
MILLION MILES--
CAN'T STOP IT AND--
GOD.
GOD HELP ME--
KKRAK
LUFTSCHUTZ
I'M NOT HERE.
HHHH. HHHH.
BEAUTIFUL.
WELCOME TO THE NATIONAL FORCE.
THIS CAN'T BE HAPPENING.

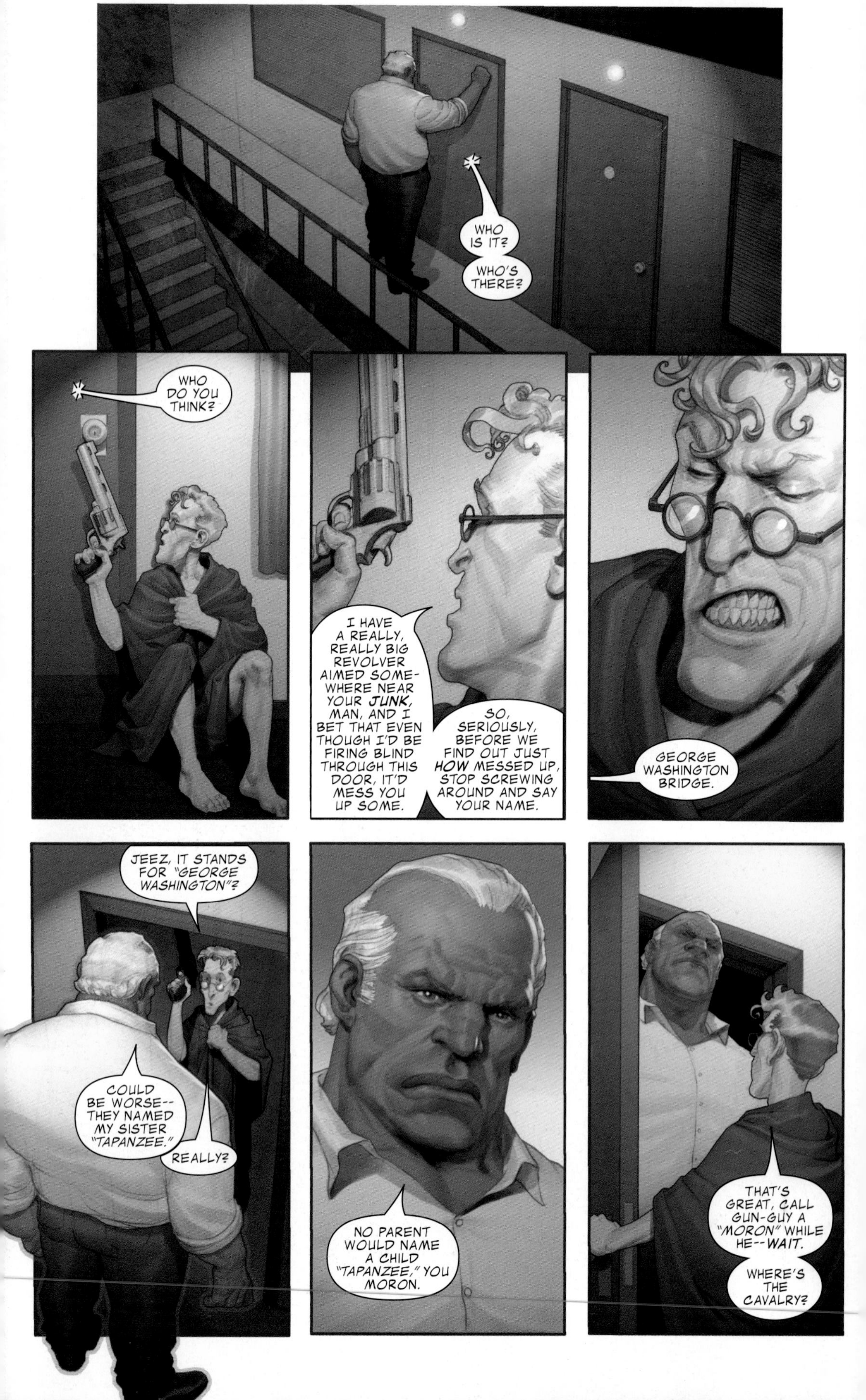

WHO IS IT?
WHO'S THERE?
WHO DO YOU THINK?
I HAVE A REALLY, REALLY BIG REVOLVER AIMED SOME-WHERE NEAR YOUR JUNK, MAN, AND I BET THAT EVEN THOUGH I'D BE FIRING BLIND THROUGH THIS DOOR, IT'D MESS YOU UP SOME.
SO, SERIOUSLY, BEFORE WE FIND OUT JUST HOW MESSED UP, STOP SCREWING AROUND AND SAY YOUR NAME.
GEORGE WASHINGTON BRIDGE.
JEEZ, IT STANDS FOR "GEORGE WASHINGTON"?
COULD BE WORSE-- THEY NAMED MY SISTER "TAPANZEE."
REALLY?
NO PARENT WOULD NAME A CHILD "TAPANZEE," YOU MORON.
THAT'S GREAT, CALL GUN-GUY A "MORON" WHILE HE--WAIT.
WHERE'S THE CAVALRY?

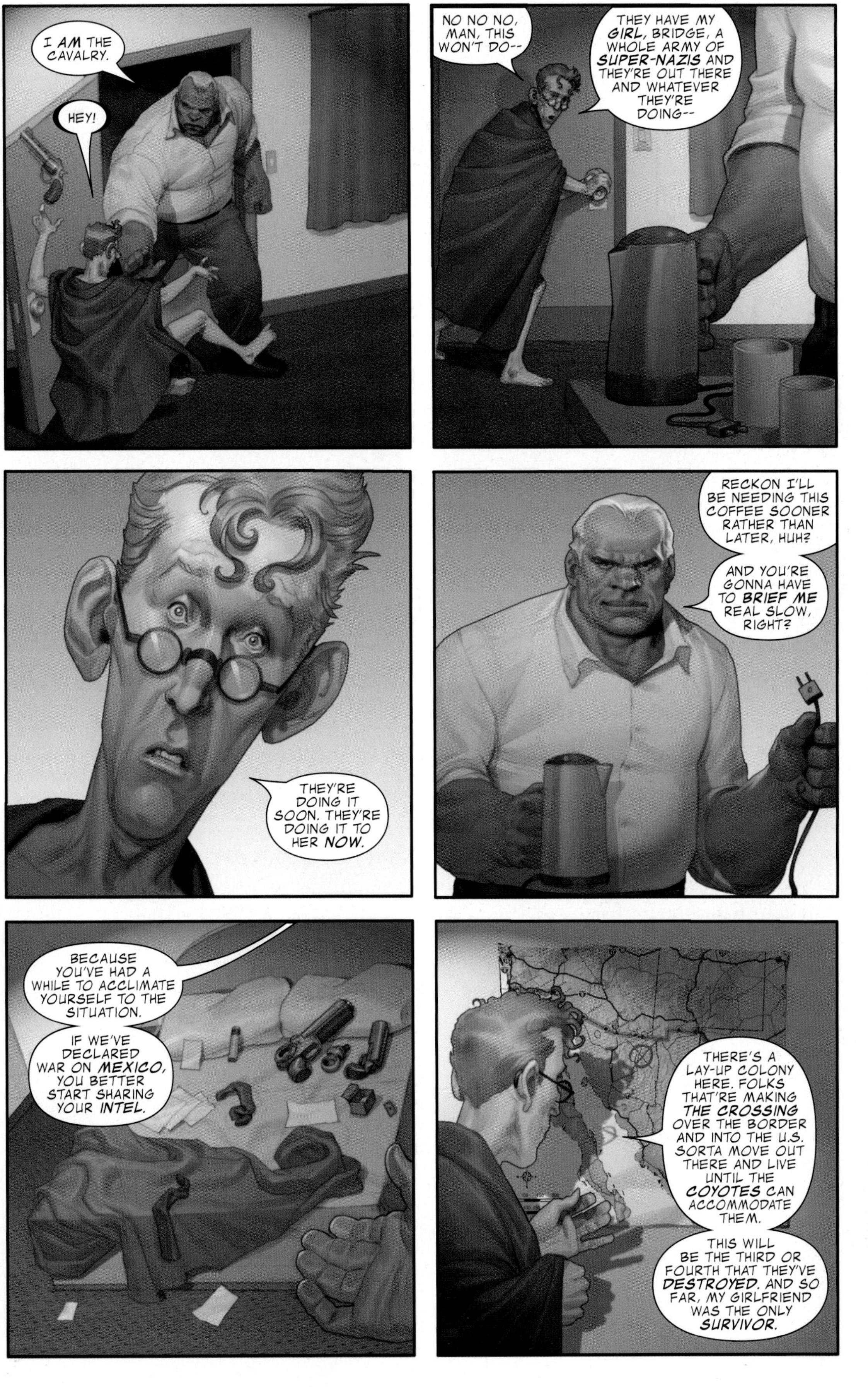
I AM THE CAVALRY.
HEY!
NO NO NO, MAN, THIS WON'T DO--
THEY HAVE MY GIRL, BRIDGE, A WHOLE ARMY OF SUPER-NAZIS AND THEY'RE OUT THERE AND WHATEVER THEY'RE DOING--
THEY'RE DOING IT SOON. THEY'RE DOING IT TO HER NOW.
RECKON I'LL BE NEEDING THIS COFFEE SOONER RATHER THAN LATER, HUH?
AND YOU'RE GONNA HAVE TO BRIEF ME REAL SLOW, RIGHT?
BECAUSE YOU'VE HAD A WHILE TO ACCLIMATE YOURSELF TO THE SITUATION.
IF WE'VE DECLARED WAR ON MEXICO, YOU BETTER START SHARING YOUR INTEL.
THERE'S A LAY-UP COLONY HERE. FOLKS THAT'RE MAKING THE CROSSING OVER THE BORDER AND INTO THE U.S. SORTA MOVE OUT THERE AND LIVE UNTIL THE COYOTES CAN ACCOMMODATE THEM.
THIS WILL BE THE THIRD OR FOURTH THAT THEY'VE DESTROYED. AND SO FAR, MY GIRLFRIEND WAS THE ONLY SURVIVOR.

"BASED ON WHAT ME AND *FRANK* KNOW, THEY'RE GOING OUT AGAIN *TONIGHT*..."

JEEZ, MAN, WHAT'S IN THAT DUFFEL?

OUR GUNS NOT GOOD ENOUGH FOR YOU?

IS IT FULLA PORNOS?

MEXICAN FIREWORKS?

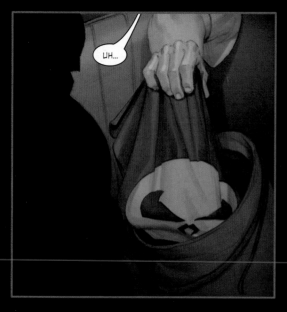

UH...

NOW YOU'VE GONE AND RUINED YOUR *SURPRISE.*

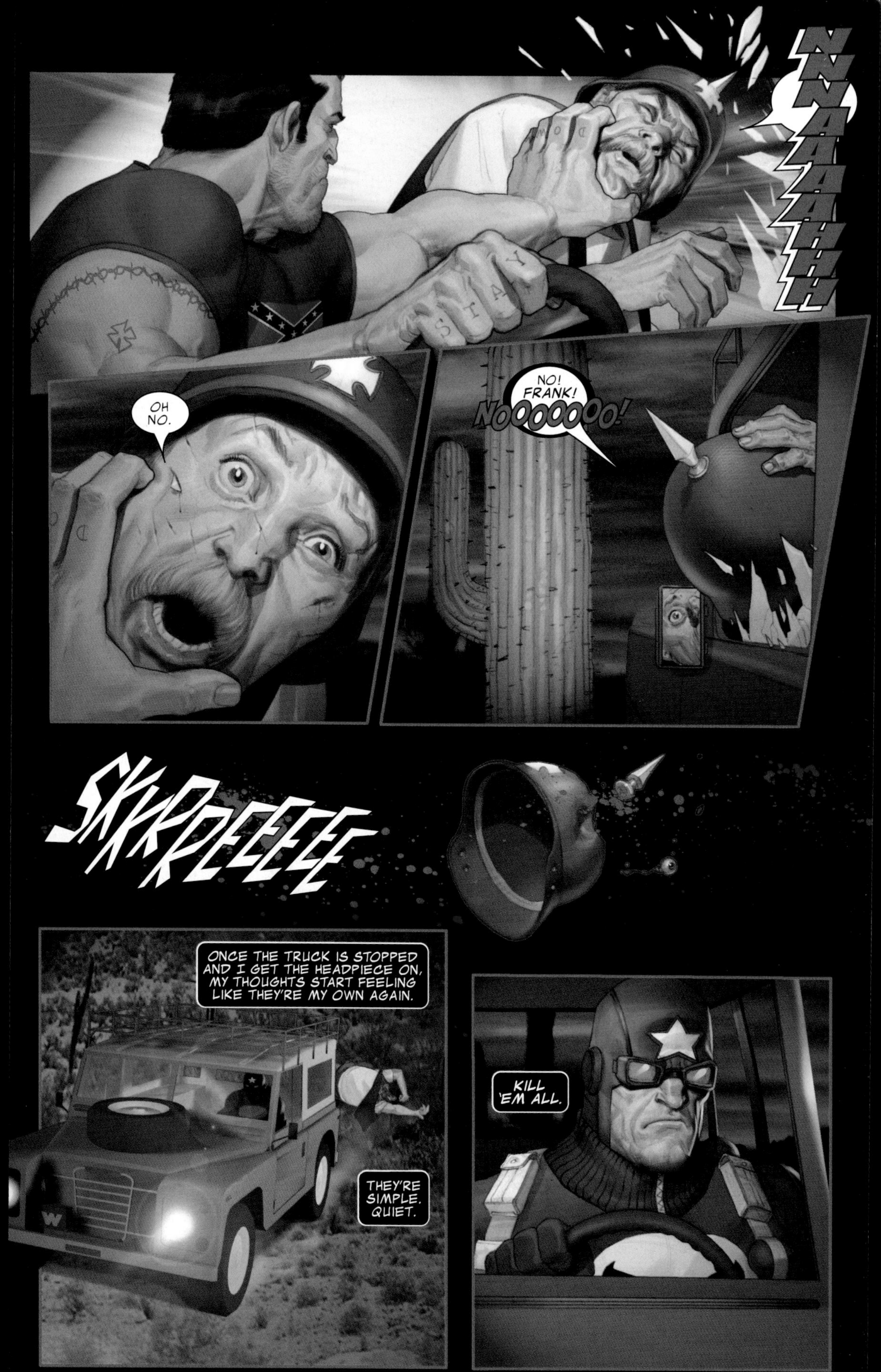
NNAAAAHHH
OH NO.
NO! FRANK!
NOOOOOOO!
SKKREEEEE
ONCE THE TRUCK IS STOPPED AND I GET THE HEADPIECE ON, MY THOUGHTS START FEELING LIKE THEY'RE MY OWN AGAIN.
THEY'RE SIMPLE. QUIET.
KILL 'EM ALL.

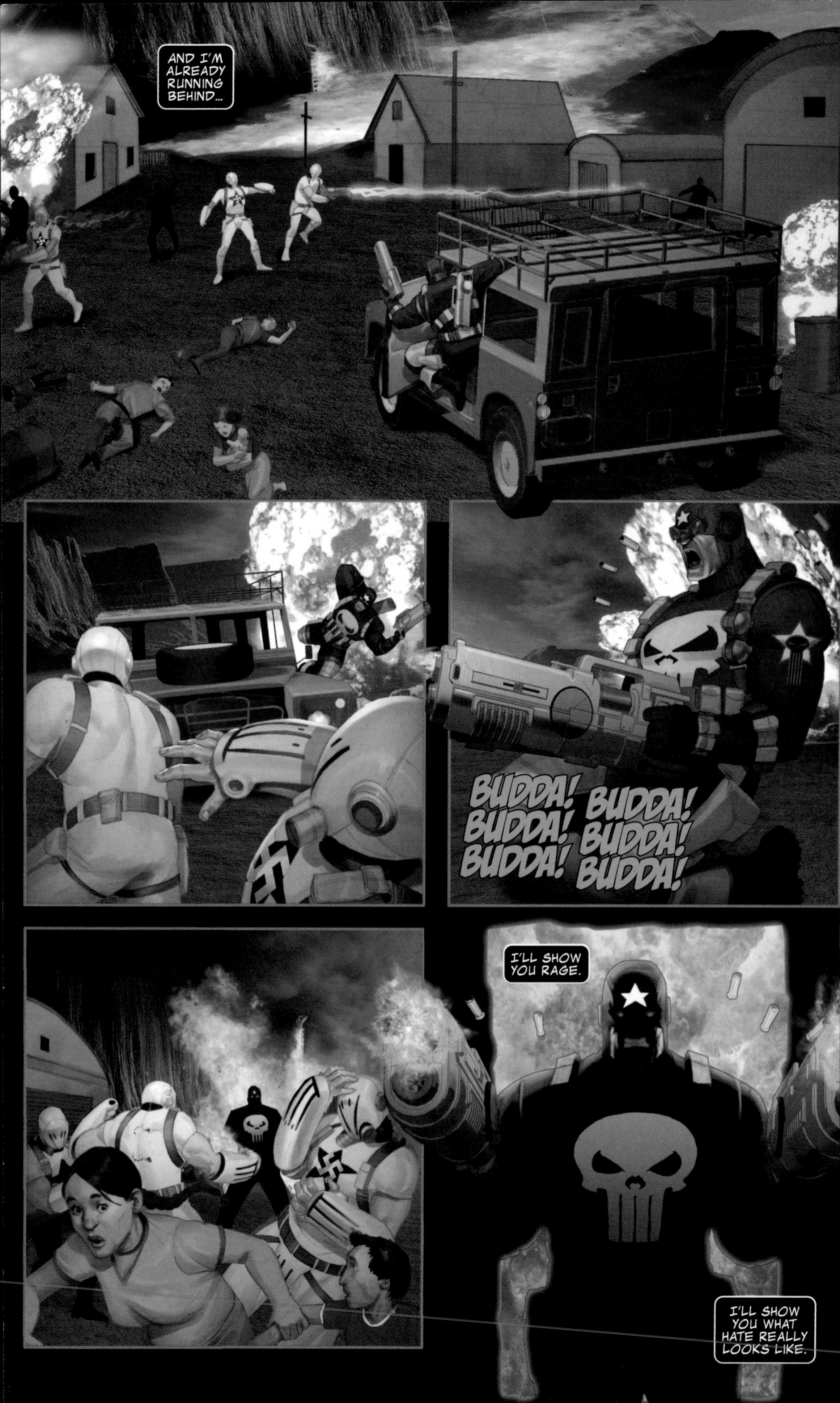
AND I'M ALREADY RUNNING BEHIND...
BUDDA! BUDDA! BUDDA! BUDDA! BUDDA! BUDDA!
I'LL SHOW YOU RAGE.
I'LL SHOW YOU WHAT HATE REALLY LOOKS LIKE.

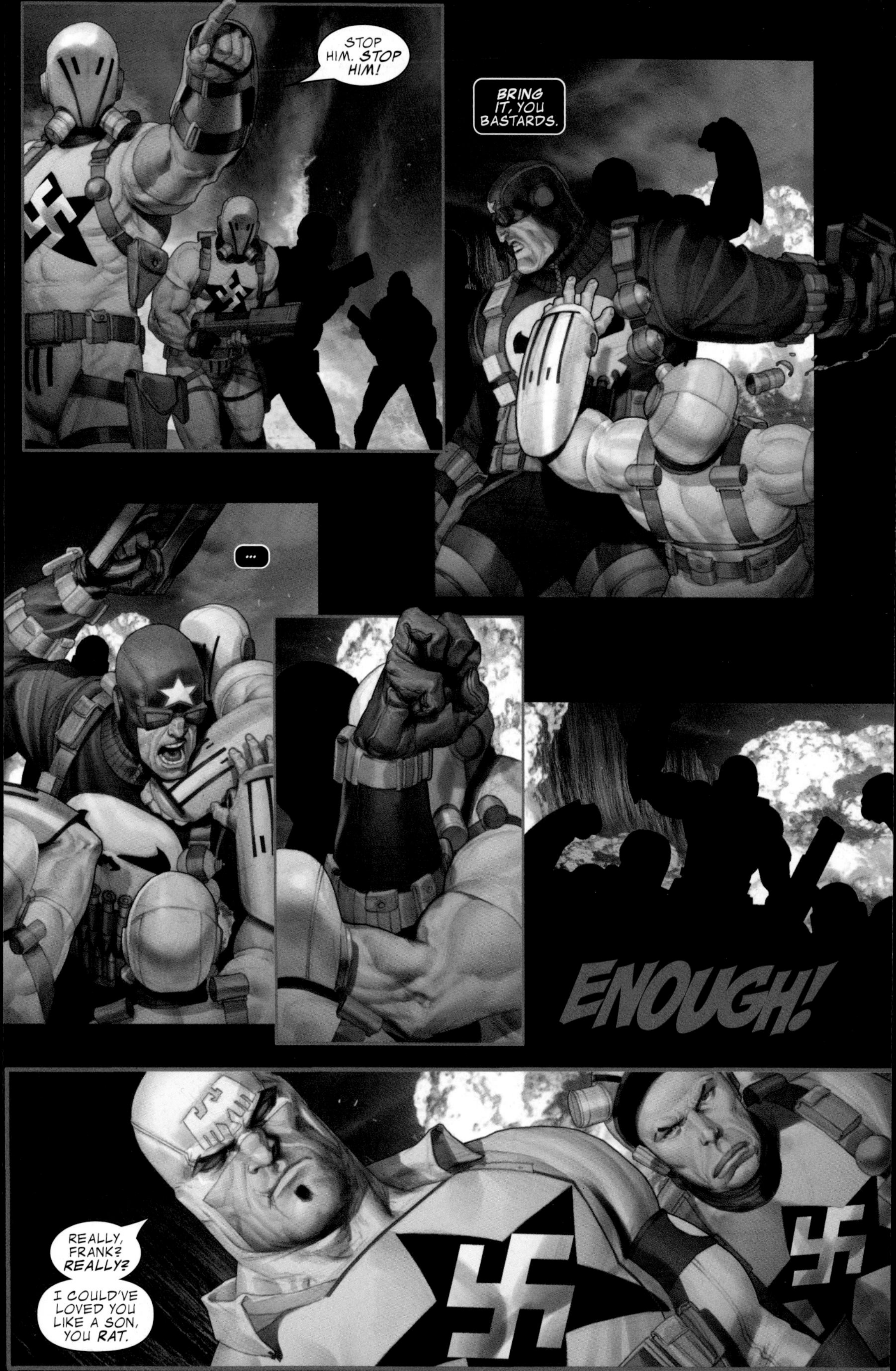

STOP HIM. STOP HIM!
BRING IT, YOU BASTARDS.
...
ENOUGH!
REALLY, FRANK? REALLY?
I COULD'VE LOVED YOU LIKE A SON, YOU RAT.

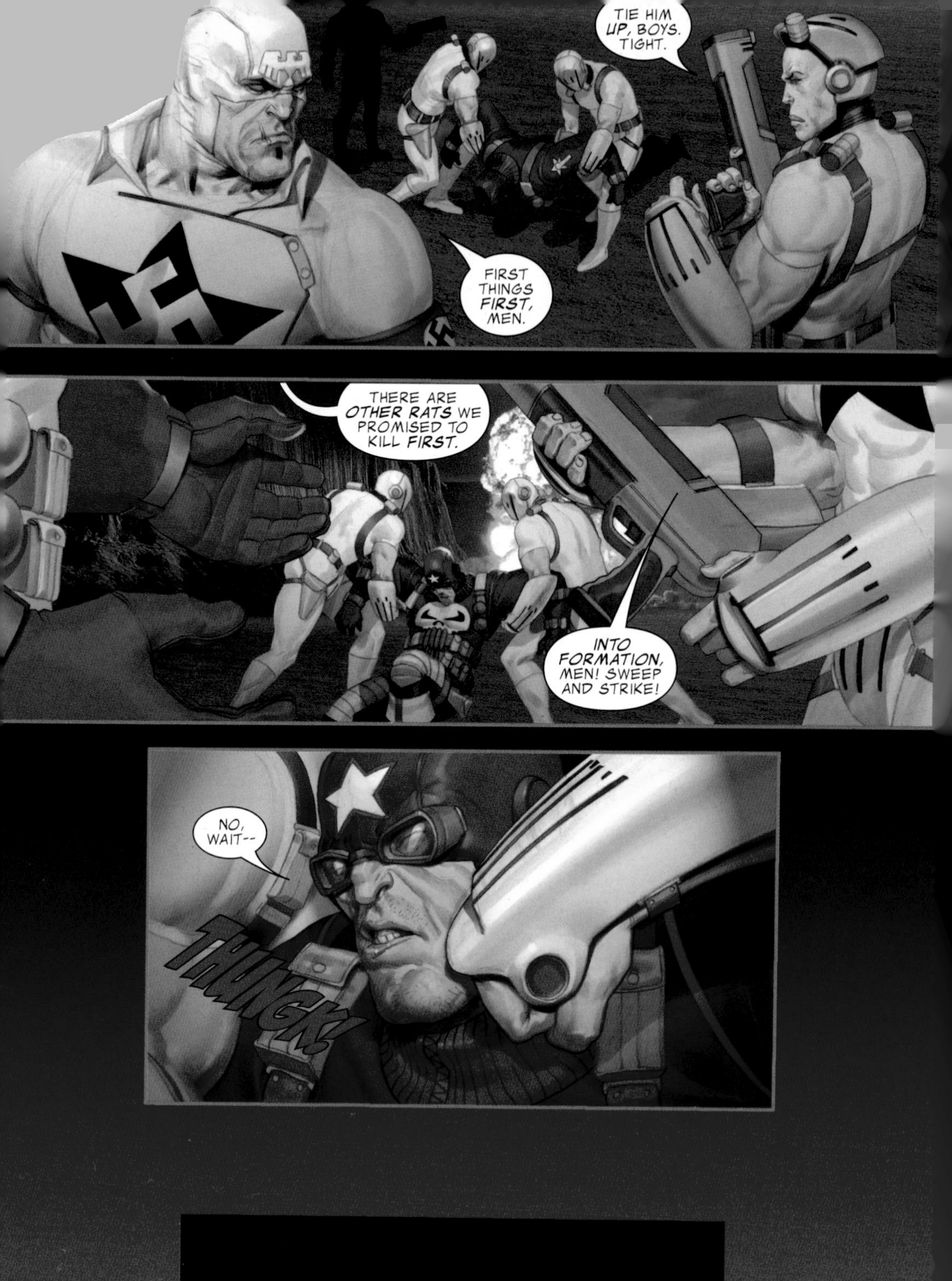
TIE HIM UP, BOYS. TIGHT.
FIRST THINGS FIRST, MEN.
THERE ARE OTHER RATS WE PROMISED TO KILL FIRST.
INTO FORMATION, MEN! SWEEP AND STRIKE!
NO, WAIT--
THUNGK!
AND I WOKE UP IN THE DESERT.

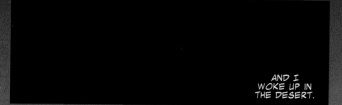

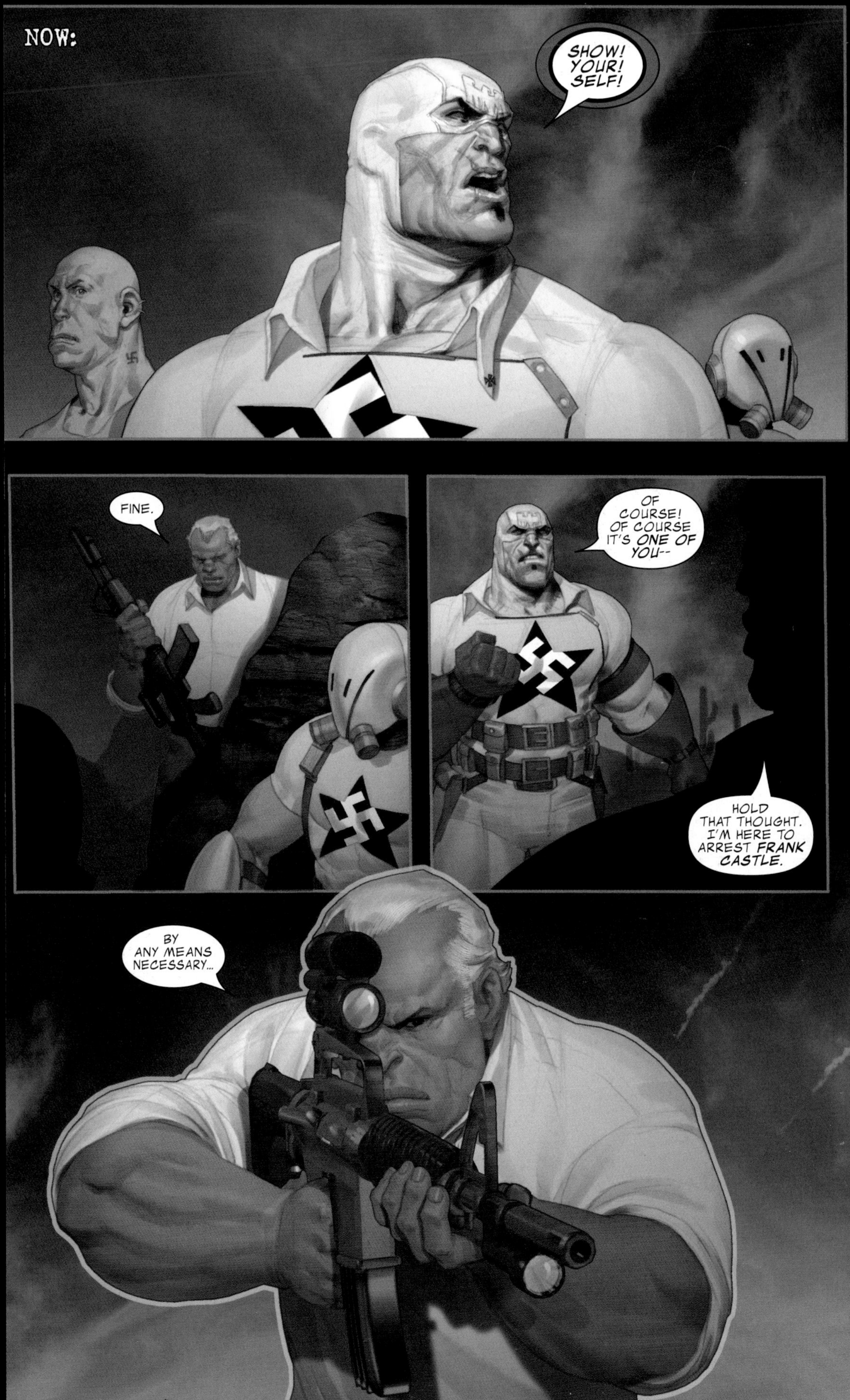
NOW:
SHOW! YOUR! SELF!
FINE.
OF COURSE! OF COURSE IT'S ONE OF YOU--
HOLD THAT THOUGHT. I'M HERE TO ARREST FRANK CASTLE.
BY ANY MEANS NECESSARY...

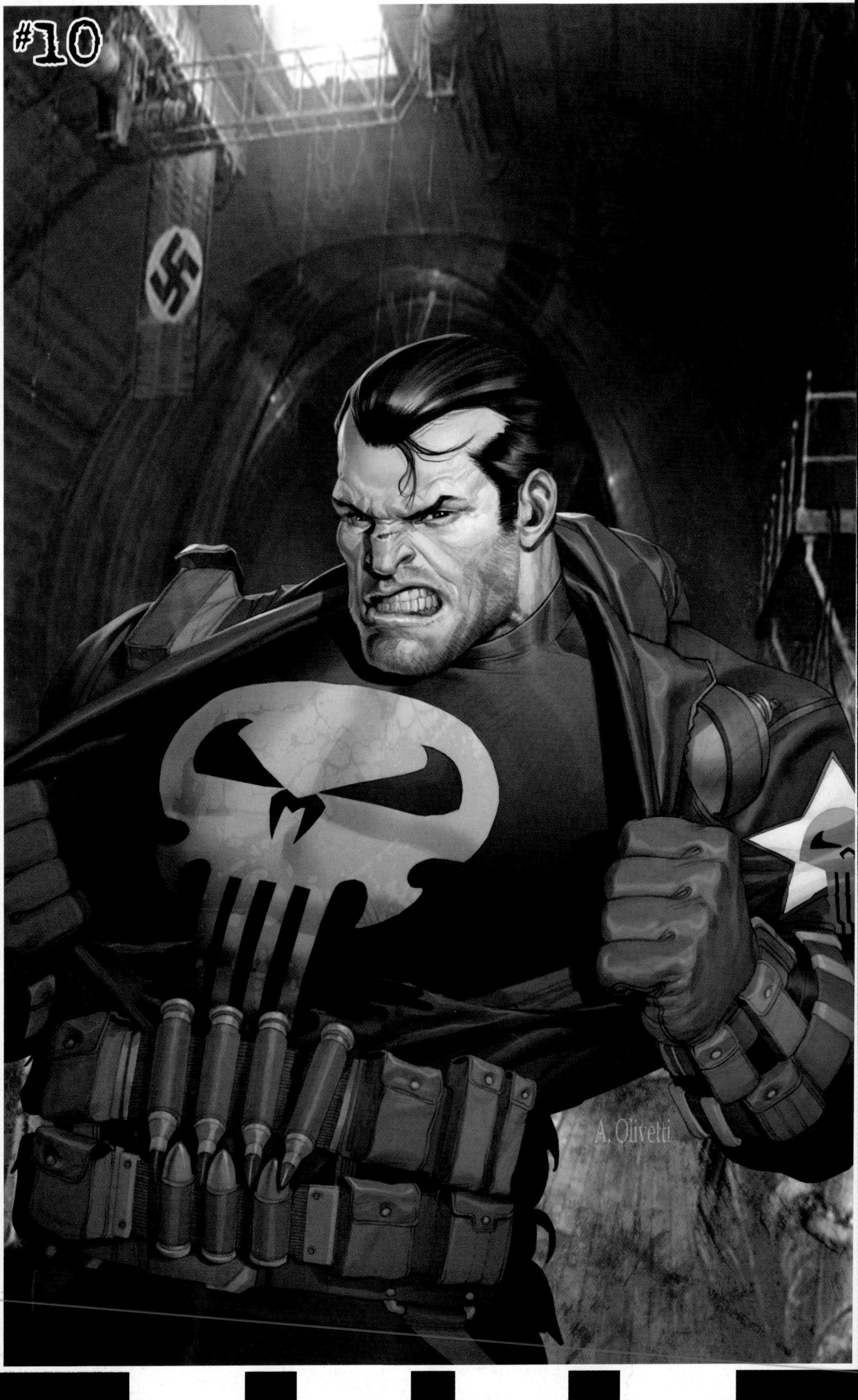

#10
A. Olivetti

NOW...

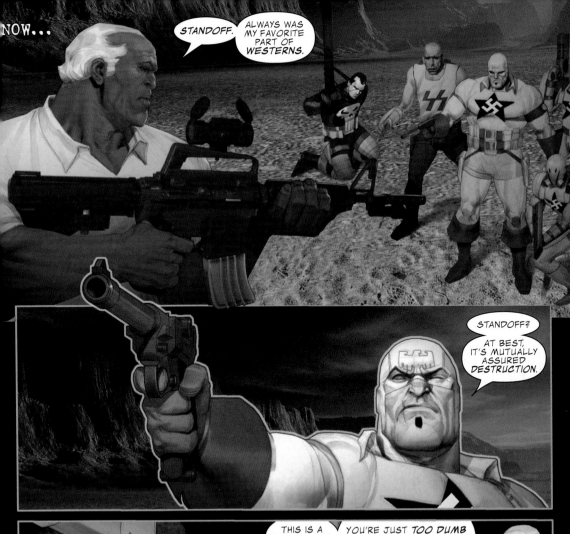

STANDOFF. ALWAYS WAS MY FAVORITE PART OF *WESTERNS*.

STANDOFF? AT BEST, IT'S MUTUALLY ASSURED *DESTRUCTION*.

THIS IS A *MASSACRE*, BOY.

YOU'RE JUST *TOO DUMB* TO REALIZE IT. WHAT IN THAT OLD ADDLED BLACK BRAIN OF YOURS MADE YOU THINK YOU COULD *STOP THIS*?

WELL. I HAVE A *PARTNER*.

AND HE FOUND YOUR *HIDEOUT*.

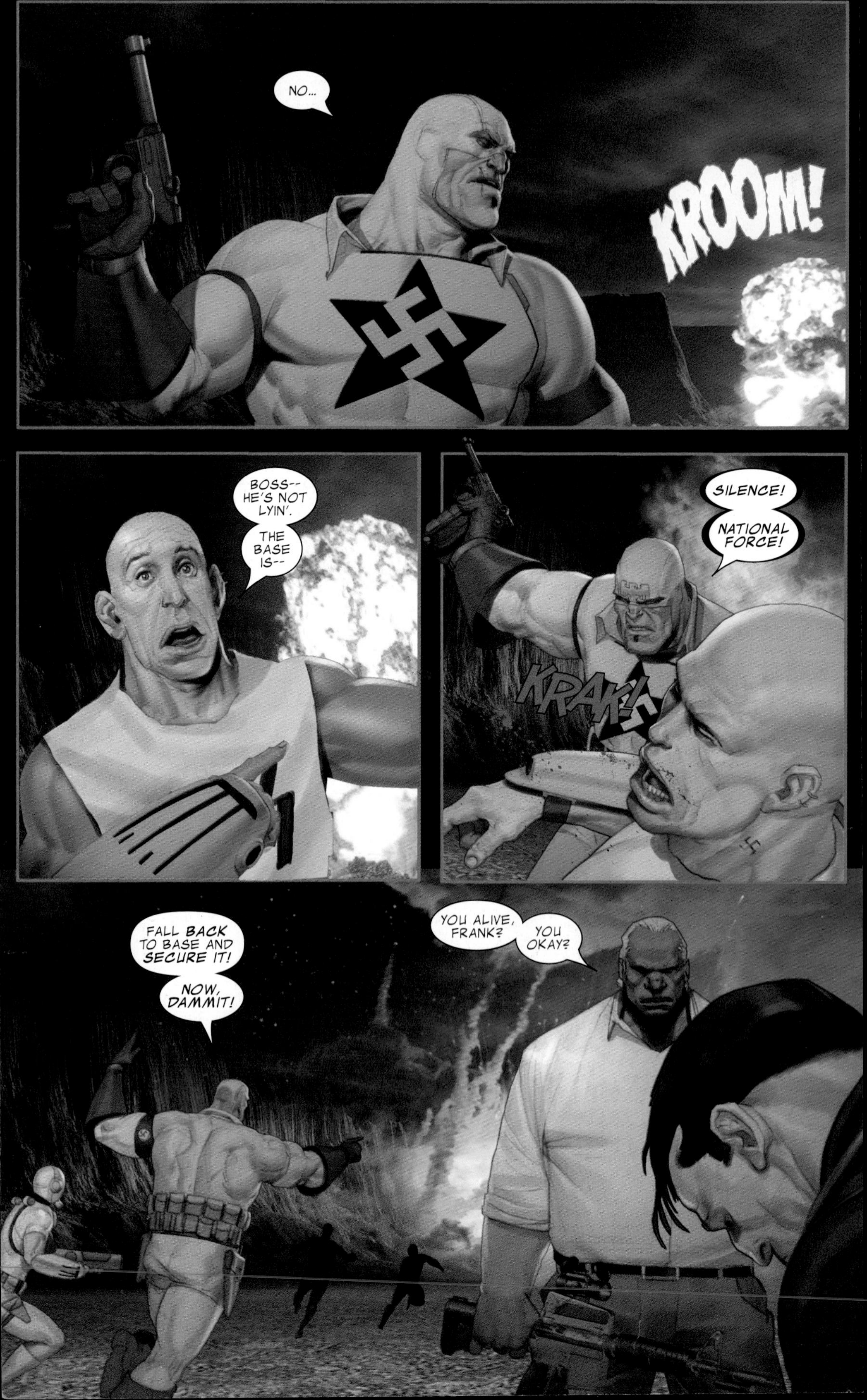
NO...
KROOM!
BOSS-- HE'S NOT LYIN'.
THE BASE IS--
SILENCE!
NATIONAL FORCE!
KRAK!
FALL BACK TO BASE AND SECURE IT!
NOW, DAMMIT!
YOU ALIVE, FRANK?
YOU OKAY?

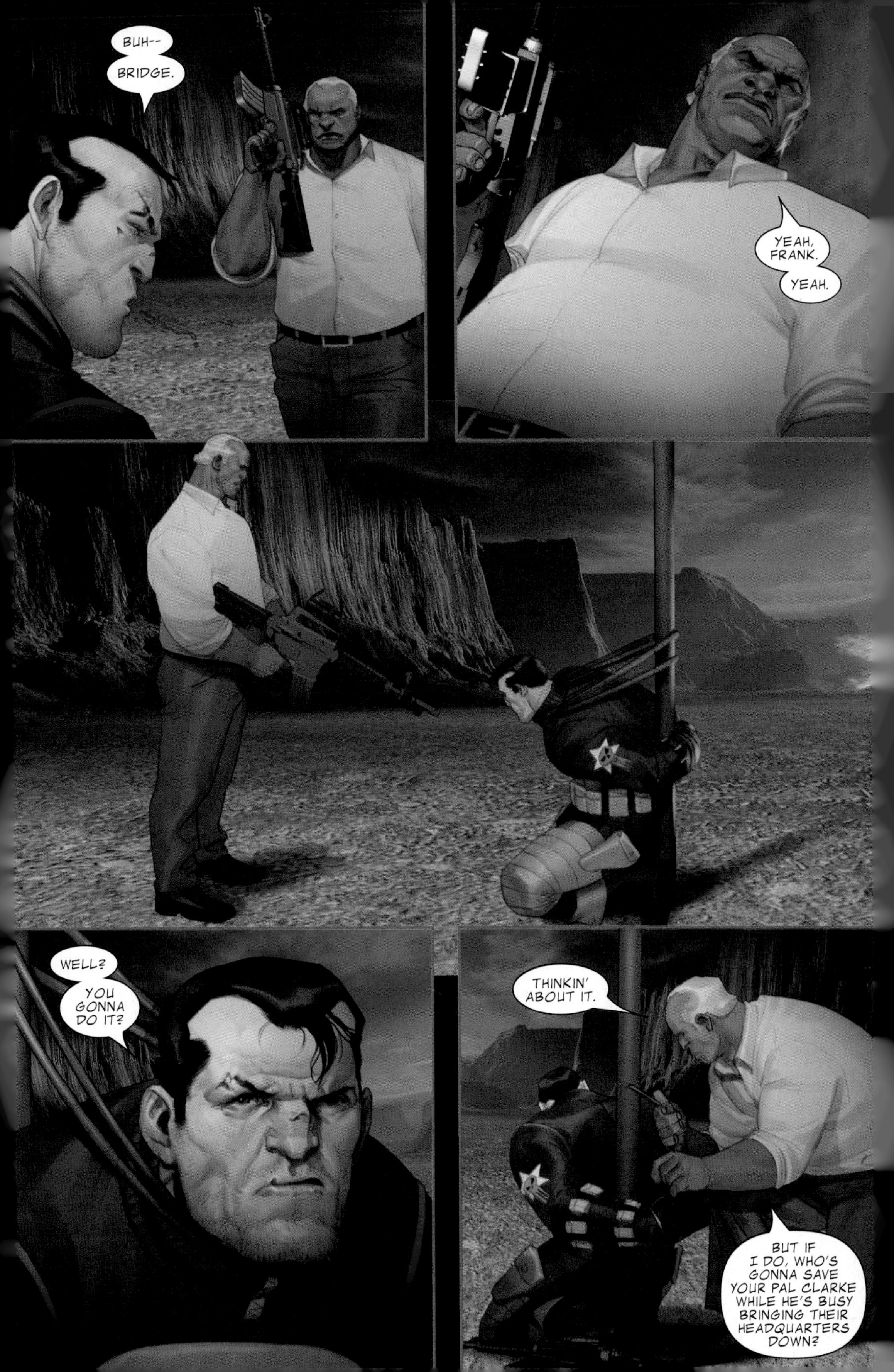
BUH--
BRIDGE.
YEAH, FRANK.
YEAH.
WELL?
YOU GONNA DO IT?
THINKIN' ABOUT IT.
BUT IF I DO, WHO'S GONNA SAVE YOUR PAL CLARKE WHILE HE'S BUSY BRINGING THEIR HEADQUARTERS DOWN?

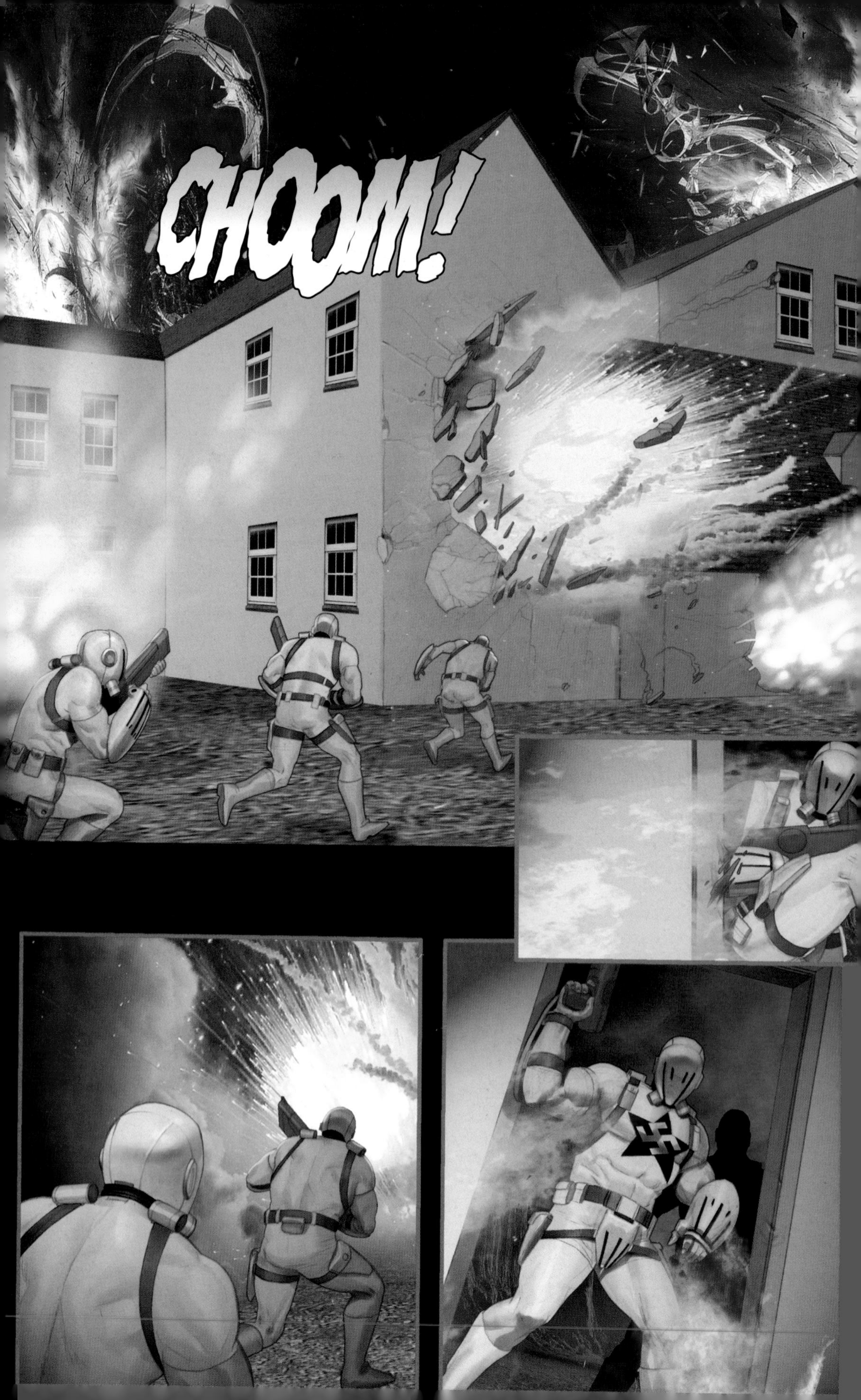
CHOOM!

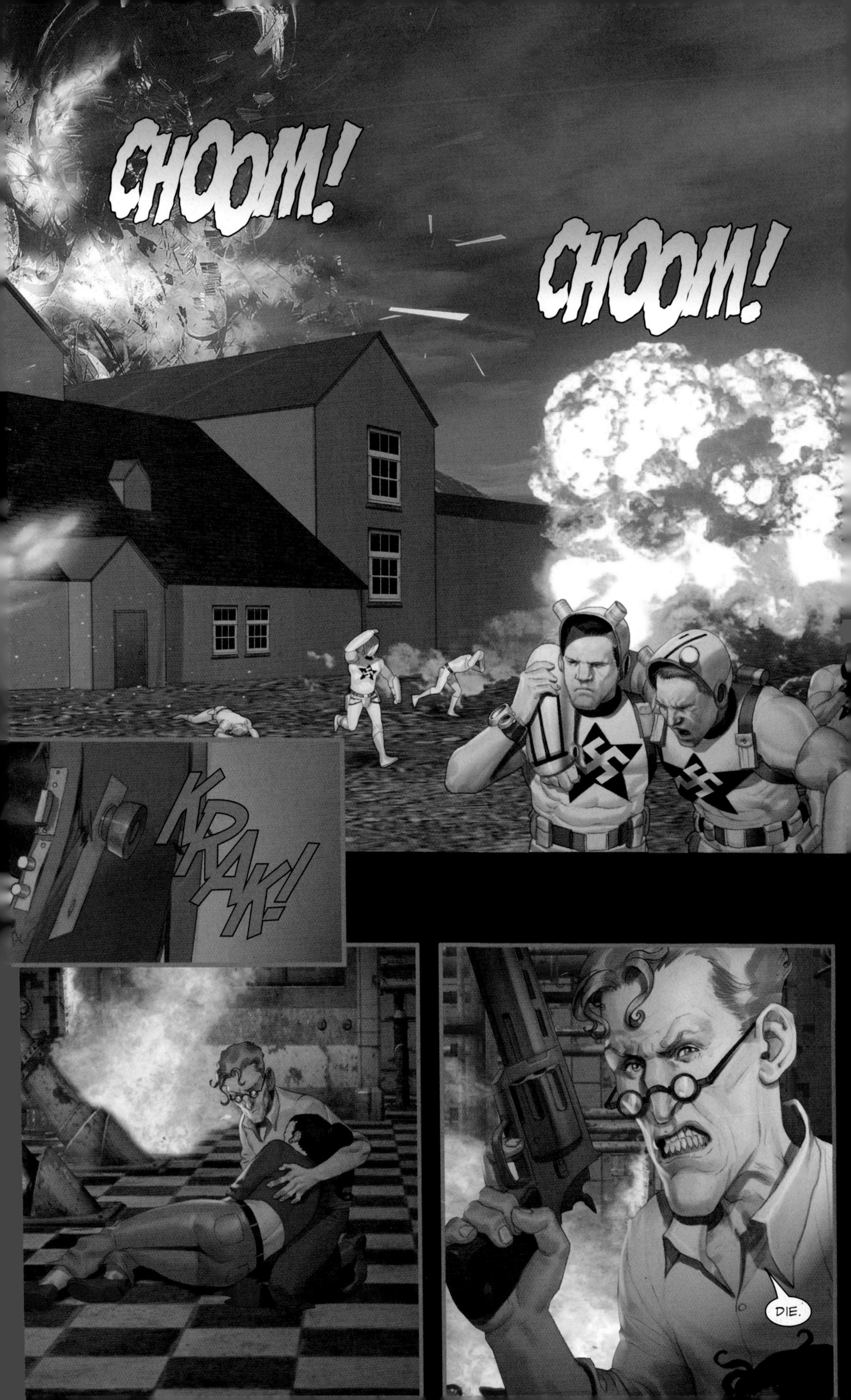
CHOOM!
CHOOM!
KRAK!
DIE.

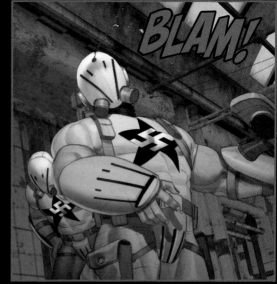

BLAM!

BLAM!

OHHH, TATI.

TATI, TATI, TATI.

I SWEAR TO GOD I'LL KILL WHOEVER DID THIS TO YOU.

I SWEAR TO GOD I'LL KILL THEM ALL.

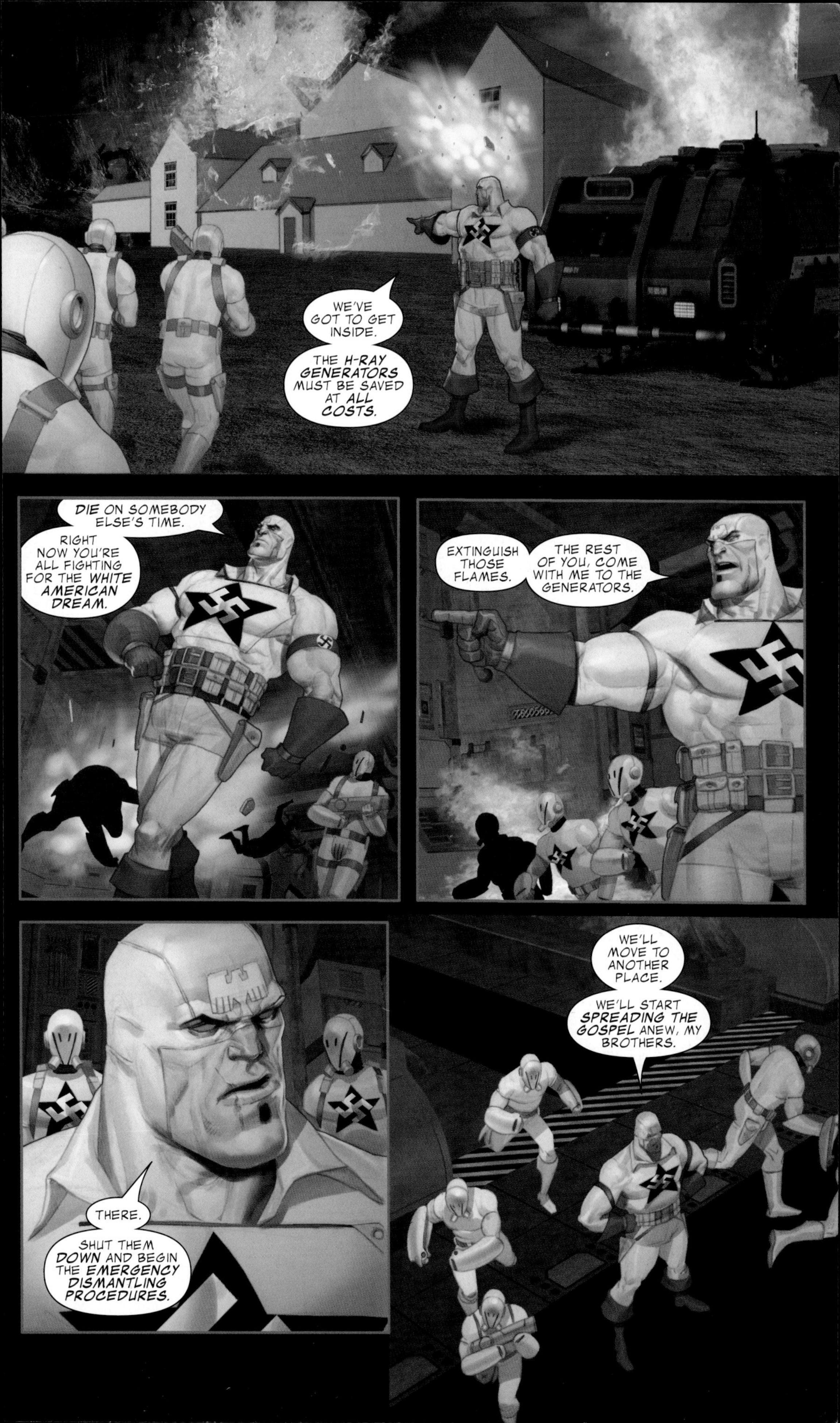

WE'VE GOT TO GET INSIDE.
THE H-RAY GENERATORS MUST BE SAVED AT ALL COSTS.
DIE ON SOMEBODY ELSE'S TIME.
RIGHT NOW YOU'RE ALL FIGHTING FOR THE WHITE AMERICAN DREAM.
EXTINGUISH THOSE FLAMES.
THE REST OF YOU, COME WITH ME TO THE GENERATORS.
THERE.
SHUT THEM DOWN AND BEGIN THE EMERGENCY DISMANTLING PROCEDURES.
WE'LL MOVE TO ANOTHER PLACE.
WE'LL START SPREADING THE GOSPEL ANEW, MY BROTHERS.

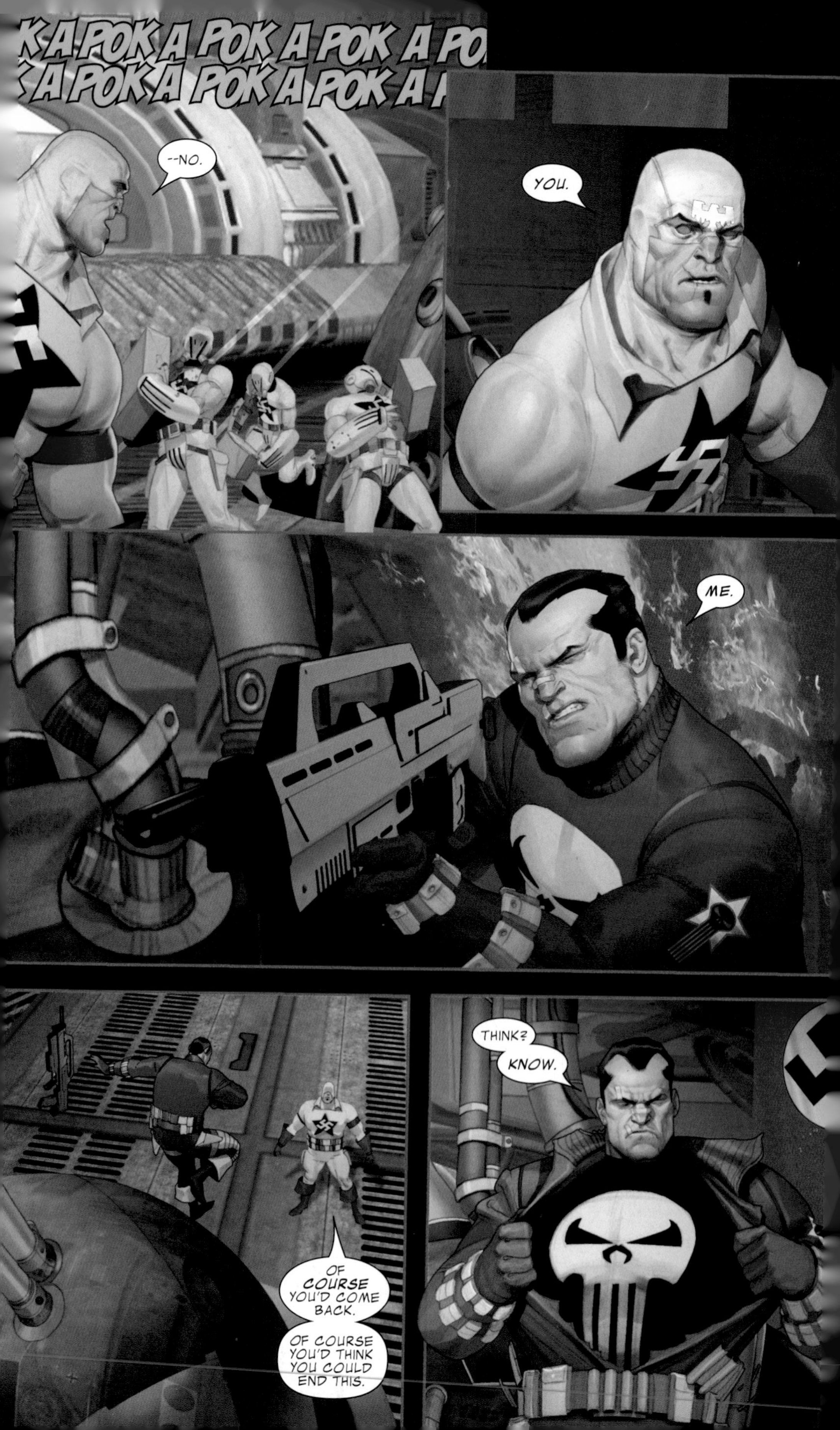
K A POK A POK A POK A PO
K A POK A POK A POK A
--NO.
YOU.
ME.
OF COURSE YOU'D COME BACK.
OF COURSE YOU'D THINK YOU COULD END THIS.
THINK?
KNOW.

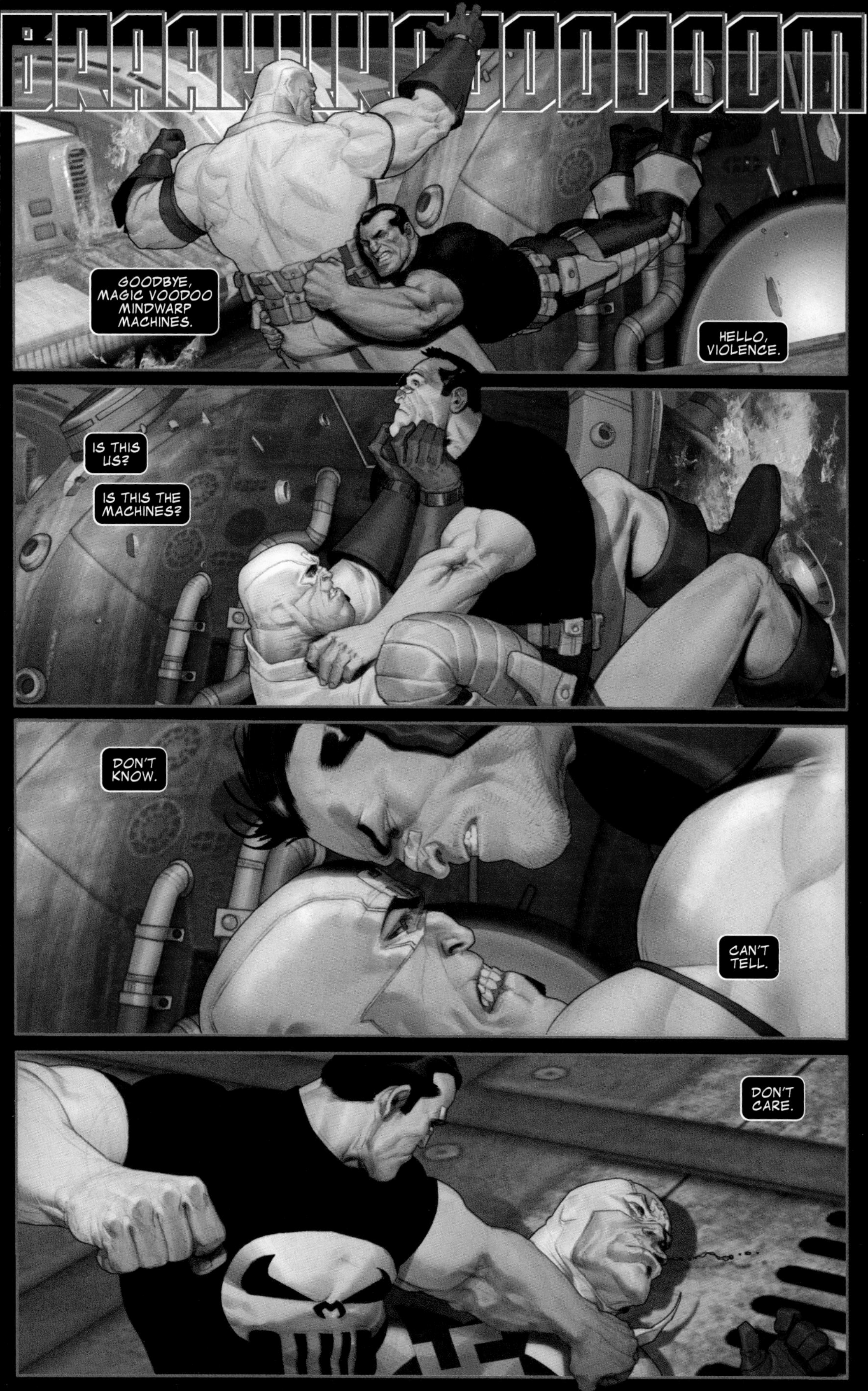
GOODBYE, MAGIC VOODOO MINDWARP MACHINES.
HELLO, VIOLENCE.
IS THIS US?
IS THIS THE MACHINES?
DON'T KNOW.
CAN'T TELL.
DON'T CARE.

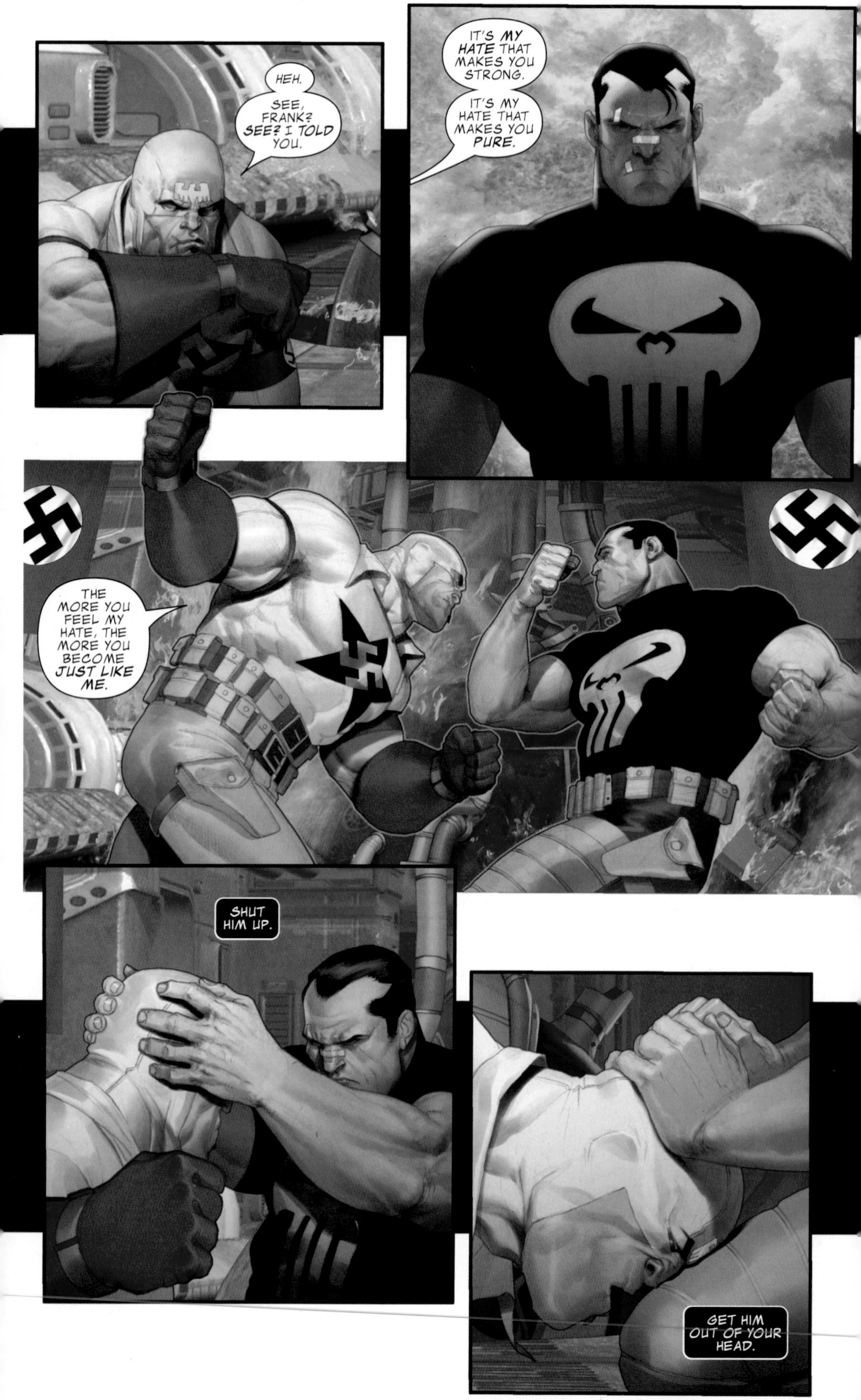
HEH.
SEE, FRANK? SEE? I TOLD YOU.
IT'S MY HATE THAT MAKES YOU STRONG.
IT'S MY HATE THAT MAKES YOU PURE.
THE MORE YOU FEEL MY HATE, THE MORE YOU BECOME JUST LIKE ME.
SHUT HIM UP.
GET HIM OUT OF YOUR HEAD.

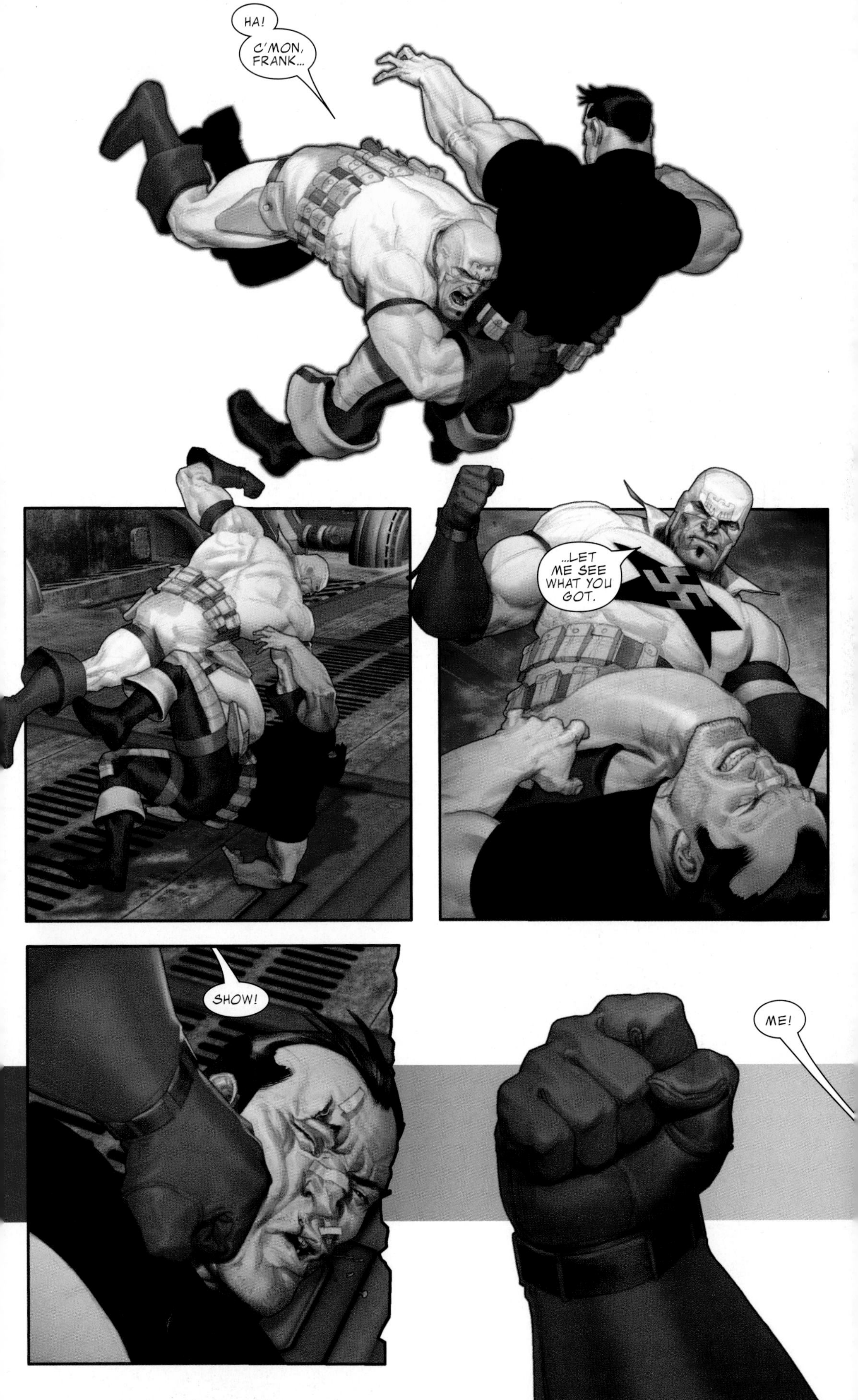
HA!
C'MON, FRANK...
...LET ME SEE WHAT YOU GOT.
SHOW!
ME!

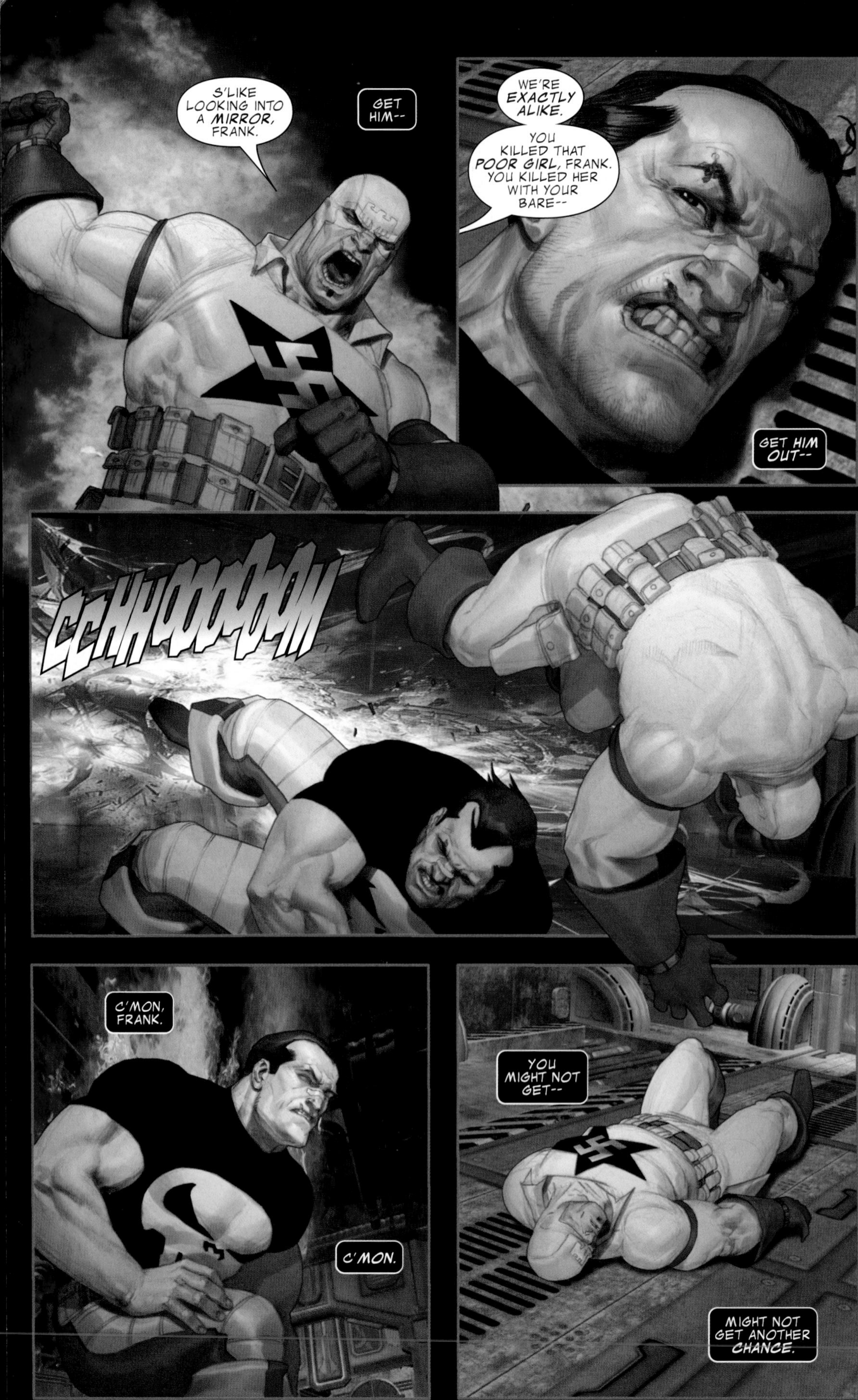
S'LIKE LOOKING INTO A MIRROR, FRANK.
GET HIM--
WE'RE EXACTLY ALIKE.
YOU KILLED THAT POOR GIRL, FRANK. YOU KILLED HER WITH YOUR BARE--
GET HIM OUT--
CCHHOOOOOOM
C'MON, FRANK.
C'MON.
YOU MIGHT NOT GET--
MIGHT NOT GET ANOTHER CHANCE.

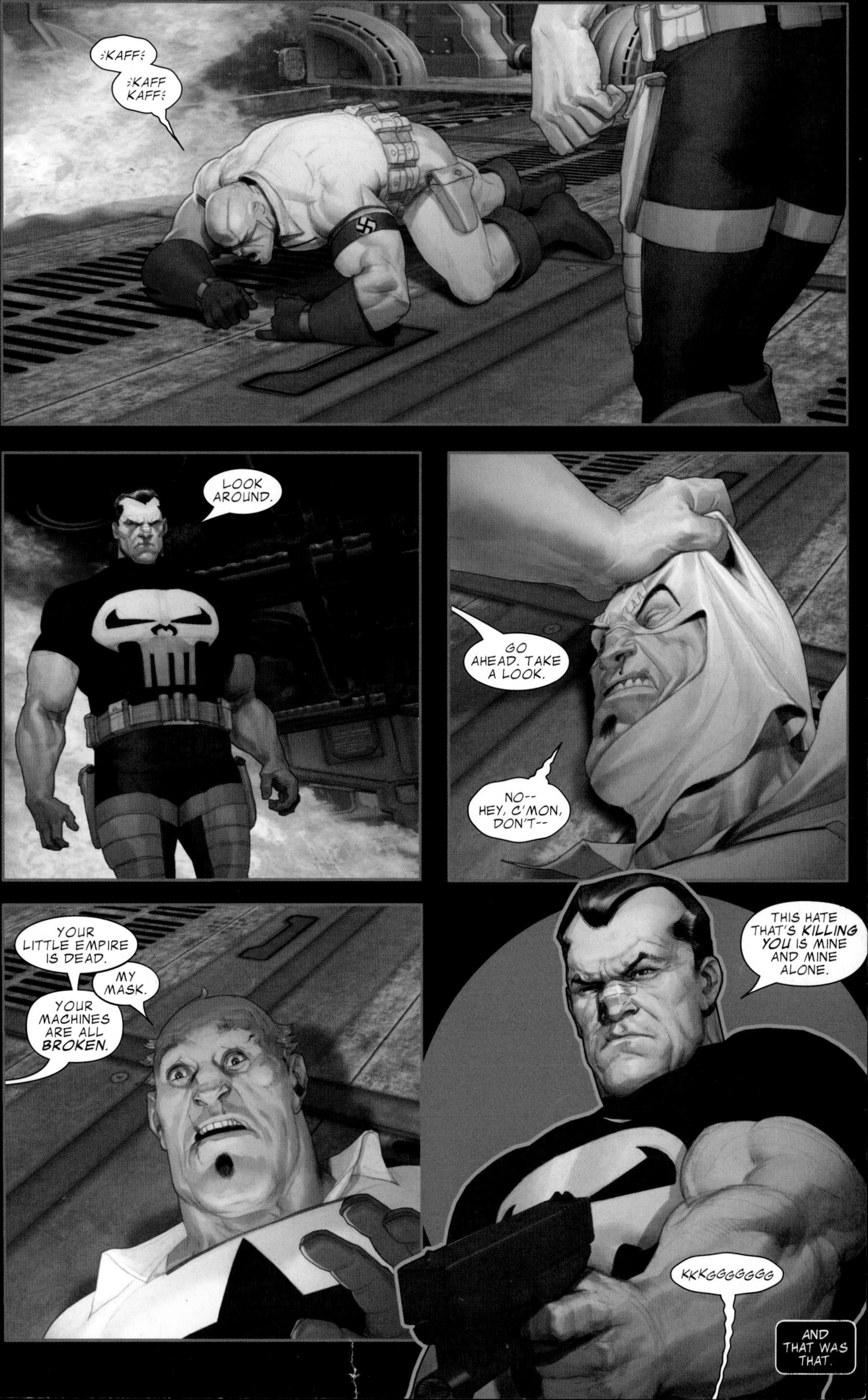
KAFF
KAFF KAFF
LOOK AROUND.
GO AHEAD. TAKE A LOOK.
NO-- HEY, C'MON, DON'T--
YOUR LITTLE EMPIRE IS DEAD.
MY MASK.
YOUR MACHINES ARE ALL BROKEN.
THIS HATE THAT'S KILLING YOU IS MINE AND MINE ALONE.
KKKGGGGGGG
AND THAT WAS THAT.

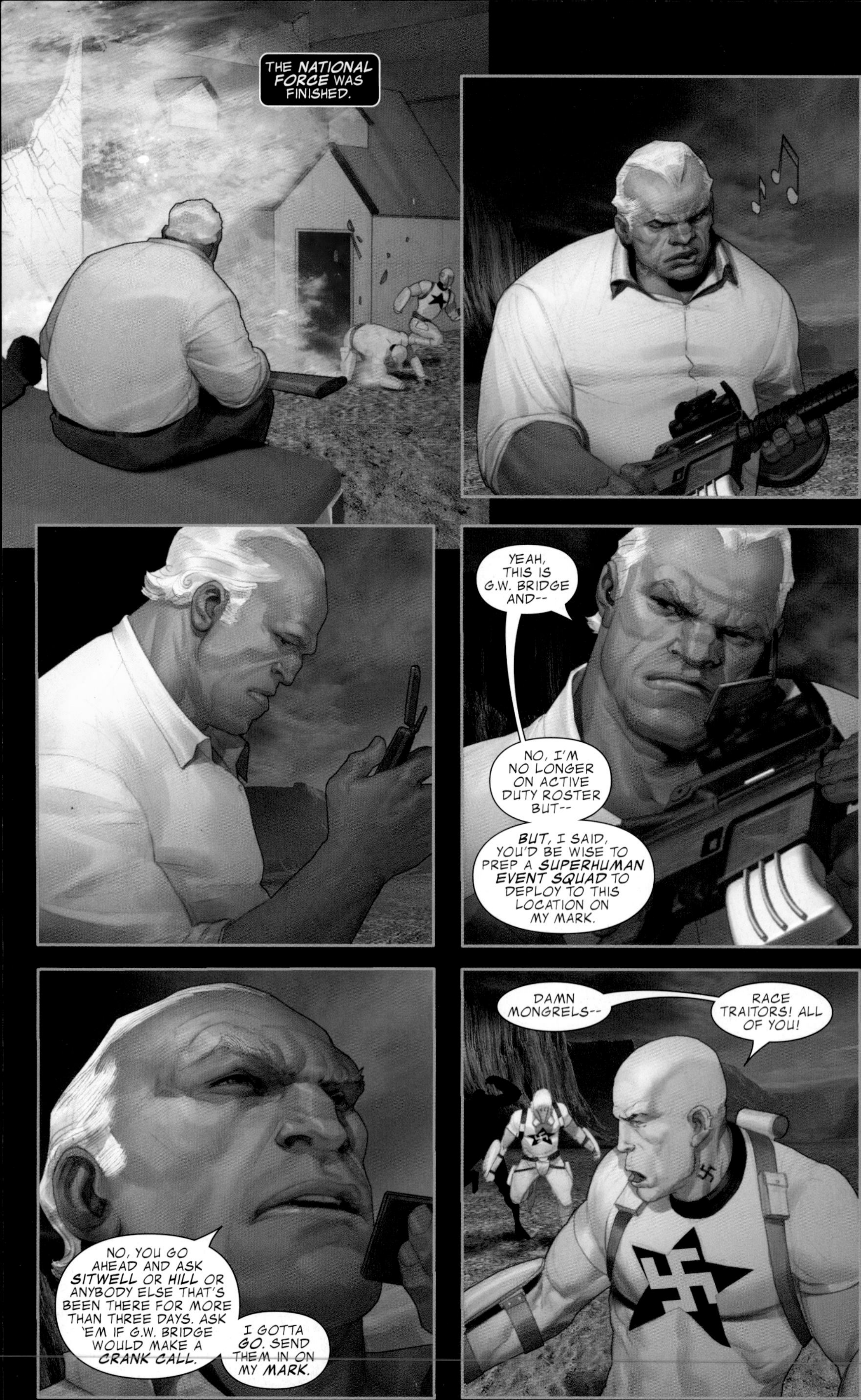
THE NATIONAL FORCE WAS FINISHED.
YEAH, THIS IS G.W. BRIDGE AND--
NO, I'M NO LONGER ON ACTIVE DUTY ROSTER BUT--
BUT, I SAID, YOU'D BE WISE TO PREP A SUPERHUMAN EVENT SQUAD TO DEPLOY TO THIS LOCATION ON MY MARK.
NO, YOU GO AHEAD AND ASK SITWELL OR HILL OR ANYBODY ELSE THAT'S BEEN THERE FOR MORE THAN THREE DAYS. ASK 'EM IF G.W. BRIDGE WOULD MAKE A CRANK CALL.
I GOTTA GO. SEND THEM IN ON MY MARK.
DAMN MONGRELS--
RACE TRAITORS! ALL OF YOU!

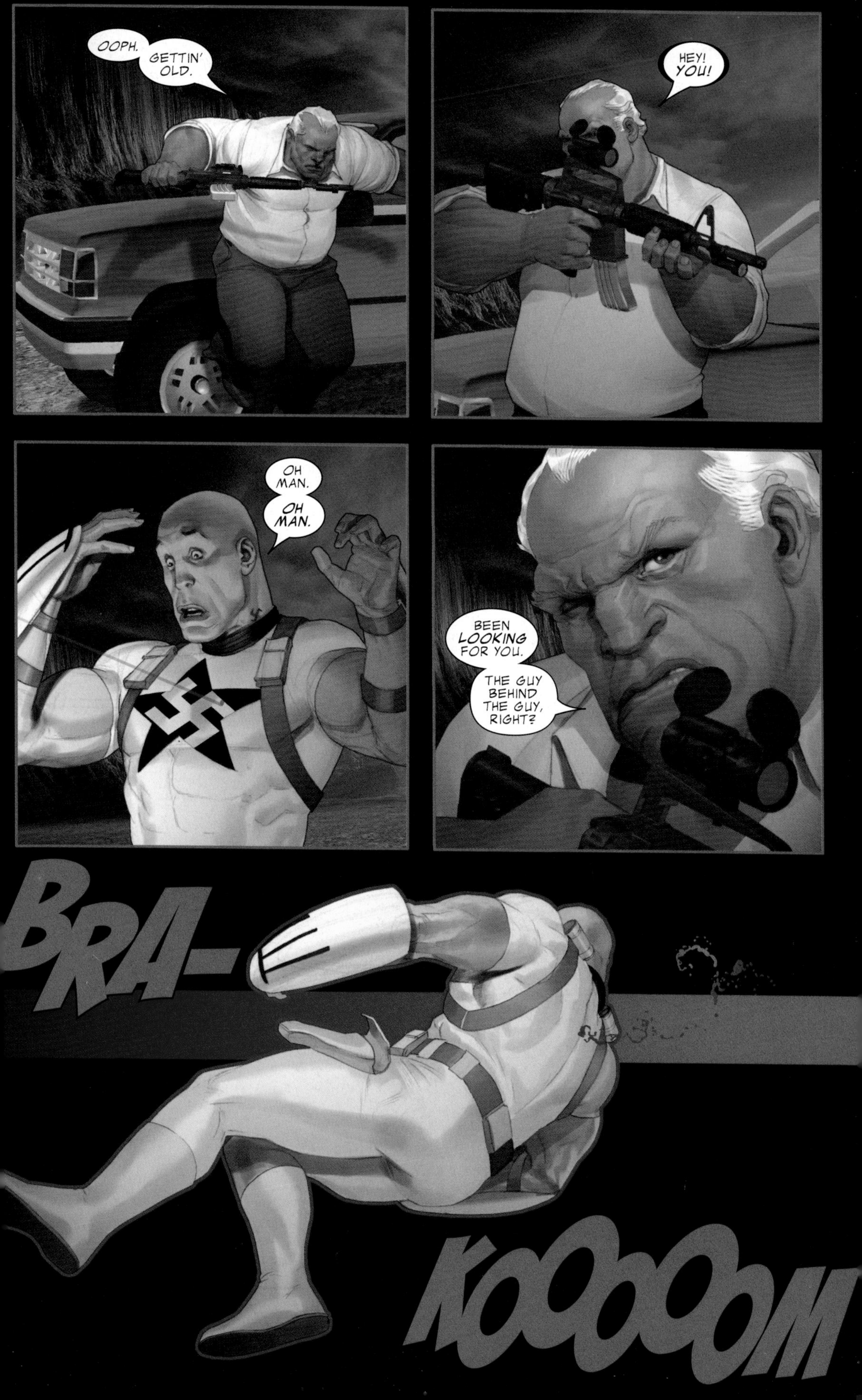
OOPH.
GETTIN' OLD.
HEY! YOU!
OH MAN.
OH MAN.
BEEN LOOKING FOR YOU.
THE GUY BEHIND THE GUY, RIGHT?
BRA-
KOOOOOM

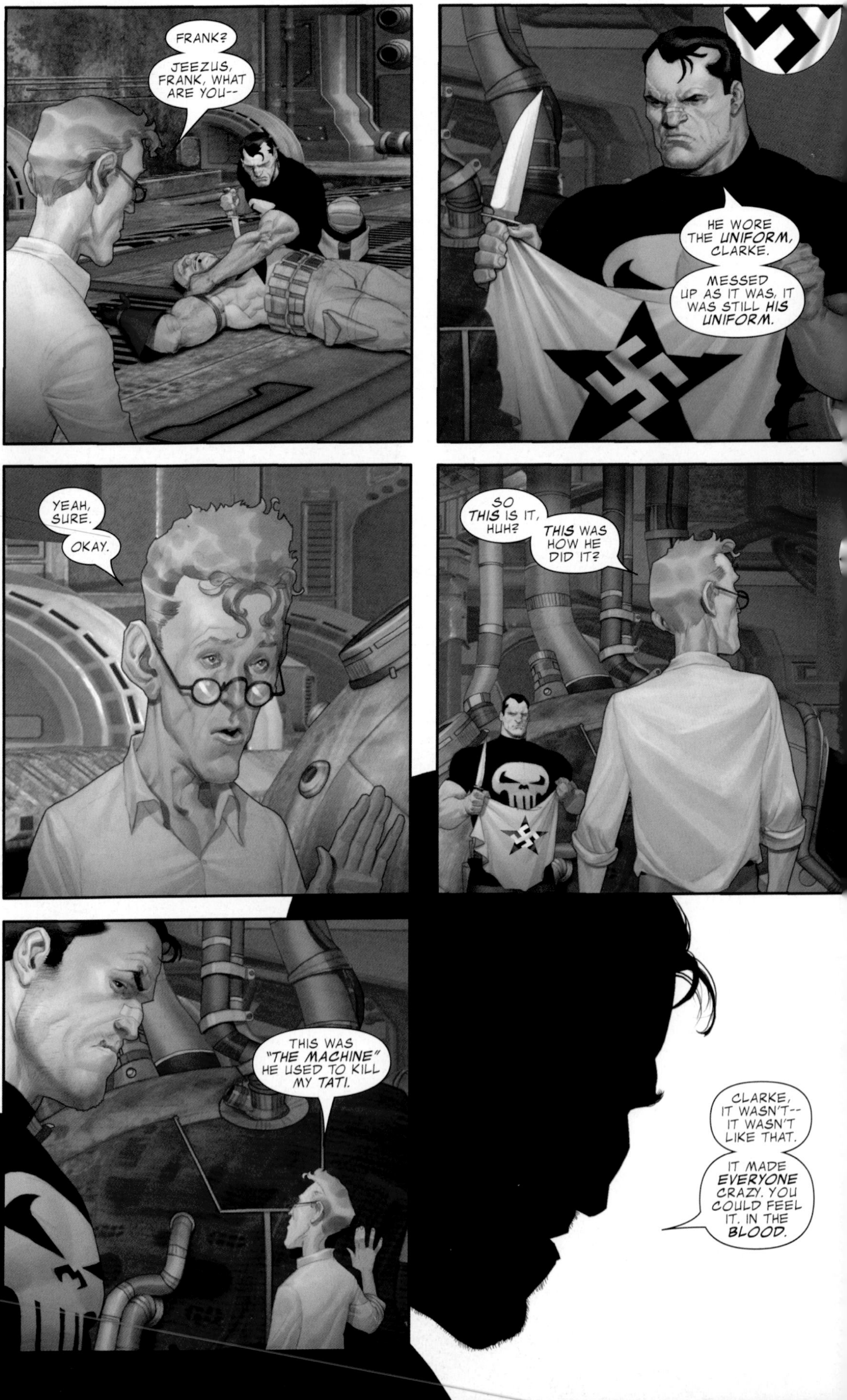

FRANK?
JEEZUS, FRANK, WHAT ARE YOU--
HE WORE THE *UNIFORM*, CLARKE.
MESSED UP AS IT WAS, IT WAS STILL *HIS UNIFORM*.
YEAH, SURE.
OKAY.
SO *THIS* IS IT, HUH?
THIS WAS HOW HE DID IT?
THIS WAS *"THE MACHINE"* HE USED TO KILL MY *TATI*.
CLARKE, IT WASN'T-- IT WASN'T LIKE THAT.
IT MADE *EVERYONE* CRAZY. YOU COULD FEEL IT. IN THE *BLOOD*.

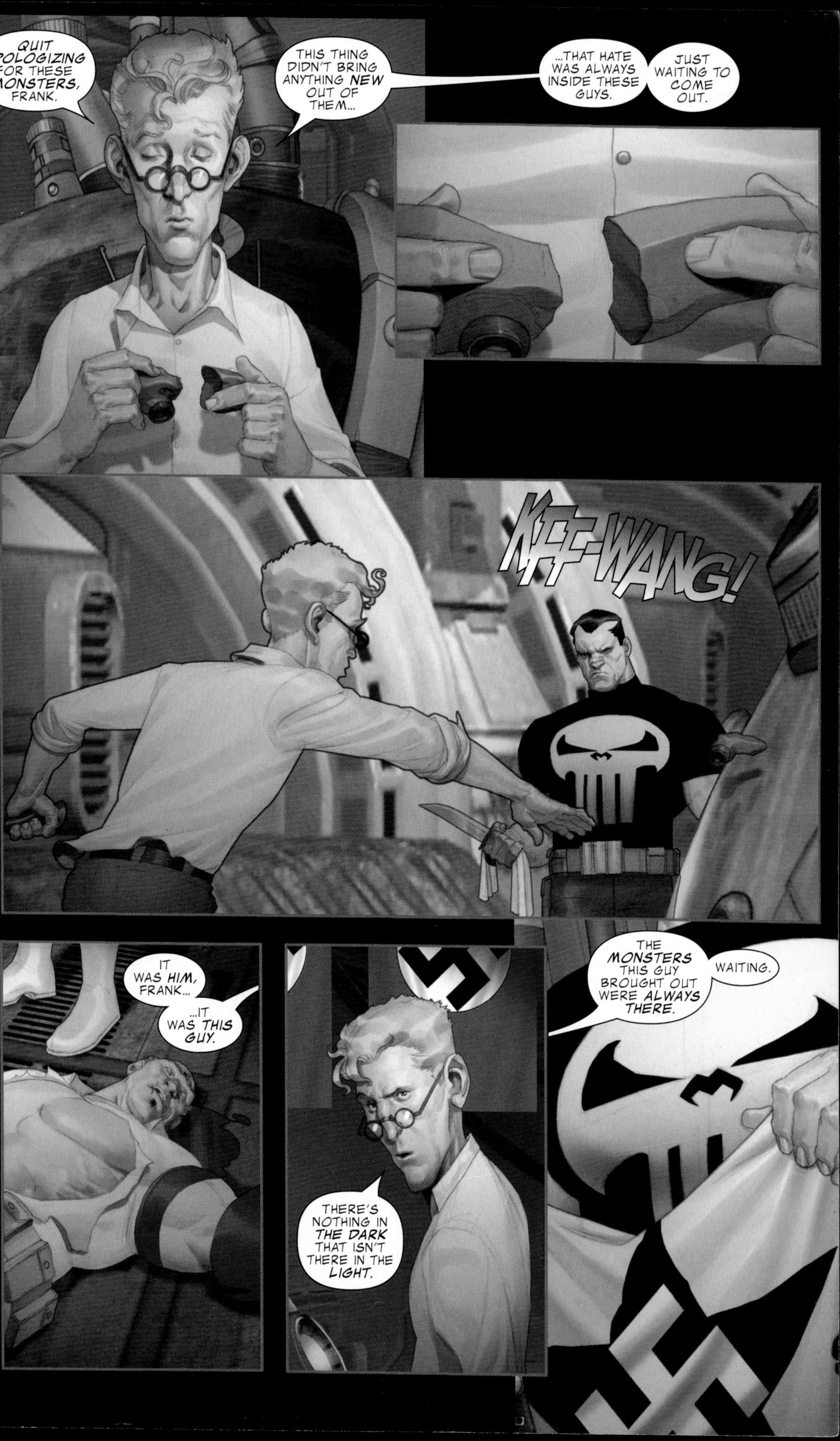
QUIT APOLOGIZING FOR THESE MONSTERS, FRANK.
THIS THING DIDN'T BRING ANYTHING NEW OUT OF THEM...
...THAT HATE WAS ALWAYS INSIDE THESE GUYS.
JUST WAITING TO COME OUT.
KFF-WANG!
IT WAS HIM, FRANK...
...IT WAS THIS GUY.
THERE'S NOTHING IN THE DARK THAT ISN'T THERE IN THE LIGHT.
THE MONSTERS THIS GUY BROUGHT OUT WERE ALWAYS THERE.
WAITING.

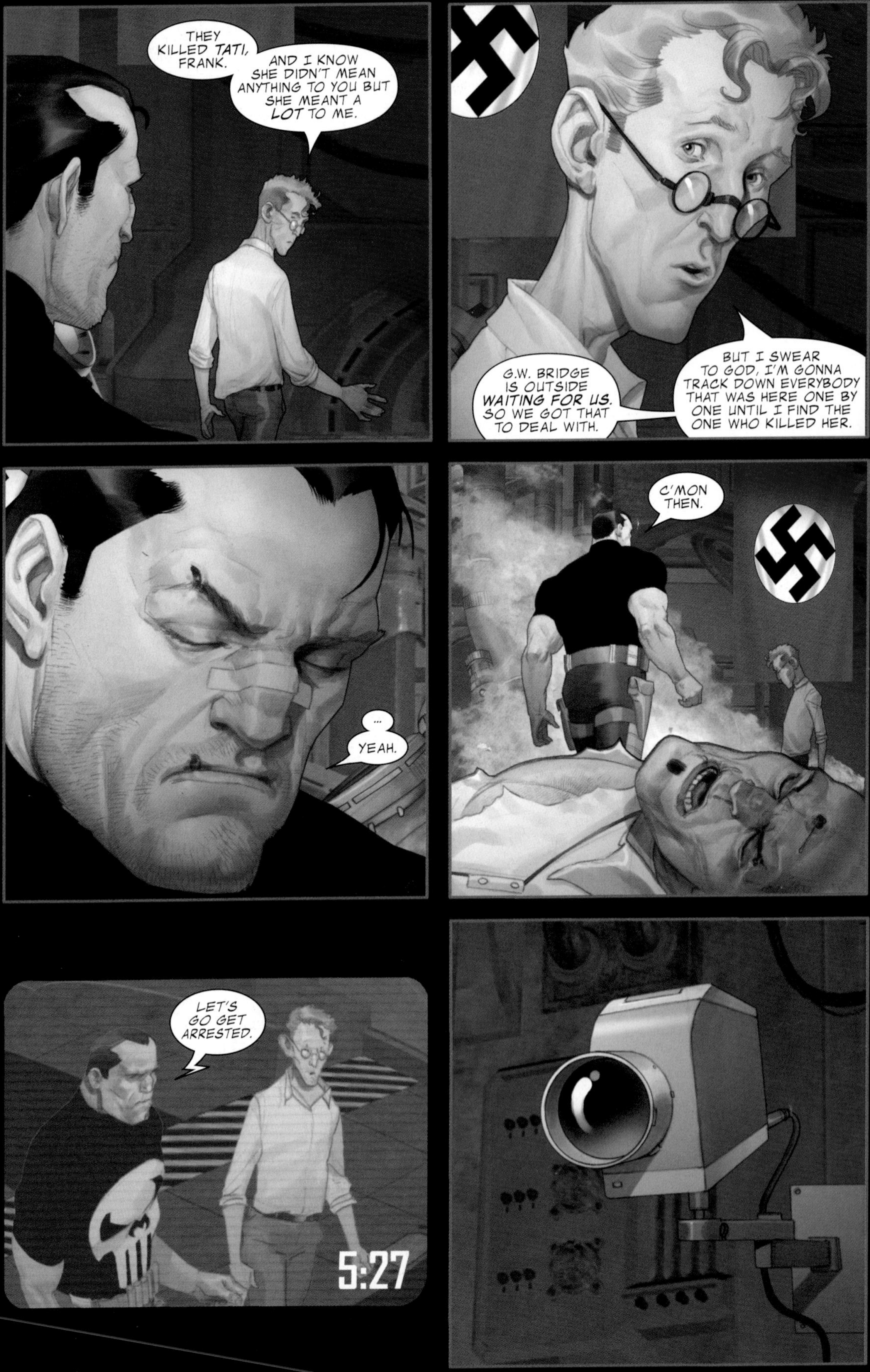
THEY KILLED TATI, FRANK.
AND I KNOW SHE DIDN'T MEAN ANYTHING TO YOU BUT SHE MEANT A LOT TO ME.
BUT I SWEAR TO GOD, I'M GONNA TRACK DOWN EVERYBODY THAT WAS HERE ONE BY ONE UNTIL I FIND THE ONE WHO KILLED HER.
G.W. BRIDGE IS OUTSIDE WAITING FOR US. SO WE GOT THAT TO DEAL WITH.
... YEAH.
C'MON THEN.
LET'S GO GET ARRESTED.
5:27

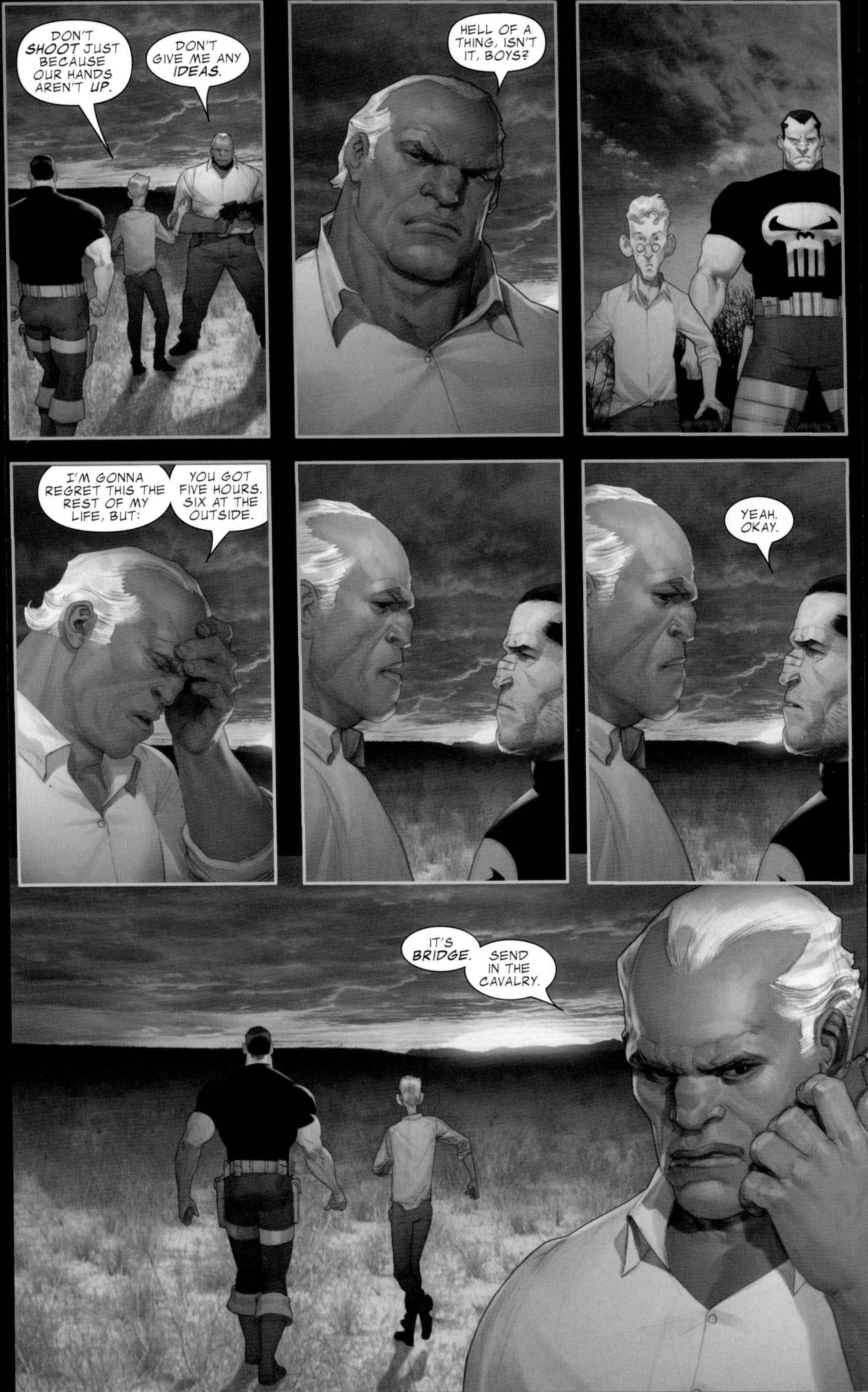
DON'T SHOOT JUST BECAUSE OUR HANDS AREN'T UP.
DON'T GIVE ME ANY IDEAS.
HELL OF A THING, ISN'T IT, BOYS?
I'M GONNA REGRET THIS THE REST OF MY LIFE, BUT:
YOU GOT FIVE HOURS. SIX AT THE OUTSIDE.
YEAH. OKAY.
IT'S BRIDGE.
SEND IN THE CAVALRY.

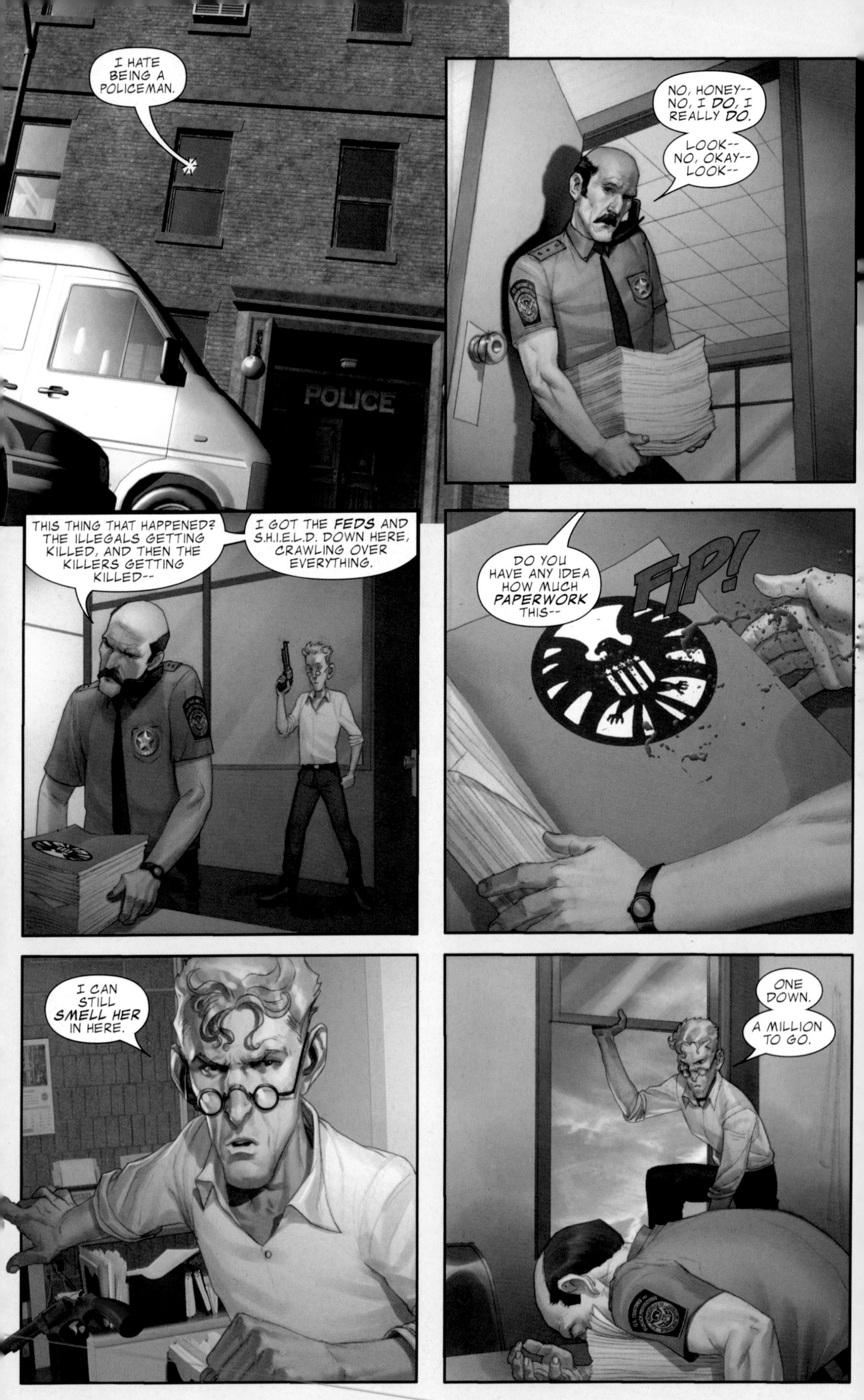
I HATE BEING A POLICEMAN.
POLICE
NO, HONEY-- NO, I DO, I REALLY DO.
LOOK-- NO, OKAY-- LOOK--
THIS THING THAT HAPPENED? THE ILLEGALS GETTING KILLED, AND THEN THE KILLERS GETTING KILLED--
I GOT THE FEDS AND S.H.I.E.L.D. DOWN HERE, CRAWLING OVER EVERYTHING.
DO YOU HAVE ANY IDEA HOW MUCH PAPERWORK THIS--
FIP!
I CAN STILL SMELL HER IN HERE.
ONE DOWN.
A MILLION TO GO.

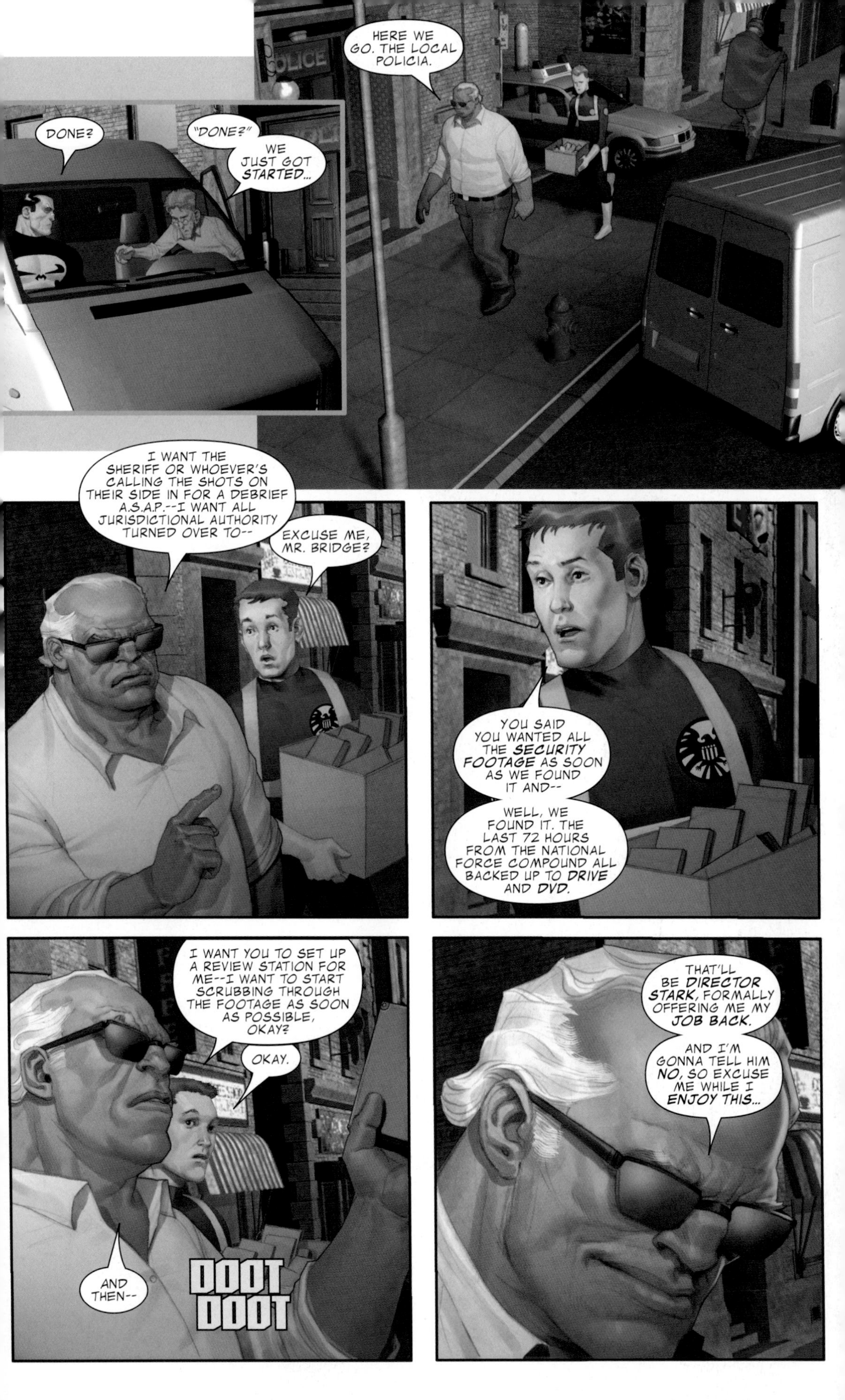
HERE WE GO. THE LOCAL POLICIA.
DONE?
"DONE?" WE JUST GOT STARTED...
I WANT THE SHERIFF OR WHOEVER'S CALLING THE SHOTS ON THEIR SIDE IN FOR A DEBRIEF A.S.A.P.--I WANT ALL JURISDICTIONAL AUTHORITY TURNED OVER TO--
EXCUSE ME, MR. BRIDGE?
YOU SAID YOU WANTED ALL THE SECURITY FOOTAGE AS SOON AS WE FOUND IT AND--
WELL, WE FOUND IT. THE LAST 72 HOURS FROM THE NATIONAL FORCE COMPOUND ALL BACKED UP TO DRIVE AND DVD.
I WANT YOU TO SET UP A REVIEW STATION FOR ME--I WANT TO START SCRUBBING THROUGH THE FOOTAGE AS SOON AS POSSIBLE, OKAY?
OKAY.
AND THEN--
DOOT DOOT
THAT'LL BE DIRECTOR STARK, FORMALLY OFFERING ME MY JOB BACK.
AND I'M GONNA TELL HIM NO, SO EXCUSE ME WHILE I ENJOY THIS...

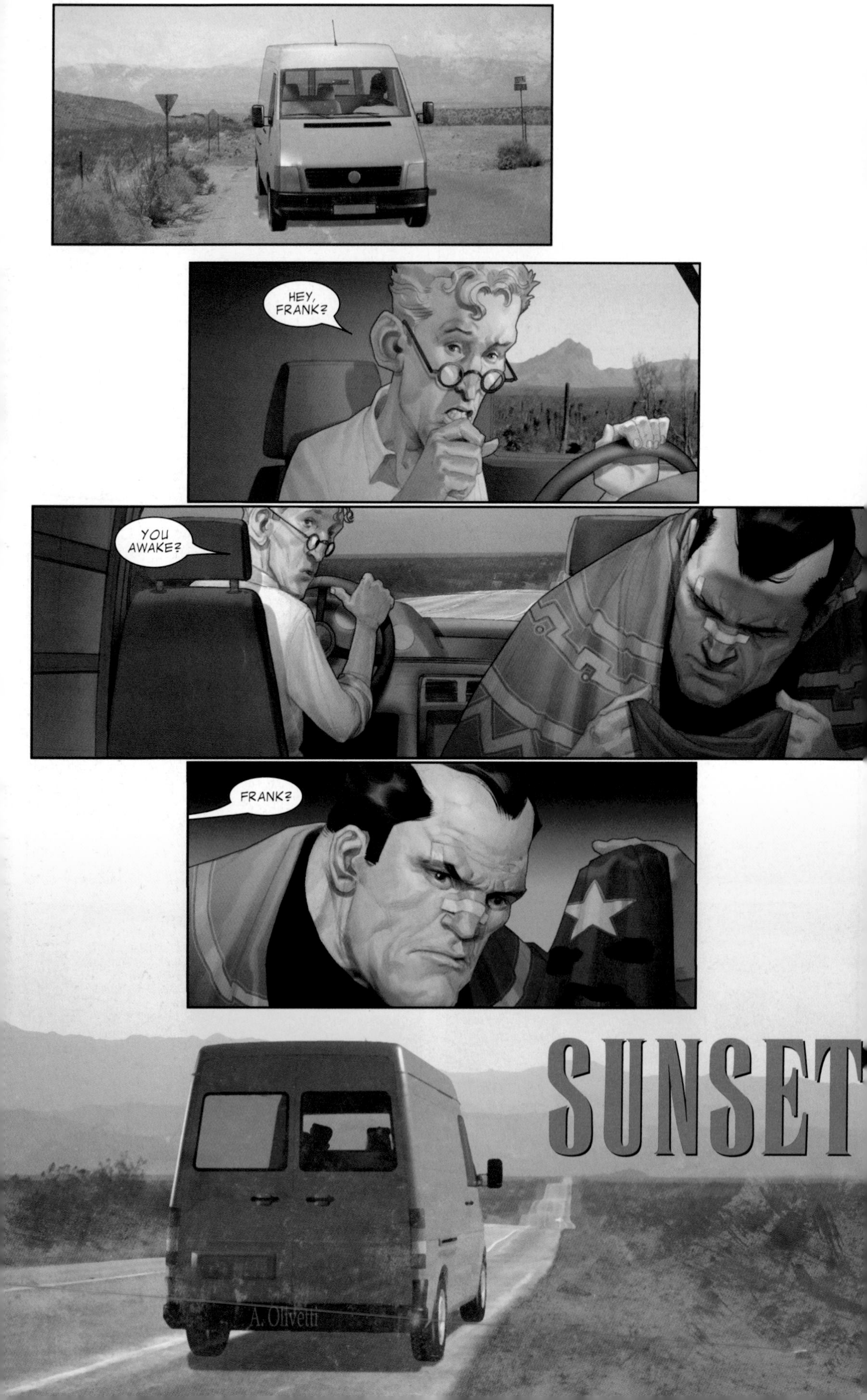
HEY, FRANK?
YOU AWAKE?
FRANK?
SUNSET
A. Olivetti

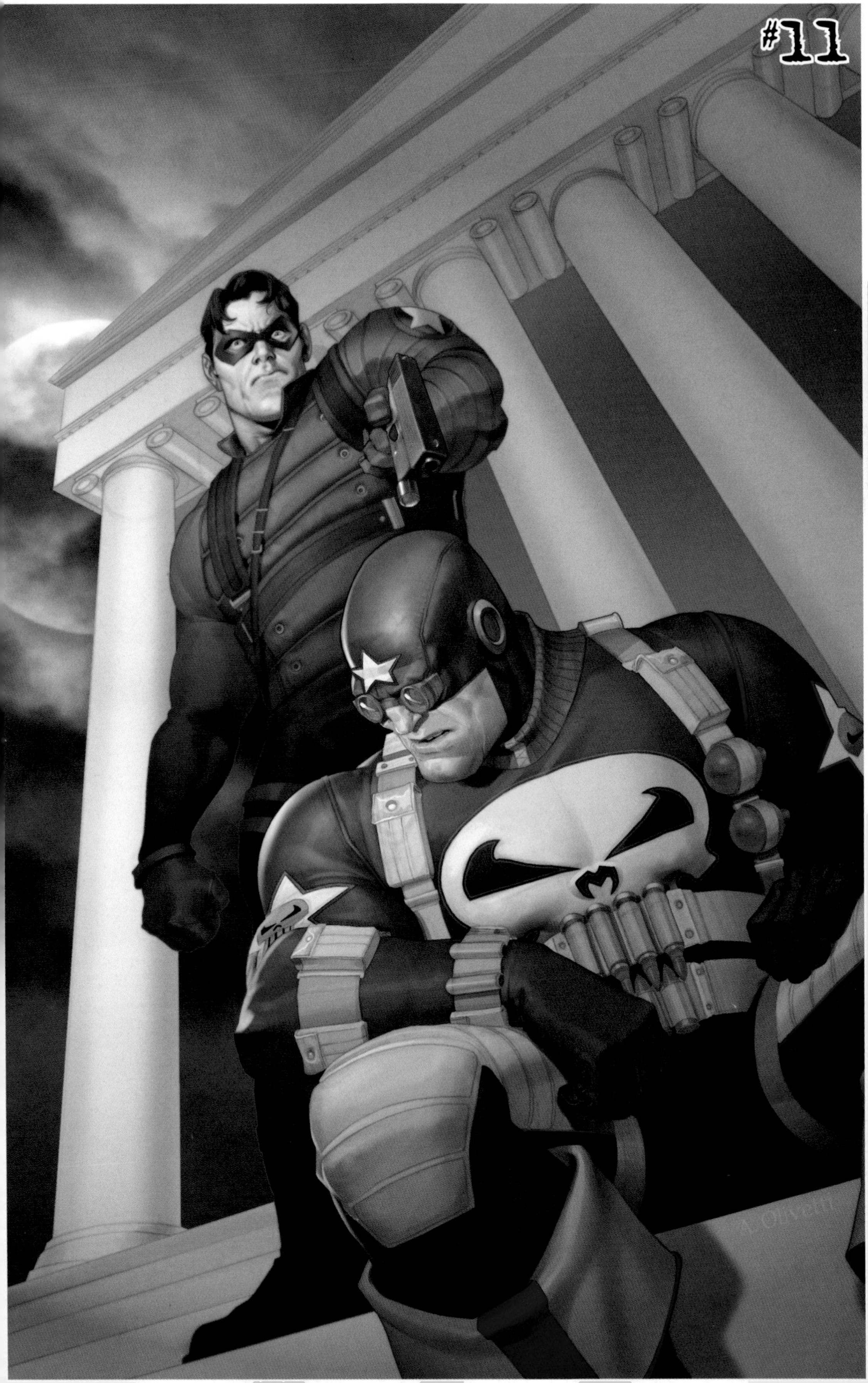
#11

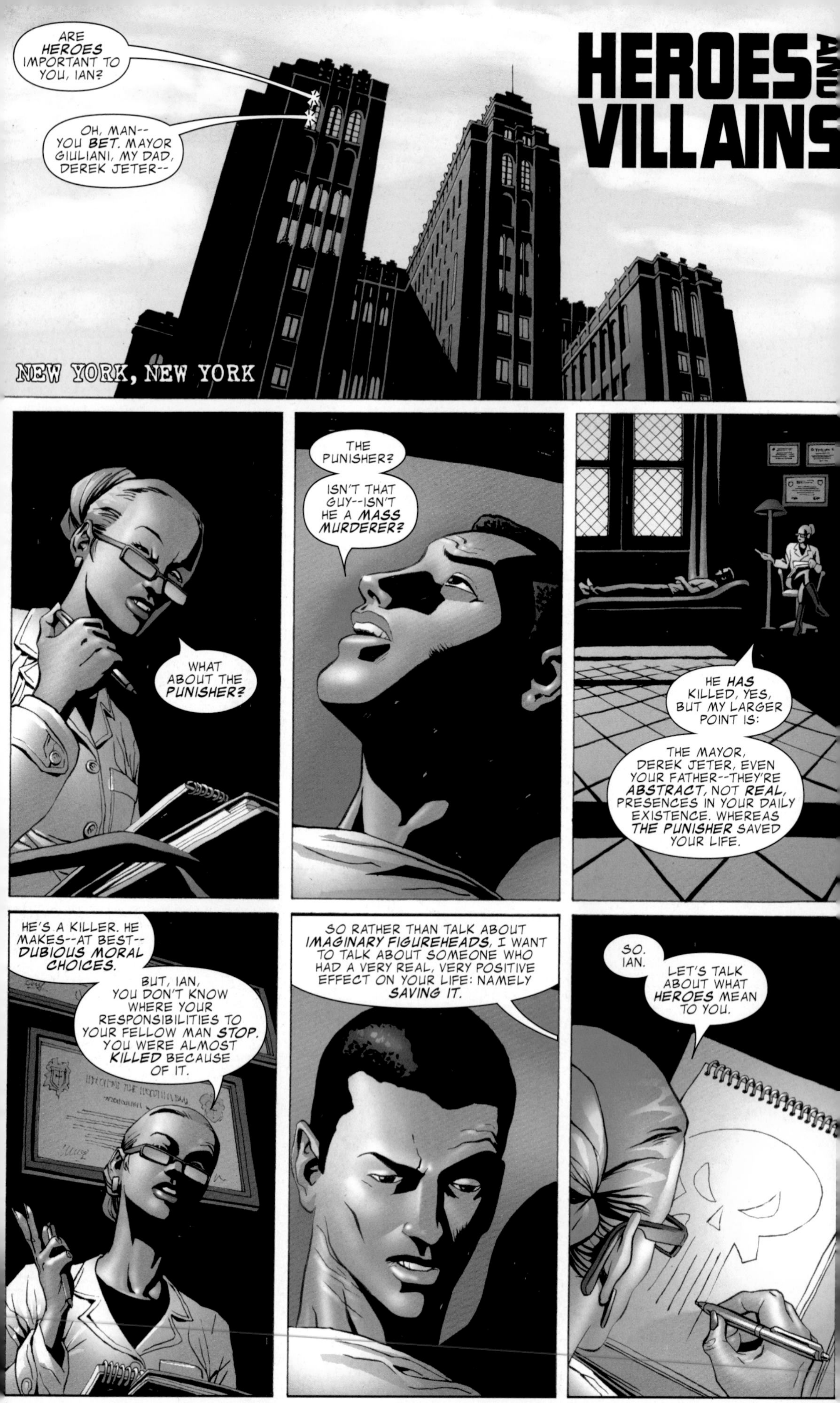
HEROES AND VILLAINS
ARE HEROES IMPORTANT TO YOU, IAN?
OH, MAN-- YOU BET. MAYOR GIULIANI, MY DAD, DEREK JETER--
NEW YORK, NEW YORK
WHAT ABOUT THE PUNISHER?
THE PUNISHER?
ISN'T THAT GUY--ISN'T HE A MASS MURDERER?
HE HAS KILLED, YES, BUT MY LARGER POINT IS:
THE MAYOR, DEREK JETER, EVEN YOUR FATHER--THEY'RE ABSTRACT, NOT REAL, PRESENCES IN YOUR DAILY EXISTENCE. WHEREAS THE PUNISHER SAVED YOUR LIFE.
HE'S A KILLER. HE MAKES--AT BEST-- DUBIOUS MORAL CHOICES.
BUT, IAN, YOU DON'T KNOW WHERE YOUR RESPONSIBILITIES TO YOUR FELLOW MAN STOP. YOU WERE ALMOST KILLED BECAUSE OF IT.
SO RATHER THAN TALK ABOUT IMAGINARY FIGUREHEADS, I WANT TO TALK ABOUT SOMEONE WHO HAD A VERY REAL, VERY POSITIVE EFFECT ON YOUR LIFE: NAMELY SAVING IT.
SO. IAN.
LET'S TALK ABOUT WHAT HEROES MEAN TO YOU.

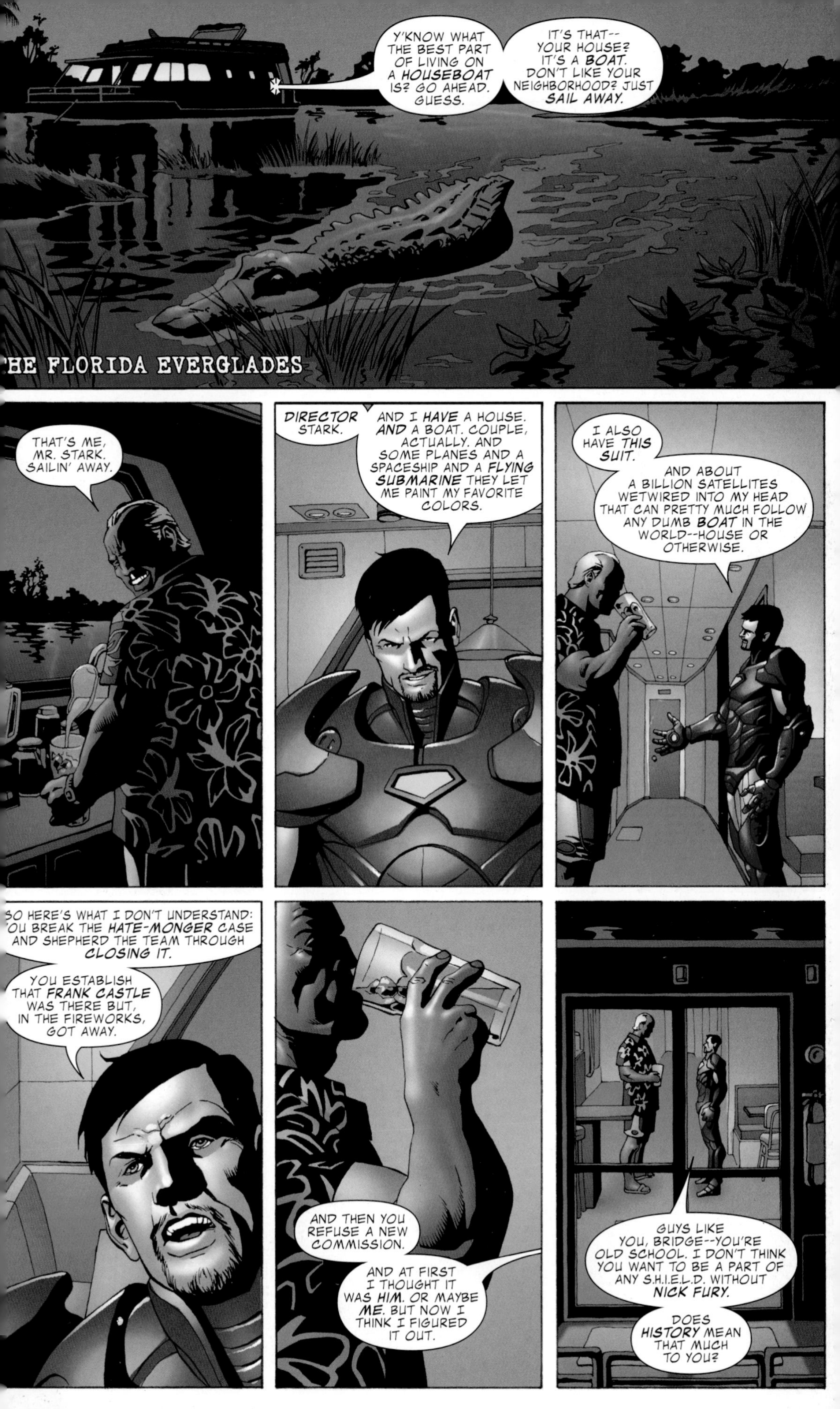
Y'KNOW WHAT THE BEST PART OF LIVING ON A HOUSEBOAT IS? GO AHEAD. GUESS.
IT'S THAT-- YOUR HOUSE? IT'S A BOAT. DON'T LIKE YOUR NEIGHBORHOOD? JUST SAIL AWAY.
THE FLORIDA EVERGLADES
THAT'S ME, MR. STARK. SAILIN' AWAY.
DIRECTOR STARK.
AND I HAVE A HOUSE. AND A BOAT. COUPLE, ACTUALLY. AND SOME PLANES AND A SPACESHIP AND A FLYING SUBMARINE THEY LET ME PAINT MY FAVORITE COLORS.
I ALSO HAVE THIS SUIT.
AND ABOUT A BILLION SATELLITES WETWIRED INTO MY HEAD THAT CAN PRETTY MUCH FOLLOW ANY DUMB BOAT IN THE WORLD--HOUSE OR OTHERWISE.
SO HERE'S WHAT I DON'T UNDERSTAND: YOU BREAK THE HATE-MONGER CASE AND SHEPHERD THE TEAM THROUGH CLOSING IT.
YOU ESTABLISH THAT FRANK CASTLE WAS THERE BUT, IN THE FIREWORKS, GOT AWAY.
AND THEN YOU REFUSE A NEW COMMISSION.
AND AT FIRST I THOUGHT IT WAS HIM. OR MAYBE ME. BUT NOW I THINK I FIGURED IT OUT.
GUYS LIKE YOU, BRIDGE--YOU'RE OLD SCHOOL. I DON'T THINK YOU WANT TO BE A PART OF ANY S.H.I.E.L.D. WITHOUT NICK FURY.
DOES HISTORY MEAN THAT MUCH TO YOU?

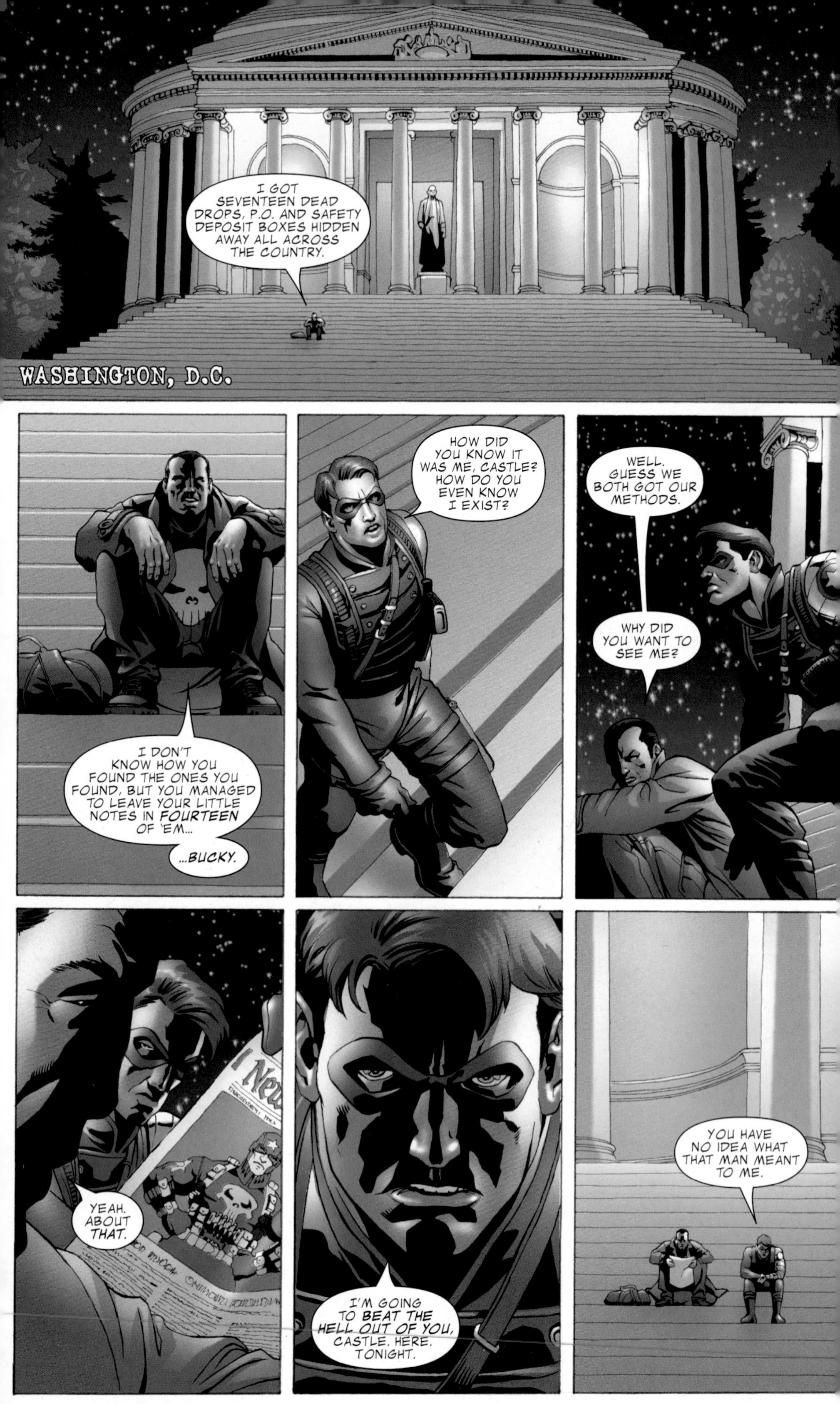
I GOT SEVENTEEN DEAD DROPS, P.O. AND SAFETY DEPOSIT BOXES HIDDEN AWAY ALL ACROSS THE COUNTRY.
WASHINGTON, D.C.
I DON'T KNOW HOW YOU FOUND THE ONES YOU FOUND, BUT YOU MANAGED TO LEAVE YOUR LITTLE NOTES IN FOURTEEN OF 'EM...
...BUCKY.
HOW DID YOU KNOW IT WAS ME, CASTLE? HOW DO YOU EVEN KNOW I EXIST?
WELL. GUESS WE BOTH GOT OUR METHODS.
WHY DID YOU WANT TO SEE ME?
YEAH. ABOUT THAT.
I'M GOING TO BEAT THE HELL OUT OF YOU, CASTLE. HERE. TONIGHT.
YOU HAVE NO IDEA WHAT THAT MAN MEANT TO ME.

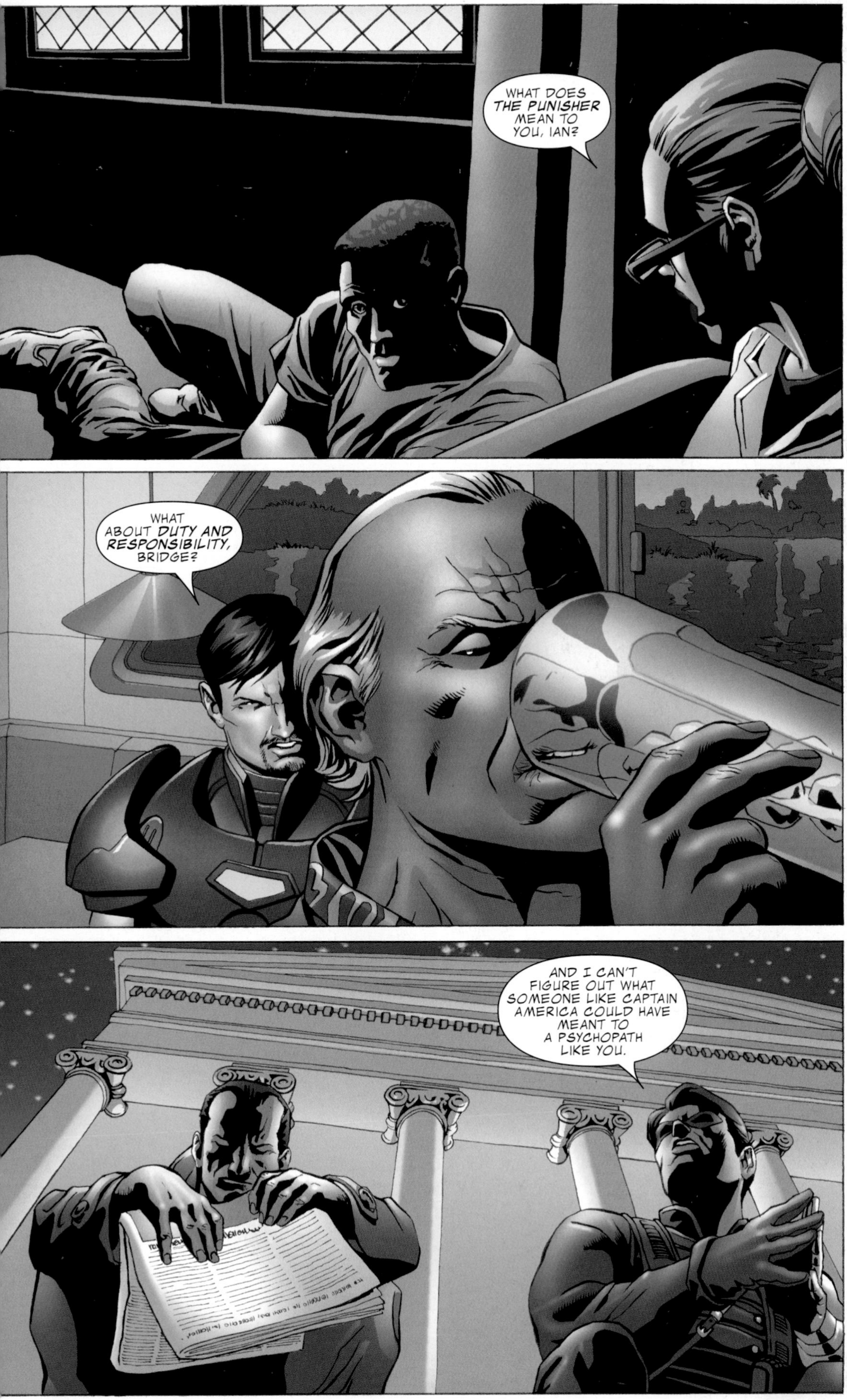
WHAT DOES THE PUNISHER MEAN TO YOU, IAN?
WHAT ABOUT DUTY AND RESPONSIBILITY, BRIDGE?
AND I CAN'T FIGURE OUT WHAT SOMEONE LIKE CAPTAIN AMERICA COULD HAVE MEANT TO A PSYCHOPATH LIKE YOU.

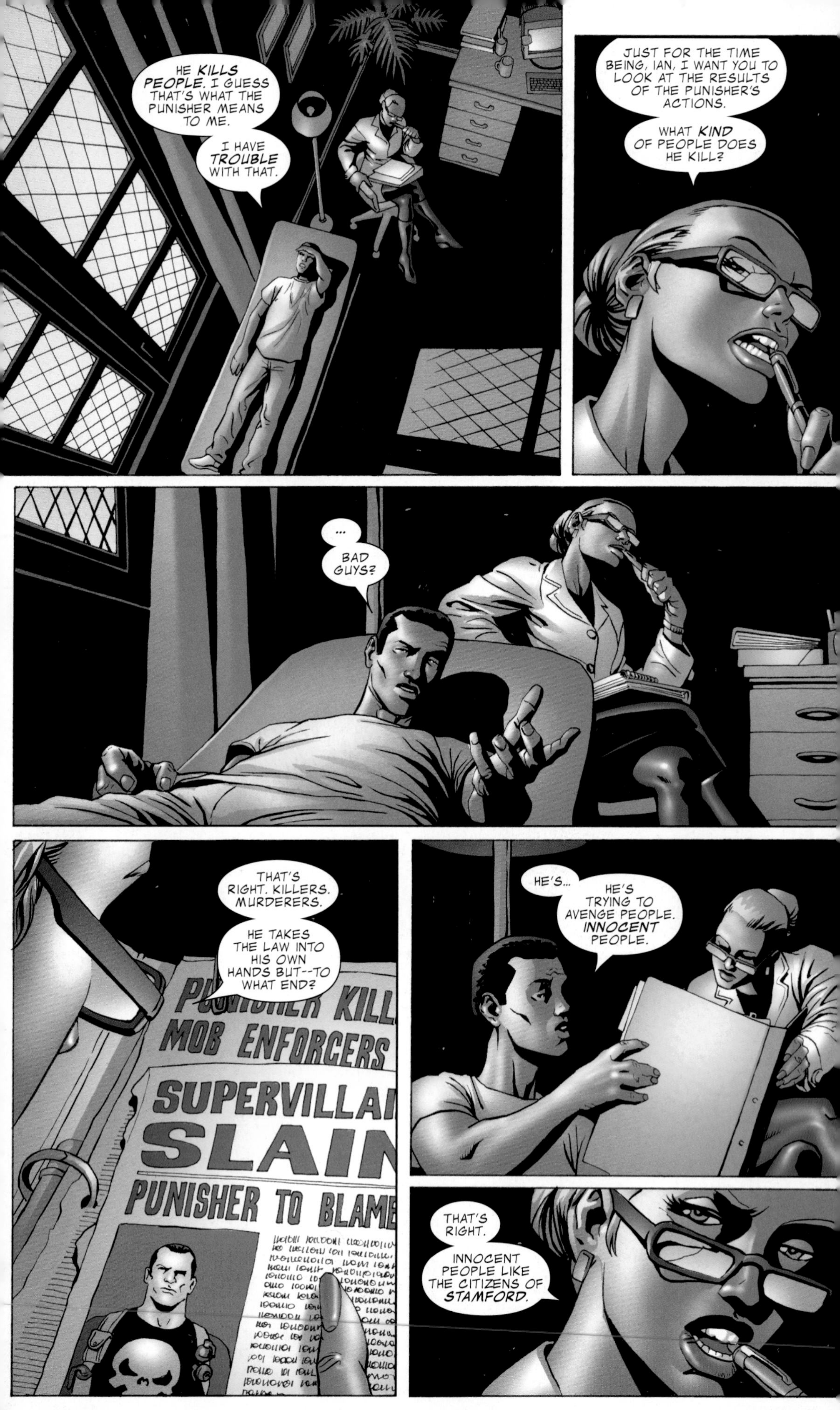
HE KILLS PEOPLE. I GUESS THAT'S WHAT THE PUNISHER MEANS TO ME.
I HAVE TROUBLE WITH THAT.
JUST FOR THE TIME BEING, IAN, I WANT YOU TO LOOK AT THE RESULTS OF THE PUNISHER'S ACTIONS.
WHAT KIND OF PEOPLE DOES HE KILL?
...
BAD GUYS?
THAT'S RIGHT. KILLERS. MURDERERS.
HE TAKES THE LAW INTO HIS OWN HANDS BUT--TO WHAT END?
MOB ENFORCERS
SUPERVILLAI
SLAI
PUNISHER TO BLAME
HE'S...
HE'S TRYING TO AVENGE PEOPLE. INNOCENT PEOPLE.
THAT'S RIGHT.
INNOCENT PEOPLE LIKE THE CITIZENS OF STAMFORD.

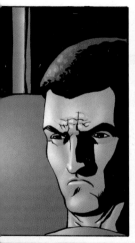

I DON'T WANT TO TALK ABOUT STAMFORD.

WE DON'T HAVE TO TALK ABOUT IT, IAN, BUT YOU HAVE TO ADMIT-- INNOCENTS DIED.

YEAH. OKAY.

LIKE YOUR FAMILY--THEY WERE *INNOCENT*. YOUR *INNOCENT FAMILY* DIED BECAUSE OF SOME SUPER-VILLAINS.

AND AFTERWARDS, YOU PRETENDED TO BE A *POLICE OFFICER* BECAUSE YOU WANTED TO DO SOME *GOOD*.

THE DIFFERENCE BETWEEN WHAT YOU DID, AND WHAT THE PUNISHER DOES, IS THAT YOU JUST PUT YOURSELF *BETWEEN* RIGHT AND WRONG.

BECAUSE I THINK... YOU WANTED TO DIE.

AND I THINK YOU WANTED TO DIE *SAVING LIVES*.

THINK ABOUT THE PUNISHER: HE'S SOMEONE WHO BRINGS JUSTICE TO THE WRONGED, AND YOU, IAN, *HAVE BEEN WRONGED*.

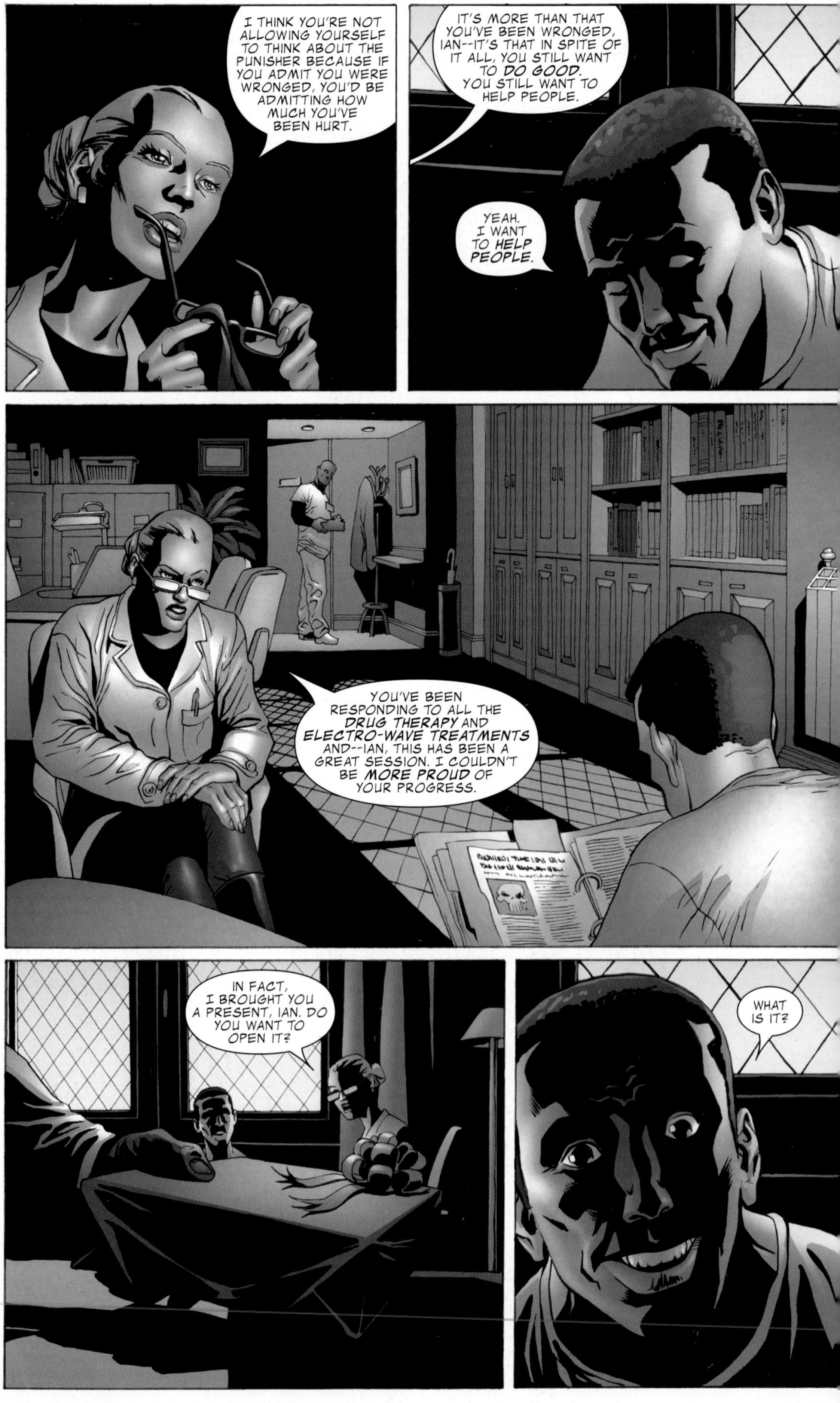

I THINK YOU'RE NOT ALLOWING YOURSELF TO THINK ABOUT THE PUNISHER BECAUSE IF YOU ADMIT YOU WERE WRONGED, YOU'D BE ADMITTING HOW MUCH YOU'VE BEEN HURT.
IT'S MORE THAN THAT YOU'VE BEEN WRONGED, IAN--IT'S THAT IN SPITE OF IT ALL, YOU STILL WANT TO DO GOOD. YOU STILL WANT TO HELP PEOPLE.
YEAH. I WANT TO HELP PEOPLE.
YOU'VE BEEN RESPONDING TO ALL THE DRUG THERAPY AND ELECTRO-WAVE TREATMENTS AND--IAN, THIS HAS BEEN A GREAT SESSION. I COULDN'T BE MORE PROUD OF YOUR PROGRESS.
IN FACT, I BROUGHT YOU A PRESENT, IAN. DO YOU WANT TO OPEN IT?
WHAT IS IT?

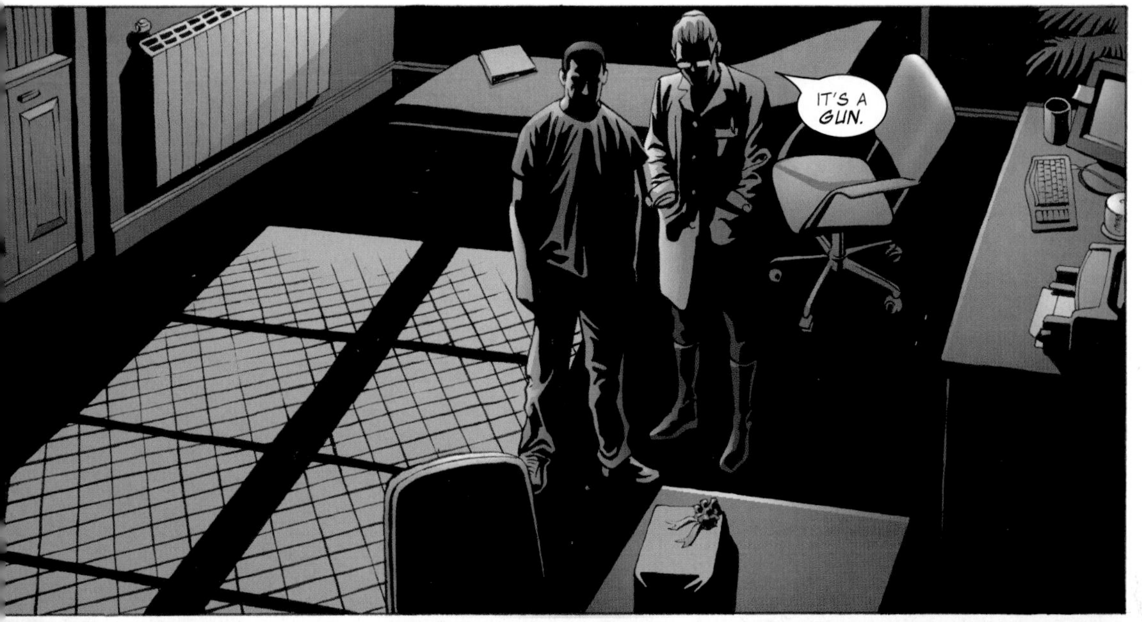
IT'S A GUN.

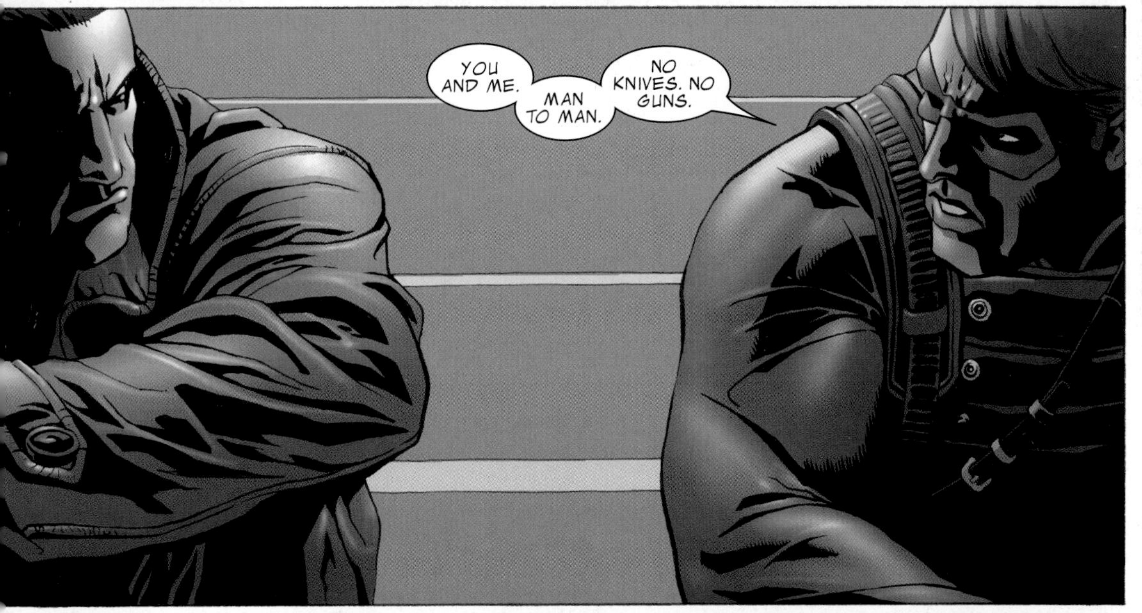
YOU AND ME.
MAN TO MAN.
NO KNIVES. NO GUNS.

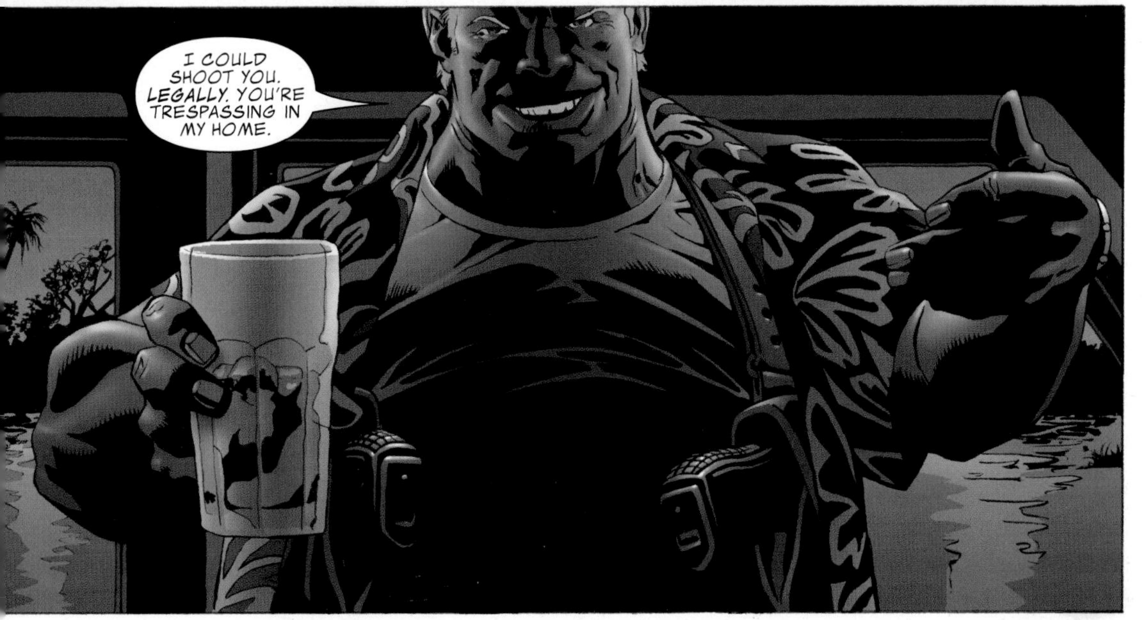
I COULD SHOOT YOU. **LEGALLY**. YOU'RE TRESPASSING IN MY HOME.

JEEZ, GEORGE. THAT WASN'T THE RESPONSE I WAS EXPECTING.

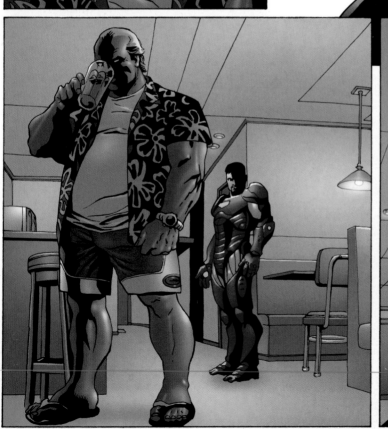

AND YOU'RE NOT *THE BOSS* I WAS EXPECTING.

THIS ISN'T *THE JOB* I WAS--

ARE YOU *ACTUALLY TWEAKED* THAT THINGS AREN'T THE WAY THEY *WERE* TWENTY YEARS AGO?

THAT THE WORLD HAS MAYBE MOVED ON A LITTLE BIT?

I'M *"TWEAKED"* BY A *TERRORIST* THAT I CAN'T EQUALLY MATCH IN METHODS PROFESSIONALLY OR MORALLY.

I'M *"TWEAKED"* THAT, SOMETIMES, HE GOES AFTER GUYS LIKE *HATE-MONGER* BY TAKING HEADSHOTS I CAN'T--AND *WON'T*--TAKE.

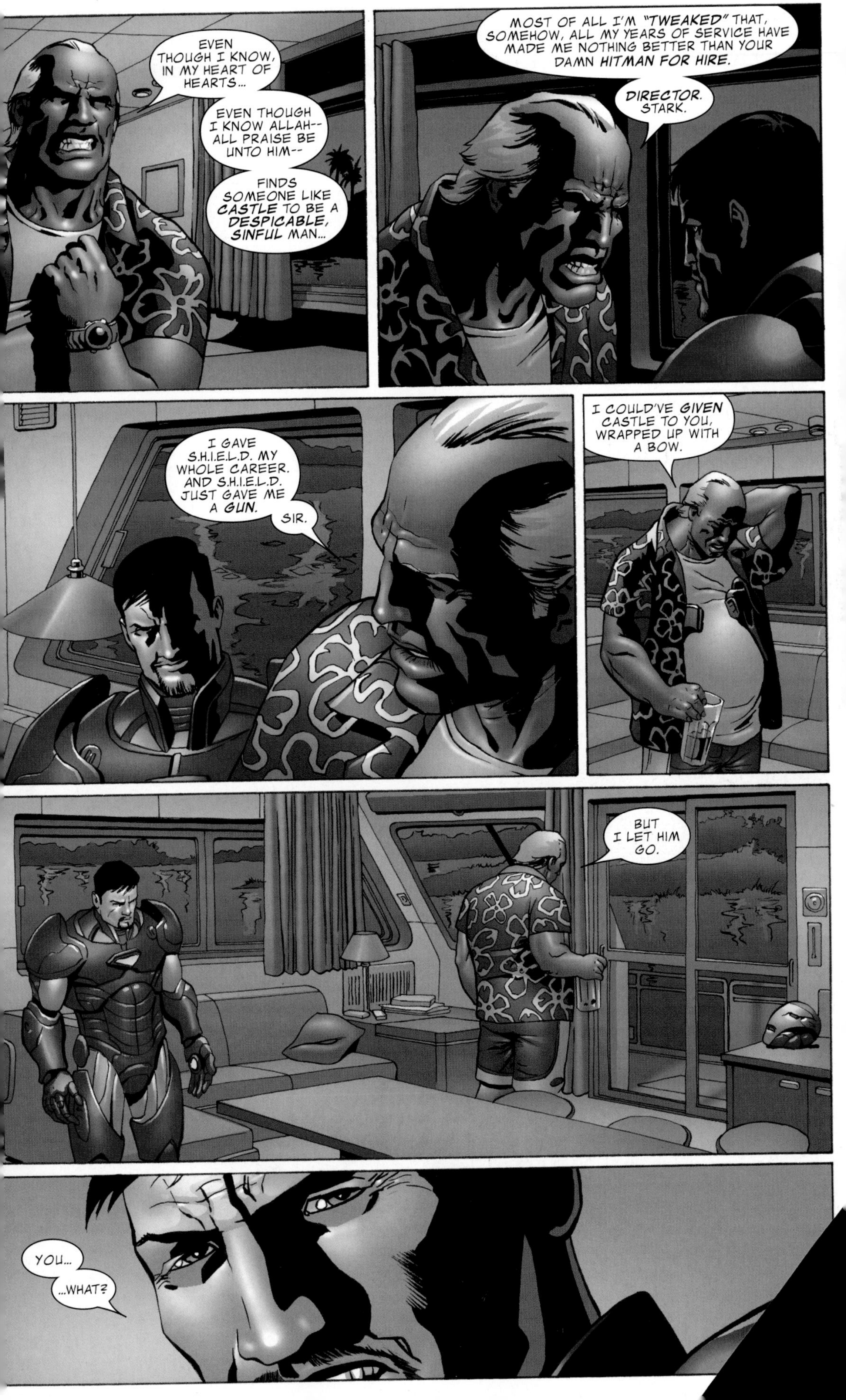
EVEN THOUGH I KNOW, IN MY HEART OF HEARTS...
EVEN THOUGH I KNOW ALLAH-- ALL PRAISE BE UNTO HIM--
FINDS SOMEONE LIKE CASTLE TO BE A DESPICABLE, SINFUL MAN...
MOST OF ALL I'M "TWEAKED" THAT, SOMEHOW, ALL MY YEARS OF SERVICE HAVE MADE ME NOTHING BETTER THAN YOUR DAMN HITMAN FOR HIRE.
DIRECTOR. STARK.
I GAVE S.H.I.E.L.D. MY WHOLE CAREER. AND S.H.I.E.L.D. JUST GAVE ME A GUN.
SIR.
I COULD'VE GIVEN CASTLE TO YOU, WRAPPED UP WITH A BOW.
BUT I LET HIM GO.
YOU...
...WHAT?

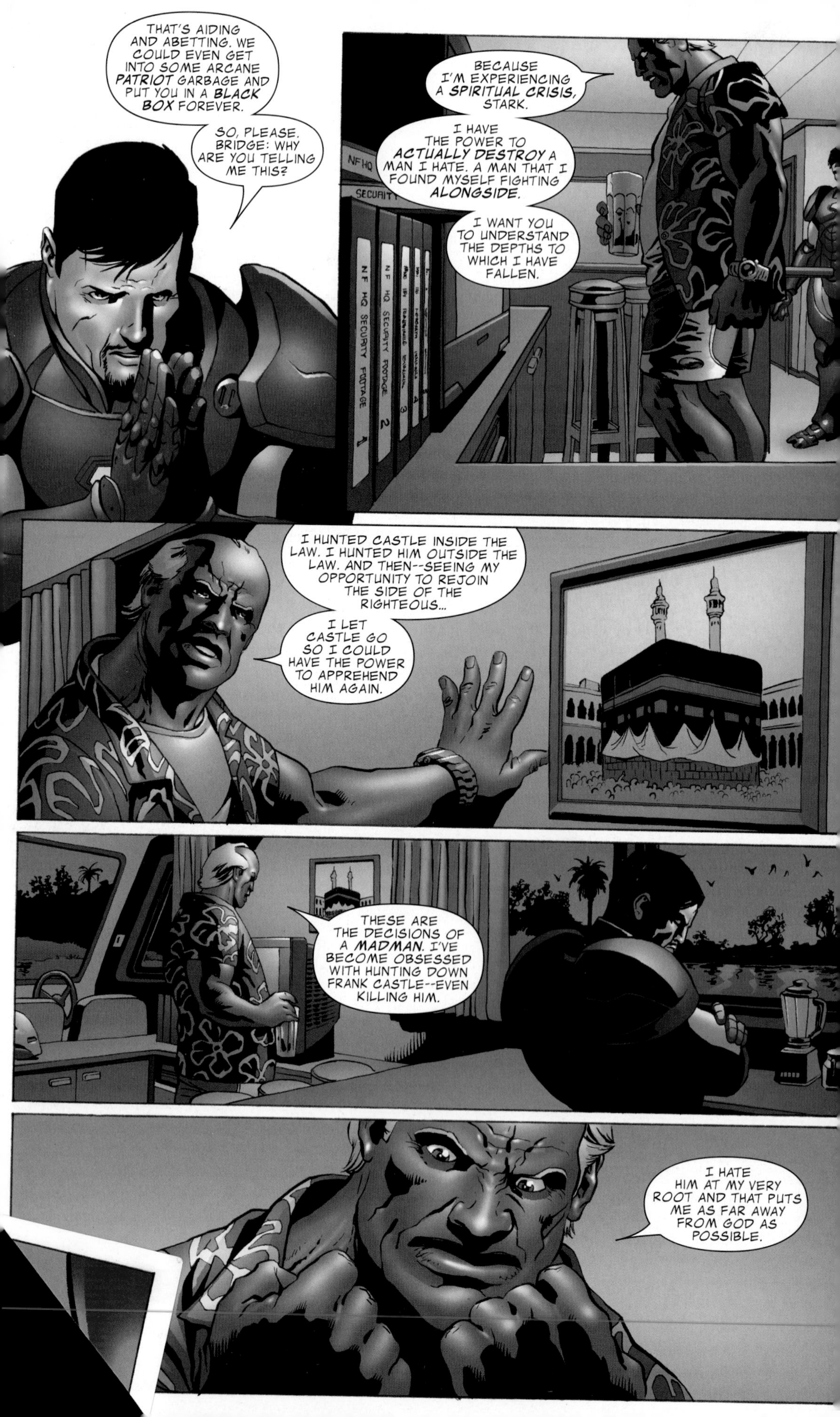
THAT'S AIDING AND ABETTING. WE COULD EVEN GET INTO SOME ARCANE PATRIOT GARBAGE AND PUT YOU IN A BLACK BOX FOREVER.
SO, PLEASE. BRIDGE: WHY ARE YOU TELLING ME THIS?
NF HQ
SECURITY
NF HQ SECURITY FOOTAGE 1
NF HQ SECURITY FOOTAGE 2
BECAUSE I'M EXPERIENCING A SPIRITUAL CRISIS, STARK.
I HAVE THE POWER TO ACTUALLY DESTROY A MAN I HATE. A MAN THAT I FOUND MYSELF FIGHTING ALONGSIDE.
I WANT YOU TO UNDERSTAND THE DEPTHS TO WHICH I HAVE FALLEN.
I HUNTED CASTLE INSIDE THE LAW. I HUNTED HIM OUTSIDE THE LAW. AND THEN--SEEING MY OPPORTUNITY TO REJOIN THE SIDE OF THE RIGHTEOUS...
I LET CASTLE GO SO I COULD HAVE THE POWER TO APPREHEND HIM AGAIN.
THESE ARE THE DECISIONS OF A MADMAN. I'VE BECOME OBSESSED WITH HUNTING DOWN FRANK CASTLE--EVEN KILLING HIM.
I HATE HIM AT MY VERY ROOT AND THAT PUTS ME AS FAR AWAY FROM GOD AS POSSIBLE.

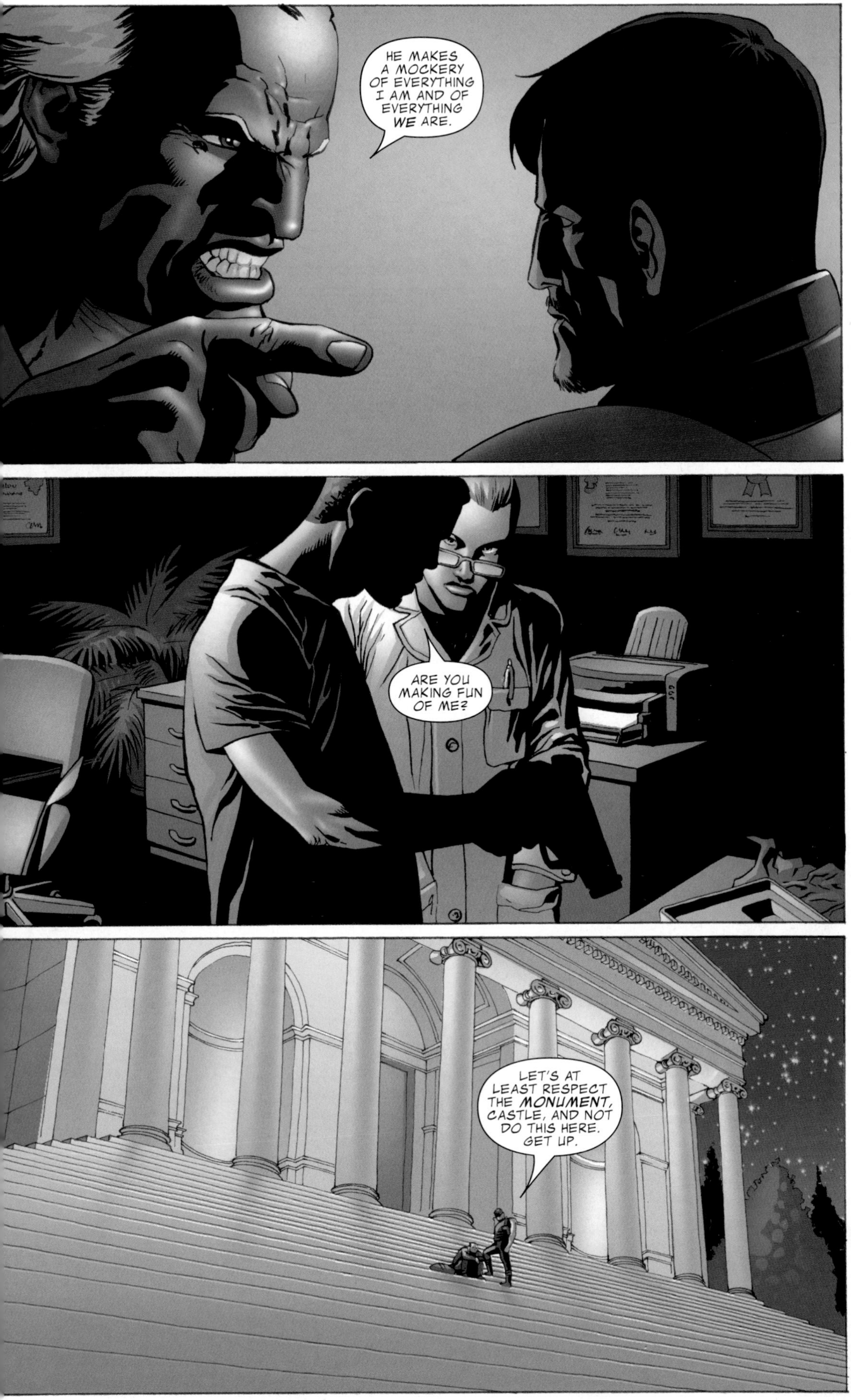
HE MAKES A MOCKERY OF EVERYTHING I AM AND OF EVERYTHING *WE* ARE.
ARE YOU MAKING FUN OF ME?
LET'S AT LEAST RESPECT THE *MONUMENT*, CASTLE, AND NOT DO THIS HERE. GET UP.

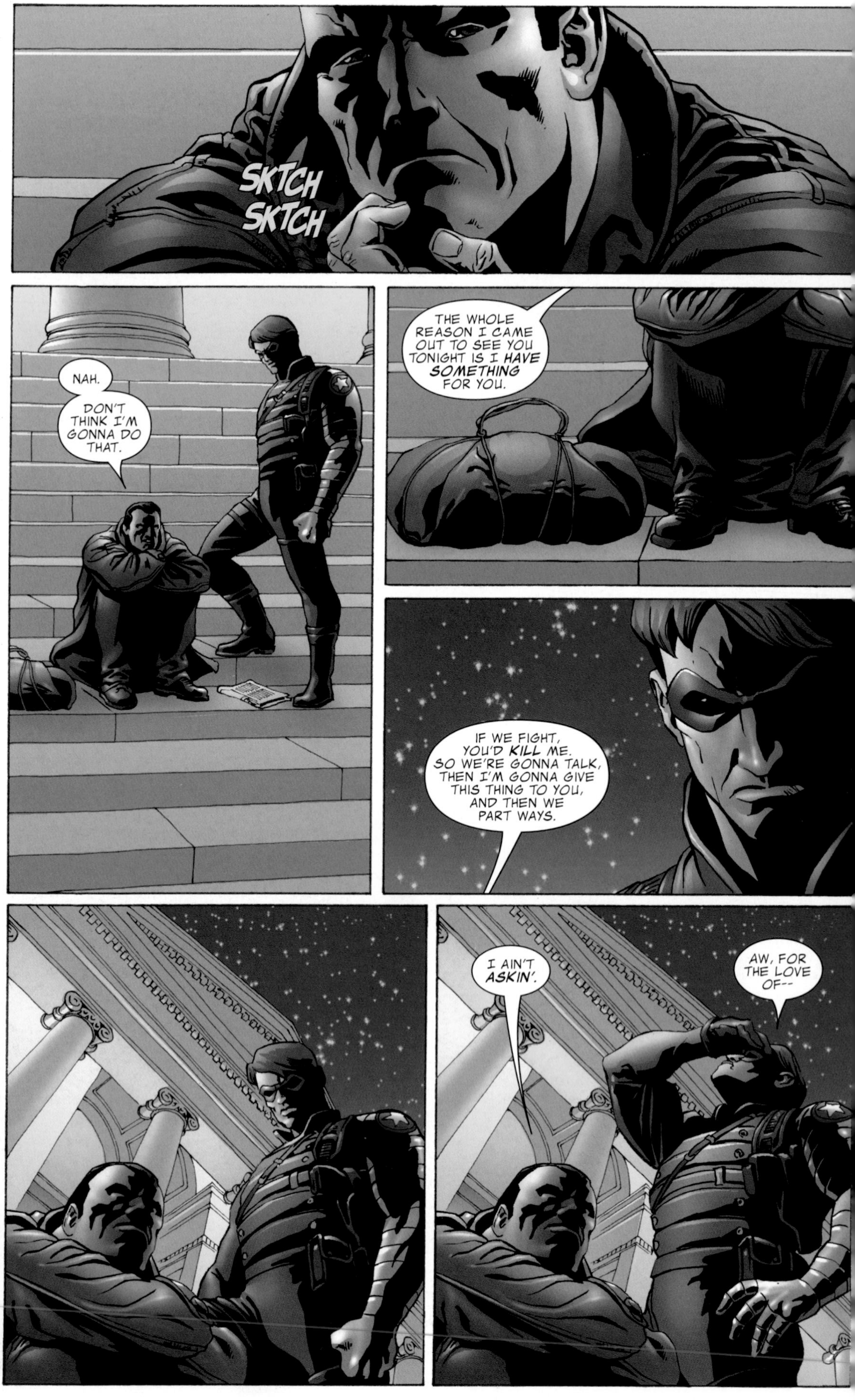
SKTCH SKTCH
NAH.
DON'T THINK I'M GONNA DO THAT.
THE WHOLE REASON I CAME OUT TO SEE YOU TONIGHT IS I HAVE SOMETHING FOR YOU.
IF WE FIGHT, YOU'D KILL ME. SO WE'RE GONNA TALK, THEN I'M GONNA GIVE THIS THING TO YOU, AND THEN WE PART WAYS.
I AIN'T ASKIN'.
AW, FOR THE LOVE OF--

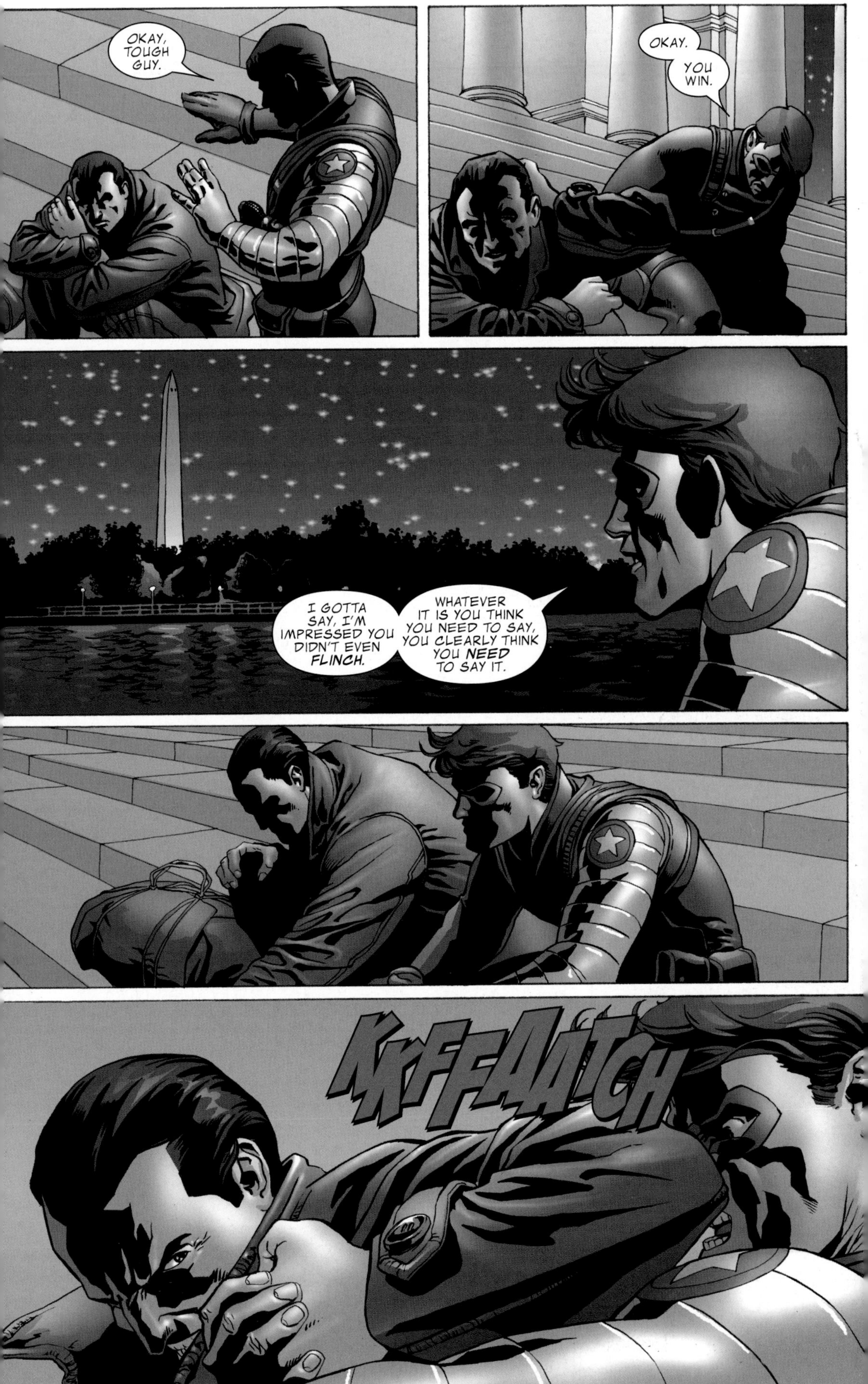
OKAY, TOUGH GUY.
OKAY.
YOU WIN.
I GOTTA SAY, I'M IMPRESSED YOU DIDN'T EVEN FLINCH.
WHATEVER IT IS YOU THINK YOU NEED TO SAY, YOU CLEARLY THINK YOU NEED TO SAY IT.
KKFFAATCH

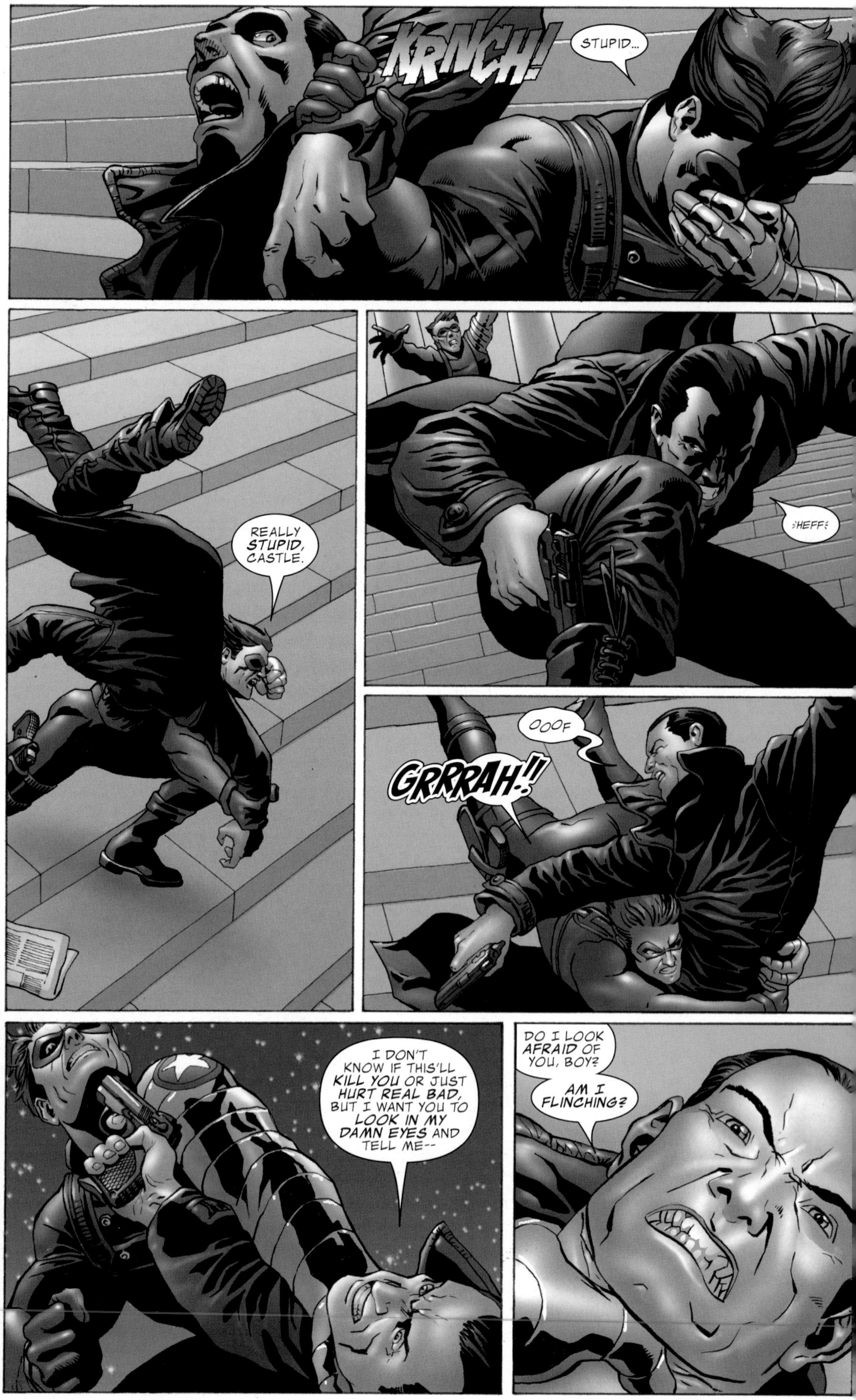
KRNCH!
STUPID...
REALLY STUPID, CASTLE.
HEFF
OOOF
GRRRAH!!
I DON'T KNOW IF THIS'LL KILL YOU OR JUST HURT REAL BAD, BUT I WANT YOU TO LOOK IN MY DAMN EYES AND TELL ME--
DO I LOOK AFRAID OF YOU, BOY?
AM I FLINCHING?

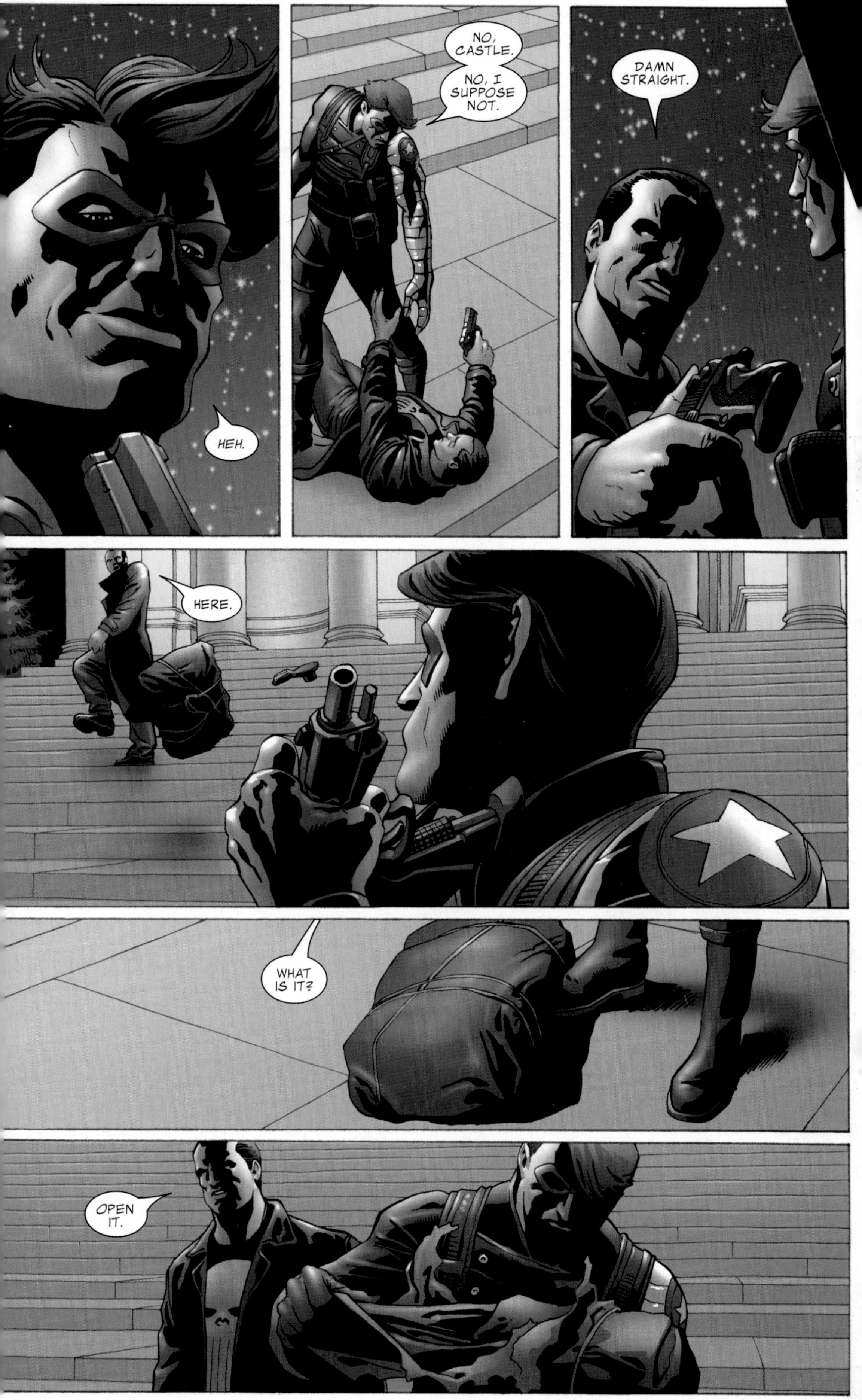
HEH.
NO, CASTLE.
NO, I SUPPOSE NOT.
DAMN STRAIGHT.
HERE.
WHAT IS IT?
OPEN IT.

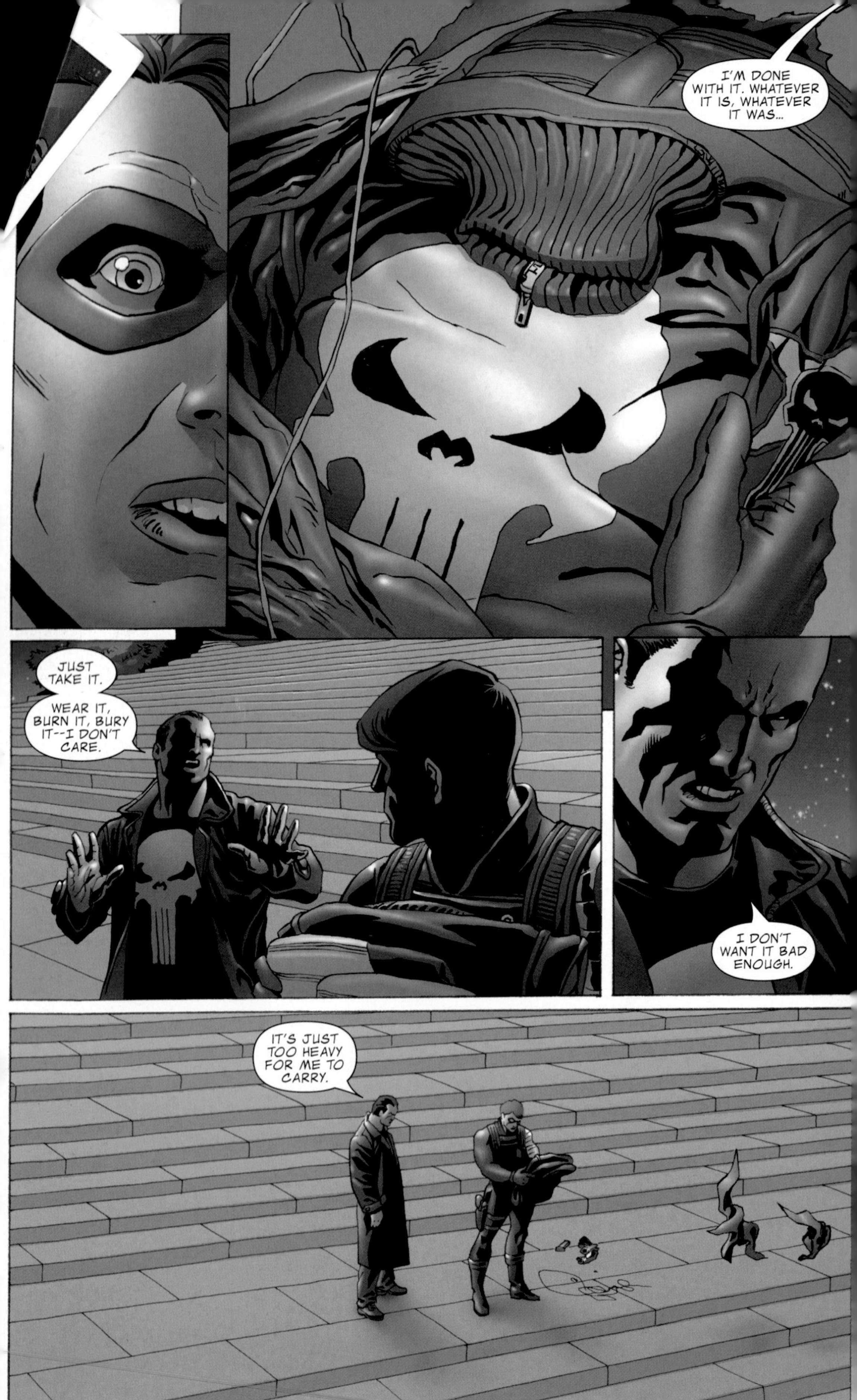
I'M DONE WITH IT. WHATEVER IT IS, WHATEVER IT WAS...
JUST TAKE IT.
WEAR IT, BURN IT, BURY IT--I DON'T CARE.
I DON'T WANT IT BAD ENOUGH.
IT'S JUST TOO HEAVY FOR ME TO CARRY.

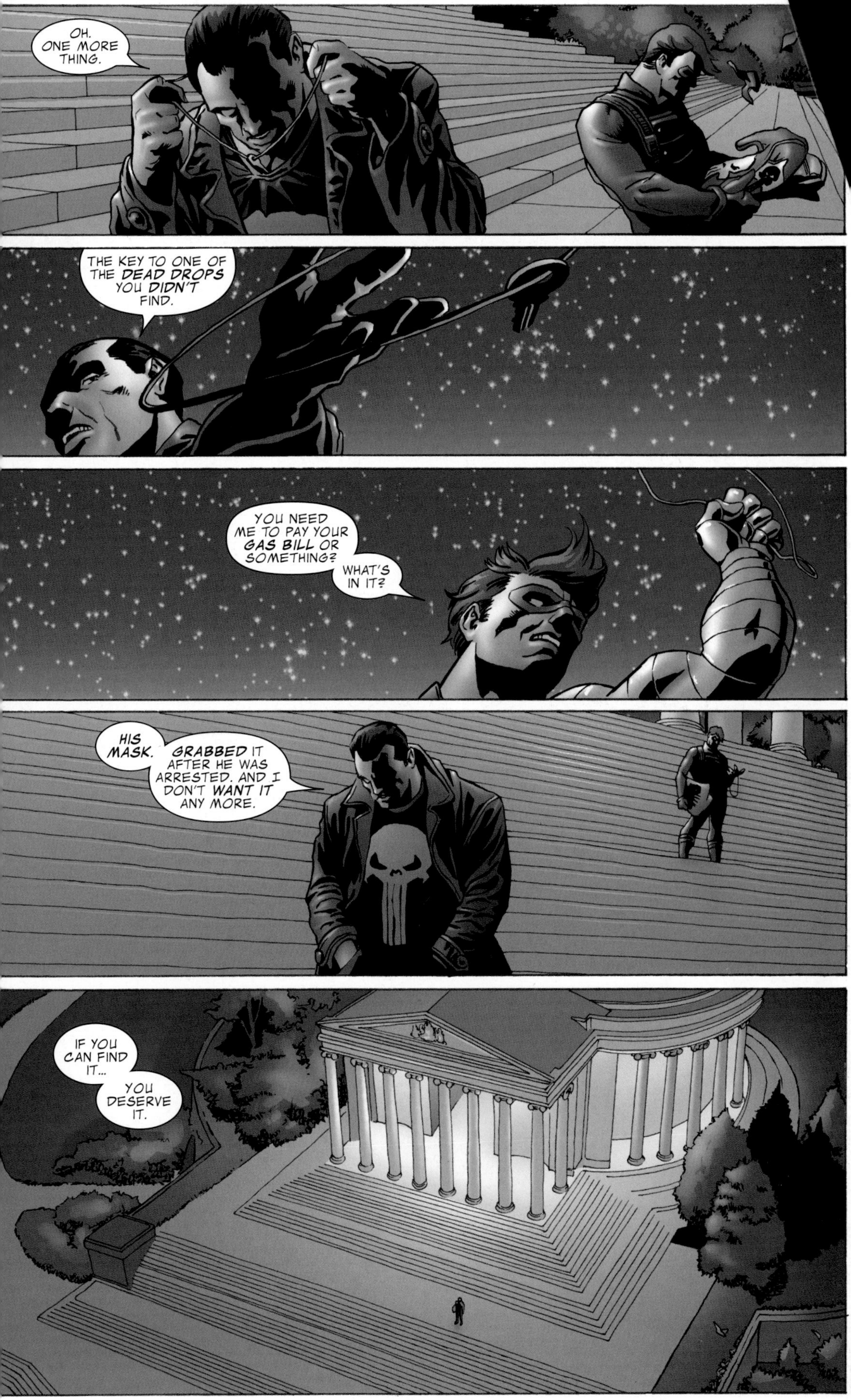
OH. ONE MORE THING.
THE KEY TO ONE OF THE DEAD DROPS YOU DIDN'T FIND.
YOU NEED ME TO PAY YOUR GAS BILL OR SOMETHING?
WHAT'S IN IT?
HIS MASK.
GRABBED IT AFTER HE WAS ARRESTED. AND I DON'T WANT IT ANY MORE.
IF YOU CAN FIND IT...
YOU DESERVE IT.

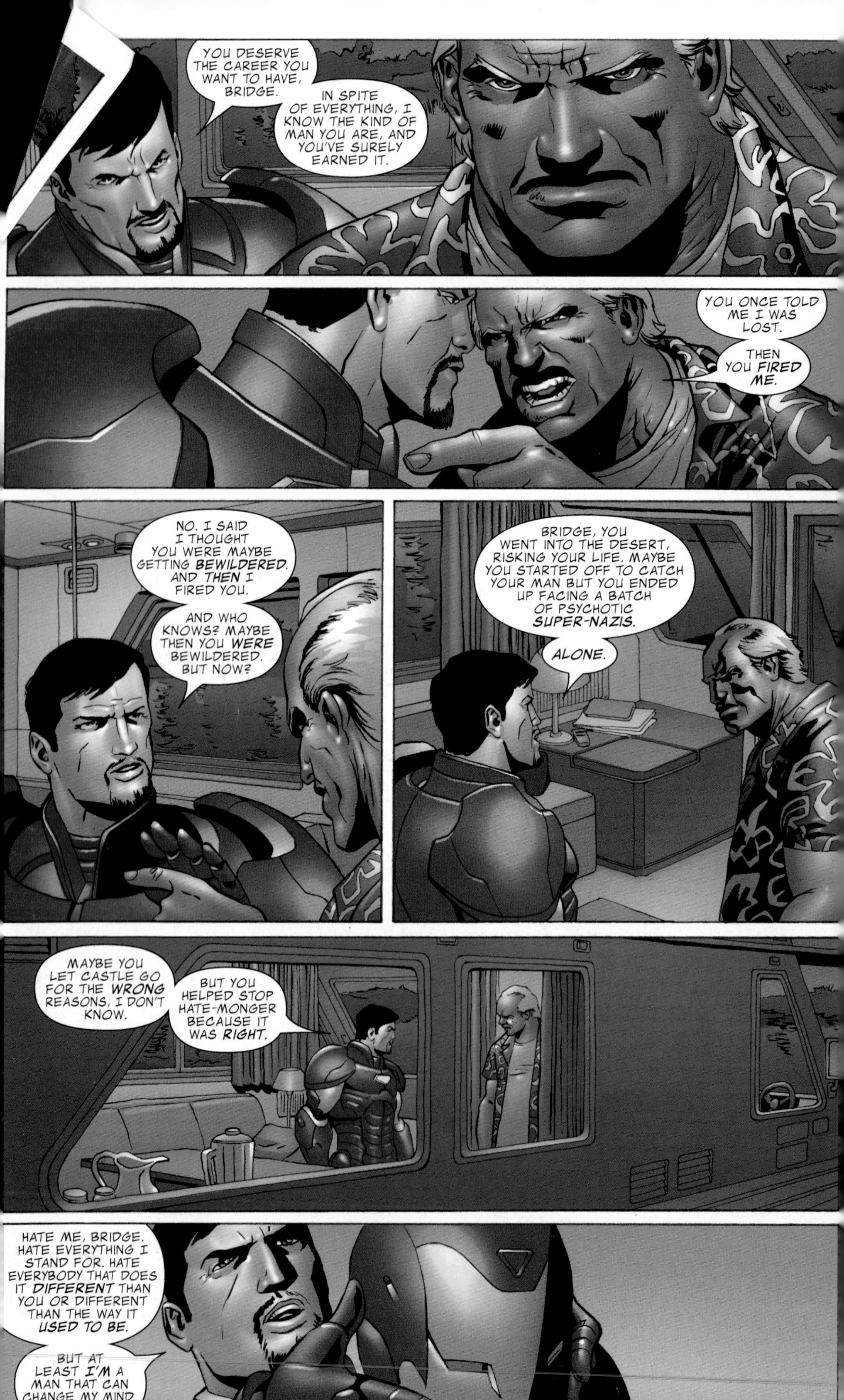

YOU DESERVE THE CAREER YOU WANT TO HAVE, BRIDGE.
IN SPITE OF EVERYTHING, I KNOW THE KIND OF MAN YOU ARE, AND YOU'VE SURELY EARNED IT.
YOU ONCE TOLD ME I WAS LOST.
THEN YOU FIRED ME.
NO. I SAID I THOUGHT YOU WERE MAYBE GETTING BEWILDERED. AND THEN I FIRED YOU.
AND WHO KNOWS? MAYBE THEN YOU WERE BEWILDERED. BUT NOW?
BRIDGE, YOU WENT INTO THE DESERT, RISKING YOUR LIFE. MAYBE YOU STARTED OFF TO CATCH YOUR MAN BUT YOU ENDED UP FACING A BATCH OF PSYCHOTIC SUPER-NAZIS.
ALONE.
MAYBE YOU LET CASTLE GO FOR THE WRONG REASONS, I DON'T KNOW.
BUT YOU HELPED STOP HATE-MONGER BECAUSE IT WAS RIGHT.
HATE ME, BRIDGE. HATE EVERYTHING I STAND FOR. HATE EVERYBODY THAT DOES IT DIFFERENT THAN YOU OR DIFFERENT THAN THE WAY IT USED TO BE.
BUT AT LEAST I'M A MAN THAT CAN CHANGE MY MIND.

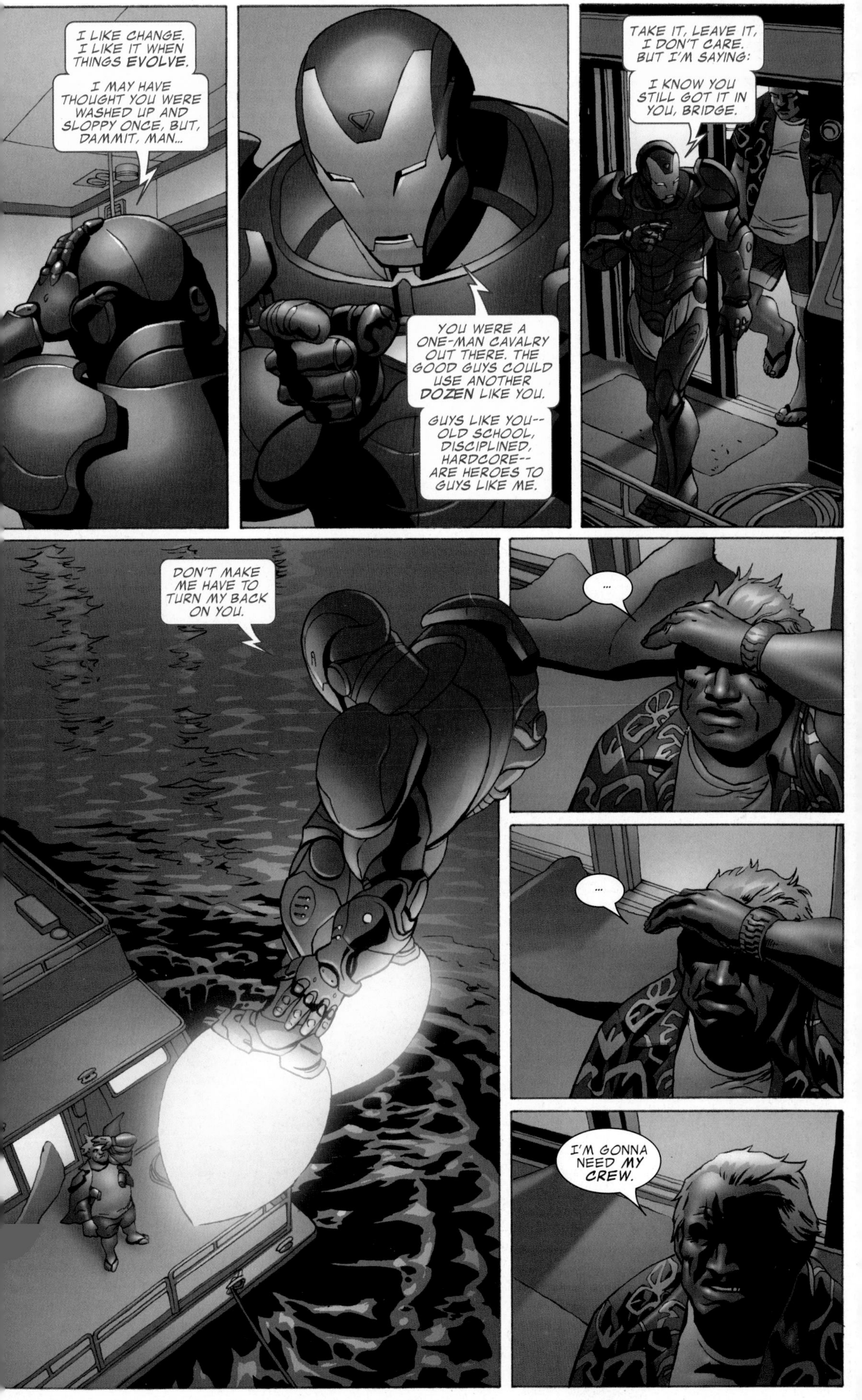
I LIKE CHANGE. I LIKE IT WHEN THINGS EVOLVE.
I MAY HAVE THOUGHT YOU WERE WASHED UP AND SLOPPY ONCE, BUT, DAMMIT, MAN...
YOU WERE A ONE-MAN CAVALRY OUT THERE. THE GOOD GUYS COULD USE ANOTHER DOZEN LIKE YOU.
GUYS LIKE YOU-- OLD SCHOOL, DISCIPLINED, HARDCORE-- ARE HEROES TO GUYS LIKE ME.
TAKE IT, LEAVE IT, I DON'T CARE. BUT I'M SAYING:
I KNOW YOU STILL GOT IT IN YOU, BRIDGE.
DON'T MAKE ME HAVE TO TURN MY BACK ON YOU.
...
...
I'M GONNA NEED MY CREW.

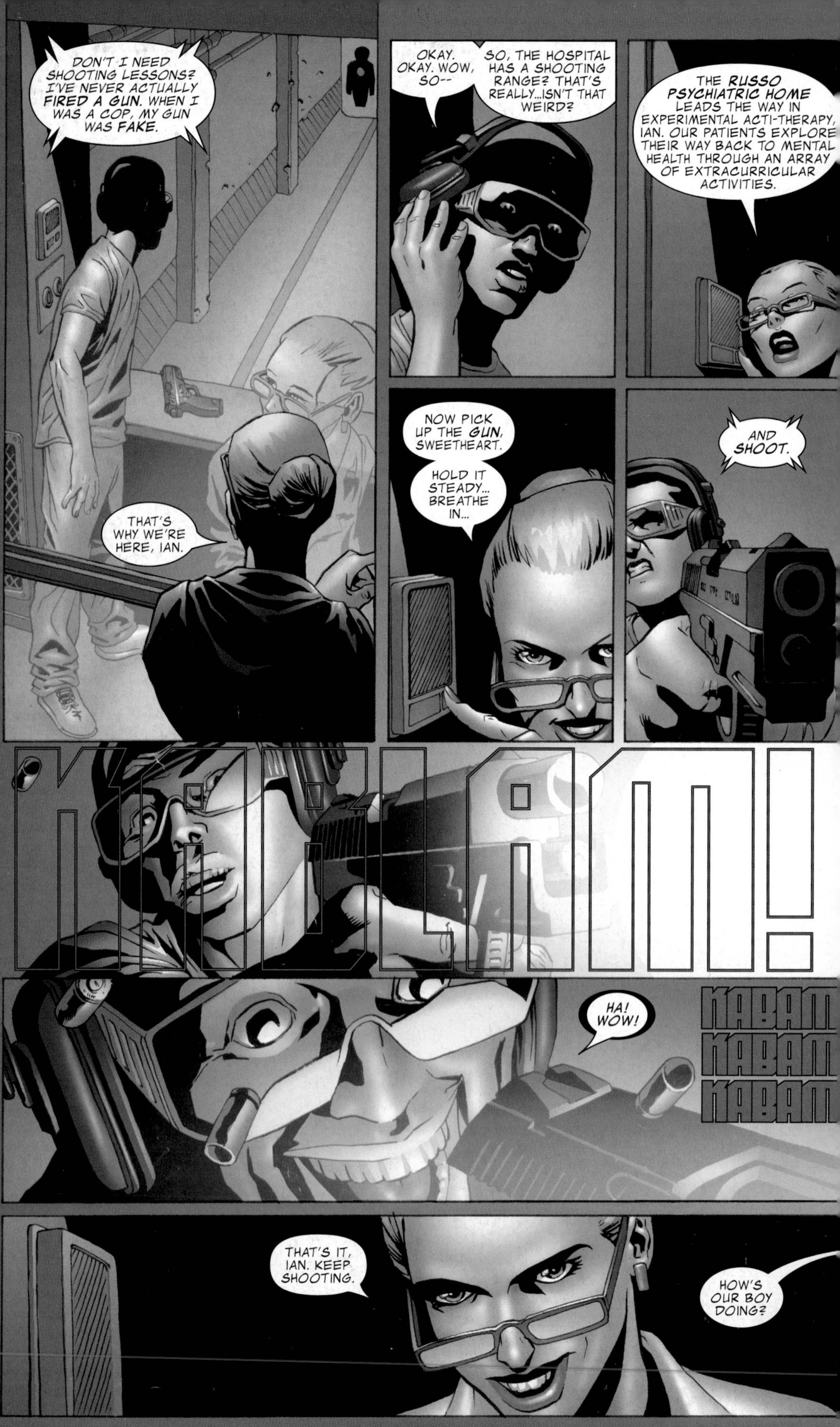

DON'T I NEED SHOOTING LESSONS? I'VE NEVER ACTUALLY FIRED A GUN. WHEN I WAS A COP, MY GUN WAS FAKE.
THAT'S WHY WE'RE HERE, IAN.
OKAY. OKAY. WOW. SO--
SO, THE HOSPITAL HAS A SHOOTING RANGE? THAT'S REALLY...ISN'T THAT WEIRD?
THE RUSSO PSYCHIATRIC HOME LEADS THE WAY IN EXPERIMENTAL ACTI-THERAPY, IAN. OUR PATIENTS EXPLORE THEIR WAY BACK TO MENTAL HEALTH THROUGH AN ARRAY OF EXTRACURRICULAR ACTIVITIES.
NOW PICK UP THE GUN, SWEETHEART.
HOLD IT STEADY... BREATHE IN...
AND SHOOT.
KABLAM!
HA! WOW!
KABAM
KABAM
KABAM
THAT'S IT, IAN. KEEP SHOOTING.
HOW'S OUR BOY DOING?

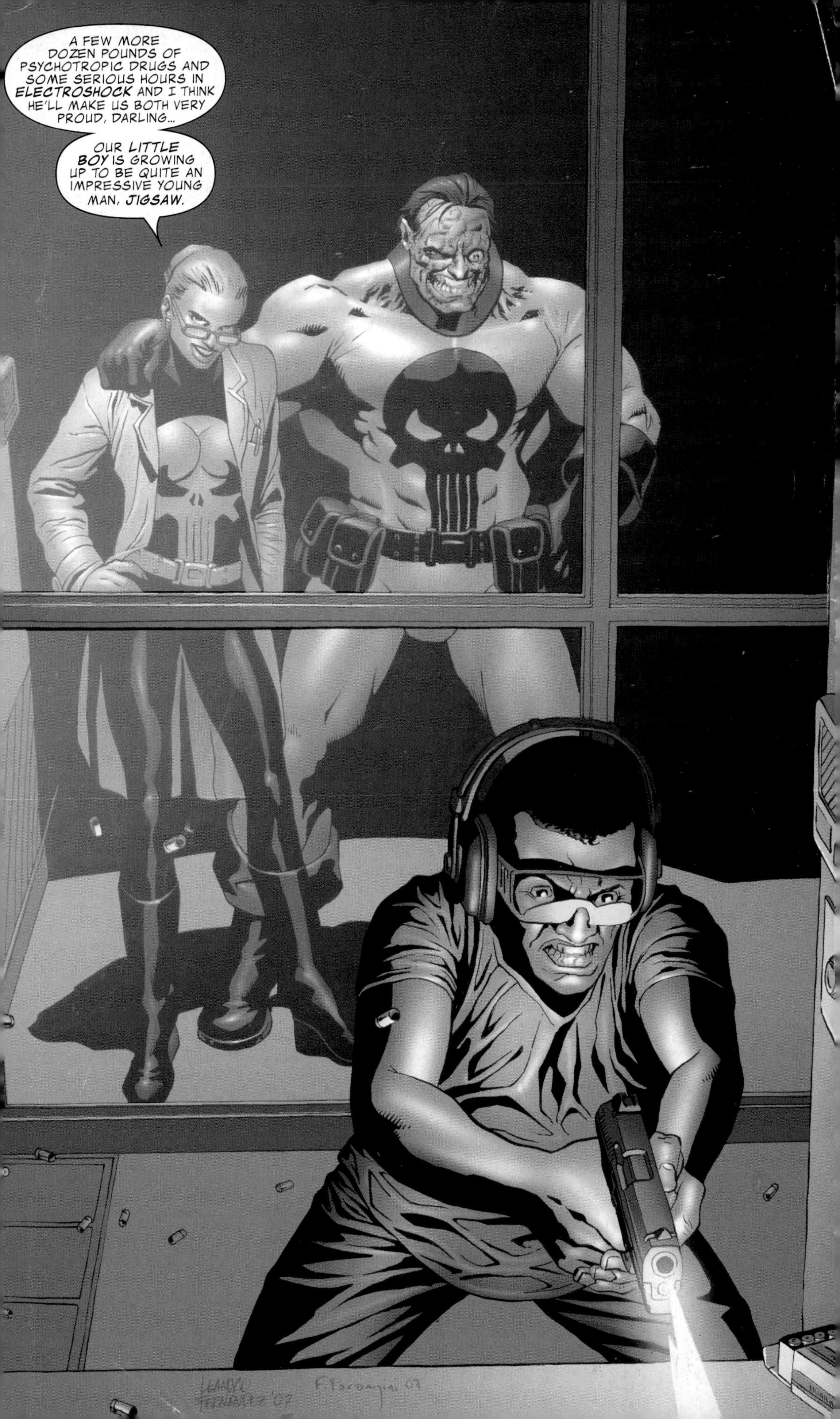
A FEW MORE DOZEN POUNDS OF PSYCHOTROPIC DRUGS AND SOME SERIOUS HOURS IN ELECTROSHOCK AND I THINK HE'LL MAKE US BOTH VERY PROUD, DARLING...
OUR LITTLE BOY IS GROWING UP TO BE QUITE AN IMPRESSIVE YOUNG MAN, JIGSAW.
LEANDRO FERNANDEZ '07
F. Taramini '07

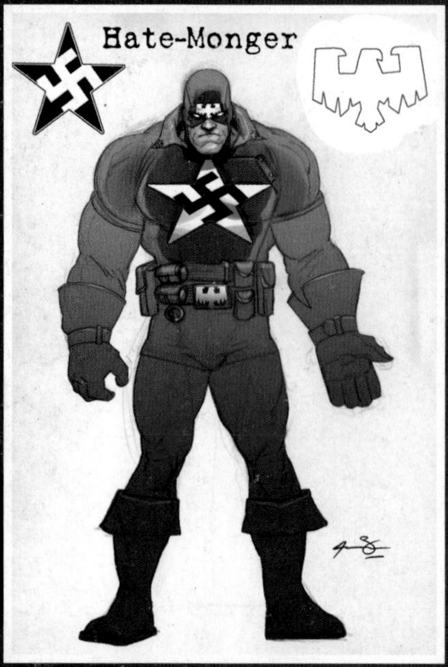
Hate-Monger

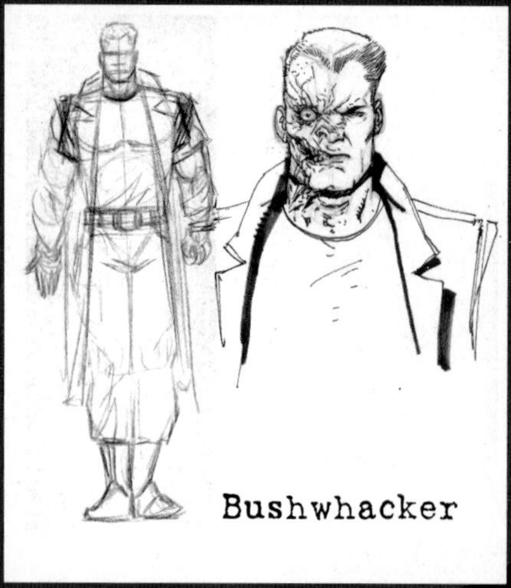
Bushwhacker

Punisher's Captian America
Costume

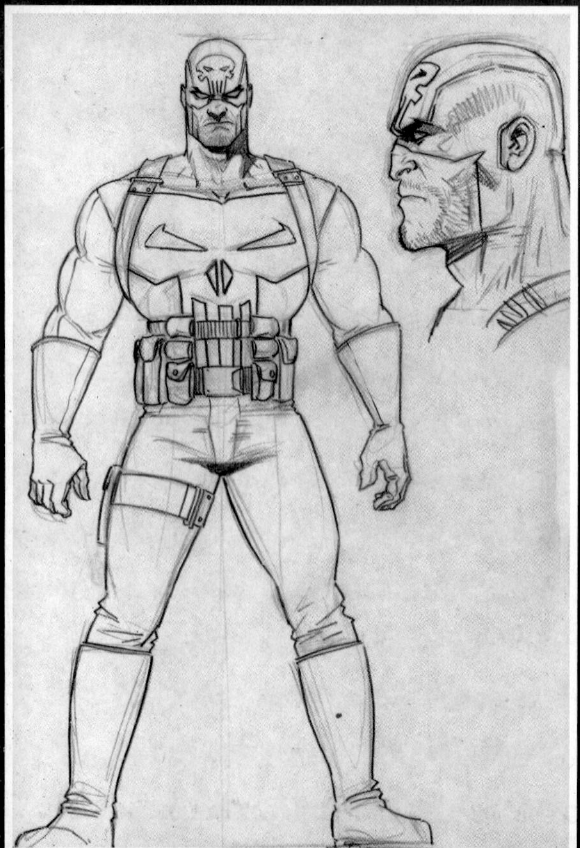

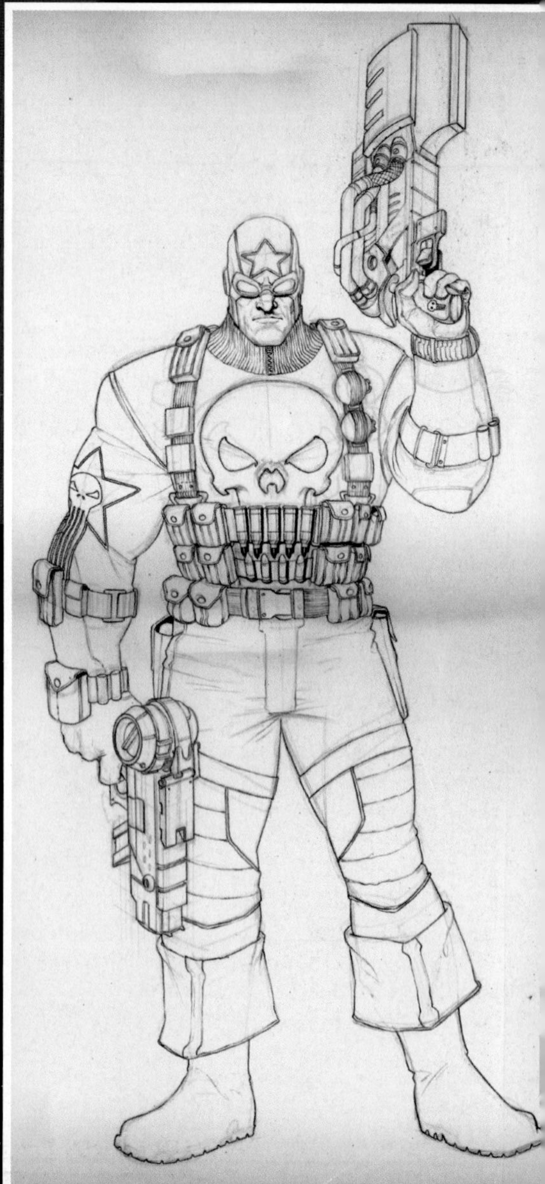